Chuck Palahniuk and
the Comic Grotesque

ALSO BY DAVID MCCRACKEN
AND BY MCFARLAND

*Chuck Palahniuk, Parodist: Postmodern Irony
in Six Transgressive Novels* (2016)

Chuck Palahniuk and the Comic Grotesque

Subversion of Ideology in the Fiction

DAVID MCCRACKEN

McFarland & Company, Inc., Publishers
Jefferson, North Carolina

LIBRARY OF CONGRESS CATALOGUING-IN-PUBLICATION DATA

Names: McCracken, David, 1962– author.
Title: Chuck Palahniuk and the comic grotesque : subversion of ideology in the fiction / David McCracken.
Description: Jefferson : McFarland & Company, Inc., Publishers, 2020. | Includes bibliographical references and index.
Identifiers: LCCN 2020041271 | ISBN 9781476678177 (paperback : acid free paper) ∞
ISBN 9781476642222 (ebook)
Subjects: LCSH: Palahniuk, Chuck—Criticism and interpretation. | Ideology in literature. | Grotesque in literature.
Classification: LCC PS3566.A4554 Z75 2020 | DDC 813/.54—dc23
LC record available at https://lccn.loc.gov/2020041271

BRITISH LIBRARY CATALOGUING DATA ARE AVAILABLE

ISBN (print) 978-1-4766-7817-7
ISBN (ebook) 978-1-4766-4222-2

© 2020 David McCracken. All rights reserved

No part of this book may be reproduced or transmitted in any form or by any means, electronic or mechanical, including photocopying or recording, or by any information storage and retrieval system, without permission in writing from the publisher.

Front cover image by CSA Images (iStock)

Printed in the United States of America

*McFarland & Company, Inc., Publishers
Box 611, Jefferson, North Carolina 28640
www.mcfarlandpub.com*

For Robert D. Newman and John J. McDermott
The better craftsmen

Contents

Preface   1

One. A Rationale for the Comic Grotesque   3

Two. The Subversive Power of the Comic Grotesque   14

Three. "Another last thing today comes down to is reality": The Subversion of Sexuality in *Snuff*   43

Four. "A rude religious revolution": The Subversion of Heaven and Hell in *Damned* and *Doomed*   66

Five. "You've become something dangerous: a woman": The Subversion of Feminism in *Beautiful You*   93

Six. "The fringe was the future": The Future of Dirty Realism in *Make Something Up: Stories You Can't Unread*   117

Seven. "To embrace the blackness": The Irony of Content and Form in *Bait* and *Legacy*   146

Eight. "Human beings don't cultivate ideas": Subverting *Fight Club* Ideology through *Fight Club 2* Mythology   168

Nine. Toward "a structure for communion": Ideological Carnival in *Adjustment Day*   200

Ten. Toward a Palahniuk Aesthetic of Comic Grotesque   229

Chapter Notes   235
Works Cited   247
Index   275

Preface

In the following pages, I contend Chuck Palahniuk exposes the manipulative and exploitative powers of ideologies through his unique application of the comic grotesque. I support this argument by applying the theories of Mikhail Bakhtin, Louis Althusser, and Slavoj Žižek to interpretations of *Snuff*, *Damned/Doomed*, *Beautiful You*, *Make Something Up*, *Bait/Legacy*, *Fight Club 2*, and *Adjustment Day*. Essentially, I assert Palahniuk is a contemporary François Rabelais, fictionalizing carnivalesque situations that reverse power hierarchies and subvert ideological authority. Imitating the Rabelaisian carnival, Palahniuk creates situations in which the marginalized exchange places with the mainstream, imploding the power center, pulling the middle of the power circle inside out. These depictions in turn encourage readers to question the efficacy of conventional normalcy and to take their own steps toward questioning the status quo, consequently challenging the ideologies manufactured to maintain, as introduced in *Fight Club*, the tension between the haves and the have nots.

I understand this all sounds extremely abstract, so as I progress through my study, I offer practical contexts to situate and to ground the theory. Trust me. The abstractions will be explained and then illustrated through close readings of Palahniuk's works.

As I have mentioned in other publications about Palahniuk's writing, I realize even the mentioning of this author's name causes some people to cringe.

A couple of years ago, at an academic conference, I noticed this firsthand. In response to a session introduction that I was reading a paper about Palahniuk's "Romance," a respected professor said under her breath to a colleague, "Palahniuk is a sexist."

Palahniuk is not a sexist, but he is also not a feminist. Reminiscent of Ralph Waldo Emerson's famous transcendentalist declaration in *Nature* that he, as a transparent eyeball, is nothing but sees everything (6), Palahniuk maintains the stance of ideological chameleon. Contrary to what critics contend, Palahniuk is neither a nihilist, nor a romantic, nor a humanist, nor the literary prototype of any other ideology. If anything, Palahniuk moves fluidly within all of them.

Honestly, Palahniuk enjoys staying untethered to any classification, although he cannot really shake his notoriety for transgressive writing, and, as you will discover, I place his topics and techniques within the American movement of dirty realism. I think Palahniuk relishes, the best he can, being a literary freelancer. He is everything (feminist, nihilist, romantic, humanist, etc.), but he is also nothing exclusively. In fact, as this book will prove, Palahniuk displays the consequences of people rigidly, tenaciously, and solipsistically tethering themselves to ideologies, when they identify with them, personify them, and embody them.

I could not have completed this project without being granted a sabbatical by Coker University. I also could not have finished this project without the assistance of my beloved wife, Wendy McCracken. I wish to thank Coker University, but I bestow my extreme gratitude and my eternal devotion to my wife. Wendy kept me focused. From the beginning, I apologize for any mistakes. My wife caught most of them, but I negligently missed the rest.

Unfortunately, COVID-19 is to blame for my tardiness in finishing the manuscript for publication more quickly. I blame the coronavirus pandemic for not completing this project in early 2020. Nonetheless, my references to 2019 events to clarify abstractions are still relevant, and my application of Bakhtin, Althusser, and Žižek to Palahniuk's writing is, of course, still pertinent.

ONE

A Rationale for the Comic Grotesque

On June 17, 2019, in a short *USA Today* article, Susan Haas remarks that actor Bella Thorne, a former child star as CeCe Jones from 2010 to 2013 on Disney Channel's *Shake It Up*, uploaded provocative selfies to her Twitter account to preempt their broadcast by a hacker threatening to release them over the Internet. According to Haas, Thorne's self-exposure of the sensual images is essentially an act of empowerment, preventing any chance for blackmail or extortion associated with the nude images. Haas cites Thorne as commenting, "For the last 24 hours I have been threatened with my own nudes.... I feel gross. I feel watched. I feel someone has taken something from me that I wanted one special person to see." In the commentary accompanying the Twitter post shown in the article, Thorne writes, "I can sleep tonight better knowing I took my power back.... U can't control my life u never will."

In the online version of this *USA Today* piece, a click of a mouse allows readers to view Thorne's photos, the items at the center of this controversy. In her summary of Thorne's situation, Haas mentions that Thorne included screenshots of her dialogue with the hacker in her Twitter post. In Haas's commentary, "screenshots of text messages" are highlighted blue, and a tap onto the hyperlink leads easily to Thorne's Twitter page. After a quick scroll down, readers may see the images in question, with Thorne's breasts clearly visible, the left nipple pierced and accessorized, posed for her "special person." Haas does not quote Thorne's warning to the perpetrator, who seems to have videos as well as photos of Thorne and other celebrities in compromising positions, but other comments are provided. Through the interconnectedness of the various media, readers can see firsthand Thorne's scathing response: "Here's the photos he's been threatening me with, in other words here's my boobies. So here fuck u, and the last 24 hours I have been crying instead of celebrating my book while doing my book press. Oh yea, the fbi will be at your house shortly, so watch. Your. Mother. Fuckin. Back." Haas also mentions Thorne had been sexually abused as a child, more intimate information about this celebrity.

Of course, this incited controversy. On June 18, Andrea Mandell and Bill Keveney report in a *USA Today* follow-up story that Whoopi Goldberg criticized Thorne publicly on the television talk show *The View* for taking the photos. Goldberg's contention referred to the initial cause for the effect described in Haas's article: if Thorne had shown some discretion and practiced some decorum by not uploading sexually compromising photos of herself in the first place, none of the resulting events would have occurred. Goldberg is cited as chastising Thorne for not thinking those images all the way through, reprimanding Thorne for the audacity to assume she could get away with uploading nudes: "When they are hacking you, they are hacking all of your stuff. So whether it's one picture or a million pictures, once you take that picture, it goes into the cloud and it's available to any hacker who wants it and if you don't know that in 2019, that is an issue." Responding to Goldberg through Instagram, Thorne accused Goldberg of victim-blaming, inferring that she has a right to "do it" with impunity. Thorne begs the question, basing her argument on the premise most agree that taking a sensual snapshot for her "special person" is appropriate; the problem rests with how someone besides the intended significant other uses the photo. In short time, Thorne rallied supporters with similar opinions. According to Thorne, Goldberg obviously fails to understand the heroic vigilantism underlying her actions. Mandell and Keveney mention Zendaya, Lily-Rose Depp, Dove Cameron, and Lucy Hale support the twenty-one-year-old's position, offering a screenshot of Hale's Instagram praise of Thorne as vindication: "This breaks my heart. But you are making a difference for other girls and women!" As Erin Jensen writes in an August 12 article in *USA Today*, Whitney Cummings also thwarted "foolish dorks" who tried to extort money for a shot of her exposed nipple. Cummings shared the image.

As the USA Women's Soccer Team progressed during the summer toward winning the 2019 World Cup, Megan Rapinoe was likewise praised and condemned for her behavior. In a June 27 article for *ThinkProgress*, Lindsay Gibbs states in her first sentence: "Megan Rapinoe is not going to the fucking White House." This is indubitably parodying Rapinoe's response to questions about visiting President Donald Trump if her team were eventually invited. A writer for the *Associated Press* cites Rapinoe as admitting that her profanities would cause her own mother to "be very upset." On July 10, Justin Kirkland recalls in an *Esquire* article that Rapinoe's exact words were "I'm not going to the fucking White House," and he points out that after she met Mayor Bill de Blasio and Governor Andrew Cuomo, Rapinoe yelled out in excitement, for all to hear through live media streaming, "New

York City, you're the motherfucking best!" CNN's video titled "US Soccer Star Megan Rapinoe Drops F-Bomb on Live TV" is worth watching about the New York City event, displaying how commentators immediately apologized to viewers for Rapinoe's word selection. As expected, there was political backlash concerning Rapinoe's words. A July 13 broadcast of Mike Allen's *Saturday Midday* on WLW out of Cincinnati is emblematic of small media market coverage of the situation. A lawyer and former judge, Allen fielded caller directives for quick, stern, and exemplary punitive actions toward Rapinoe's disrespect for President Trump and her vulgarity toward the American people. Echoing the sentiments of many, callers advocated Rapinoe's exile from organized soccer to exclusion from impending endorsements. Only a few callers supported Rapinoe's choice of language. As CNN's Jeanne Moos points out, Rapinoe, who first claimed to be at a loss for words, should have let one in particular stay lost. Moos goes on to scold Rapinoe: "Megan, Megan, your mother is going to have to wash your mouth out with soap." Needless to say, conservative media in small and large markets questioned Rapinoe's ethical character based predominantly on her propensity to express "fuck" during less than opportune public moments.

Without a doubt, Thorne's and Rapinoe's situations illustrate the changing perspectives concerning what is proper, acceptable, civilized, and, dare say, moral behavior in American society. Forty years ago, in the 1980s, before widespread Internet accessibility, Thorne would not have been capable of posting a nude photo of herself for someone to hack so easily. Nudity was certainly uploaded into the World Wide Web, but leaking photos was definitely not the same issue as it is in the twenty-first century. Another major difference is news services would not have so readily covered this kind of incident. A story such as Thorne's would have probably been seen as low culture, bad taste, or lowbrow, definitely not front-page news. During a time when paper copies of *USA Today* were available in airports and at hotels and threatened to outsell homegrown newspapers, readers would neither see the word "fuck" in any story nor would they have access to nudity. Likewise, coverage on television would have censored any extemporaneous utterance of "fuck" when watching a national team honored during daylight or primetime viewing hours. Even in the early 1990s, the verb "suck" was monitored for sexual innuendo. Granted, Goldberg has a point that if Thorne had not taken that skinshot then she would not have needed to preempt the hacker to the broadcast of her "boobies." In other words, she would have had no reason technically to exploit herself, turning a demeaning act of misogynistic objectification into a publicity opportunity leading to her sexual empowerment. Allen is also likely correct that Rapinoe should more effectively consider her audience while she is interviewed. However, the distinction between what is right or wrong or ethical or unethical is currently not always clear. Case in point, the Supreme Court recently decided a company may use FUCT as its clothing brand name. As Richard Wolf remarks in a *USA Today* piece, Associate Justice Elena Kagan stated while announcing the decision, "The First Amendment does not allow the government to penalize views just because many people, whether rightly or wrongly, see them as offensive." Needless to say, the real dilemma is defining what is currently "offensive." As the Supreme Court case confirms, what is, to use the conventional connotation, dirty for some is certainly clean for others. Andrew Joseph affirms that media are mostly relinquishing any duties as social and cultural gatekeepers, and he offers the Fox News postgame report after the Americans won the World Cup as evidence. Joseph points out that clearly articulated pronouncements of "fuck" were heard in declarations associated with President Trump during this broadcast. In 2020, a scan of Thorne's Twitter photos indicate she has no problem displaying her body (other recent media indicate she is okay with sexualizing herself), and even though Rapinoe has toned down her language, media coverage suggests she is still a bit unpredictable during public events.

In *I Am Charlotte Simmons*, the recognized social and cultural commentator Tom Wolfe attempts to fictionalize the shifting perspectives associated with sexuality and language, particularly reflective of young people around the traditional college age, eighteen to twenty-two, roughly the age of Thorne (Thorne is twenty-two, and Rapinoe, thirty-four now, would have been in the same age group as the characters when the novel was published in 2004). In a 2004 interview with Brian Lamb on C-SPAN's *BookTV*, Wolfe describes observing this demographic with anthropological intensity, visiting Duke, Stanford, the University of North Carolina, the University of Florida, and the University of Michigan to form a collective vision of this group. To give credence to his portrayal, C-SPAN devoted two academic panel discussions—one from a BookExpo America event ("Book Tour") and another from the Independent Women's Forum ("Discussion")—to debate the book's accuracy. During these sessions, scholars David Brooks and Christina Hoff Summers argue Wolfe's fictional presentation is inaccurate, but just a walk across any collegiate campus could provide observational evidence otherwise. An illustration is Wolfe's scandalous section devoted to the etymology of "fuck." Early in the novel, during a pick-up basketball game, Dupont University senior Jojo Johannsen blurts out profanities after being thoroughly embarrassed by the play of the freshman phenom Vernon Congers. The narrator explains, in Wolfe's undisguised sarcasm:

> Without even realizing what it was, Jojo spoke in this year's prevailing college creole: Fuck Patois. In Fuck Patois, the word fuck was used as an interjection ("What the

fuck" or plain "Fuck," with or without an exclamation point) expressing unhappy surprise; as a participial adjective ("fucking guy," "fucking tree," "fucking elbows") expressing disparagement or discontent; as an adverb modifying and intensifying an adjective ("pretty fucking obvious") or a verb ("I'm gonna fucking kick his ass"); as a noun ("That stupid fuck," "don't give a good fuck"); as a verb meaning *Go away* ("Fuck off"), *beat*—physically, financially, or politically ("really fucked him over") or *beaten* ("I'm fucked"), *botch* ("really fucked that up"), *drunk* ("You are *so* fucked up"); as an imperative expressing contempt ("Fuck you," "Fuck that"). Rarely—the usage had become somewhat archaic—but every now and then it referred to sexual intercourse ("He fucked her on the carpet in front of the TV") [35–36].

Making sure readers see the satire, Wolfe writes in his next sentence: "The fucking freshman in question was standing about twenty fucking feet away" (36). Noted feminist critic Elaine Showalter argues that Wolfe provides mostly vacuous caricature, only reinforcing established stereotypes: "But don't be fooled by the eponymous heroine. Charlotte Simmons is still primarily about masculinity and male contest…. Indeed, it takes a writer as snobbish, superficial, and insecure as Tom Wolfe (who got his own undergraduate degree from Washington and Lee University, where he played baseball) to write such puerile rubbish" (B14). College-level instructors recognize that they must tread lightly through this section in the novel unless they want to be called for a meeting in a dean's or a provost's office. Ironically, even though students vociferously curse on campuses with complete impunity, once they visually view profanity on a page in a book assigned for a college-level course, something interesting happens. Unexpectedly, they start to consider the appropriateness of the language in the controlled atmosphere of the classroom. The same people (largely classified demographically within Generation Z) who post nude selfies and speak in obscenities are surprisingly appalled by Wolfe's survey of "fuck."

Showalter's caustic criticism of Wolfe resembles the tone in many of the negative commentaries leveled against Chuck Palahniuk's fiction, and adverse student reactions imitate corresponding attitudes toward Palahniuk's subjects. In many ways, Wolfe and Palahniuk are similar writers, although they are not usually compared. Both have a penchant for questioning the beliefs, values, and attitudes that are sacrosanct to many Americans, and, consequently, they both have a propensity to expose the subtle as well as the blatant ways Americans hypocritically promote their allegiances to them. In particular, Wolfe and Palahniuk draw attention to how Americans seem to display a fierce attachment to these ideologies when they are challenged by various factors, especially those affiliated with socioeconomic inequities and injustices, delving into nebulous and tempestuous controversies associated with political correctness. For instance, in "Hooking Up," Wolfe foresees the collapse of traditional class distinctions and a redefinition of what is considered "working-class." He predicts that in the 2000s a distinction such as "proletariat" will only be recognized by a "few bitter old Marxist academics with wire hair sprouting out of their ears" because the "average electrician, air-conditioning mechanic, or burglar-alarm repairman [would live] a life that would have made the Sun King blink" (3). Wolfe prophesizes the typical Marxian worker would partake of the stereotypical middle-class existence, vacationing in "Puerto Vallarta, Barbados, or St. Kitts," dining on a terrace of "some resort hotel with his third wife, wearing his Ricky Martin cane-cutter shirt open down to his sternum, the better to allow his gold chains to twinkle in his chest hairs" (3).

Along the same lines, Palahniuk announces a similar merging of socioeconomic classifications in "Foreword: The Fringe Is the Future," the introduction to Read Mercer Schuchardt's essay collection. Palahniuk's prognostication is more so a switching of roles or a swapping of places. Considering the layout of the power circle, those wielding control firmly occupy the middle, while those possessing lesser degrees of authority dissipate into the fringes, along the margins or the boundaries. Palahniuk projects an inversion, an ideological implosion, pulling the middle inside out, that would install a "new form of social structure" empowering those who are on the outside looking in toward the seemingly inviolable innermost point. Palahniuk admits that his fiction depicts the process by which this reversal of fortune occurs, and he portrays how individuals take on the responsibilities of reformulating ideologies to serve their particular social, cultural, and political agendas. In an extremely relevant passage for the remainder of this extensive study of this writer's work, Palahniuk conveys how he undertakes this tremendous literary challenge: "People ask me why I write about characters who seem to live on the margins of society, and my answer is always that the fringe is the future. Outside the mainstream, people are engaged in constant small experiments, testing new social models, new hierarchies, new personal identities. The most successful of those experiments—what begin as cults, fads, crazes, or manias—the ones that serve people best grow to become the new mainstream" (9). Palahniuk consequently shares what has become his mantra, a significant theme explored throughout this book as a guiding principle that underpins many of his texts, "The fringe is the future" (9). These words resonate over a decade after Palahniuk published them in 2008. Evidently, many supporters of President Trump do not necessarily resemble Wolfe's old Marxist professors or Palahniuk's own liberal professor Emmitt Brolly in *Adjustment Day*. If anything, the 2016 presidential election confirms Wolfe's and Palahniuk's predictions about the shifting class tides of power in America. Ironically, proletarian voters identify with the ideology promoted by the bourgeois Trump, and one could surmise many Americans ignore the socioeconomic gulf demarcating them from their president. In fact, Trump's fight against the liberal onslaught of attacks has endeared him to many fringe groups. Upper-class Trump is subsumed by many working-class and under-class Americans as one of their own.

Although coming at the factors that influence social and cultural change from different perspectives, Wolfe and Palahniuk unquestionably address the contemporary significance of status, one's particular place within an ideological framework. In *I Am Charlotte Simmons*, working-class Charlotte eventually achieves notoriety by association with Jojo Johanssen; in *Fight Club*, the grass roots creation of fight club (with the narrator holding a white-collar job but aligning himself with the proletariat over the bourgeoisie) evolves into counter-capitalistic Project Mayhem.[1] Many people were flabbergasted by Wolfe's etymology of one of the most infamous of the taboo words in American society, one surely to precipitate a thorough mouth washing from Mrs. Rapinoe or any other traditionally conscientious American mother. These readers were also probably upset, if they got that far in the book, by Charlotte's sexual experimentation culminating in her date rape after a fraternity dance. Although *Fight Club* does not contain the graphic sexuality—and Wolfe's intention is surely not to entice sexually but to incite socially—Palahniuk's 1996 novel certainly makes up for this through what is largely perceived as gratuitous violence. In either case, readers are offended by fictional presentations that fall outside the comfortable spaces of modesty and propriety.

Wolfe and Palahniuk do not provide typical situations that are scripted according to dominant ideologies. Instead, they offer satirical representations that provoke readers toward questioning the dominance of those ideologies. As Thorne and Rapinoe help to prove, good, moral, and reputable people say "fuck." Likewise, the recent Supreme Court decision illustrates that profanity is clearly interpretative and a matter of taste rather than law. This calls into question the impetus behind such strong reactions against those who deviate from the mainstream. In a 2014 interview with Ed Cumming, Palahniuk describes his creative agenda: "I try to achieve high-culture effects through low-culture methods. I'm fascinated by low fiction that generates a physical response: disgusts the reader, makes them hungry or sexually aroused." Regardless of what he says, none of Palahniuk's fiction, however, whets appetites toward food or sex. Just like Wolfe, Palahniuk takes advantage of tropes to inspire readers to look closely at why they follow, often blindly, authority reinforced by ideology, which is essentially doctrine, principles, or precepts sanctioned by a ruling or a controlling faction—whomever is in power designs the matrix or creates the hegemony that functions to control the actions of the serving population. Both authors motivate readers toward examining why they consider certain behaviors to be either profane, vulgar, or obscene, and, in turn, to acknowledge their own social and cultural hypocrisies.[2] In "The Power of Persisting," after discussing how readers mature as they gain reading experience, Palahniuk comments, "For the sake of argument, I hereby reject first impressions of 'good' or 'bad.' Over time, readers will remember strong writing; time passes, and the reader changes. What's considered tasteful and readily acceptable to one era is easily dismissed by the next, and while the audience for bold storytelling might start small, as time passes it will continue to grow" (3).[3] He points out that a "hallmark of a classic long-lived story is how much it upsets the existing culture at its introduction," and readers are ironically attracted to the repulsion, gaining something beneficial from finally "embracing" what "challenges" (3).[4] As Palahniuk says, the everchanging and divergent "fringe is the future" ("Foreword" 9), and, more so than Wolfe, Palahniuk challenges readers with unorthodox and offensive stories that often precipitate discomfit and distress because they do not pander to prevailing ideological prescriptions.

The purpose of this book is to prove that Palahniuk practices what he preaches. To be more direct, Palahniuk exposes social, cultural, and political paradoxes in ideologies through his unique application of the comic grotesque. Undoubtedly, Palahniuk's subject matter as well as his presentation of this content causes some readers anxiety, stress, and uneasiness. Most people defend their beliefs, values, and attitudes based upon the ideologies that they trust, the paradigms that they faithfully follow as beneficial, equitable, and providential. Justifiably, they respond with anger, frustration, and confusion when tenets that give their lives purpose and meaning are opposed and challenged. Palahniuk provokes readers to examine their preconceptions, ones instilled through formal education and other institutions that promote ruling-class ideologies. To refer to the introductory illustrations, the conflict between Thorne and Goldberg is at its core a difference in ideology, a fundamental disagreement in what is appropriate and suitable conduct according to trusted codes that serve as standards and that foster norms. The same is true for Rapinoe and those who question her integrity simply by her choice of words. As Wolfe contends, whether they like it or not, the times are changing, and people might need to reassess the criteria, as difficult as this would be, upon which they make their judgments. As Palahniuk says in "The Power of Persisting," "What you resist persists" (4). He understands change is inevitable, unavoidable, and inescapable; therefore resiliency, flexibility, and adaptability are admirable virtues. In this era of strictly partisan allegiances, even during the COVID-19 pandemic, these are not widely held let alone practiced.

Palahniuk's brilliance as an author is his ability to uncover flaws in existing paradigms and to call into question allegiances to totalizing systems, most of which are, if the structuralist notion of the "death of man" is believed, only configurations perpetuated to ensure the political status quo. Furthermore, his artistic gift is creating literary stories that allegorically show readers how they are either being deceived or manipulated by ideologies. His strength is an uncompromising and steadfast dedication to presenting this with a simplicity that is almost too accessible, communicated in a minimalist style with ordinary language in literary forms and genres easily understood by his audience. Notwithstanding, Palahniuk creates transgressive fiction considered improper and impolite according to mainstream etiquette and manners. The reality is, however, what he offers could be the ordinary and the commonplace for most of his marginalized and disenfranchised readers, those along the proverbial fringes, and there are more of them than there are those occupying the mainstream—mostly because the lines of demarcation between the two areas is blurring, becoming progressively murky and unclear. Those who defend the markers likely benefit from maintaining the socioeconomic delineations. Actually, the so-called center might be only a faceless bureaucratic amalgam, not concretely populated but only abstractly maintained. Regardless, Palahniuk (and Wolfe) fight against passive adherence to dominant ideologies manifested in the controlling power structure. Palahniuk's fiction is not realistic in terms of presenting a one-to-one corresponding vision of the world. The descriptions on his pages do not provide a mirror-like reflection of everyday occurrences. Instead, Palahniuk relies on imaginative depictions that resemble actual events but then swerve toward the fantastic or the magical to emphasize the message of inconformity and resistance.

An application of several reputable critical theories will help to demonstrate how Palahniuk accomplishes all of this. Mikhail Bakhtin's theory will explain the reversal of high and low social and cultural principles (mostly through the carnivalesque comic grotesque), and Louis Althusser's and Slavoj Žižek's theories will clarify the construction and implementation of ideologies. In the next chapter, there will be a thorough discussion of these theories. In the following chapters, these theories will be applied to several of Palahniuk's fictional works: *Snuff* (Chapter Three), *Damned* and *Doomed* (Chapter Four), *Beautiful You* (Chapter Five), *Make Something Up: Stories You Can't Unread* (Chapter Six), *Bait* and *Legacy* (Chapter Seven), *Fight Club 2* (Chapter Eight), and *Adjustment Day* (Chapter Nine). In the conclusion, attention will be devoted to Palahniuk's aesthetic theory concerning the comic grotesque in conjunction with theories of ideology. Importantly, the argument throughout this book is Palahniuk's fictional carnivals, full of different and distinct narrative voices, portray characters struggling with ideological discordance, a form of cognitive dissonance adapted from Žižek's theory, in which the master belief system no longer seems to work. Characters discover the truths that were once trusted as sacred are essentially falsehoods created to manipulate them toward prescribed and orchestrated behaviors. Readers may laugh at the characters, believing themselves superior, but in actuality, Palahniuk portrays personalities that are fundamentally ordinary and commonplace. Just like students who arrogantly assume the moral high ground while reading *I Am Charlotte Simmons*, readers might not notice on the surface the affinities they have with these characters, but when they dig into the substance of the stories, hopefully they will identify with what Palahniuk presents.

To contextualize his strategy, every chapter will begin with relevant information (mostly from last year, 2019) to demonstrate how Palahniuk responds to currently controversial issues. These introductions are necessary to show how Palahniuk situates his stories within provocative contemporary settings. The contention repeatedly made throughout this book is that Palahniuk seditiously veils his message behind satirical fantasy or hyperbolic realism, performing the act of carnival by masquerading common occurrence and ordinary life in his fictional accounts. For this reason, examples of similar real-life incidents are necessary. Many of Palahniuk's settings are imaginary, such as Madison's hell or Talbott's territories, or are embellished, as with Cassie's gang bang or Maxwell's nanobots, but Palahniuk reinforces these fictional representations with how real flesh-and-blood people respond when confronted with dominant ideologies set out to manipulate their behaviors, their attitudes, and their decisions. Palahniuk wants his readers subsequently to apply what they learn by taking ownership of their own lives. In *Adjustment Day*, Shasta contemplates how the same sun that warms her also warmed Hitler (267), which inadvertently speaks to the temporality of ideological repression. Although references to current situations might seem extraneous or superfluous, they embed Palahniuk's creative rhetoric in his works within the decade of 2008–2018, from *Snuff* to *Adjustment Day*.

Dorothy Parker is generally attributed as saying, "A little bad taste is like a nice dash of paprika" ("Dorothy"). Although Palahniuk's fiction might seem to be overly seasoned, his peppering (actually splashing) of literary transgression sufficiently presents his currently apropos axiom, one that will be validated and verified throughout this book: the fringe is moving toward the center ("Foreword" 9). Fair warning is now given to readers who are not interested in the critical background, the esoteric theories of Bakhtin, Althusser, and Žižek. The information in the second chapter is needed but is not necessary to understand the content in the third through the tenth chapters. If readers do not want background theory—about significant reviews of Palahniuk's work and criticism that will be applied to his work—they should move past the second chapter to the third chapter. The information in the second chapter is for those who want to understand background concerning the comic grotesque (broken down into comedy and grotesque) in addition to an explanation of significant details pertaining to the applicable theories of ideology. To entice readers into the next chapter, one needs only to consider the real-world application of Bakhtin's carnival. In a *USA Today* photo spread titled "The Best Pop Culture-Themed Hotels and Rentals of 2019: Barbie, Harry Potter, Lisa Frank, More," a caption reads, "Fandoms around the world in 2019 had the opportunity to live like their favorite characters: Airbnbs and other hotel booking sites collaborated with some major brands to bring on-screen places to life." People pay to live like the characters who occupy their favorite stories. They also want to reside within the lap of American consumerism, staying in places decorated to resemble a Taco Bell restaurant, albeit on a hyperreal scale, and other commercial-themed hotels. Carnival is what people crave in entertainment, and it is also what they yearn for in their own lives. Palahniuk adds Parker's dash to how art imitates life, or, conversely, how life imitates art.

Here is another reason to proceed to the next chapter. In "The Second Coming," William Butler Yeats might have been correct when he portrayed the cyclical give-and-take of belief systems, competing saviors alternatively empowered within a perpetual gyre. Yeats writes, "Things fall apart; the centre cannot hold; / Mere anarchy is loosed upon the world" (3–4). In the Palahniuk cycle, those who inhabit the fringe will inevitably replace whatever constituency occupies the central point. This relates to the lines of Yeats's poem in which "The best lack all conviction, while the worst / Are full of passionate intensity" (7–8). There is a constant back-and-forth tidal motion between those that "lack all conviction" and those "full of passionate intensity." Cultural mavericks, those such as Thorne and Rapinoe, feel their "intensity" is lost upon those who exhibit a loss of the appropriate "conviction." Hence, the fringe moves toward the center. This book will help readers to understand how Palahniuk enables readers to see, as Yeats claims in the ninth line, a revelation is inevitable. Currently, things are falling apart, the centre is not holding, and the fringe is becoming the new normal. As Palahniuk forecasts, those on the margins will establish their presence in the mainstream ("Foreword" 9).

Two

The Subversive Power of the Comic Grotesque

In "The Guts Effect," Chuck Palahniuk claims that nobody fainted when he initially read his famous story "Guts" during a 1991 workshop meeting with his friends. He shares in this essay, "Each week, I would read another of the short stories I planned to include in a novel to be called *Haunted*. My goal was to create horror around very ordinary things: carrots, candles, swimming pools. Microwave popcorn. Bowling balls." He continues by claiming "Guts" is based on real-life experiences heard from friends, anecdotes about masturbation that had "gone wrong. Horribly wrong." In a 2004 article in *The Guardian*, Dan Glaister recalled that Palahniuk, after a public reading of the story, testified that "Guts" could "damage your health" because of its emotional assault on the senses, specifying that forty people had fainted while listening to the tale. The number of those who experienced a visceral response to "Guts" has well surpassed one hundred by 2020. Glaister acknowledges Palahniuk's exaggerated self-confidence to evoke illness, but he also recognizes this author's writing has an uncannily noticeable effect on readers. Through his prose, Palahniuk has a knack for influencing people at a gut level, emotionally as well as physically. Unequivocally, the visceral "effect" of Palahniuk's transgressive descriptions is a defining quality of his literary expertise.

Applied as literary criticism, the Marxist theories of Mikhail Bakhtin, Louis Althusser, and Slavoj Žižek will help to demonstrate the philosophical nature of the extensive Palahniuk effect. Bakhtin's theory of carnival serves as the baseline for this study. More precisely, an application of Bakhtin's "comic grotesque," grotesque realism combined with comic elements of transgression, will function as the central critical concept in this examination of Palahniuk's work. Before addressing the comic grotesque, in addition to Althusser's and Žižek's theories of ideology, a rationale for this investigation needs to be established as a defense of Palahniuk's effect against relevant criticism. As mentioned in the previous chapter, this book

Two. The Subversive Power of the Comic Grotesque

will defend Palahniuk's literary approach against critics who are unable to unpack the messages beneath his mediums. Palahniuk takes advantage of the comic grotesque to warn readers against the exploitation of dominant ideologies. This chapter will explain what this means in theoretical and in practical terms.

To be fair from the onset, a taste of negative criticism of Palahniuk should be surveyed.[1] In a *Paste* article about *Fight Club 2*, after referring to the "Guts Effect" as well as Madison severing her grandfather's penis in *Doomed*, Tyler R. Kane portrays Palahniuk as the "dude who has, more or less, mapped a career from finding meaning in your family's worst story." In a *New York Times* review of *Damned*, Janet Maslin writes, "By any definition of the word 'decency' it's been a long time since Chuck Palahniuk wrote a decent book," and tracing the progression from *Snuff* to *Tell-All* to *Pygmy*, she concludes, "These books have been skimpy and tired enough to suggest that this *Fight Club* author has had all the fight drained out of him." Evaluating *Damned* for *GQ*, Eric Sullivan jibes, "Chuck Palahniuk is not the worst writer in the world, but he is certainly one of the most frustrating. His phoned-in, half-baked drivel reads like a deviant 7th grader's diary." Referring to Palahniuk's belief in what is termed "dangerous writing," when an author addresses personally troubling material, Tim Martin states in *The Telegraph*, "The impression is of a writer phoning in his stuff with cynical abandon. It's genuinely dispiriting to see Palahniuk reduced to the Garbage Pail Kid of contemporary literature, prodding gently in book after book at the disgust reflexes of bored teens," wisecracking that these "glib compendiums of adolescent humour" are only "dangerous" to a person's reputation if others find out he or she purchased them. Critiquing *Beautiful You* for National Public Radio, Jason Sheehan grouses, "So I wanted to remind [Palahniuk] that veiled satire needs, at minimum, two things to succeed: First, a veil, however thin. Second, it has to actually *be* satire, and not just 200 pages of telling everybody on earth how dumb they are." Reviewing *Adjustment Day* for *The Observer*, Alexander Larman sees the book as boring, chastising Palahniuk, "While his descriptions of Project Mayhem in *Fight Club* suggested a real nihilistic rage, there is little more here than tired shock tactics. At a time when parents and children are being forcibly separated at US border control and imprisoned, there is hardly a need for this oddly dated polemic...." These critics also concede Palahniuk's appeal. Maslin believes Palahniuk is revitalized through *Doomed*, Sullivan admits Palahniuk is nonetheless successful, Larman sees bright spots in *Adjustment Day*, and Martin finally grants, praising *Fight Club* counter-culturalism, Palahniuk attracts those who crave stories that will "grab them by the throat."

Of all the negative commentary, four scorching reviews display open derision for Palahniuk's technique. Beyond the acrimony, these writers believe they are fulfilling their professional obligations to their readers. In the section assigned for criticism on the "Chuck Palahniuk" page on *Wikipedia*, Laura Miller's review in *Salon* stands out as the representative negative assessment of Palahniuk's work. To add injury to insult, because this is the criticism most easily searched and downloaded, this passage resurfaces frequently in other places (such as hastily composed undergraduate essays). Miller begins by asking readers to consider horrible prose, full of sophomoric mistakes emblematic of novice creative writers. Then she drops the hammer: "Does it hurt yet? Now, imagine that every five pages or so the author of these novels will describe something as smelling like shit or piss because the TRUTH is fucking ugly, man. Imagine that he affects to attack the shallow, simplistic, dehumanizing culture of commodity capitalism by writing shallow, simplistic, dehumanized fiction." Miller finishes this passage by sarcastically reprimanding Palahniuk for hastily pumping out superficially developed books each year. In an often-cited section, Miller takes shots at what most would consider Palahniuk's strengths, his style and his presentation, by comparing the technique of a great novelist with that of Palahniuk, whom she deems a bad writer: "The bad writer, it turns out, picks exactly the wrong detail, flubs it, and then tosses it like a stink bomb in the path of the reader dutifully struggling to follow him. This is a signature Palahniuk technique." During a rare occasion in which he responds to critical attack, Palahniuk retorts (in a published declaration in *Salon*), "Until you can create something that captivates people, I'd invite you to just shut up. It's easy to attack and destroy an act of creation. It's a lot more difficult to perform one. I'd also invite you to read the reviews Fitzgerald got for 'Gatsby' from dull, sad, bitter people—like yourself." Unfortunately, Miller's words are often viewed as the definitive critical commentary because they appear on Palahniuk's *Wikipedia* page.

In her review of *Make Something Up* for *The Guardian*, Sandra Newman offers opinions that have been embraced by many academics, calling into question Palahniuk's status as an author worthy of attention in scholastic settings. Her most vitriolic comment expresses how many feel about the insubstantiality and superficiality of Palahniuk's work: "No one would call Chuck Palahniuk a writer's writer. He isn't even, strictly speaking, a reader's writer. He's the sort of author who's admired by people who don't usually care for literature, and correspondingly scorned by those who do." What is remarkable about this review, however, is the love/hate relationship critics (as well as general readers) form with this author. Newman admits that Palahniuk's characters are banal and his style is pedestrian, but she gives in that some of his transgressive stories are "startling" and are not loaded with profanity solely for juvenile shock effect. Newman admires at least aspects of Palahniuk's technique when she commends his ability to create engaging plots out of implausible occurrences. Nonetheless, Newman calls out Palahniuk for repetitively misusing words, inferring that neither Palahniuk nor his editors corrected the errors because his stereotypically unacademic readers (victims of "genuine illiteracy") would not even notice them. Confirming the intended effect of the stories, Newman argues that Palahniuk "leans heavily on gross-out humour," which she contends is not funny because it is often laced with varieties of discrimination. Unfortunately, she loses sight of the purpose behind the satire. Newman makes the connection between Palahniuk and both Rabelais and Burroughs (a significant comparison between comedy and transgression that will be focused upon later in this chapter), and she concludes ultimately that Palahniuk is an author who is good at what he does but who refuses to do anything good with it, only expressing literary tantrums that his editors apparently ignore if not enable.

Paula Bomer's critique of *Beautiful You* in *The New York Times* has been cited by critics for its sardonic first sentence. For instance, in his post for *Barnes & Nobles Reads*, Jeff Sommers urges readers to take a chance on reading Palahniuk's work even though the critical reception is vastly divided, and he praises the underrated Palahniuk as the voice of his generation. Notwithstanding, Sommers begins his discussion by citing Bomer's famous statement, "Palahniuk is a novelist of ideas, I suppose, but that doesn't necessarily mean they're good ones." In her review, Bomer berates Palahniuk for his unflattering characterization of C. Linus Maxwell. Considering all of the technically clinical descriptions of female genitalia during arousal and orgasm, Bomer writes, "It's as if the reader is vicariously experiencing a particularly uncomfortable gynecological exam. And while the novel delivers moments of awkward humor and some nominally feminist plot twists, the language and the ridiculousness of this particular concept remain hard to digest." After praising Palahniuk for all of his research in preparation for his meticulously esoteric coverage, Bomer claims that readers might laugh at Palahniuk's satirical mockery of sociocultural clichés, but the major problem is above and beyond anything else Palahniuk's unsexy depiction of sexual material. Again, similar to Newman's review, Bomer's criticism is mostly negative but has iridescent flashes of praise. Likewise, comparable to Newman, Bomer fails to recognize that what she considers a weakness is indeed the novel's greatest strength. Palahniuk is scrutinizing the sexualization of American capitalist consumerism, and his rather effective strategy is to go right at the feminine personal pleasure device industry.

The harshest of Palahniuk's reviews is unmistakably Lucy Ellmann's critique of *Snuff* in *The New York Times Book Review*, and her commentary, like the opinions of Bomer and Miller, has an intertextual life by appearing in other criticisms dispersed all over the Internet. Deciding whether Salman Rushdie, William Burroughs, or Chuck Palahniuk received the worst *New York Times Book Review* commentary, a writer for *Vulture* concludes, "But the gold medal goes to Chuck Palahniuk's *Snuff*, which as it happens is the target of—and there's no nicer way to put this—a snuff review by Lucy Ellmann, one that offers the queasy-making sight of a book being shot dead by a reviewer bent on mayhem." Ellmann's first paragraph presents succinctly the aversion many readers have with Palahniuk's work: "What the hell is going on? The country that produced Melville, Twain and James now venerates King, Crichton, Grisham, Sebold and Palahniuk. Their subjects? Porn, crime, pop culture and an endless parade of out-of-body experiences. Their methods? Cliché, caricature and proto-Christian morality. Props? Corn chips, corpses, crucifixes. The agenda? Deceit: a dishonest throwing of the reader to the wolves. And the result? Readymade Hollywood scripts." Sarcastically, Ellmann admonishes Palahniuk for achieving sensationalist fame by relying on the success of "Guts," a story that "excellently delineates the shallowness of American life," only to conclude afterward, "Whatever point Palahniuk meant to make seems to have been lost in a self-induced miasma of meaninglessness—onanism of a more dispiriting sort." After questioning many aspects of the plot in *Snuff* (the movie titles, the sex factoids, the sex products, etc.), Ellmann sees little moral or ethical value in a novel that seems only to mock and ridicule. She views little artistry in Palahniuk's weak attempt to cobble together porn language in an innovatively productive way. In a review of *Snuff* for *The Los Angeles Times*, Carolyn Kellogg acknowledges Ellmann's points but also recognizes Palahniuk's large audience probably fails to appreciate canonical literature. Kellogg also responds, however, readers might not see themselves portrayed in Palahniuk's characters. Importantly, Kellogg and Ellmann miss the point that Palahniuk is neither asking readers to identify with his characters nor requesting they imitate the language. Ellmann neglects to account for Melville's absence in the highbrow American literary canon until critics such as Van Wyck Brooks called for the substitution of provincial Melville for Eurocentric (stuffy and boring) New England writers who did not reflect indigenous American ideology. Palahniuk's opponents' posture on so-called higher ground, obviously believing Palahniuk caters to a homespun low-class readership along the uncouth, uncivilized, and inherently uneducated fringe. Ironically, Melville was also once considered lingering along the fringe.

Granted, most of these critics (and readers) feel this way because of Palahniuk's transgressivity. Thinking about Thorne's and Rapinoe's situations, the transgressive includes words such as "fuck" and describes women's breasts with nipple piercings. In "Chuck Palahniuk's *Beautiful You*, Alfred Kinsey's *Sexual Behavior in the Human Female*, and the Commodification of Female Sexual Desire," I write that transgressive writing rebels against conventional standards, "exposing the darker shades, bleaker terrains, and rougher contours of humanity than presented in most mainstream fiction; focusing on the nihilistic and existential vicissitudes associated within the human experience. Transgressive fiction often includes content that is considered obscene, vulgar, and profane; and it frequently raises questions concerning what is proper or improper, acceptable or unacceptable, and even right or wrong" (102). In "Preface to Transgression," Michel Foucault set the standard in 1963, although abstractly, for the contemporary definition of this genre: "transgression prescribes not only the sole manner of discovering the sacred in its unmediated substance, but also a way of recomposing its empty form, its absence, through which it becomes all the more scintillating. A rigorous language, as it arises from sexuality, will not reveal the secret of man's natural being, nor will it express the serenity or anthropological truths, but rather, it will say that he exists without God" (30). In an influential *Los Angeles Times* article, Michael Silverblatt explains in 1993, acknowledging Foucault's emphasis on experience, "The body becomes the locus for the possibility of knowledge.... AIDS is throwing everyone's sexual norms into disarray, and the already embattled nuclear family is under attack by the new rhetoric of incest, abuse and dysfunction" (17). In an *Atlantic* "Word Watch," Anne H. Soukhanov describes transgressive fiction in 1996 as "a literary genre that graphically explores such topics as incest and other aberrant sexual practices, mutilation, the sprouting of sexual organs in various places on the human body, urban violence and violence against women, drug use, and highly dysfunctional family relationships, and that is based on the premise that knowledge is to be found at the edge of experience and that the body is the site for gaining knowledge" (128). In her seminal *New York Times* article, Rene Chun comments in 1995, "Subversive, avant-garde, bleak, pornographic—and these are compliments. Such words are used to describe transgressive fiction, books pitched to young adults, written by authors descended from William Burroughs and the Marquis de Sade, that explore aberrant sexual practices, urban violence, drug use and dysfunctional families in graphic detail" (49). In *Transgressive Fiction*, Robin Moorkerjee views writers such as Palahniuk as "continuing the venerable tradition of social satire but making it more transgressive" (2). He adds, "Transgressive satirists treat flashpoint subjects without taking any kind of moral stand and treat bizarre behavior as if it were absolutely normal" (2). These descriptions certainly apply to Palahniuk's mode of writing.

More pertinent for this study of Palahniuk, however, is how Peter

Stallybrass and Allon White define transgression, drawing connections between counterculture or anti-social behaviors—those considered improper, impolite, or rude—with Bakhtin's theories concerning comedy, grotesque, and carnival. In their influential *The Politics and Poetics of Transgression*, Stallybrass and White see Bakhtin's theory of carnival as a vehicle perfect for transgressive fiction. As they point out, carnival as an event is therapeutic, cleansing, and rehabilitative: "There is now a large and increasing body of writing which sees carnival not simply as a ritual feature of European culture but as a *mode of understanding*, a positivity, a cultural analytic" (6). The controlled chaos of carnival motivates people to accept behaviors that would normally be chastised as improper. These two theorists continue,

> Carnival is in its widest, most general sense embraced ritual spectacles such as fairs, popular feasts and wakes, processions and competitions ..., comic shows, mummery and dancing, open-air amusement with costumes and masks, giants, dwarfs, monsters, trained animals and so forth; it included comic verbal compositions (oral and written) such as parodies, travesties and vulgar farce; and it included various genres of "Billingsgate," by which Bakhtin designated curses, oaths, slang, humour, popular tricks and jokes, scatological forms, in fact all the "low" and "dirty" sorts of folk humour. Carnival is presented by Bakhtin as a world of topsy-turvy, of heterglot exuberance, of careless overrunning and excess where all is mixed, hybrid, ritually degraded and defiled [8].

Furthermore, they explain that carnival laughter has an "earthy" quality, full of "abusive language" and "mocking words" that contrasts starkly with the official and bureaucratic dominant or privileged discourse affiliated with the empowered, consequently claiming this language is "used for parody, subversive humour and aversion" (8). They interpret Bakhtin's grotesque realism as "flesh conceptualized as corpulent excess" (8–9) that exploits physical hyperbole and sexual utility: "The openings and orifices of this carnival body are emphasized, not its closure and finish" (9). Significantly, especially for applications in this study of Palahniuk's work, they assert that Bakhtin's carnival evolved, eventually transforming into what is currently perceived as the transgressive.[2]

In traditional literary criticism, an appeal to humor falls within the purview of comedy. In his seminal *Anatomy of Criticism*, Northrop Frye places the comic within the fourth of five classifications of the heroic modes: "If superior neither to other men nor to his environment, the hero is one of us: we respond to a sense of his common humanity, and demand from the poet the same canons of probability that we find in our own experience. This gives us the hero of the *low mimetic* mode, of most comedy and of realistic fiction" (34). However, from a contemporary perspective, and one only has to consider any popular situation-comedy, especially affiliated with one of the major television networks, audiences are amused and find comfort laughing at characters and not necessarily laughing with them, particularly in the imitative mimetic way. Audiences exhibit traits of schadenfreude, pleasure felt from others' misfortunes. This would perhaps correspond to Frye's last category: "If inferior in power or intelligence to ourselves, so that we have the sense of looking down on a scene of bondage, frustration, or absurdity, the hero belongs to the *ironic* mode. This is still true when the reader feels that he is or might be in the same situation, as the situation is being judged by the norms of a greater freedom" (34). Frye illustrates his fourth mode by explaining how Lysistrata in Aristophanes's Greek play evokes emotions of "sympathy and ridicule" of comedy, comparable to the ones of "pity and fear" in tragedy, asserting the "comic hero will get his triumph whether what he has done is sensible or silly, honest or rascally" (43). Frye reiterates that this hero "is seldom a very interesting person: in conformity with low mimetic decorum, he is ordinary in his virtues, but socially attractive" (44). Frye places the concepts of the *alazon* (self-aggrandizing) and the *eiron* (self-deprecating) figures in the last mode predicated on both exhibiting ironic behaviors in that they are versions of the self-deceived personality (40).[3]

Similarly, Roger B. Rollin asserts readers believe themselves to be better than comic characters. He points out in *Hero/Antihero* that the "Lowly Man," the fifth type of hero, "is at best inept and at worst disreputable" (xix). Rollin claims this character "is clearly not one toward whom we aspire. Indeed, we may be able to identify with him only during our most self-deprecating moods or in his moments of transcendence" (xix). Rollin places the Lowly Man within the realm of comedy, and readers feel superior to this person because they are too intelligent to find themselves in the Lowly Man's circumstances (xix). Audiences are more likely to laugh at a low figure, one toward whom they feel superior, but they are also prone to relish the fall of a high character. Although this fall is traditionally in the domain of tragedy—an elevated figure falls because of a flaw (hamartia), usually excessive pride (hubris), and has a revelation only after the damage is done—there are surely those who enjoy seeing the great brought down to the common level. People like to see someone particularly deserving of retribution get exactly what he or she is entitled to receive, no more or no less. Referring to the beginning of this book, there are likely those who would be entertained via schadenfreude if Thorne or if Rapinoe were publicly reprimanded for their lapses in what is considered mainstream moral judgment. The punishment would pertain to mainstream rules concerning fair and equitable justice. The addition of transgressive behaviors always increases the public delight. Case in point is the infamous Puritan justice enacted upon Nathaniel Hawthorne's Hester Prynne for her act of adultery in the American classic *The Scarlet Letter*. Hawthorne's addition of a child spawned from the promiscuity increases the transgressive appeal of the story. If current celebrities are now synonymous with ancient royalty, media sensationalize the ascension as well as the decline in status. In this regard, one only needs to consider Bill Cosby, once praised for his virtuous work with children, now in prison for multiple sexual assaults.

Incidentally, a transgressive component also influences the variety of laugh evoked by the comedy. In many world literature survey courses, students react toward the women's sex strike in *Lysistrata* similarly to how many responded to Tom Wolfe's etymology of "fuck" in *I Am Charlotte Simmons*. These readers incorrectly perceive Lysistrata's call for celibacy as a literal action and not as Aristophanes's literary satirical farce. As a result, they definitely do not laugh at references to sex toys, erect penises, and aroused vaginas (refer to my article "'Just hear that potty mouth!': An Argument for Sarah Ruden's Translation of *Lysistrata*"). Stallybrass and White's association of the transgressive with Bakhtinian concepts is pertinent in this regard. Granted, concerning Thorne's situation, there is nothing humorous about possible extortion or blackmail. Furthermore, in Rapinoe's case, sexism and homophobia are not funny. Yet, the implications of both situations are interesting. Since these situations were covered by the national media, people evidently were interested in what happened. In terms of heroism, both women exhibited fortitude and were steadfast in their beliefs. However, both chose to express themselves in less than appropriate ways according to mainstream notions of moral and ethical behavior. When people read the *USA Today* articles about the indiscretions, some might feel self-righteous superiority because the circumstances relate to sex and to profanity. Palahniuk plays with this dynamic, anticipating how readers might hypocritically position themselves on slippery high ground. As will be demonstrated, Palahniuk's depictions of how Americans confront problems related to their belief systems expose the same hypocrisies. Hawthorne understood this when he allowed Hester ultimately to gain moral and ethical traction in his story. Many contemporary readers' responses toward Palahniuk characters are not very different from Renaissance readers' reactions to Rabelais's *Gargantua and Pantagruel*. Actually, in the next few chapters, Bakhtin's interpretation of how Rabelais fictionalized his world will correspond closely to how Palahniuk depicts his own.

Before summarizing Bakhtin's ideas, however, a specific look at Rabelais's fiction helps to illustrate this point. A couple of representative passages selected from the *Norton Anthology of World Literature* show what Rabelais achieves in *Gargantua and Pantagruel*. Comparable to how some react to references to dildos and erections in *Lysistrata*, many readers do not understand the satire in Rabelais's story, therefore not seeing the purpose underlying the profanity and vulgarity—inaccurately taking the references at face value instead of integrating them within the fabric of the story's overall texture. These readers fail to understand, as Bakhtin contends in his study of Rabelais's work, ruling authority is subverted and power systems are parodied, and transgression accentuates and intensifies both. For instance, in a section devoted to the education of Gargantua (and his hugeness reflects spectacular embellishment and elaborate farce), the student reads from a desk weighing more than thirty tons an actual book used during Rabelais's time, *De modis significandi* (*The Methods of Reasoned Analysis*), which contains philosophical discussions from noted scholars Broken Biscuithead, Bouncing Rock, Talktoomuch, Cuntprober, and many others with similar nomenclatures (2596). Before his tutelage under his professor, aptly named Powerbrain, Gargantua "shat, pissed, vomited, belched, farted, yawned, spat, coughed, sighed, sneezed and blew his nose abundantly" (2600). In the description of the Abbey of Thélème, Rabelais mocks church protocol. When Gargantua asks why there will be no walls, he is told "it won't be necessary to build walls all around it, because all the abbeys are brutally closed in" (2608). Likewise, the typical inhabitants will not serve as occupants: "because in these times of ours women don't go into convents unless they're blind in one eye, lame, humpbacked, ugly, misshapen, crazy, stupid, deformed, or pox-ridden, and men only if they're tubercular, low born, blessed with an ugly nose, simpletons, or a burden on their parents ... it was decreed that, in Thélème, women would be allowed only if they were beautiful, well formed, and cheerful, and men only if they were handsome, well formed, and cheerful" (2608). In line with the hyperbolic nature of the story, the decree of Thélème is "DO WHAT YOU WILL" (2615).

Emphasizing physicality while lampooning the abstract and the theoretical, Rabelais stages an absurd scholastic debate between Pantagruel's roguish friend Panurge and a pedantic Englishman who communicates through sign language. As Thaumaste puffs out his cheeks as if he were "inflating a pig's bladder," Panurge counters: "At which Panurge stuck one finger of his left hand right up his ass, sucking in air with his mouth, as if eating oysters in the shell or inhaling soup. Then he opened his mouth a bit and slapped himself with the palm of his right hand, making an immensely loud sound which seemed to work its way up from the very depths of his diaphragm all along the tracheal artery. And he did this sixteen times" (2627). After Thaumaste thumbs his nose, Panurge offers the decisive blow: "So Panurge put his forefingers on each side of his mouth, pulling back as hard as he could and showing all his teeth. His thumbs drew his lower eyelids as far down as they would go, making an exceedingly ugly face, or so it seemed to everyone watching" (2628). Readers laugh at Rabelais's sixteenth-century comedy while they cringe at the grotesque, feeling both attraction and repulsion to the preposterousness of the actions described in the scene. The legacy of Rabelais's craft can be seen in current programs such as *Family Guy*, *American Dad*, and *Rick and Morty*, cartoon satires of contemporary issues that rely on comic hyperbole and grotesque metaphor, popular for their flaunting of bad taste and blasting of social decorum. Other Adult Swim programs undoubtedly fit into this mold. Unmistakably, Palahniuk also portrays the contemporary world through the Rabelaisian lens.

A consideration of the transgressive implicitly calls for a definition of the normative revered in the mainstream. If the transgressive (abhorrent or deviant) is typically associated with the fringe, then its meaning depends on its binary (normal or average) firmly placed in the center. Of course, whomever controls power usually decides what is inside and, by the same token, outside. This is addressed in disability studies in which normalcy is synonymous with "ableness," but ableism holds the same pejorative connotation as sexism, racism, or homophobia. To be able-bodied infers normalcy, so those who are not able-bodied are inferior, are disabled, and are subsequently abnormal. In turn, those who are abnormal are linked with characteristics of the grotesque, something that is neither attractive nor desired because of its otherness. In *Narrative Prosthesis*, David T. Mitchell and Sharon L. Snyder explain that normalcy is contextual: "While differing conditions—in the jargon of the field, sensory impairments, orthopedic impairments, neurological impairments, language and speech disabilities, emotional disturbances—have particular consequences for the individuals involved, in each instance it is the interplay between the condition and the environment which determines the extent to which a disability becomes a handicap" (2). In *Dis/ability Studies*, Dan Goodley contends "not abled" signifies abnormality: "Disability haunts and produces humanity (a humanity often rested on ableist ideals). When the good life, a functioning body, being sound of mind are understood they can only ever be done so in relation to their apparent opposites: the monstrous lives of the poor, the broken bodies and those lacking intellect" (56). Goodley argues that on the "neoliberal ablest landscape" (38), normalcy is determined by its identification with white heteropatriarchal ideology (36–39). In *Contours of Ableism*, Fiona Kumari Campbell concurs that definitions of normalcy are ideological: "Inscribing certain bodies in terms of deficiency and essential inadequacy privileges a particular understanding of normalcy that is commensurate with the interests of dominant groups (and the assumed interests of subordinated groups)" (11). Campbell defines "disablism" (synonymous with ableism) as "a set of assumptions (conscious or unconscious) and practices that promote the differential or unequal treatment of people because of actual or presumed disabilities" (4), and she recognizes that "disability is always present (despite its seeming absence) in the ableist talk of normalcy" (14).[4] In "Screening Stereotypes," Paul Longmore asserts that writers characterize those with disabilities as three stereotypes: "disability is a punishment for evil; disabled people are embittered by their 'fate'; disabled people resent the nondisabled and would, if they could, destroy them" (67).[5] Significantly, Mitchell and Snyder point out, "The power of transgression always originates at the moment when the derided object embraces its deviance as value. Perversely championing the terms of their own stigmatization, marginal peoples alarm the dominant culture with a canniness about their own subjugation. The embrace of denigrating terminology forces the dominant culture to face its own violence head-on because the authority of devaluation has been claimed openly and ironically" (35). Traditionally, the abnormal has been associated with the grotesque, considered the "derided object" that opposes, by nature of its difference, the desired normal object.

Through his writing, Palahniuk exposes the hypocrisy underlying mainstream allegiance to the broadly accepted definition of normalcy based on dominant ideology. He reveals, to borrow Friedrich Engels's term (reaffirmed by György Lukács), the false consciousness upon which people base their values, beliefs, and attitudes.[6] Hence, Palahniuk is just as subversive as Rabelais in using literature to illuminate for readers the illusions upon which they obediently base their life decisions. In their comprehensive study in this area, Justin D. Edwards and Rune Graulund start off with two denotations per the *Oxford English Dictionary*, "the grotesque is incongruous or inappropriate to a shocking degree" and "comically distorted figures, creatures or images'" (2). Afterward, they ponder that a "grotesque body that is incomplete or deformed forces us to question what it means to be human" (3). In a significant passage, they situate the grotesque within the context of normalcy:

> Grotesque figures can cause the dissolution of the borders separating the normal and abnormal, inside and outside, internal and external.... After all, we must remember that normalization is a powerful discourse for control and institutionalization, for dominant institutions sanction certain forms of "normalcy," and this always comes at the expense of others, which are constituted by contrast as abnormal, inferior or even shameful.... The ab/normal aspects of the grotesque, and the provocative way in which that lack of normality is represented, have inspired some critics to condemn it as a marker of what is "uncivilized," thereby offensively reinscribing the distinctions between the norm and its deviations ... grotesquerie revolves around the categories of inclusion (the norm) and exclusion (the abnormal) in order to preserve marked distinctions between "us" and "them," "self and other" [9].

In his fiction, Palahniuk often blurs these divisions. Although his portrayals appear sometimes fantastically beyond the realm of reality, at least outside most routine experience, he is close enough in his pseudo-parabolic stories for reader identification with the situations and contexts. For readers familiar with Palahniuk transgression, normalcy is a matter of subjective opinion, not objective definition. In fact, normal as an entity is more a representation perpetuated by those in power to reinforce their dominance than a description that refers to the average, the commonplace, or the everyday. To many Palahniuk readers, the grotesque situated in the fringe is the new normal. To be grotesque is therefore to be average, a simple semantic inversion of meaning.

There are several pertinent studies of the grotesque, tracing the concept historically and critically from a physical deformity to a psychological psychosis. In the respected *A Handbook to Literature*, the perennially trusted reference source for anything related to literary studies, William Harmon offers the standard denotation applicable "to any decorative art characterized by fantastic representations of human and animal forms often combined into formal distortions of the natural to the point of absurdity, ugliness, or caricature. It was so named after the ancient paintings and decorations found in the underground chambers (*grotte*) of Roman ruins. By extension, *grotesque* is applied to anything having the qualities of *grotesque* art: bizarre, incongruous, ugly, unnatural, fantastic, abnormal" (223). Afterward, Harmon presents the contemporary meaning:

> [The] *grotesque* is the merging of the comic and tragic, resulting from our loss of faith in the moral universe essential to tragedy and in a rational social order essential to comedy. Where nineteenth-century critics like Walter Bagehot saw the *grotesque* as a deplorable variation from the normal, Thomas Mann sees it as the "most genuine style" for the modern world and the "only guise in which the sublime may appear" now. Jorge Luis Borges echoed Mann's sentiment. Flannery O'Connor seems to mean the same thing when she calls the *grotesque* character "man forced to meet the extremes of his own nature" [223].

Edwards and Graulund provide an excellent survey how the grotesque has functioned as a literary trope associated with subversion. Importantly, they note that the grotesque cannot be "locking into" one meaning but is transformative (15), and they offer succinct, cogent, and comprehensive summaries of the most respected scholars writing about this area: Wolfgang Kayser, Dieter Meindl, Bernard McElroy, Geoffrey Galt Harpham, Philip Thomson, James Goodwin, and Irving Howe (1–15).[7] Edwards and Graulund trace the grotesque through critical theory (including Foucault and Julia Kristeva) as well as devote chapters to the grotesque stereotyped as monstrosities, deformities, outcasts, and commodities. They also contextualize the grotesque within Bakhtin's carnival, queer theory, and postcolonial theory, conceptualizing the grotesque as the Other in cultural terms. Synthesizing Mookerjee's ideas about transgression with Kathryn Hume's concerning "aggressive fiction," Douglas Keesey writes, "Both scholars note that one of the most potent weapons of satire is the grotesque or 'monstrous' body, one whose unruly corporality defies repressive rules and regulations ... and upsets society's rigid order.... Palahniuk frequently uses the grotesque or 'monstrous' body as a satiric attack on social norms" (13). Keesey offers this discussion while categorizing Palahniuk's characters within the literary tradition of "social misfits and protesters" having physical deformities or possessing psychological psychoses (11–13).

For a better understanding of how grotesque is applied in this study of Palahniuk, Robert Dunne's discussion in *A New Book of Grotesques* is especially relevant.[8] Dunne astutely analyzes Sherwood Anderson's eponymous treatment of the grotesque as a metaphor to describe the disconnectedness and alienation felt by the inhabitants of his stories collected in *Winesburg, Ohio*. Dunne explores how these distinctly modernist themes are manifested in the personalities of Anderson's characters. In "The Book of the Grotesque," Anderson's narrator explains that when people embrace an ideology as truth, assimilating the belief into their lives, the result is their transformation into grotesques: "It was the truths that made the people grotesques" (5).[9] Dunne asserts that "Anderson succeeds in subtly depicting the milieu in which his grotesques grasp onto truths, lead frustrated lives, and seek to communicate their grotesqueness to someone, often George Willard, who will provide understanding" (*New* 5). He also argues that the author reaches "a moment in which he realized that if characters become grotesques by molding their lives around absolute truths, he as author could not authoritatively describe this process. Hence, the narration in most of the *Winesburg* tales undercuts the 'truth' of the storytelling through repeated intrusions by the narrator that destabilize the accuracy and objectivity of the tale he is telling" (*New* 8). Essentially, Dunne posits that Anderson understood the difficulty of representing the ideological dissonance resulting from the realization that a belief system is only illusory. This is precisely what occurs when Palahniuk's characters discover the ideological "truths" they believe are equally as false.

A difference between Anderson and Palahniuk might be their perceptions of "truth." Undoubtedly, *Winesburg, Ohio* is a canonical text in American literature. Anderson occupies space alongside William Faulkner and Ernest Hemingway, whom he directly influenced, as well as other major American modernist writers. Unquestionably, Palahniuk's fiction is representative of American postmodernism, and whereas there might have been a stable truth underlying modernist works, there is definitely an instability of truth in postmodern texts. Truth is now subjective, contextual, and elusive, and agencies that lay claim to it, inferring they accurately present it, are deceptive, manipulative, and evasive. Palahniuk practices his craft within Jean-François Lyotard's vastly influential declaration in *The*

Postmodern Condition, "Simplifying to the extreme, I define postmodernism as incredulity toward metanarratives" (xxiv). In their introduction to *Postmodern American Fiction*, Paula Geyh, Fred G. Leebron, and Levy Andrew define "antifoundationalism," the deconstructing of authoritative principles, based on Lyotard's proclamation: "If any one common thread unites the diverse artistic and intellectual movements that constitute postmodernism, it is the questioning of any belief system that claims universality or transcendence. For the past thirty years, both within and outside the American academy, the guiding principles of nearly every discipline and branch of knowledge have been called into question" (xx). Explaining Lyotard's mantra, they claim the French theorist advocates a skepticism toward any of the "grand narratives" of modernity:

> Like the "official story" ..., these narratives, such as the progress of humanity through reason, have legitimated the "discourses" (the systems of language and thought) of philosophy, science, and many other fields. This skepticism extends to any philosophy or theory, such as Marxism, which claims to provide a complete explanation of culture and society. Lyotard argues that there is no longer any hope of a single conceptual system or discourse through which we might aspire to understand the totality of the world. Indeed, one can no longer speak about "totality" at all. Instead, we have a plurality of worlds and multiple, often mutually incompatible discourses through which to understand them [xx].

Through the comic grotesque, Palahniuk demonstrates the ideological dissonance, the realization that a belief system no longer provides security, inherent in postmodern experience. Moreover, similar to Anderson, he populates his stories with ordinary characters with whom readers identify, although his settings certainly differ from Anderson's small-town venue. Through this perspective, grotesques are the normal people inhabiting typical life. Palahniuk motivates readers to differentiate truths eventually from so-called truths within this conventionality, to cultivate a skepticism toward grand or master narratives endorsed by those who control power. Ultimately, readers will realize that these narratives are subsidiaries of dominant or privileged ideologies advocating mainstream definitions of normalcy. Similar to Anderson, Palahniuk calls for a new different way of perceiving what is normal.

Although there is no direct link between Palahniuk and Bakhtin—no one has proven that Palahniuk set out to put Bakhtin's theory into practice or that he wanted to become the contemporary Rabelais—the connection between the two is remarkable. For the sake of economy, only the most relevant points in Bakhtin's theory will serve as touchstones for the following chapters.[10] According to Simon Dentith in *Bakhtinian Thought*, "Bakhtin traces a pattern in which extensive analogues can be found for Rabelais' writing and the carnival forms is an attitude in which the high, the elevated, the official, even the sacred, is degraded and debased, but as a condition of popular renewal and regeneration" (68). In *Mikhail Bakhtin*, Alastair Renfrew offers a thorough synopsis of the quintessential idea of carnival:

> Derived from the ritual spectacle of the Middle Ages, *carnival* is Bakhtin's distillation of the spirit of the "non-official," "second life of the people" in its opposition to any conception of truth as eternal and indisputable. Carnival is a symbolic shorthand for openness, growth and potential in opposition to closure and reification, to all that is "ready-made and completed," and is hence closely related to the concept of *unfinalizability*. Bakhtin's key exemplar of the moment of transmission is Rabelais, particularly his *Gargantua and Pantagruel*. The key mode of a carnivalized literature is *grotesque realism*, which seeks to incorporate and reconceive the parodic-travestying forms that have been so central to both the *dialogized heteroglossia* and the *chronotope* [143–44].[11]

Moreover, Renfrew describes a significant trademark Bakhtinian principle, "*Heteroglossia* describes the internal stratification of a national language into a series of 'social dialects,' which are ideologically saturated with the world views of their speakers; it is the internal correlative of *polyglossia*, which describes the mutual inter-animation of national languages, the moment at which language in general is distanced from itself, and from which its essentially double-voiced nature becomes undeniable—actively constitutive of a new form of linguistic consciousness" (110). Renfrew clarifies that satire and parody are "the key means by which literature is carnivalized, ..." (136). He states about another vital concept, "Grotesque realism is, essentially, the dominant manifestation of the carnival spirit in literature and culture after the demise of carnival as a maximally free ritual spectacle" (137). In addition, Michael Holquist writes in the introduction to *Rabelais and His World*,

> carnival was a kind of safety valve for passions the common people might otherwise direct to revolution.... Bakhtin's carnival, surely the most productive concept in this book, is not only an impediment to revolutionary change, it is revolution itself. Carnival must not be confused with mere holiday or, least of all, with self-serving festivals fostered by governments, secular or theocratic. The sanction for carnival derives ultimately not from a calendar prescribed by church or state, but from a force that preexists priests and kings and to whose superior power they are actually deferring when they appear to be licensing carnival. *Rabelais and His World* is a hymn to the common man; at times it makes excessive claims for the people [xviii].

Holquist proclaims, "The significance of Rabelais in this view is not only the unique place he occupies in the history of literature but also the lessons he provides for political history" (xxii). Bakhtin's carnival is an occasion for people from opposite socioeconomic polarities to swap positions—to act, to dress, to speak, and essentially to become their dialectical other within the festive binary substitution, at least for a short time. Transgression rules, as ideologies are temporarily open to scrutiny, which, potentially, could lead to reassessment of those ideologies.

In *Rabelais and His World*, Bakhtin explains all of this theory. In a very important passage, he states, "Rabelais' basic goal was to destroy the official picture of events. He strove to take a new look at them, to interpret the tragedy or comedy they represented from the point of view of the laughing chorus of the marketplace. He summoned all the resources of sober popular imagery in order to break up official lies and the narrow seriousness dictated by the ruling classes. Rabelais did not implicitly believe in what his time 'said and imagined about itself'; he strove to disclose its true meaning for the people, the people who grow and are immortal" (439). Bakhtin stresses the reversal of social roles during carnival, as serious rituals were replaced with comic ceremonies, swapping chivalric formality with foolish informality (5). Significantly, Bakhtin asserts carnival was necessary to ensure order: "In the framework of class and feudal political structure this specific character could be realized without distortion only in the carnival and in similar marketplace festivals. They were the second life of the people, who for a time entered the utopian realm of community, freedom, equality, and abundance.... Actually, the official feast looked back at the past and used the past to consecrate the present" (9). Bakhtin considered the practice of carnival egalitarian and democratic, as an event or occurrence that would be experienced by everyone, not relegated to one group or population (7). Pointedly, Bakhtin proclaims that all official protocols were suspended: "As opposed to the official feast, one might say that carnival celebrated temporary liberation from the prevailing truth and from the established order; it marked the suspension of all hierarchical rank, privileges, norms, and prohibitions. Carnival was the true feast of time, the feast of becoming, change, and renewal. It was hostile to all that immortalized and completed" (10). He reiterates this in a highly pertinent passage:

> The suspension of all hierarchical precedence during carnival time was of particular significance. Rank was especially evident during official feasts; everyone was expected to appear in the full regalia of his calling, rank, and merits and to take the place corresponding to his position. It was a consecration of inequality. On the contrary, all were considered equal during carnival.... These truly human relations were not only a fruit of imagination or abstract thought; they were experienced. The utopian ideal and the realistic merged in this carnival experience, unique of its kind [10].

During carnival, language was allowed, even expected, to become what Bakhtin calls "billingsgate" (5), "marketplace style of expression" (10), or what Dentith terms "market-place abuse" (69): the vulgar and profane speech attached to those of the lower class.

In other words, Bakhtin attributes qualities of the transgressive to the language and the actions of Rabelais's carnival. Bakhtin explains, "This temporary suspension, both ideal and real, of hierarchical rank created during carnival time a special type of communication impossible in everyday life.

This led to the creation of special forms of marketplace speech and gesture, frank and free, permitting no distance between those who came in contact with each other and liberating from norms of etiquette and decency imposed at other times" (10). Bakhtin remarks that linguistic registers change. He writes that speakers use different styles of communication from what is normal, swapping what might be typically appropriate for what is usually inappropriate:

> A new type of communication always creates new forms of speech or a new meaning given to the old forms. For instance, when two persons establish friendly relations, the form of their verbal intercourse also changes abruptly: they address each other informally, abusive words are used affectionately, and mutual mockery is permitted. (In formal intercourse only a third person can be mocked.) These two friends may pat each other on the shoulder and even on the belly (a typical carnivalesque gesture). Verbal etiquette and discipline are relaxed and indecent words and expressions may be used. But obviously such familiar intercourse in our days is far from free familiar communication of the people in carnival time. It lacks the essentials: the all-human character, the festivity, utopian meaning, and philosophical depth [16].

Simply put, public profanity and cursing are suitable during carnival (16–17). Bakhtin stresses repeatedly that Rabelais glorifies humanity indulging in eating and drinking, defecating and copulating, all in hyperbolically physical exaggerations, which Bakhtin terms "conditionally the concept of grotesque realism" (18). In other words, body gestures considered obscene during normal situations are not ridiculed during carnival:

> In grotesque realism, therefore, the bodily element is deeply positive. It is presented not in a private, egoistic form, severed from other spheres of life, but as something universal, representing all the people. As such it is opposed to severance from the material and bodily roots of the world; it makes no pretense to renunciation of the earthy, or independence of the earth and the body. We repeat: the body and bodily life have here a cosmic and at the same time an all-people's character; this is not the body and its physiology in the modern sense of these words, because it is not individualized. The material bodily principle is contained not in the biological individual, not in the bourgeois ego, but in the people, a people who are continually growing and renewed. This is why all that is bodily becomes grandiose, exaggerated, immeasurable [19].

Bakhtin concludes, "The essential principle of grotesque realism is degradation, that is, lowering of all that is high, spiritual, ideal, abstract; it is a transfer to the material level, to the sphere of earth and body in their indissoluble unity" (19–20). References to the physical taboo is also appropriate: "This means that the emphasis is on the apertures or convexities, or on various ramifications and offshoots: the open mouth, the genital organs, the breasts, the phallus, the potbelly, the nose. The body discloses its essence as a principle of growth which exceeds its own limits only in copulation, pregnancy, childbirth, the throes of death, eating, drinking, or defecation" (26).[12] In *Problems of Dostoevsky's Poetics*, Bakhtin connects references to body functions—often classified as slapstick humor—with comedy that produces robust laughter. He writes, "Carnivalistic laughter likewise is directed toward something higher—toward a shift of authorities and truths, a shift of world orders" (127). Importantly, Bakhtin claims comedy produces something more significant than simply an expression of feeling.

The purpose of all of this information about Bakhtin, comprised of extensive quoting of the author in addition to renowned scholars, is to tie Palahniuk's transgressive fiction with Rabelais's depiction of the carnivalesque world. Those who negatively criticize Palahniuk's work do not notice how well "Guts" and other texts resemble Rabelais's carnivalesque literary landscape. Those who condemn Palahniuk's use of language and his provocative content do not understand how Palahniuk is imitating exactly what Bakhtin praises in Rabelais. Reviewers who criticize Palahniuk for overly simplistic plots or, said another way, lack of any meaningful complexity refuse to account for Palahniuk's masterfully created carnivalesque tales that move readers in a similar manner to how Rabelais influenced his contemporaries—and still entertains readers fortunate enough to peruse *Gargantua and Pantagruel*. Simple style does not equate to simplistic meaning. Comparable to Rabelais (and to Anderson), Palahniuk subversively challenges readers through the comic grotesque to question the grand narratives that are held as sacred. Critics such as Miller, Newman, Bomer, and Ellmann prove just how Rabelaisian Palahniuk actually is. These critics verify that Palahniuk's rhetorical agenda is not didactically obvious, and they fail to notice the artistry comparable to how many readers fail to recognize Rabelais's brilliance in what appear absurd tales. In the introduction to the first-year composition reader *Signs of Life*, Sonia Maasik and Jack Solomon refer to Roland Barthes's theory to frame the included readings for composition studies: "But Barthes's point ... is that all social behavior is political in the sense that it reflects some personal or group interest. Such interests are encoded in what are called ideologies, or worldviews that express the values and opinions of those who hold them. Politics, then, is just another name for the clash of ideologies that takes place in any complex society in which the interests of all those who belong to it constantly compete with one another" (11). In a later section about paradox, Maasik and Solomon show how Americans hypocritically hold onto Puritanical values while simultaneously claiming liberally inclusive and pluralistic stances (483). Students usually grapple with what this means. Many Americans have difficulty recognizing the irony between their thought and their actions. This is why satirists such as Rabelais and Palahniuk are so vitally important—they show readers what they would not notice otherwise. In particular, Palahniuk's transgressive fiction allows readers to laugh at characters with whom they relate or toward whom they may feel superior. Spectators might claim they are much too experienced or much too intelligent to put themselves in Palahniuk's fictional situations. Truth told, if they are honest with themselves, they have probably already been in similar contexts, just not to the extent or to the extreme as they are portrayed in the stories. Palahniuk realizes his fiction challenges his readers' self-perceptions of their own places in their worlds, but he also knows that he must move them toward relinquishing their holds on safe ideas that they deem as sacred before they are capable of recreating them into something more beneficial.

Whereas Palahniuk's application of the comic grotesque shows *how* this happens, Althusser's and Žižek's theories of ideology clarify *why* this happens. In "Ideology and the Ideological State Apparatus," Althusser explains—drawing on the ideas of Karl Marx—how ruling class hegemony indoctrinates through the teaching of values, beliefs, or concepts to "ensure *subjugation*" (106).[13] Althusser points out that religious, educational, familial, political as well as media-driven Ideological State Apparatuses (ISAs) promote obedience.[14] This is merely a revitalization of Marx's famous statement in *Capital* that defines workers blind allegiance to a paradigm: "In order to relate their products to one another as commodities, men are compelled to equate their various labours to abstract human labour. They do not know it, but they do it, by reducing the material thing to the abstraction, *value*." Aggressively, Repressive State Apparatuses (RSAs) affiliated with government, army, police, court, or prison enforce systems of control (96–106). Citing Marx's *The German Ideology*, Althusser points out, however, that ideology is an "imaginary assemblage" (108) of bricolage, a "pure illusion" or a "pure dream" (108), that only *"represents the imaginary relationship of individuals to their real conditions of existence"* (109). Althusser states that the "real" is predicated on what he terms "*a material existence*" (112), the practice of myth and ritual that supports ideology. Through what Althusser designates as "interpellation," when agents of the ideology "hail" deviants toward allegiance, people become ideology (literally are the subjects of ideology) and are incapable of functioning normally outside the system (118–19). Althusser offers the example of someone altering his or her behavior in response to being called ("hailed"), and in this manner, a person gives into authority because of "guilt feelings" affecting his or her conscience (118). Basically, a person responds instinctively to a call (initiated by an RSA) that he or she intuitively relates to an abstract principle (promoted by an ISA) considered important. When people understand the conflict between the bourgeois and proletariat that fosters this response, they are able to break free from what is essentially blind subservience. The ISAs implement soft manipulation; the RSAs apply hard coercion. Typically, people follow this ideological framework without questioning their motivation for doing so.

Although his theory builds off of and even extends Althusser's claims, Žižek has a fundamental disagreement in how people react after they begin to understand the nature of this motivation. Žižek's theory is also structuralist in the sense that meaning proceeds from significations. Althusser is a "structuralist Marxist" because he calls for an identification of signs that would liberate those ruled by dominant ideology. Once the signs are identified (and the ISAs and RSAs exposed), people can better understand their almost subconscious responses to authoritative appellations—why they act without questioning the authority prompting those actions. Žižek argues, however, people are instinctively complicit in following ideologies even after they recognize how they are being manipulated by those in power to adhere to subjective interpretations of normalcy.[15] In *Absolute Recoil*, Žižek acknowledges that comedy (inferring the transgressive) serves as a mediator toward revealing this manipulation (an extensive passage worth quoting in its entirety):

> The Althusserian theory of ideology fully asserts the gap that separates our ideological sense-experience from the external material apparatuses and practices that sustain that experience. The theory distinguishes two levels of the ideological process: external (following the ritual, ideology as material practice) and internal (recognizing oneself in interpellation, believing). Although Althusser refers to Pascal to account for the passage between them—follow the external rituals and inner belief will come—the two dimensions remain external to each other; their relationship is that of the parallax: we observe ideological practice either from the outside, in bodily gestures, or from the inside, as beliefs, and there is no intermediate space or passage between the two. Nevertheless, (theatrical) comedy seems to provide a kind of intermediate space here, a place for passage in both directions—acting as if one believes and believing that one merely acts. When a character in a comedy feigns to believe or just acts as if he believes, he enacts (in his external behavior) an internal belief, or, vice versa, when he gets caught in his own game, actual belief can arise out of his conviction that he just believes that he acts [51].

In *The Sublime Object of Ideology*, Žižek warns, "The ruling ideology is not meant to be taken seriously or literally. Perhaps the greatest danger for totalitarianism is people who take its ideology literally..." (24). Referring to Marx's definition of ideology as something that is done but not realized, he contends, drawing on Engels's (and Lukac's) description, "The very concept of ideology implies a kind of basic, constitutive naiveté: the misrecognition of its own presuppositions, of its own effective conditions, a distance, a divergence between so-called social reality and our distorted representation, our false consciousness of it. That is why such a 'naive consciousness' can be submitted to a critical-ideological procedure" (24). Referring to Peter Sloterdijk's *Critique of Critical Reason*, Žižek points out that people illogically obey appellations even after they have identified their function within a dominant ideology: "The cynical subject is quite aware of the distance between the ideological mask and the social reality, but he none the less still insists upon the mask. The formula, as proposed by Sloterdijk, would then be: 'they know very well what they are doing, but still they are doing it'" (26). Žižek terms this a "paradox of an enlightened false consciousness" in which one understands the contradiction but does absolutely nothing about it, continuing to affirm instead of renounce the ideology (25–26).[16]

In the section of *The Sublime Object of Ideology* titled "Ideological Fantasy," Žižek discusses the cognitive dissonance that influences why people are reluctant to stop responding to what they know is blatant manipulation. He again contemplates the apparent contradiction between the "ideological mask" and the "social reality":

> So now we have made a decisive step forward; we have established a new way to read the Marxian formula "they do not know it, but they are doing it": the illusion is not on the side of knowledge, it is already on the side of reality itself, of what the people are doing. What they do not know is that their social reality itself, their activity, is guided by an illusion, by a fetishistic inversion. What they overlook, what they misrecognize, is not the reality but the illusion which is structuring their reality, their real social activity. They know very well how things really are, but still they are doing it as if they did not know. The illusion is therefore double: it consists in overlooking the illusion which is structuring our real, effective relationship to reality. And this overlooked, unconscious illusion may be called the *ideological fantasy* [29–30].

In other sections of *The Sublime Object of Ideology*, speaking about the "fundamental dimension of 'ideology,'" Žižek avoids calling ideology a false consciousness, an "illusory representation of reality," because people believe the reality as true (16). Since the most powerful ideology is unobtrusive and stepping outside of ideology is so difficult (Althusser generally claims it is impossible), people would rather maintain a false sense of who they are rather than acknowledge the reality that is their lives: "Ideology is not a dreamlike illusion that we build to escape insupportable reality; in its basic dimension it is a fantasy-construction which serves as a support for our 'reality' itself: an 'illusion' which structures our effective, real social relations.... The function of ideology is not to offer us a point of escape from our reality but to offer us the social reality itself as an escape from some traumatic, real kernel" (45). This gives credence to the adage "ignorance is bliss," although better put "ideology, as our social reality, is bliss."

In additional passages of *The Sublime Object of Ideology*, Žižek asserts people can only break free by self-consciously identifying ideology as fantasy. This occurs by unveiling the "true" as the "false," taking power from that ideology by recognizing its inherent duplicity and not feeling guilt or shame as a consequence of the revelation (48). Once the false is unmasked, the ideology loses its control. In Freudian terms (as Žižek relies heavily on Jacques Lacan's psychoanalytical theory), a person acts through the id more so than the ego and is thus reluctant to heed any hailing generated through the superego's sense of obligation. The ego projects a reality representative of the dominant ideology. When a person succumbs to the id, the result is a feeling of enjoyment by transgressively acting as he or she desires and ignoring the psychological pressure of ISAs and the physical censure of RSAs. A person does not give into the superego's sometimes paralyzing self-criticism. Therefore, the identification of the false consciousness is an essential step for productive change. To put this in context, one only needs to think about Whoopi Goldberg's condemnation of Bella Thorne's selfies described in the first chapter. There are American laws against profanity, but these are not really deterrents. Most people do not take nude selfies simply because their ideologies make them feel guilty for what is implied to be an indecent act. Thorne refuses to acknowledge the hailing. Moreover, Megan Rapinoe has not really given in to authoritative condemnation of her language. Thorne and Rapinoe see the oppressive signs for what they are, subjective opinions expressed to conform their behaviors to perceived normalcies. Thorne and Rapinoe are giving up to the liberating id and are not giving into the oppressive superego. They intuitively recognize that social restrictions inherently call for their transgressive violation. This is precisely what many of Palahniuk's characters understand.

Pertinent to this study, Žižek applies his ideas to Palahniuk's *Fight Club*, praising the film (although he acknowledges the novel) for illustrating how taking power away from oppressive ideologies is successfully accomplished. In "The Violence of the Fantasy," speaking about postcolonial issues, Žižek asserts the marginalized are resisting those occupying the dominant power center through discourse that questions the validity of this relationship (278). Referring to violence in films, he remarks that viewers are self-deceived if they believe this discourse rebels against ruling ideologies, suggesting this actually reaffirms the dominance of ruling entities (280–81). Applauding the film as well as the story, Žižek calls *Fight Club* "an extraordinary achievement" (285) that exemplifies, on the other hand, the taking charge of one's power. Specifically, Žižek focuses on the scene in which the narrator hits himself brutally in his boss's office to extort pay, inflicting upon himself the aggression metaphorically held by his superior (285). Žižek calls this the "first act of liberation" as the narrator assumes control by taking the desire to harm him away from his boss, essentially usurping the power to harm him from the surprisingly astonished man who is only capable of dumbfoundedly watching this masochistic self-mutilation (286). Ultimately, the narrator's guiltless self-punishment negates anything his boss's ideological agency potentially could muster. In a traditional master/slave dichotomy, this type of action substitutes control by allowing one the freedom, to follow Žižek's logic, to beat the aggressor "to the punch," so to speak. In a sense, this gives control to the individual, enabling one the ability to manipulate personal destiny, by, to turn around a proverb, doing unto oneself before others do unto him or her. Referred to in the first chapter, Thorne did this when she forestalled her extortionist by posting her nude image.

In "The Violence of the Fantasy," Žižek mentions that the narrator's self-inflicted wound on top of the Parker-Morris Building is another example of preempting control, in this case the exertion of Tyler's influence upon his psyche. Žižek points out, "When, toward the end, Norton shoots at himself (surviving the shot, effectively killing only 'Tyler in himself,' his double), he thereby also liberates himself from the dual mirror-relationship of beating. In this culmination of self-aggression, its logic cancels itself, Norton will no longer have to beat himself—now he will be able to beat the true enemy (the system)" (286). Žižek asserts *Fight Club* provides the model for personal empowerment, one centered in the body and not the mind, with liberation rooted in physical self-assault rather than intellectual contemplation or rationalization (286). Ideally, this emphasis on physicality refers to the transgressive, and the relevance of the atypical over what is consider normative. Commenting on The Monkees' song "I'm a Believer" at the end of *Shrek*, Žižek claims, "This is how we are today believers—we make fun of our belief, while continuing to practice them, that is, to rely on them as the underlying structure of our daily practices" (280). Importantly, a person's desire to transgress, to break the law or act against rules, provides the opportunity for freedom from repressive ideology.[17]

In the "Ideological Fantasy" section of *The Sublime Object of Ideology*, Žižek discusses a term that is similar in meaning to ideological dissonance, an extremely important concept concerning how people respond to the influences of dominant ideologies. This concept is also similar to cognitive dissonance in that a person feels the discomfit of trying to understand two conflicting ideas. Žižek refers to "discordance," but, especially concerning how Palahniuk's characters struggle to mediate belief systems, Žižek's concept will hereafter be referred to as "ideological discordance." This designates a character's discomfort when he or she realizes that a grand narrative or a master paradigm, anything he or she has trusted as a valuable ideology through which he or she bases life decisions, no longer serves its intended purpose. In other words, a character realizes that a system that has been considered true is exposed as false, a revelation that what was once sacred is full of flaws and inconsistencies. The result is often, as in the case of Anderson's characters, alienation and disconnectedness, but the effect could stimulate a character into retaliating against those behind the system. Considering this recognition of what is essentially the false consciousness of ideology, Žižek writes,

> If we want to grasp this dimension of fantasy, we must return to the Marxian formula "they do not know it, but they are doing it," and pose ourselves a very simple question: where is the place of ideological illusion, in the "*knowing*" or in the "*doing*" in the reality itself? At first sight, the answer seems obvious: ideological illusion lies in the "knowing." It is a matter of a discordance between what people are effectively doing and what they think they are doing—ideology consists in the very fact that the people "do not know what they are really doing," that they have a false representation of the social reality to which they belong (the distortion produced, of course, by the same reality) [27].

Most of Palahniuk's major characters experience some degree of ideological discordance, a disconnection between what they think they should believe and what they actually do believe. When they recognize the falsity in what they once perceived as true, they either have an epiphany that moves them toward positive action, taking charge of their own destinies, or, as Žižek claims, they remain exactly where they are, just hoping everything works out for the best.

As will be demonstrated in the following chapters, Palahniuk takes advantage of the comic grotesque to show how his characters function within repressive ideologies. As his critics declare, Palahniuk writes transgressive stories full of seemingly abnormal characters who interact within extraordinary circumstances. Many of the settings are indeed fantastic, but they are based on typically routine occurrences. Moreover, the characters are actually, when it comes right down to it, plausible reflections of regular readers experiencing life events. Even though, for several instances, not every reader participates in a gang bang, confronts global domination, or descends into hell, Palahniuk's presentations offer the necessary verisimilitude for reader empathy, or at least for readers to think to themselves, "That could happen, probably would not, likely never would, but there is the chance." True, these presentations are low-culture rather than high-culture, but in actuality, popular culture currently reigns supreme, and Palahniuk imitates the language and the actions of what could be perceived as the average working-class American. The fantastic in his fiction is perhaps allegorical, but as readers react to the comic (not laughing the guffaw associated with pleasant amusement but probably the emission attributed to nervousness or uncertainty), they are well aware of the grotesque (related to both the psychological and to the physical). Hopefully, readers will then be more likely to apply this knowledge to their own lives, their own experiences, their own realities. *Fight Club* has permeated into the American collective storehouse of information and has infiltrated into American cultural literacy. Palahniuk's other works certainly have the same potential.

Palahniuk has definitely started this process through his first book after *Fight Club*. In his 2005 collection of short fiction called *Haunted*, termed a "Novel of Stories" in the book title, Palahniuk offers a tale that starts off describing a homemade porn movie and concludes with what could be interpreted as a metaphor for ideological discordance. In "Post-Production," Tess Clark narrates how she and her husband decided to stop "wasting their sex" by shooting a film to earn some much-needed money (141). Tess and Nelson then assumed the personas of porn actors and meticulously shot their video. Unfortunately, when they reviewed the recording, what they saw in the objectivity of film did not match how they subjectively perceived themselves. Tess states, "The difference between how you look and how you see yourself is enough to kill most people" (144). The result of their efforts was a disappointing porno, a bill for Tess's cosmetic surgery, and an unexpected pregnancy. When Nelson left to return the video equipment, he never returned, and Tess eventually burned the tape (146). In "The Nightmare Box," Tess's fifteen-year-old daughter, Cassandra, looks into a uniquely shaped contraption at an antique store and subsequently becomes completely despondent. No specific description is given for what Cassandra sees, but there is insinuation that inside the Nightmare Box is the reflection of the worst that people could possibly see in themselves, or, put another way, a glimpse into what they actually are, an extremely unsettling vision. A crucial point concerning the box is that its ticking is seemingly random—functioning by a Random Interval Timer (212)—so the moment when a person may view what is inside is unpredictable. Evidently, Cassandra must have witnessed something devastating, a vision Rand, the shop owner, calls "a glimpse of the real reality": "It's something that goes beyond life-after-death. What's in the box is proof that what we call life isn't. Our world is a dream. Infinitely fake. A nightmare" (222). Clark writes in her notes that the Nightmare Box either hypnotizes or reprograms a viewer's brain, making "everything you know wrong. Useless" (220). In the story "Cassandra," Tess reports her daughter admitted that the Nightmare Box had inspired her to "want to be a writer" (347), which probably led her to Roland Whittier's Writer's Retreat, but at the end of this story, Tess confesses she had killed her daughter with sleeping pills because the young woman had changed so much when she returned home after her long absence (353).

Palahniuk infuses comedy with tragedy in this story, but the transgression is what lingers. Tess and her husband lead desperate, boring, monotonous lives until they come up with the idea to create a porn video. Everything goes well during the taping, as they imitate their impressions of how adult stars copulate on film. Ironically, when they see on film the reality of who they are, they cannot withstand that stark honesty. The vision of truth is too much for Nelson, but Tess is left with the product of the enterprise, Cassandra. In Greek mythology, Cassandra is the daughter of Trojan King Priam and the sister of the brave warrior Hector. Falling in love with her, Apollo gives Cassandra the gift of foresight. In retaliation for Cassandra rebuking his affection, Apollo transforms this gift into a curse, leaving Cassandra to predict the Greek ruse of the Trojan Horse and the ultimate sacking of the city. Citizens consider Cassandra's prophesy the product of insanity, and after Cassandra is raped, pulled from an Athenian temple during the invasion, the Greeks are punished for invading the sanctuary, which is partially the reason for Odysseus's meandering trip to Ithaca. The Nightmare Box offers a stark glimpse of the ideology that falsely provides a sense of security. The granting of Cassandra to view this reality consequently causes her to renounce the superficial and the insignificant materialistic commodities—what Žižek terms "commodity fetishes" (*Sublime* 18–22) associated with ideology. Tess does not understand the profound effect on her daughter until she joins the Writer's Retreat. In fact, giving into materialistic consumer ideology, Tess burns herself with cigarettes to coerce Cassandra to "make an effort to be pretty" (346) according to conventional standards of femininity. Cassandra understands the hypocrisy of succumbing to the media-driven behaviorism necessary to "be popular" (347).

Cassandra's similarity to her mythological namesake is surely no coincidence. Perhaps in the development of his literary ethos, Palahniuk perceived the revelation of one's true self, the unadulterated vision of self-awareness, is overwhelming, a weight not many are prepared to bear. In the case of Tess's story, Cassandra capitulates to this burden, unable to function after the veil of self-deception has been lifted, thereby erasing all of the subtle fabrications that construct her sense of who she is. In her case, Tess's Cassandra is simply incapable of rewriting her life narrative, of reconstructing her psyche after it has been decimated through the glimpse inside the Nightmare Box. Cassandra has seen at point-blank range the truth that destroys all the falsehoods that collectively form her persona, her sense of self. In mythology, Cassandra is raped by Ajax in Athena's sacred temple, thus evoking Athena's wrath that caused Greeks a tempestuous journey home. Eventually, Cassandra became King Agamemnon's concubine, only to be murdered by Queen Clytemnestra and her lover. Cassandra's death in Tess's story is just as bleak. For both women, the gift of clarity causes ideological discordance, and in both situations, the results are disastrous. As will be discussed later, knowledge of the exploitative effects of ideology need not be destructive. On the contrary, this insight can be liberating.

Thankfully, Palahniuk's stories do not have the same effect as the

Nightmare Box, but they similarly expose the fiction manufactured by dominant ideology, as ideology could indeed be compared with the dream state of a nightmare. Both Althusser and Žižek concur, in different ways, that ideology is an inescapable illusion, fantasy, projection. Just as an operating system is needed to drive a computer, humans need paradigms to determine their decisions and to justify their actions. Currently, people are pulled toward all kinds of ideological alliances, those related to the 2020 presidential election, those connected with political correctness, and those associated with cultural diversity. COVID-19 has certainly complicated matters. In the following chapters, an argument will be presented that Palahniuk is the Rabelais of the twenty-first century, and his satire of master systems and parody of socioeconomic hierarchies reveals the inconsistencies, inequalities, and incompetencies affiliated with grand narratives. On July 22, about a month after Bella Thorne posted her nude selfies online, Charles Trepany reports in the *USA Today* article "'I'm Actually Pansexual': Bella Thorne Gets Real About Her Sexuality and Struggles" more information about this actress. Apparently, Thorne came out as bisexual in 2016, but now she admits to liking people as "beings," simply for whom they are as people, no matter gender or sexuality. Although Thorne is still miffed by Goldberg's criticism, she is outwardly comfortable with who she is and the decisions she has made. A loyal Palahniuk reader might wonder if Thorne does not seem a little like (although not to the extreme) Shannon, Brandy, or Evie in *Invisible Monsters*. One also remembers Palahniuk's fascination with pop icons in *Tell-All* and his pieces about Juliette Lewis and Marilyn Manson in *Stranger Than Fiction*, and Reese Witherspoon is likely lampooned in a *Bait* story. Nonetheless, Thorne has certainly garnered ample time in the media spotlight as she uses popular ideological markers to explain the current version of herself. As Tyler tells the narrator in *Fight Club*, "It's only after you've lost everything ... that you're free to do anything" (70). Palahniuk demonstrates how loss leads to freedom—people must be willing to substitute their allegiance to false consciousnesses for principles that provide more pragmatic and practical guidance. People are so attached to ideologies they count on to define themselves that they lose focus upon broader implications. As Palahniuk contends, "the fringe is the future" ("Foreword" 9), but people populating these fringe subcultures are slowly but methodically assimilating into the new normal that is redefining the mainstream.

Undoubtedly, Palahniuk addresses subjects that are not just taboo but are highly sensitive and touching them borders on bad taste simply because they are so emotionally charged. Take for example the extremely sensitive subject of mass shootings, not an easy one to treat for a number of reasons. On August 4, 2019, Americans awoke on a Sunday morning to discover there were two, not just one, shooting tragedies within twenty-four hours. As Susan Miller reports in "El Paso, Dayton Make 251 Mass Shootings in the US in 216 Days, More Shooting Than Days in the Year," the frequency and the devastation of domestic gun violence has increased at a previously unfathomable rate. In *Pygmy*, Palahniuk included a mass shooting at a mock United Nations event that was intended to cultivate diversity and promote inclusivity (106–10), and, of course, there is the university lecture hall massacre in *Adjustment Day* (195–96). In his fiction, Palahniuk focuses attention on significant social and cultural problems that most Americans would rather not examine. He directs light toward controversies that many would rather remain in the dark. Looking at issues related to something as painful as mass shootings is difficult, as is directing attention toward provocative issues associated with sexuality, race, gender, in addition to politics and religion. Palahniuk is willing to tackle these tough subjects. In a way, Palahniuk's fiction has a similar effect as the Nightmare Box by displaying unattractive yet true glimpses into the realities of readers' lives. Before the final page of this book, readers will agree that Palahniuk's fictional carnivals, full of different and distinct narrative voices, portray characters struggling to make sense of their worlds and fighting to take ownership of their own destinies. Reciprocally, in the Rabelaisian tradition, Palahniuk's readers enjoy carnivalesque experiences that might empower them eventually to move from the fringe into the mainstream.

Three

"Another last thing today comes down to is reality"
The Subversion of Sexuality in Snuff

In an August 1, 2018, article in *USA Today*, William Cummings covers a rather bizarre story. Cummings reports that Leslie Cockburn, a Democrat competing at the time as a Virginia delegate for a seat in the U.S. House of Representatives, accused Republican opponent Denver Riggleman in a tweet of being "a devotee of Bigfoot erotica." This claim is significant not because Riggleman was apparently preparing to release a book titled *The Mating Habits of Bigfoot and Why Women Want Him*, which Riggleman calls a "parody of an anthropological study and a 'long-running prank,'" or because someone actually would want to view, for heaven's sake, anything of a sexual nature attributed to what is, supposedly, a fictitious entity (in this case, possibly possessing lustful traits associated with a mythological woodlands satyr). More important, as Cummings notes, Cockburn's publicized insinuation caused an incredible spike in searches for "Bigfoot" videos on the website Pornhub, an astonishing 8,000 percent increase of those wanting to view Bigfoot pornography, which, of course, takes for granted that there is a consumer niche for this brand of entertainment. Cockburn is the mother of actor Olivia Wilde and herself a respected investigative journalist and renowned filmmaker, so her lowbrow claim was astonishing considering her highbrow affiliations. Briefly, Bigfoot erotica was red hot. As Cummings jokes, referring to Leonard Nimoy's *In Search Of* episode from the 1970s devoted to the mythical man/animal, "But the shift to adult entertainment is a new front in the search for the elusive creature."

In an August 13, 2019, news release, the Associated Press shares that Bella Thorne has directed a porn film for Pornhub through the Visionaries Director's Series titled *Her & Him* ("Former"). The critically acclaimed movie is a porn retelling of the traditional *Romeo and Juliet* story about lovers who face obstacles, overcome challenges, and, as expected in porn, have sex. The stars of the film series are two celebrities, rapper Young M.A. and singer-rapper Brooke Candy. Besides directing, Thorne has recently published a collection of poetry, *The Life of a Wannabe Mogul: Mental Disarray Vol. 1*, which mostly chronicles her personal struggles and hardships. Thorne has previously published three semi-autobiographical novels. In "The Real (and Fake) Sex Lives of Bella Thorne," Megha Mohan and Yousef Eldin of *BBC News* clarify that several porn videos of Thorne in Pornhub and elsewhere are "deepfakes." According to Mohan and Eldin, Thorne's posted images were the first authentic nudes of her online, and they describe how she became a victim of a deepfake: "One particular video disturbingly takes audio from a recording of Thorne crying about her dead father ... and edits her face on to a video of a woman masturbating." By releasing her own nude photos, Thorne is countering the exploitation of her body through what is similar to "revenge porn." Comparable to participants in Palahniuk's fight club taking ownership of their bodies through brutal combat, Thorne is certainly taking charge of her sexuality through her posting and directing. Thorne has previously been manipulated by agendas dictated by those who held authority over her. Not one to shy away from provocative issues, Thorne is now taking charge of how she is portrayed sexually, and media are certainly following her progress.

There are, however, still rules of etiquette and decorum that most Americans expect to be enforced per the social contract that governs daily public and private behaviors. As stated previously in regard to Thorne's posted nude images, conventional mainstream opinion likely suggests, for example, a person should not snap sexually explicit selfies, let alone upload those images to any online outlet, no matter whether this is Facebook, Instagram, Twitter, or any cyber cloud that supposedly ensures confidentiality and security. Along these lines, a person should probably not use profanity, in speech or in writing, and should use discretion at all times concerning what he or she wears, how he or she acts, or how he or she expresses values, beliefs, or opinions. As explained thoroughly in the preceding chapter, Louis Althusser theorizes how various agencies—internal ones such as intuition and conscience through interpellation and external ones such as police or military through force—mandate what is largely accepted as appropriate behavior. Moreover, as also previously explained, Slavoj Žižek contends people often continue to follow tenets associated with ideological systems even though they realize these are corrupt, abusive, or exploitative. In the case of the Bigfoot porn searches, as most would concur, even if Bigfoot is considered at least half-human, watching him (or her) have sex is bestiality, still a practice against the law in most (if not all) states. This said, Cummings's report that there was an 8,000 percent increase in searches pertaining to this sexually taboo enterprise proves that there are many along the fringe who are apparently interested in what would be deemed aberrant behavior by most Americans. Riggleman eventually won the election, so the accusation that he was interested in Bigfoot erotica did not appear to hurt him too badly. Conventional wisdom still dictates that ideologically, considering mainstream belief systems, Bigfoot sex is not widely considered proper viewing material.

Nonetheless, the definition of what is lewd, obscene, or pornographic is rather fluid now. Styles change, and what was once out is now in, and as discussed in the preceding chapter, Chuck Palahniuk recognizes this cyclical flow in power hierarchies. Indeed, ideologies also adapt to the pulse of the zeitgeist. One only has to consider the changes in sodomy laws. Whoopi Goldberg might have chastised Bella Thorne for posting nude selfies, but Thorne will certainly not be arrested for uploading nude images, and she will definitely not be arrested for directing a porn movie. In fact, Thorne is currently praised for her directing talents. Times have certainly changed when pornos were termed "stag" and "dirty" films because of a distinctively male audience and their seedy and low-life status. Chances are Farrah Fawcett's erect nipples in her famous poster and Cheryl Tiegs's semi-exposed breasts through a fishnet swimsuit would not garner much media attention in 2020, especially when *Sports Illustrated* swimsuit issues now feature models only covered in body paint, but they were quite salacious and provocative in the mid–1970s when they were released.

Of all the issues related to ideology, those linked with sexuality are understandably the most sensationalized. In her discussion of disability studies, Fiona Kumari Campbell points out many people fetishize the abnormal, becoming sexually stimulated by images of the disabled (such as amputees) (179–81). *Playboy*'s 1987 pictorial of twenty-three-year-old paraplegic college student Ellen Stohl is not, however, ideologically the same as the various porn videos displaying amputees in sexual encounters. *Playboy* was considered tasteful in its coverage, as Judith Cummings covered the pictorial for *The New York Times* titled "Disabled Model Defies Sexual Stereotypes." *Playboy* does not exploit Stohl's condition, as none of the photos portrays her nude in a wheelchair, making sure its images differ from similar ones shown in *Hustler* years earlier. Stohl is nude in the same positions as previous models (although a Google search yields that Stohl later posed nude, for a philanthropic cause, in her wheelchair). Americans appear all too eager to tap into their Puritan collective unconscious to condemn zealously what seems ideologically improper behavior. One only needs to think of the Janet Jackson and Justin Timberlake 2004 Super Bowl XXXVIII fiasco. Yet, Americans really like their porn, and they defend their right to view it even though it is ostracized publicly in polite, refined, and sophisticated circles as indecent.

Unquestionably, Palahniuk's *Snuff* addresses this very sticky paradox. Given ample attention earlier in this book, Lucy Ellmann fails to see the literary merit in Palahniuk's transgressive depiction of Cassie Wright's record-setting gang bang, and Ellmann's reaction reflects what is surely the conservative mainstream reception to what appears on the surface a story about female sexual exploitation within heteropatriarchal date-rape culture. Ellmann sounds the indecency alarm. According to this mindset, because of its subject, the book must be lewd, obscene, and lascivious, harking nostalgically back to condemnations of all porn (cheaply made street productions as well as expensively casted films). Palahniuk surely welcomes these preconceptions; he simply expects them. Fortunately, many reviewers acknowledge that Palahniuk's setting takes place during an obviously sexual situation but is assuredly not sexually enticing. Concerning representative reviews, Keir Graff says there are "indistinct voices and characterizations, repetitiveness, and research that's not integrated but quoted from one character to another" (30), Neil Hollands writes, "Don't expect titillation here: every detail underlines the degradations of sexual obsession and the pornography industry" (78), a commentator for the *Kirkus Reviews* reports, "After reading the novel, ... it might be difficult for anyone to become aroused from watching pornography or find any redeeming social value in it," and most of the others poke fun at Palahniuk and/or his plot. Owen Williams and Brian Gallagher state in articles about the proposed movie version that the novel addresses male bonding. Writing for *The Advocate*, Austin Bunn remarks the real-world information in this novel is particularly attractive to young heterosexual males, adding, "The appeal, [readers] say, is that [Palahniuk's] books are restless, funny, and physical, as if they are impatient with being books. But it's also that they are oddly informative. 'True facts' about the Vatican's drawer of penises, the origins of the vibrator, and the legalese of gang bangs filter throughout *Snuff*." A representative blogger critic, Robert concludes on *Fantasy Book Critic*, "The book can be offensive, vulgar, and unsettling. Then again, it can also be hysterical, informational, and insightful.... Definitely recommended to Chuck Palahniuk fans and anyone who's not afraid of a little debauchery."

Through his "unsettling" and "hysterical" use of the comic grotesque, Palahniuk actually undermines prejudices about pornography. Through Bakhtinian heteroglossia, the combination of various dialogues expressed through alternating narrative testimonies, Palahniuk pieces together a story about essentially a young woman's ideological discordance. Palahniuk tricks readers from the onset concerning Cassie Wright's presumed death wish, recorded through what technically would become a snuff film (with her dead), to provide financial stability for her lone heir, taken for granted to be male and possibly Mr. 72. In plot twists, readers discover that Sheila is surprisingly Cassie and Branch Bacardi's daughter, she introduced the idea for this epic porno to Cassie, and she is finally left juggling resentment, admiration, and affection for the focus of the sexual extravaganza, her mother. By the time readers get to Sheila's epiphany at the end, most are so desensitized to the inferences to pornography, viewing the situation as one in which people interact within what is fundamentally a work environment, that they forget any predilections that they had going into the story. This carnivalesque transformation of setting is *Snuff*'s greatest attribute. Importantly, Palahniuk challenges ideologies about sex in a novel that is about sex but is not really about sex. In *Chuck Palahniuk. Parodist*, I address this novel thoroughly in "'True fact': Hyperreality in *Snuff*" (37–53). In *Understanding Palahniuk*, Douglas Keesey devotes about half a dozen pages to *Snuff* (81–87). For the most part, Palahniuk is not given the credit he deserves for tackling the controversial subject with such satirical acumen, not going too far with sexual descriptions, yet offering just enough to irritate and to chide any puritanical readers.

In 2008, Palahniuk does this at the opportune time. Academically, attitudes are shifting toward pornography as a recognized area of study. In "Why It's Time for the Journal of *Porn Studies*," Alexis C. Madrigal concedes that the proliferation of pornography through various media and its accessibility through electronic devices has necessitated serious scholastic consideration. In "Why Pornography Deserves Its Own Academic Journal," Lynn Comella responds, "for many of us working in the growing field of porn studies—myself included—we reacted to the news with a collective 'Hurrah!'" John Dugdale writes in *The Guardian* that *Porn Studies* editors Feona Attwood and Clarissa Smith argue that their Routledge publication should have started prior to 2014: "In acknowledging that 'pornography studies are still in their infancy,' the editors implicitly criticize [the tardiness of] cultural studies [influenced by] debate within second-wave feminism between those viewing pornography as liberating (Angela Carter's *The Sadeian Woman*) and opponents (Kate Millett, Andrea Dworkin) who saw it as epitomizing and reinforcing phallocratic oppression." In "Porn Sites Get More Visitors Each Month Than Netflix, Amazon, and Twitter Combined," starting her article with the ironically famous refrain, "The Internet is for porn," Alexis Kleinman claims thirty percent of all data transferred through the Internet is categorized as pornography. Concerning mainstream ideologies, Emma Green points out in "Most People Think Watching Porn Is Morally Wrong" that the majority of Americans in a variety of polls see pornography as negative but advocate for "the right to voluntarily work in the erotica industry without harassment, the right to enjoy sex work, the right to watch porn without interrogation from your government." According to Steven W. Thrasher in "What Tumblr's Porn Ban Really Means," the broadscale elimination of sexually explicit material on Tumblr has extensive implications: "The move doesn't just affect how people look at and exchange nude photos ... it portends a broad shift in how we experience intimacy and connection online."

The debate rages over the propriety of porn, mostly consumed via the Internet. In "Is Pornography Adultery?" Ross Douthat blames online porn as the reason for many celebrity marriages breaking up, and he raises the question whether or not looking at porn constitutes infidelity. Belinda Luscombe in "Porn and the Threat to Virility" examines how porn becomes a substitute for real-life sexual interaction, causing sexual isolation. In "This Is What Porn Does to Your Brain," Melinda Carstensen contends porn consumption (seventy percent of men and thirty percent of women admit to viewing) could lead to problems comparable to alcohol, drug, or gambling addictions.[1] Nevertheless, she cites psychotherapist and sex counselor Ian Kerner who claims masturbating to porn helps to alleviate depression, watching "feminist pornography" (with storylines) enhances monogamous activity, and self-pleasuring individuals leads to increased couple fidelity. As Kerner states, "porn is actually a really positive way to smooth over those libido gaps" (qtd. in Carstensen). In "Porn Sex Versus Real Sex," based on their study's findings, Cassandra Hesse and Cory L. Pedersen argue that widespread online consumption of sexually explicit material does not negatively influence viewers' perceptions of actual sexuality. According to them, looking at Pornhub all day might be positive. Synthesizing information from reputable studies in the field, Hesse and Pedersen mention that "sex" is the most researched subject (2008), online porn grosses more than thirteen billion dollars per year in America (2007), and, amazingly, 28,000 people search for porn online every second, with 244 million porn websites operating in the United States alone, many more operating abroad (2009) (755). They begin their study by claiming previous research has not shown any adverse effects of porn on young people. The consumption has vastly increased, but data have "largely generated inconsistent and conflicting findings" (754). If anything, these statistics and all of the opinions illustrate that the sex industry is moving from the fringe into the mainstream. Palahniuk claims during a 2014 interview in *The Guardian*, "Pornography is the giant thing in the internet age that nobody will talk about. It's a big secret that is generating so much traffic, at the leading edge of the new Wild West. It is a pure, nonverbal example of commodified experience; books are another example. Commodified formulae for a fake sense of intimacy." In this interview, Palahniuk calls himself more a romantic than a nihilist because he writes stories that promote community rather than individualism ("Chuck"). Taken all together, pornography's omnipresence online has desensitized viewers concerning censorship or decency issues, therefore decreasing stigma attached to recreational masturbation.

Dare say, porn is experiencing a paradigm shift. In fact, one only has to flip through television channels (cable or otherwise) to see the prevalence of softcore porn through adult situations, partial nudity, or explicit language. Sometimes, the division between mainstream production and adult production is only the difference in camera angles, as displayed in typical sex scenes between Jamie and Claire in Starz's *Outlander* (refer to Mehera Bonner's "Inside the Making of the Greatest 'Outlander' Sex Scenes"). A different camera shot, and, *voilà*, softcore romance becomes hardcore pornography, as one is designed to elicit warm emotions of sentimental desire, the other the hot feelings of full-blown sexual instinct. Differentiating the two is literally a matter of degree. Palahniuk understands this, and he exploits reader expectations, playing with what they anticipate versus what they receive. In most of his so-called sex scenes, there is little sexual enticement but a lot of physical grossness. If Palahniuk is right, online porn diminishes person-to-person intimacy, and he does not want to continue that trend through his fiction. With all the hullabaloo over Felicity Huffman, Lori Loughlin, and other high-profile parents bribing their children into the University of Southern California and comparable schools, porn star Tasha Reign (Rachel Swimmer) recently earned a graduate degree in journalism at the hard-to-get-into USC, after earning an undergraduate degree in women's studies at the University of California at Los Angeles. Reign is a contributor to *MEL* magazine and posts several of her stories on the website ("Tasha"). Many other female porn stars have broken through the stereotype of "air-headed bimbos" to succeed in intellectual professions. These include Asa Akira, Laurie Wallace, Sasha Grey, Asia Carrera, Savanna Samson, Brandy Love, Stoya, and Nina Hartley, but there are many more who are like Annabel Chong (who was a gender studies grad student at USC) than their porn female predecessors. In a 2018 CNN article, Carol Costello reports that Reign is visiting fraternities to teach members that "no means no." Costello states, "Reign told me young men don't understand porn is fantasy—not reality. This begs the question of whether some men realize the sex they see depicted in adult films—especially rape porn—is not what young, inexperienced women crave."

In *Snuff*, Palahniuk balances reader preconceptions about sexuality with deeper issues concerning mainstream ideological dictates related to pornography. He portrays the sex industry as neither glamorous nor exploitative, and he neither idolizes nor demonizes anyone affiliated with the skin trade. The "business" is portrayed as what it is—just another job, work completed for a monetary wage. In several interviews, Palahniuk seems to respect Susan Faludi, currently a gender studies guru whom he mentions in his famous Afterword (hereafter capitalized as Afterword) attached to the Norton edition of *Fight Club* (212). Faludi has two significant studies of gender expectations, *Backlash* (about women) and *Stiffed* (about men), and her 1995 article "The Money Shot," which objectively looks at the pressure placed on male porn stars (with a focus on Cal Jammer and Jill Kelly), possibly influences the direction of Palahniuk's approach. J. Michael Clark's essay "Faludi, Fight Club, and Phallic Masculinity" addresses the emasculation of men by American consumerism. Considering Bakhtinian grotesque realism, there are plenty of descriptions of bodily emissions (e.g., "money shots") that would rival Rabelais's depictions. Simply put, physicality has an unattractive utilitarian purpose in *Snuff*. To the participants in the gang bang, sex is only an occupational requirement. Service is primary, orgasm is secondary, and for most participants, a minute of the first does not guarantee the luxury of the second.

Similar to an athlete, Cassie Wright must reach the top of her game, completing oral, anal, or vaginal sex acts lasting at least sixty seconds with a minimum of 600 men. The goal is to sustain the physical assaults upon her body, but just as an older competitor gets not only his or her body prepared, Cassie needs to develop the mental stamina to go the distance as well. Sheila serves as Cassie's assistant, but she is also her coach and her manager. Cassie needs Sheila as her strictly no-nonsense facilitator for the entire event, one that rivals every other premier sporting event, as Cassie's action compares with Evil Knievel's 1974 televised jump over Snake River Canyon, Cal Ripken, Jr.'s 1995 breaking of Lou Gehrig's consecutive professional baseball game record, and every Atlantic City hot dog eating contest on July 4. Not that ABC would have risked broadcasting Cassie's gang bang on its pre–ESPN *The Wide World of Sports*, but Cassie's performance is not that different—except, of course, the sex—than those in many of the heavily physical reality shows. Cassie is literally *Naked and Afraid*. Palahniuk creates his own version of the sporting spectacular, and the drama depends upon Cassie's endurance to withstand what is indeed a record-breaking heteropatriarchal "sausage party," a sexual lollapalooza. Anything coital takes on the onus of practicality, and exposed physicality starts to resemble camera shots of Olympic swimmers, gymnasts, or sprinters preparing by lathering on gels and creams to avoid friction, stretching skimpy garments worn to avoid restriction, and stimulating the circulation of blood to body parts for efficiency. In *Snuff*, Palahniuk undermines the conservative guilt attached to porn by displaying it as just another vehicle for gratification through good old American capitalistic consumption. In short, people have legal sex for fast cash.

Regardless, Sheila becomes less stoic as the story progresses. Palahniuk's application of the comic grotesque establishes the context for her ideological discordance at the end of the novel. Considering the Bakhtinian inversion of social hierarchies in carnival, men who would consistently have power outside the basement, which is for all intents and purposes a bullpen for Cassie's 600 sex partners, must adhere to protocols determined by Cassie but enacted through Sheila. Although men appear to be in control, they are subservient to the wrangler's call to action. If Sheila does not call their names, they do not perform, so she in effect determines their usefulness in the sexual assembly line. Technically, Sheila controls male sexual potency; if a number is not called, that person is rendered impotent for the intended function (no money shot). In reality, Sheila needs every one of these performers—no one can be excluded to reach 600—but she does not reveal this negotiation disadvantage (although at least one person pushes her to give in to his demands to see Cassie quickly). In Chapter 4, Sheila considers that this day is certainly not about reality (25), and she is correct as normal gender-power relationships are flipped. The monitors display the traditional dynamic of men as sexual predators and women as their prey, but clearly twenty-one-year-old Sheila runs this show. When she calls a name, the man must be "camera ready" (4), so she in a sense controls the rigidity of the fully erect penis by demanding immediate compliance at her beckoning. As such, she might be the only one with truly phallic power. Sheila thinks about all the money she is accruing from bribes (20–22), and she jokes with participants (especially taking pokes at Mr. 137 about dosing himself with Viagra). Consequently, she maintains absolute authority, inciting perturbation in the impatiently waiting men, which she openly relishes.

Significantly, Sheila's chapters are attributed to her name. The male speakers are enumerated, as their sections are only designated by numbers: Mr. 72 (Darin Johnson), Mr. 137 (Dan Banyan), and Mr. 600 (Branch Bacardi). Sheila is the only character given the freedom of undisguised and direct expression, even though readers ironically never know her true identity, at least directly, until the last few chapters. Douglas Keesey reports that Palahniuk inserted Sheila's sections so the combined male voices would not be too "claustrophobic" (85), with Sheila serving as a literary mediator organizing the narratives. In this role, Sheila influences indirectly reader perceptions of the characters. For instance, most of what readers learn about Cassie's motivation is told through Sheila's chapters, and Sheila's derision toward Branch—as she identifies him as Cassie's rapist—shapes how they perceive his intentions. As in carnival, with role reversals dependent upon social status, those normally empowered follow orders from the young woman least likely to have control.

Considering the narrative structure, Palahniuk allows the characters to express themselves using the vocabulary appropriate for the context.

The profanities and obscenities correspond to their relevance in various situations. Through Bakhtinian heteroglossia, the diverse voices construct a multifaceted discourse community inside the text. These various voices counter the language of the ruling class—or the language reflecting the dominant ideology, as in the case of a standard, official language—so they naturally would classify as transgressive. Thus, the exchanges between the four narrators exemplify this Bakhtinian linguistically diverse community. The official language is conveniently exterior to the story, completely outside the text, as mainstream opposition against pornography would likely represent this dialogue. Fortunately, Palahniuk does not allow this ruling-class speech thread to intrude and allowing it access would certainly be uncomfortably out of place. This would be comparable to allowing a non-partisan woman to argue with Lysistrata concerning the morality of using sex as a weapon; it would undermine the comedy and be out of place in a fertility play. Instead, Palahniuk allows words to flow such as "fuck," "cock," "cunt," and other such nomenclatures as vernacular for the vocations of the speakers and as predicable terminology devoid of discriminatory demarcations. Granted, the transgressive language is exactly why many people dislike this novel. Semantically, these are the correct and appropriate words, rhetorically if not ethically. A reader would expect to see "suck off" in place of "fellate" during a gang bang. Annabel Chong, Tasha Reign, and other porn stars are intelligent, but they would likely use the vocational language for the job and not worry about Standard English or proper speech. Thorne writes "fuck" in Twitter responses, Rapinoe uses the profanity among soccer teammates, and Jojo in *I Am Charlotte Simmons* blurts out the same expletive to express his frustration after getting burned on the basketball court. In this carnivalesque world, anything but this register of language would be out of place. This said, Palahniuk does not gratuitously throw out f-bombs for the sake of shocking readers; contrary to what his critics think, he is much too smart for this amateurish literary tactic.

When one thinks about it, readers are never allowed access to the set where this porno is being filmed until the end of the novel. This limits commentary about what is happening upstairs to those downstairs who impatiently await entrance to the main event. More important, this arena functions as an imitative microcosm of a Rabelaisian feast. The first paragraph provides the tenor for the general grossness of the waiting area: "One dude stood all afternoon at the buffet wearing just his boxers, licking the orange dust off barbecued potato chips. Next to him, a dude was scooping into the onion dip and licking the dip off the chip. The same soggy chip, scoop after scoop. Dudes have a million ways of peeing on what they claim as just their own" (1). Coincidentally, this area resembles the stereotypical locker room breaming with toxic masculinity. If Cassie is the matriarch, then Mr. 600 serves as patriarch, as his testimony opens the narrative and, as the old-timer in a profession obviously dominated by youth, he is the elder "woodsman" (3). His narrative describes the line of plastic Tupperware containers filled with condoms and the various salty, sugary, and sticky treats on the table. He introduces the men wearing wing-tipped shoes on cell phones talking about business matters as well as those men with seemingly no place else to go in flip-flops. He establishes the democratic inclusivity of this community (2–3). When Mr. 137 is introduced, he comments how the powdery spices on the snack foods make their way on the participant's body parts, and this combined with the bronze toning creams describes the communal color of light brown that unifies this diverse group. He points out ugliness in the setting: the bathroom sink and toilet are layered with creams, and the floor is sprinkled with stubble from requisite shavings (13–14). Mr. 600's comments about the likelihood of Cassie's demise anticipates the "snuff" motif: "Ain't no human body that can take a pounding from six hundred hard-ons," soon followed by "We're talking one pussy fart getting pounded in too deep. Or eating snatch, one puff of air up inside her works and a bubble gets into her bloodstream" (27–28). Mr. 600 later mentions the carnivalesque rancor and stench of men. The farting, belching, spitting, shitting, and pissing combined with the smells of Sheila's black marker, Mr. 72's wilting roses, and deodorant products resemble a Rabelaisian landscape (51–52). Although Sheila is not performing, Palahniuk includes her in the grotesqueness by brushing off flakes of dandruff while penning numbers on contestants (116). Considering physical repulsion, Branch's admission of urinating inside his first-love's vagina as a form of contraception might win the prize, especially since he could not, as his father advised, emit only a trickle but released a stream of urine after their first (and last) lovemaking (157–58).

Palahniuk's meticulous attention to detail increases the Rabelaisian (and Swiftian) aura in the novel. Case in point, Mr. 72 remembers how his father, a successful and prosperous accountant, maintained a train diorama that replicated with minute precision the physicality of prostitutes and gang members (imitating distinctive tattoos and noticeable characteristics) and other seedy qualities of the city, focusing on the counterculture aspects and not those associated with his own socioeconomic class or in the mainstream (35–37). Mr. 137 talks about replica sex toys, copied from porn celebrities such as Ron Jeremy. As Banyan mentions, Cassie's vagina is reproduced with her episiotomy scar, and Branch's penis has all of his identifiable veins and warts. Banyon sincerely asks, "How's it feel seeing your dick and balls, or your clit and cunt flaps, cloned a zillion times?" (41). These low-culture dildo reproductions are contrasted by high-culture artistic phalluses kept in the Vatican (44). Mr. 72's disclosure about his masturbatory habits are particularly transgressive. Not only was he caught by his adoptive mother in a moment of onanistic pleasure, but this woman tells him the porn star to whom he is "jacking off" is his birth mother (87). To continue, Mr. 72 admits fondling Cassie's manufactured vagina, pressing the button substituted for the clitoris, as well as squeezing, tweaking, and licking her synthetic left breast, what he terms the better of her two. He humps the blow-up version of Cassie, the product purchased secondhand (82–87), and readers surmise how it was "used" previously. Mr. 137 offers a more repugnant anecdote when he reveals his friend Carl thought he had worms when he actually discovered pink pieces of plastic from a deteriorating "Branch Bacardi Special" that he "used" for anal stimulation (42). In an interview for *AdultDVDTalk*, porn star Lisa Ann Corpora (famous for her porn impersonations of Sarah Palin) comments that she stays busy marketing merchandise that she trademarks. In this way, she claims that she sells "herself" to her admirers. She is only one example of countless other porn celebrities who profit from this brand of consumerism. A simple online trip to *Sextoy.com* proves this point, and the price of a product is based upon how authentically it resembles the original.

The commercialism of this enterprise naturally lends itself to Marxist interpretation. Cassie might be attempting to break this record for the noble and courageous reasons attached to the popular motif of the aging artisan, athlete, or warrior trying to recapture epic accomplishment through one more feat or challenge. One only has to consider the industry Sylvester Stallone has created from the *Rocky* film dynasty (as Tom Cruise has tried in a *Top Gun* sequel or Bruce Willis has carried out through the *Die Hard* films; Sigourney Weaver's roles in the *Alien* movies bring to mind a female counterpart). In canonical highbrow literature, one might think about the last lines in Alfred, Lord Tennyson's "Ulysses," in which an aged Ulysses inspires his elderly comrades to set out on one last adventure:

> Tho' much is taken, much abides; and tho'
> We are not now that strength which in old days
> Moved earth and heaven, that which we are, we are;
> One equal temper of heroic hearts,
> Made weak by time and fate, but strong in will
> To strive, to seek, to find, and not to yield [65–70].

In not so high culture, as Charles Bukowski is perhaps the marquee transgressive author, "Roll the Dice" is a comparable solicitation to greatness, a call to respond to the exigence in spite of the risk. In his much appropriated poem, recently exploited to motivate athletes as well as to sell merchandise, Bukowski recasts Tennyson's message to address readers directly. Through the second-person "you," Bukowski commands readers to invest everything they have, their proverbial hearts and souls, toward

Three. "Another last thing today comes down to is reality" 55

accomplishing their goals (27–28). If they are willing to put forth the efforts, Bukowski promises incredible rewards existing on a celestial level (29–33). In other words, Bukowski reiterates that Ulyssean sacrifice produces epic greatness.

A romantic portrayal of Cassie would elevate her status, and considering ideology, she would probably be relegated or forced by circumstance to engage in this gang bang even though her integrity would withstand a conflict of conscience. Although Palahniuk calls himself a romantic, there is no recitation of Tennyson or Bukowski promoting mood during this gang bang. Cassie's incentive is initially financial, neither courageous nor heroic. Sheila's proposition for Cassie to go out with a "bang" might first appear educational, albeit in a porn-film approach, as the adult film will be based loosely on a script treatment about Adolf Hitler's production of the first sex doll (in the same sense Thorne's *Her & Him* is aesthetic). Sheila is obviously motivated by getting the insurance payout after Cassie is "snuffed" while attempting what seems a physically overwhelming feat (48–49). Cassie is not having sex with 600 men for altruistic purposes, even though Palahniuk often interjects within the various narratives that she is now being a good mother by providing income for her "porn baby" given up for adoption. The truth is that Cassie is doing this for herself, and just like Lisa Ann comments during her interview (and elsewhere), porn is now mainstream big business supported by consumers who no longer care about public shame or ridicule attached to the stigma of (like Mr. 72) "rubbing one out" to currently respected adult actors. Tasha Reign as well as porn personalities such as Reena Sky, India Summer, and Samantha Ryan have fared well in lucrative softcore productions by Nitro Video and other companies satisfying late-night carnal appetites of consumers who only browse mainstream pay-for-view movie providers such as Showtime, HBO, Epix, Starz, and Cinemax, instead of checking channels created by the major porn providers like Vivid, Playboy, Hustler, and Penthouse. In short, people will pay to see Cassie have sex with a lot of men, and Cassie understands her role as a sexual commodity, much like a highly salaried athlete realizes he or she is, regardless how well loved in a venue, paid to play. There is no sugarcoating the business of physical performance.

As the story progresses, however, Cassie's reasoning turns away from greed and vanity to higher purposes. Before this occurs, Palahniuk's juxtaposition of fictitious porn movie titles with mainstream productions draws attention to the high/low difference signifying the socioeconomic stereotypes attached to those who participate in the adult industry. Based upon their ideologies, many people believe, with strong and unwavering conviction, porn is nasty, consumed by deviants, degenerates, and perverts. No matter, porn makes money. Although *Snuff* was published a decade ago, Palahniuk predicted accurately the merging of what has been historically considered two morally and ethically divergent film media. The purpose behind Palahniuk's close attention to Hollywood backstory is to demonstrate that fact is often more vulgar than fiction, and he illustrates how mainstream Hollywood stars were not very different from subculture porn icons. Cassie informs Sheila about the difficulty Norma Talmadge, John Gilbert, Mary Pickford, and Karl Dane, among others, experienced making the switch from silent to talking films, many of whom just faded out of the spotlight (47–48). Cassie reveals how the canine Terry, Toto in *The Wizard of Oz*, could not perform for two weeks because of a broken leg (69–70), and then she reports rather morbidly that a stuffed and mounted Terry was sold in 1996 for $8,000 (74). Cassie explains how Buddy Ebsen had an allergic reaction to aluminum paint that caused him to lose his role to Jack Haley (70), how Lucille Ball wrapped her hair around toothpicks and then secured them to a wig cap (122), and how Lon Chaney blinded one eye by fitting an egg membrane over his iris to appear blind in *Phantom of the Opera* (125). Cassie summarizes how many people committed suicide after discovering that Rudolph Valentino had died in 1926 (147–48). More gruesome, Cassie mentions the unique deaths and unorthodox burials of Ernie Kovacs, Bela Lugosi, Walt Disney, Greta Garbo, Marlon Brando, Peter Lawford, Wallace Reid, and Marie Prevast, including details that her dog partially ate her corpse (150–51).[2] Palahniuk contrasts this with Sheila's comments about the suicides of porn stars Megan Leigh, Cal Jammer, Shanna Grant, and Shannon Wilsey, divulging that Leigh killed herself only after she had purchased a home for her mother, while Jammer, Grant, and Wilsey all shot themselves (53–54). Sheila combines subject matter by mentioning previous gang bang benchmarks: in Candy Apples's 721 sex acts with fifty men, Jasmin St. Claire's famous 300 sex acts, Spantaneeus Xtasy's 551 sex acts, and Sabrina Johnson's reported 2,000 sex acts, noting that Johnson later confessed she only had 500 sex acts with thirty-nine men (7).

Palahniuk addresses ideological issues when he alludes to Annabel Chong and Valeria Messalina. Whereas Cassie knows Hollywood trivia, Sheila's forte is porn. Preceding her review of previous records, Sheila mentions that Chong had 251 sex acts, commenting that only one-third of the eighty men attending the event could "perform" (7). Without calling direct attention to this designation, Palahniuk crafts Sheila as a third-wave feminist in this novel. Sheila is the one who pitches the idea for the event, she is the one who keeps the men in line, and she is the one who almost executes an ingenious scheme of vengeance against her mother while pocketing an expensive insurance payout. Sheila follows Chong's strategy for crowd management, herding five performers in at one given time on stage (22), and she justifies this by comparing "pud-pullers" to cattle: "Basing porn films on modern dairy-farm procedures. Trade secrets that can destroy the romance of any good gang bang" (23). Sheila tells Cassie that Chong, whose real name is Grace Quek, based her gang bang in 1995, probably the most recognized event of its kind in American cultural literacy, upon Messalina, a Roman empress with a voracious sexual appetite.[3] An excellent student, Quek did not match the stereotypical persona of a porn actress. Supposedly, Quek participated in porn after she became, according to Robin Askew of *Spike*, "enraged by feminist theory." Today, one only needs to compare her profile to the notorious Duke University then-freshman Belle Knox (Miriam Weeks), acting in porn to pay off hefty school costs (Jones). Sheila comments that Quek's aim was to be the "stud" (24), assuming the role of insatiable sexual predator mythologized by Messalina in her sex challenge with prostitute Scylla, and she claims *The World's Biggest Gangbang* was the best-selling porn video of all time (96). This statement about sales of the 1999 film release might not be completely correct, and porn star Kelly Trump starred in the Italian adult film *Messalina* in 1996. Nonetheless, the historical progression from Messalina to Quek to Cassie helps to elevate the ideological importance of this event. This all supports Sheila's promotion of feminist ideology within the context of the porn business. Assuredly, Sheila confesses that Cassie asked her about a life insurance policy while watching the Quek performance, but Sheila had clearly set up this sequence from her initial contact with Cassie. When Cassie discloses that she thought Messalina should have just killed herself when confronted with her adultery, this might suggest she is prepared to martyr herself for the life insurance money (97). A more likely interpretation is that Cassie sees the gang bang as a chance for empowerment as she can go out on her own terms. As the novel progresses, Cassie becomes more of an advocate for feminist rights. If she were given her own narrative stream, Cassie might communicate to readers that she has always been motivated by compassion and charity.[4]

This elevation in Cassie's status consequently prepares readers for Sheila's revelation at the end. Besides his leading readers toward anticipating Cassie's death by embolism or some other sex-related cause, Palahniuk offers seemingly conflicting comments about Branch and Cassie's recorded sexual encounter that was produced as *Frisky Business* and started Cassie's career in the porn industry. In Chapter 15, through obvious answers to her questions, Sheila indirectly tells Mr. 137 that Cassie was relegated to a life in porn after being raped: "The sick fuck who talked her into this awful business? The living piece of shit who slipped her Demerol and Drambuie, then set up cameras and fucked her from every angle?" (92–93). In Chapter 17, Mr. 137 confronts Branch by inferring he date-raped Cassie: "Why not drug your son? You already drugged his mother" (102). In Chapter 19, Sheila calls

Branch Bacardi a "rapist" who wanted the baby aborted (115). In Chapter 22, Branch Bacardi offers his side, however, and he contends that Cassie instigated the filming: "It was Cassie wanted to shoot a porn loop to escape her folks' house. Cassie asked could I score her something to help her relax" (140). Significantly, he tells Mr. 72 that Cassie has planned her own demise through cyanide poisoning: "it's what she wants most" (140). Nonetheless, Branch Bacardi tells Mr. 72 what is probably the true story in Chapter 32, how Cassie Wright planned to attend drama school, remembering how she had said sarcastically that "maybe if she was stupid and desperate, really clutching at straws and emotionally needy, utterly destroyed," she would have stayed with him. He admits: "If you got to know, Cassie never planned to make that first movie" (186). This disclosure seems to indicate that Cassie was indeed raped. The meeting when Branch laces Cassie's drink with betaketamine and Demerol and then films their sexual intercourse is nothing more than sexual assault (185). All of this is relevant because the films, beginning with her first blockbuster *World Whore One*, trace Cassie's participation in the porn business out of necessity and not ambition.

Cassie refused to assume the role of victim, however. Placing this situation within the context of Žižek's theory, Cassie might have started in the porn industry willingly, as there is no indication that she was forced to make skin flicks according to pre-1980s stereotypes associated with the underground production of this media. If she began in the 1980s or even the 1990s, she might have done so reluctantly but not forcibly. In other words, Cassie understood the problems with porn but continued nonetheless. After her pregnancy, and her attempt to seek sanctuary with her parents back home in Montana, Cassie returned to porn because of its lucrative appeal (59). Sheila mentions to Mr. 137 that Cassie told her giving up the child for adoption was the biggest mistake in her life (174). Dan confesses to Mr. 72 that early in his career he had performed in *Three Days of the Condom*, a gay porn film that he participated in to earn money to pay off debts. Ten years later, he became famous for his role in *Dan Banyan, Private Detective*, and he was later discriminated against after his role in the film was broadcast (106–07). Mr. 72's restatement of Dan's comment, an allusion to what is inscribed over the gate into hell in Dante's *Inferno*, could apply to some extent also to Cassie: "Porn, he says, is a job you only take after you abandon all hope" (107). If the porn world resembled the underworld, then Cassie would be more comparable to the mythological Persephone, who could return from the depths, rather than the Catholic sinner doomed to pay for her sins. Cassie's career had trailed off, and as Mr. 137 goes through her oeuvre, he mentions one of her recently dubious projects, *Lassie Cum, Now!* (17). Regardless, Mr. 137 emphasizes how diligently, conscientiously, and seriously Cassie prepared for her roles (9–10). Evidently, Cassie put as much effort and energy into her histrionics as her counterparts in mainstream films, even though her audience might not have appreciated her care and devotion to authenticity. Her viewers were not, to concede the nature of her films, interested in her lines as a thespian.

Palahniuk's mimicking of real movie titles closes the distance between the two motion picture industries, and when the films are cited, Cassie's performances are praised. Notwithstanding, these titles are comic farces, and they are definitely placed in the story for comic relief. Considering the purpose of simulation during carnival (similar to children wearing costumes during Halloween), these imitations of feature films provide intertextual meaning as well as poke fun at "serious" mainstream films. Cassie portrayed Mary Todd Lincoln in the Civil War epic *Ford's Theatre Back Door Dog Pile*, re-released as *Private Box*, then re-released as *Presidential Box*. Humorously, Mr. 72 comments to Mr. 137, "in the scene where Cassie Wright gets double-reamed by John Wilkes Booth and Honest Abe Lincoln, thanks to her research, she truly does make American history come alive" (10). Cassie promoted stunning verisimilitude in *Emergency Room* (9–10), *Titanic Back Door Dog Pile* (9), *The Da Vinci Load* (12), *To Drill a Mockingbird* (12), *The Postman Always Cums Twice* (12), *Chitty Chitty Gang Bang* (12), *The Wizard of Ass* (15), *On Golden Blond* (26), *The Blow Jobs of Madison County* (110), *The Italian Hand Job* (106), *The Miracle Sex Worker* (144), *Butt Pirates of the Caribbean* (40), and *Smokey and the Ass Bandits* (40). There are also references to literature, such as *The Gropes of Wrath* (15), *Moby Dicked* (16), *A Midsummer Night's Ream* (16), *Much Adieu About Humping* (16), *The Ass Menagerie* (29), *Catch Her in the Eye* (29), *Bang the Bum Slowly* (29), *The Importance of Balling Ernest* (55), and *Slut on a Hot Tin Roof* (76). Cassie's best performances relate to world war: *World Whore One: Deep in the Trenches*, *World Whore Two: Island Hopping*, and *World Whore Three: The Whore to End All Whores*. In the World War II adaptation, scenes of Cassie's oral sex with Hirohito are shown concurrently with shots of the *Enola Gay* approaching Hiroshima (16–17).[5] Ironically, Cassie's porn baby is contextualized within history as the child's father is referred to as Benito Mussolini, as Cassie did a reverse cowgirl on top of Branch, who played that role (17–18).

Furthermore, Palahniuk cultivates the carnivalesque additionally through paratexts, ancillary media that supplement what occurs in *Snuff*. Palahniuk is known for his tedious factoids, and this novel includes research that is extraneous—such as anthropologist Catherine Blackledge's premise that a human fetus masturbates (23) or that the vibrator was the third electrified appliance behind the sewing machine and fan (44)—but he ignores porn star Houston's event in 1999 with 620 different men or Lisa Sparxxxs's truly record-holding occasion in 2004 when she had sex with

919 men (videos of both are available online). At the time of the book's publication, there was a Cassie Wright venue on *Myspace*, but now there is little uploaded at the site. Accessible via *You Tube*, there are 1980s-retro trailer parodies for *The Twilight Zone, The Wizard of Oz*, and *Chitty, Chitty, Bang, Bang*. Doubleday Publishing produced three interviews between Cassie (portrayed by a transgendered person) and Palahniuk (imitating an investigative reporter). This quintessential carnivalesque role-playing is Palahniuk satirizing his own satire, especially since this Cassie is not likely who most would picture in their minds, almost a Cassie imitating Cassie. The trailers show a traditionally "normal" porn blond, thin, young porn actor, resembling qualities attributed to Hitler's love doll (49). Although not buxom, she resembles the typical female actor portrayed in popular 1980s porn. In the novel, Cassie works by inserting Kegel-stones (71) to strengthen her vaginal muscles, basing this on ancient folklore and citing Casanova's mandate that his lovers insert silver balls as a prophylactic (73). The person in the Doubleday Publishing videos is certainly not the physically toned and in "porn shape" Cassie. Significantly, in one of the segments, Palahniuk asks, "How does it feel to know that, that really, every woman in the world is measured against you?" Masculine Cassie responds without hesitation, "I think they have set an awfully high standard, certainly." All three videos are available through YouTube. There is neither nudity nor profanity in the videos, demonstrating how imaginative innuendo and sexual suggestion are perhaps more entertaining than actuality, which is certainly offered in the online Houston and Sparxxx gang bang videos. Nevertheless, Palahniuk provides a dichotomy between high and low (actual and fantasy) that set up the surprising end of the story.

Although Cassie is the focus of the action in the novel, an argument could be made the main character is Sheila, the character who undergoes more of a change. Sheila is the one who struggles with ideological discordance, working through the resentment that she holds toward Cassie. Compared with Sheila, the three male characters develop subtly but do not experience a transformation to the degree of Sheila. After Darin Johnson finds out there is no possibility that he is the porn child, he regains his long-lost erection and comes close to assaulting a surprised and astonished Cassie, who sarcastically asks to be toweled off after he almost "drowns" her with his discharge (168). Darin changes somewhat from being complicit in the plan to kill Cassie to becoming Sheila's only trusted ally. Mr. 137 also changes when he reveals himself an imposter and wants to marry Cassie after she changes the "HIV" marked on his head to "How I loVe U" (144). For the most part, Dan remains pompous, egotistical, and self-conscious. Mr. 600 seems admirable in the beginning as Cassie's accomplice in this record-setting event, distinguished as the last participant, but he becomes less likable. Finally, he is only portrayed as a washed-up has-been who wants to go out (one way or another) with Cassie through a blockbuster climax. Sheila is the sole character, however, who changes radically. She wrestles with the psychological conflict either to hate or to love her mother, and most of what appears extraneous information seems to shape her final revelation. Importantly, Sheila evolves from blaming "sick fuck" (92) Branch for orchestrating Cassie's rape to helping him survive his dramatic electrocution. Ironically, after giving Sheila celebrity beauty secrets, Cassie asks, "Didn't your momma teach you anything?" (123) and confides that she did not "set out to be a porn star" (126). After Sheila finds out the true meaning behind Zelda Zonk, breaking down her fragile defensive attitude of self-centered superiority, she has her moment of understanding: "All along, the woman knew who I was. Who she really was. She played along, knowing she would die. Cassie Wright would willingly fuck six hundred pud-pullers to make me rich.... That *bitch*" (184). In Chapter 32, after deceptions to exploit Cassie fail, Sheila evolves realistically from the final sequence of events. Emotionally, Sheila has the most to lose and to gain of all the characters; she is more psychologically invested than anyone in the outcome of the gang bang. Still, Sheila is not the one taking on the physical assault her mother endures.

Interestingly, there are several comparisons in how both *Fight Club* and *Snuff* address the control of dominant ideologies. Of course, Palahniuk omits any blatant acknowledgment of Althusserian Ideological State Apparatuses and Repressive State Apparatuses. There are obviously no worries about possible raids to stop the gang bang, and there are no moral or ethical censures except a slight condemnation of Darin's potentially incestuous sexual proclivities. Intercourse between mother and son is strictly prohibited, and even Palahniuk's toughest detractors know this line would never be crossed. This said, the protocols structuring the gang bang follow conventional rules; there is a pattern to the business of filming the sex. In fact, taste and decorum dictate even the most lurid descriptions. When Cassie decides to mount Branch's engorged penis to ensure the breaking of the world record, her action is not very different from the narrator in *Fight Club* inflicting pain upon himself in his boss's office. Cassie controls her destiny—she makes the decision to jump on even after she realizes what Branch has done to sabotage the entire enterprise. This compares with the moment in *Fight Club* that Žižek praises, when the narrator takes control of the situation in his boss's office, in effect empowering himself against ruling ideology.

Cassie is not going to allow Branch to have his heteropatriarchal moment of dominance by robbing her of stardom, so she straddles his torso knowing Branch is about to get shocked with defibrillators. She exclaims,

"Upstage me ... you prick piece of shit.... You stole my biggest scene, you rat bastard" (193). Comparable to earlier scenes, Cassie demands that this moment is recorded. When her pseudo-son is ferociously humping her, she asks her production crew, "You guys getting this?" (168). Before lowering herself onto Branch's penis, she queries, "Are you getting this?" (192). Significantly, Cassie wants this definitive moment of personal empowerment saved for future broadcast, potentially for posterity. She wants her third-wave feminist action recorded, documenting (á la Andrea Dworkin and Catherine A. MacKinnon) heteropatriarchal aggression toward the female body, dehumanizing women as sexual commodities. This is when Cassie becomes empowered similar to the narrator in *Fight Club*, and this moment is unabashedly comic grotesque. Branch and she melted together into a "human X" (196) signifies ideological defiance. In Freudian terms, Cassie goes with her id over her ego and will not give in to her super-ego—she will have her moment of authority and control. This is humorously offset by Sheila thinking she smells "meat smoke. Barbecue" (191). Cassie is willing to barbecue herself, and, to heighten the uniqueness of the occurrence, Sheila has her epiphany because of this sexual shish kabob. On this day, Cassie is *the* epic porn star, who, comparable to Messalina and Chong, goes all the way to achieve greatness.

Through the course of events, the back-and-forth of the disparate voices through their individual chapters in a dialogic carnivalesque exchange, Sheila has worked through her resentments and finally made amends with her parents. In fact, she interprets the unexpected monstrosity of her burned-together parents (comic and grotesque) as symbolic of their love, and this is the impetus for her apotheosis to become "real" by exposing her "secret name" (197). Of course, readers cannot insinuate necessarily that Sheila could become the next iteration of porn entrepreneur, but she has proven herself as both knowledgeable and experienced in the staging of a record-setting gang bang. Her name Zelda Zonk reflects the cerebral side, the serious side, of Marilyn Monroe, who attended the famous Actors Studio run by Lee Strasberg, not the notoriously ditsy sex object. At the end of this novel, the "real" Sheila might progress into this profitable consumer industry as a fourth-wave feminist. Sheila has dealt with rape culture and with women's productive rights issues, so she would be the perfect candidate to lead the next generation of executives in the porn industry. Sheila has not rebelled against dominant ideology in the same manner as Cassie, but she has still transformed into a self-confident and self-reliant woman who appears ready to continue what her mother has started. Sheila asks, "What do you do when your entire identity is destroyed in an instant? How do you cope when your whole life story turns out to be wrong?" (184). In other words, what happens when the beliefs upon which one has based her life turn out to be unfounded and untrue? Sheila's final comments indicate that she is willing to move forward: "Raising my hand just a tiny bit higher, so someone might finally look and see me" (197). As her parents are simmering as a smoldering lump of commingled flesh, Sheila bashfully decides to move out of the fringe toward the middle, no longer hiding behind the scenes, assuming a stance center stage in her own "Me Too" moment. This novel is not a porn Cinderella story, but considering Sheila's evolution from someone in the margins to one demanding recognition, *Snuff* is definitely not about a woman's death but her awakening. Sheila states at the beginning of the novel, "Another last thing today comes down to is reality" (25) as well as toward the end (184). Even though the ending is surreal, Sheila is faced with the reality of her life. She knows who she really is, and she finally understands her mother's sacrifice to help her achieve this self-actualization. Without this entire experience, Sheila would live a life based on a false consciousness, directed by false principles, a false ideology.

Irrespective of the subject matter, this novel is essentially a romance. Even though Palahniuk might appear nihilistic in some of his transgressive depictions, he exhibits faith in humanity by the time a reader gets to the end of his books. In a 2015 interview in *Esquire* aptly titled "Chuck Palahniuk Is Really Just a Misunderstood Romance Novelist," Palahniuk admits, "I think it's just a matter of time before everybody realizes that I'm kind of a romance novelist … that these are all stories about people kind of falling back in love or struggling with relationships. Even *Fight Club* was just a big romantic ending." Technically, thinking about the "falling back" in this book, Cassie and Branch get back together—they *really* hook up again. Darin turns out to be all right, and he and Sheila seem to be particularly friendly. Palahniuk could have provided a much more pessimistic conclusion. In a 2015 interview in *Men's Health*, Palahniuk reveals that he probably went too far in *Fight Club*, for instance, by having Marla wish she were pregnant just so she could have an abortion ("Chuck"). Palahniuk could have actually "snuffed" Cassie as well as Branch, allowed Dan Banyan to be ridiculed as a fraud and Darin to be condemned as a pervert, and left Sheila either despondent, confused, or self-righteous (or all of these) while still trying to figure out how her intentions fail to correspond with her actions.

Palahniuk is too much of a humanist to allow such a bleak ending. Just as the case concerning Belle Knox's story portrayed in the Lifetime film *From Straight A's to XXX*, Palahniuk offers a positive message advocating women's rights to control their bodies. Palahniuk could have imitated "Porn Star's Requiem" on *Law & Order: Special Victims Unit*, with Sheila, just like the character based on Knox, jaded and resentful. Sheila is thankfully more the Lifetime version—the softer rather than the harder product of porn. In a 2015 interview for *Nightmare*, Palahniuk says, "My books are always about someone obtaining a power to replace the previous sort of power that they held" ("Interview"). In a 2018 interview for the *Matador Review*, following up on this comment in *Nightmare*, he states, "I guess I see romance (attachment) and power (self-reliance) as polar opposites. My perception is that we ping-pong between needing attachment and needing isolation. When one becomes too horrid we create the circumstances that drive us to the other extreme" ("Heaven"). To illustrate, one only needs to consider former porn star Jenni Lee (Stephanie Sadorra), a highly successful performer who was discovered in August of 2019, according to Bruce Golding in the *New York Post*, by a Dutch television crew living homeless in a Las Vegas drainage tunnel. Appearing accustomed to her situation, Lee shares, "People down here are good to each other, which I don't think you find much." Unbelievably, Lee seems comfortable in her seclusion, even while people reach out to help her.

Regardless what Palahniuk claims, Sheila regains power through attachment and self-reliance. Truth be told, Sheila is not exactly the conventional romantic hero depicted even in the Hollywood films that Palahniuk parodies. She looks forward to a new definition of feminism, perhaps one that acknowledges women's opportunities to revitalize porn for the mainstream. *Snuff* might be the perfect novel for a new configuration of porn moving into the third decade of the twenty-first century. In an October 10, 2019, article in *USA Today*, Sonja Haller covers Katie Couric's new podcast that warns parents about the detrimental effects of pornography. Haller remarks that Couric's curiosity why one in four women were frightened during sexual intercourse led her to the conclusion that both males and females are acting out the hurtful sex that they witness in porn videos. Couric cites experts who claim porn teaches girls to please boys, and boys are indoctrinated to carry out what is comparable to assault against girls. Couric repeats the statistics mentioned in the beginning of this chapter: Pornhub gets more monthly visits than Amazon, Netflix, and Twitter combined. Couric concludes porn is devoid of feminine sexual passion, that "hardcore porn is absent of women's desire to engage in sex" ("Katie"). Ironically, Haller reports in a July 28, 2019, *USA Today* article that using technology in another sexual direction is not so bad. In "Caught Your Teen Sexting? Don't 'Freak Out,' Experts Say. Study Found It Can Be Healthy," Haller summarizes research that supports adolescents' "exploration of their sexual identity" is necessary for development. Although Haller includes disclaimers about harmless effects of sexting, she presents an overall conclusion that adolescent sexting is "no big deal." One statistic Haller notes is that 15 percent to 27 percent of teens between twelve and seventeen sext, a higher number than what most people would assume. Again,

Three. "Another last thing today comes down to is reality" 65

Palahniuk simply responds to provocative issues that do not necessarily get mainstream attention. Through *Snuff*, he addresses subject matter that likely does not shock readers who understand the pervasiveness of sexual media content and acknowledge the paradigm shift concerning sexual mores and behaviors. Case in point, people are going on Pornhub to watch Bigfoot sex.

FOUR

"A rude religious revolution"
The Subversion of Heaven and Hell in Damned and Doomed

Former Democratic presidential candidate Marianne Williamson fuses spiritual mysticism with political liberalism. During the Democratic debates in June and July of 2019, whereas her opponents were dogmatically defending their own agendas while proselytizing the virtues of their plans for closing the socioeconomic gap between the haves and the have nots, she cogently pontificated about the merits of a different way to attack American problems. In an August 5 essay in the *National Review*, Kathryn Jean Lopez reports that many people appreciate this distinctly apolitical approach, which, unfortunately for Williamson, made candidacy for the Democratic Party nomination an impossibility from the beginning. Lopez writes that Williamson is not "serving up the usual soundbites" when she refers to the "dark psychic force of the collectivized hatred," and her advocation of national healing is neither farfetched nor outlandish. This commentator points out that Williamson "shows us something about our poisonous culture," a perspective overdue and needed in 2019 with accusations flying all over the place about Russian collusion and abuses of powers.

There were other Williamson supporters in the media. In a June 24 article in *USA Today* titled "Hello, New Zealand: Williamson Says First Act as President Would Be a Phone Call Across the World," Ledyard King concurs with political pundits that Williamson's suggestion that love would defeat incumbent President Trump threw many of her Democratic opponents off-balance. In separate late-July opinion pieces in *USA Today*, Scott Jennings and Kristen Powers pronounce Williamson a stand-out during the second debate, Maeve McDermott reports that Williamson has the support of #MeToo activist Alyssa Milano ("Alyssa"), and N'dea Yancey-Bragg and Jordan Culver declare Williamson was the "most–Googled candidate" during the July debate in every state except Montana.

Americans may be attracted to Williamson because of her ideological eclecticism, blending many types of paradigms, ones that people recognize and others they do not. During the June and July Democratic debates, she exhibited self-reliance à la Ralph Waldo Emerson coupled with common sense per Thomas Paine with the plurality of yoking together the secular with the religious reminiscent of Jonathan Edwards. Nonetheless, she was labeled "kooky" by *Salon* writer Ashlie D. Stevens, called a "dangerous whacky" by *Daily Beast* journalist Jay Michaelson, and indirectly seen as "bizarre" by Julia Louise-Dreyfus (McDermott, "Marianne"), in addition to being the only female candidate excluded from a special forum in *Vogue* about having a woman as president (Morin). However, in July, she accurately scolded her peers on stage for the "wonky" attention to intangibly abstract and self-promoting rhetoric and struck at the heart of the matter, advocating to cut the oratorical and bureaucratic fluff and to get back to substantial strategies to confront current American problems.

Some people have always seen this spiritual pragmatism in Williamson. In "The Curious Mystical Text Behind Marianne Williamson's Presidential Bid," Sam Kestenbaum traces one of the primary exigences for Williamson's beliefs to her understanding of *A Course in Miracles*, a manual, a treatise, a bible rolled into one document published in 1976 by the Foundation for Inner Peace that contains the dictations of wisdom bestowed by Jesus Christ to Helen Schucman.[1] Kestenbaum mentions that this book is a composite of principles taken from Christian Science, New Thought, nineteenth-century philosophy, and Freudian psychology. He explains Williamson views reality as an illusion and looks to love and forgiveness to initiate miracles, citing the first three sentences in Williamson's book to demonstrate her doctrine: "Nothing unreal exists. Nothing real can be threatened. Herein lies the peace of God." Kestenbaum wrote his *New York Times* essay after attending a watch party for Williamson during the first debate, and he comments that the New Age prophetess/politician energized her supporters with the few words she was allowed to speak among all the chaotic cacophony of candidates wanting to be heard: "'Mr. President, if you're listening, I want you to hear me, please: You have harnessed fear for political purposes, and only love can cast that out.' She went on, building now: 'I'm going to harness love for political purposes. I will meet you on that field. And, sir, love will win.'" While campaigning in Iowa, Williamson confessed repeatedly that her agenda was not based on conventional political ideology. As Christal Hayes reports, Williamson said politics is currently not "aligned with the deep goodness" necessary for prosperity, adding that she is not opposed to President Trump but to "the system that produced him" ("2020").

The main character in Chuck Palahniuk's *Damned* (2011) and *Doomed* (2013) is neither a replica of Marianne Williamson nor a personification of her spiritual and political agendas, but Madison Spencer shares with Williamson an ethic that springs from the intuition, is cultivated by common sense, and rejects (most of the time, although there are prodigious lapses) the cardinal sins of vanity, pride, and greed. If she practices what she preaches, Williamson might share Madison's naïve altruism, although Williamson appears more ambitious in garnering power. Admittedly, Madison may be following Williamson's lead. Along this line, Williamson's *A Politics of Love*, her thirteenth book, explains how love can be manifested in productive ideology. In his *New York Times* piece, Kestenbaum comments that Williamson became a celebrity guru—consulting the Clintons, Oprah Winfrey, and Elizabeth Taylor, among others—whose Detroit megachurch congregation threatened separation if she did not stop her political rhetoric. Kestenbaum also acknowledges Jon Mundy's point that "the Course" is not political whereas Williamson definitely is. During her political campaign, at least in public forums, Williamson balanced the long-standing constitutional division between church and state theoretical frameworks.

Similarly, Madison expresses an innovative approach to power through her writing. In *Damned*, Maddy naïvely writes correspondence to Satan, in the vein of Judy Blume's 1970 book *Are You There God? It's Me, Margaret*, about her rise to power through the candy-based socioeconomic system in hell.[2] In *Doomed*, a much more diplomatically mature Madison realizes that her empowerment was predestined and her role in the political battle for humanity has been preordained. Still the self-proclaimed optimist as she was in *Damned*, Madison is not a Williamson caricature, yet she advocates through tweetish blogs what is almost a platform based on love as she confronts demons and other obstacles in the underworld, intuitively doing what she considers right, good, and moral according to conventional Judeo-Christian standards. In *Doomed*, Madison assumes the persona of detective in figuring out why she is in purgatory (unseen among the living) and why Satan has apparently composed the story of her life. Madison is particularly curious why Satan is unable to finish what could be perceived as her divine conclusion. Through Madison, Palahniuk anticipates someone like Williamson in his novel. This is not equating the American political arena as hell with Williamson as the hopeful optimist bequeathed with the dubious honor of saving American souls from the threat of eternal damnation. On the contrary, this situates *Damned* and *Doomed* within the current political climate and allows readers to identify with someone espousing a secular yet spiritual ideology based on love. Palahniuk has admitted in various interviews that Dante's medieval journey inspired these two novels, and he has confessed during a conversation with Royal Young that his third book in this series will take Madison through paradise: "Madison goes to hell first—she's stuck in purgatory in the second book, which

Four. "A rude religious revolution" 69

I'm writing now—and eventually she ends up in heaven." Love will likely see Madison through the travails that she encounters as she makes her way toward paradise.

Through these two novels, Palahniuk uses the comic grotesque to show how Madison experiences ideological discordance as she attempts to understand her purpose in the epically titanic struggle between God and Satan for human souls. Just as during Halloween when actors, no matter how terrifyingly costumed, rely on the haunted house to stage their frightful performances, Palahniuk depends tremendously on setting for effect in *Damned*. Palahniuk must have enjoyed creating his hellish landscape full of sexual imagery and populated with a wide array of tormentors (not all from Dante's predominantly Catholic depiction). In fact, most people shopping Barnes & Nobles or other bookstores likely do not realize the cover of the Doubleday hardback edition of *Doomed* displays a person drenched with what appears to be white goo. As those who have read *Damned* know, this figure is covered in male ejaculate from what is surely the Great Ocean of Wasted Sperm, the product of Onanistic masturbatory discharge since the beginning of time (44). The fictional hell in *Damned* is very unlikely to match what most children learn in Sunday school or even comes close to Hollywood productions (although Tim Burton might get within range). In *Snuff*, Palahniuk counts on allusions to actual movies, allowing the tie between the fictitious porn movie and its real-life referent to accentuate meaning and to supply humor through the puns. In *Damned*, he simply constructs a ghastly underworld not dependent upon hellish allusions where anything goes concerning profanity, vulgarity, and obscenity, a landscape full of transgressive hyperbole. In this fictional atmosphere, Palahniuk can design elaborate comic grotesque creatures within the muck and vileness while concurrently superimposing historical personalities onto this terrain. Literally, Palahniuk is allowed to play God (or Satan) by deciding on the inhabitants and their particular punishments. Satan rules not as religious demonic dictator but as secular heteropatriarchal capitalist.

Interestingly, there is less of this masculine white washing in *Doomed*. By moving her back on Earth, thereby placing her into purgatory, Palahniuk allows Madison to encounter comparable perversity in what are reasonably ordinary events, and just as Sheila experiences in *Snuff*, Madison must decide what action to take when trusted truths are undermined as falsehoods. Fortunately, in *Doomed*, Madison rises to the occasion by assuming the role of divine mediator between Satan and God, determined to resolve their conflict and consequently reconcile heaven and hell (329). On the surface, this conflict appears religious, subjugated by principles, codes, and tenets comprising doctrine within predominantly Christian ideology. Beneath the surface, Palahniuk applies a more corporate structure. The resolution is likely somewhere in between, perhaps what Williamson promotes as a "politics of love." Regardless, not to minimize Sheila's importance, Madison is empowered to save the world, not simply to rescue two seared-together porn parents. Similar to Virgil in Dante's *Divine Comedy*, based on the grand narrative pertaining to the paradigm of Catholicism, thirteen-year-old Madison evolves from a pedestrian traversing (the *homo viator*, although in this case "woman" on a journey) through the underworld in *Damned* to heroic status in *Doomed*.

Deceptively, Bakhtin's comic grotesque might seem more applicable to these two novels than *Snuff*. In the Judeo-Christian tradition, the hierarchal switch between heaven and hell is prototypically an archetypal swap. Clearly differentiated concepts contrast: good/bad, virtue/sin, moral/immoral, reward/punishment, etc.—hell is full of demons, heaven full of angels. Palahniuk muddies the proverbial holy (or unholy) water. Traditionally sharp religious distinctions are blurred by cultural consumerism. In Dante's vision of hell, the abandonment of hope is the most punitive of punishments, but Madison is allowed to maintain faith (albeit more secular than religious) regardless of her situations. Palahniuk's hell is certainly an unattractive place to end up for eternity, but there is a socioeconomic hierarchy in which those who adhere to the rules and regulations, contrasted with those who do not, are given perks and provisions and are not punished as one would expect in a venue avoided for its eternal damnation. Considering divine justice, Madison only experiences the slightest of discomforts, and as she mentions, hell is, as these kinds of places go, remarkably not so bad, not really stacking up to all that is advertised. Palahniuk parodies the dogma attached to Althusserian Ideological State Apparatuses of the church, but he politicizes these so that they are identifiable with secular bureaucracy. In fact, there is a striking absence of religious ritual and sacrament. Nonetheless, the authority of Satan and God serve as the supreme arbiters of Repressive State Apparatuses. There are divine laws promoted by the two premier divinities and enforced by their demonic and angelic minions—but the standard Christian rules do not necessarily apply.

Similar to reader saturation with so much information related to porn in *Snuff*, readers might forget the locale of *Damned* is indeed hell. Dare say, they might become so amused and entertained by the almost unthreatening docility of a setting that resembles the children's game Candy Land or Willy Wonka's Chocolate Factory that they forget this place is associated with endless pain. Palahniuk's hell typifies the carnivalesque reversal of power, as nerdish Madison ultimately reigns over historically influential personalities. On Earth, the substitution is illustrated in Boorism, which glorifies Rabelaisian cursing, farting, and other base conventionally impolite actions. Moreover, followers of Madison's pseudo-religion believe that abiding by

Four. "A rude religious revolution" 71

Boorism's repugnant yet hilarious strictures will guarantee them a place in heaven. According to this belief system, traditionally moral behavior is punished and not rewarded. To emphasize the carnivalesque nature of these plots, the result of sperm extracted through fellatio is the anti–Madison, functioning as doppelgänger as well as antichrist, and the apocalypse is diverted to, of all locations, the Pacific Gyre on a trash-compacted plastic volcano aptly named Madlantis. There is no way any major religious leader could have predicted the apocalyptic showdown would happen on a bunch of trash. Granted, no major leader could have anticipated a global shutdown as a result of COVID-19. Without question, Palahniuk subverts religious ideology, and her ultra-liberal parents would have predictably supported Marianne Williamson's candidacy for president.

Many reviewers of *Damned* make the obvious connection between this novel and Dante's *Inferno*. Although these reviewers mention the apparent influence of the *Inferno* upon *Damned*, they do not explore in any depth the literary implications of Palahniuk's parody of Dante. In "Chuck Palahniuk's Latest an Empowering Inferno," Claude Peck reports Madison Spencer, who has died of a marijuana overdose and finds herself in hell, will appear in two future Palahniuk novels, *Doomed*, which will follow her journey through purgatory, and *Delivered*, describing her eventual trip to paradise, clearly tracing Dante's progression in *The Divine Comedy*. Peck mentions Palahniuk researched Dante as well as Sartre's *No Exit* to create his pack of teenage stereotypes (geek, jock, punk, cheerleader, etc.) reminiscent of the 1985 movie *The Breakfast Club*. As Chris Barton comments, "When it comes to drawing up a vision of hell, there are few American writers better suited to the job than Chuck Palahniuk." In a 2011 interview with Adam Weinstein for *Mother Jones*, Palahniuk confirms plans to write this Dante-inspired trilogy. Weinstein portrays Madison as "Our Virgil" who leads readers through what the first-edition book jacket describes as "the *Inferno* by way of *The Breakfast Club*" ("Chuck"). Mentioned in the first chapter, Janet Maslin notes Palahniuk's domestication of hell, claiming that he "appreciates that hell has great visual potential. And he exploits the idea a girl raised by a movie star (her mother) and a producer (her father) with bankrupt show-business values would actually find hell kind of homey." Neil Hollands represents the negativity toward Palahniuk's presentation: "As in *Tell-All*, Palahniuk takes a high concept and kills it with a meandering plot and an unsatisfying conclusion. His humor occasionally scores, but the best jokes are repeated until they become more annoying than funny." In his review of *Doomed*, in which he compares it to *Damned*, Cameron Woodhead writes, "It isn't as vigorous and riddled with pithy insights as the first installment, and without those qualities, the grossness seems gratuitous. Nor is it especially funny. One for die-hard fans only." In "Death and Dying as Literary Devices in Brite's *Exquisite Corpse* and Palahniuk's *Damned*," Claudia Desblanches examines death as a literary trope in Palahniuk's novel. In "Chuck Palahniuk's US Culture and Economic Policy Discussion in *Damned*," Thiago Martins Prado addresses hell as an ideological construction influencing the creation of Madison's persona.

Many reviewers of *Doomed* reiterate the blatant connection to Dante's progression in *The Divine Comedy*, particularly Madison's progression from hell to purgatory. These critics also notice Palahniuk's application of the comic grotesque without exactly calling this by name, yet they fail to see the relevance of this strategy. In an essay for *Publishers Weekly*, a reviewer comments, "At the heart of the rollicking story is a girl's relationship with her parents, but Palahniuk embroiders the tale with myriad poop jokes and gratuitous vulgarity with scant comedic value," concluding the novel is "like a YA novel from hell whose threadbare premise only sporadically entertains" ("Doomed"). Before blasting Palahniuk's writing style as simplistic, a commentator for *The New Yorker* pens, "Read generously, the narrative might be seen as a satire of contemporary materialism and spirituality. But, while satire need not necessarily be funny, it should, at least, be clever. This novel is neither: Palahniuk considers old ideas—celebrities are vacuous; liberals are intolerant; organized religion relies on hypocrisy" ("Doomed"). In separate reviews, Natasha Harding and Dan Pountney praise the book as "funny" while inferring Madison is the typical teenager. Brooke Bolton claims, "Our eccentric, sharp-witted tween narrator walks the line between hilarity and sorrow throughout." David Pitt disagrees, "Spencer isn't the most likable of girls; she's self-centered, in-your-face, and almost too aggressively clever for her own good—but so was Holden Caulfield." A writer from *Kirkus Reviews* settles for the middle ground: "As a notoriously unreliable narrator, Madison can grate on the nerves, but it's sort of peek-between-your-fingers interesting to learn more of her gruesome back story" ("Doomed"). Emma Hagestadt emphasizes the transgressive qualities of the story: "Grossness on a grand scale is the order of the day, and much depends on the reader's threshold for such eschatological and ejaculatory flights of fancy. An inventive pillorying of modern America." In "Dispatches from the Great Beyond," Ben Machell commends *Doomed* for its Bakhtinian transgressive language and physicality, even though he calls some of Palahniuk's writing "morbid slapstick" reminiscent of "Philip Pullman's *Dark Materials* trilogy by way of *Mad* magazine." Machell's descriptions of Madison's parents as New Age enthusiasts desiring constant publicity reiterates the connection with Marianne Williamson and seemingly unorthodox spiritualism. What reviewers claim as narrative liabilities in these novels are actually their literary assets, especially interpreted through the lens of the comic grotesque.

Palahniuk's brilliance is that he obscures his seditiousness just enough through fantasy to avoid creating mere political fable. He has agendas, but they are not always articulated as overtly polemic. Unlike Bizarro writers who rely on comedy and grotesqueness to create whimsically off-center fiction that entertains without being satirical, Palahniuk maintains the delicate balance between addressing controversial ideological issues while also maintaining his allegiance to the aesthetics of literary technique. For instance, in *The Haunted Vagina* or *I Knocked Up Satan's Daughter* (two of many works), Carlton Mellick III does not appear to have a rhetorical motive underlying his plots. The stories are whacky, weird, and extremely grotesque, but they are generally easy to read and to understand, unencumbered by masked references to contemporary hot topics. Palahniuk's proposed trilogy (comparable to the horror trio of *Haunted*, *Lullaby*, and *Diary*) provides him with more creative options than if he addressed Madison's plight in one story or novel. *Damned* is the more transgressively provocative of the two completed works, with *Doomed* referring more to various problems sensationalized through media. This is not to imply *Damned* is more imaginative than *Doomed*, but a landscape full of human waste (such as mountains made of nail clippings) is less political than keeping up with Madison's reactions to Boorism. In short, Palahniuk has more creative opportunities in hell than he has moving Madison back among the living.

Palahniuk clearly takes advantage of the traditional *bildungsroman*, typically called the story of initiation, in which a character, usually a young person, moves from innocence to experience, immaturity to maturity, ignorance to knowledge, or adolescence to adulthood. This corresponds also to one of the options of the hero's journey identified through Joseph Campbell's paradigm of the monomyth laid out in *The Hero with a Thousand Faces*, a universal pattern for the hero that has been applied to countless popular culture texts (30–37). In various forums, Palahniuk has credited Campbell for providing him with a mythical/ideological model through which to contemporize traditional archetypes (more on this in the eighth chapter). As he admits during a 2015 interview for *UPROXX*, "Now, I've recognized that so much of my work was pioneered by Joseph Campbell" ("Chuck"). In the basic sequence, although there are deviations, the hero follows a complete circuit (with the aid of helpers along the way) of separation from his or her community in response to a call to adventure, initiation through overcoming numerous obstacles and adversities until he or she achieves a goal (i.e., boon or elixir), and return to his or her community to give what he or she has gained through the experience. Significantly, the hero encounters a dark night of the soul (a low or bottom point), but through a transformation (similar to an apotheotic rebirth), he or she is able to recover fully revitalized and rejuvenated to complete the journey.

Campbell's theory has more complexities and nuances, yet Madison's journey, anticipating the last stage into paradise, corresponds with this basic sequence. At the end of what Palahniuk provides thus far, as readers await the third novel, a reenergized and refocused Madison is prepared for the next phase of her heroic development. Palahniuk parodies the initiation model to cast Madison as the warrior whose purpose is to save humanity, and she will consequently achieve this by reconciling good and evil, a pretty big job for a thirteen-year-old nerdy outcast. Nonetheless, as Palahniuk likes to mock or to deconstruct totalizing systems, as the monomyth falls into this category, Madison does not have the usual qualities in this regard. In *Inferno* (a spiritual hero story), Dante says to Virgil, who urges Dante to venture forth into hell, "I am not Aeneas, I am not Paul" (2.32). Palahniuk surely portrays Madison as an unlikely hero, and she could exclaim to follow suit, "I am not Virgil." In a 2017 interview in *Impulse Gamer*, Palahniuk admits his apparent animosity toward the tidiness and the predictability of such an ideological apparatus. After being asked if "good guys are too one-dimensional and boring," Palahniuk answers, "You nailed it. Heroes are a little tedious. No matter what Joseph Campbell said, I'd rather read a book called 'The Antihero with a Thousand Faces'" ("Chuck").

Madison easily serves as the quintessential antihero, parodying strategies implemented by traditional heroes as well as those tried by figures in emblematic teen coming-of-age stories.[3] Pitt's comparison of her to Holden Caulfield, another counter-culture antihero (run-of-the-mill, not extraordinary), is appropriate. Palahniuk successfully balances the two sides of his main character: a sarcastic, know-it-all solipsism with a naïve, oversimplistic self-deception. Madison is at once confidently insecure. These dualities coexist effectively through Madison's narrative confessions, first in correspondence and then in blogs. In "Fact and Fiction: An Introduction," Palahniuk writes, "In support groups. In hospitals. Anywhere people had nothing left to lose, that's where they told the most truth" (xix). First in hell and then in purgatory, Madison in her dis-ease has nothing to lose. Granted, she is unreliable at times, but this is because of her inexperience, and perhaps Palahniuk actually wants this unreliability to enhance Madison's credibility as a typical adolescent. There are no divergent voices in the *Damned* and *Doomed* novels, only Madison's point of view, the opposite of the heteroglossic narrative structure in *Snuff* with the interplay of several perspectives describing a central experience. Madison controls the narrative direction, and all other dialogue is filtered through her unique frame of reference as paradoxically a privileged yet marginalized young woman. Madison relies on her sophisticated language skills to display what she perceives as well beyond average critical thinking abilities. In her mind, she is smart, particularly according to standard markers of intelligence, plus she has the benefit of a sharply intuitive level-headedness about practical matters. Palahniuk demonstrates through Madison's writing that she is capable of articulating what she thinks and feels but may not truly understand what she is reporting. This is why Madison is such a great choice for the narrator. She can provide the form but not necessarily understand the content, and readers "grow" into meaning with her. As she matures, Madison becomes much more aware of the various nuances of understanding attached to every situation. Madison cannot avoid the anxiety of ideological discordance when faced with uncertainties about her life, but she certainly seems to take ownership of her destiny at the conclusion of the second book.

In this regard, she develops her linguistic repertoire as she cultivates her writing. For example, Madison is certainly proud of her mature vocabulary. As she mentions at the beginning of *Damned*, "How to best convey the exact sensation of being dead.... Yes, I know the word *convey*. I'm dead, not a mental defective" (1). Two pages later, she remarks, "Yes, I know the word *absentia*. I'm thirteen years old, not stupid—and being dead, ye gods, do I comprehend the idea of absentia" (3). She later admits what readers will eventually discover: "My mom would tell me I'm too flip and glib about everything. My mom would say, 'Madison, please don't be such a smart aleck'" (5). Speaking about the "Mr. Pervy McPervert" mortician who perversely touched her virginal corpse, Madison claims, "You can call me glib, but death is about the biggest joke around. After all the permanent waves and ballet lessons my mom paid for, here I am getting a hot-spit tongue bath from some paunchy, depraved mortuary guy" (5). She repeats this attitude in *Doomed*: "My name is Madison Desert Flower Rosa Parks Coyote Trickster Spencer, and I'm a ghost. Meaning: Boo! I'm thirteen years old, and I'm somewhat overweight. Meaning: I'm dead *and* fat. Meaning: I'm a piggy-pig-pig, oink-oink, real porker" (8). In *Doomed*, recognizing that she is communicating to "blogosphere busybodies" (13), Madison instructs readers about correct protocol: "To you predead people, like it or not, postalive people are not your bitches. The dead have better things to do than respond to your dumb-ass Ouija board queries concerning lottery numbers and who's going to marry you. You and your séance games, your table-tipping, ghost-baiting shenanigans. I had, at best, four hours of darkness to gather Kit Kat bars, and here I was getting summoned by a giggling cadre of Miss Coozey Coozenheimers" (10–11). She confesses how she covered the summoning "Miss Sleazy O'Sleazenicks" in "their own fragrant upchuck and gummy doo-doo" (12).

Madison's word creations are transgressively hilarious. After introducing herself in *Doomed*, Madison's fake diary entries intended for her mother are grotesquely chatty as she deceptively writes to herself that she "daubed hallucinogenic jellyfish toxin on my exposed woo-woo" (75), "sipped the *most divine* absinthe using a dried monkey dingus as a drinking straw" (76), and "sucked mind-altering lungfuls of Maui Wowie through a bong filled with bubbling, lukewarm elephant semen" (77). She maniacally adds, "Please remind me to never mainline stale hyena urine with a dirty needle every again! I was awake all night, standing over my sleeping parents with a Wushof butcher knife in one hand. Had either of them stirred I'm certain I would've hacked them both to bloody ribbons" (78). Needless to say, this colloquial register is not the Standard Written English of formal writing, but the syntax almost always abides by conventional academic decorum. In both stories, Madison intersperses neologisms, but no matter what she claims, they are tech-oriented in *Doomed*. For instance, Madison comments, "And, yes, I fully intend to use words like *vertiginous*, so get used to it. I might be a dead heifer, but I'm not going to play dumb just because you feel Ctrl+Alt+Insecure about your puerile vocabulary. And, no, nope, I definitely am *not* going to use slangy Internet lingo. Jane Austen made a deliberate choice not to enliven her wry narratives with emoticons, so I shan't either" (19–20).

Madison's creation of her identity sometimes clashes with Satan's construction of *The Madison Spencer Story* (*Doomed* 13), her scripted existence. As such, readers discover by the end of *Doomed* that God and Satan have both influenced Madison's opportunities, which ultimately calls into question if Madison's life is predetermined or if she has free will. Furthermore, this also raises the question whether or not she is capable of breaking out of any ideological structure working within the heaven/hell framework established in the novels. Palahniuk does not resolve any of this at the end of the second book. In *Damned*, once Madison gains confidence in the merit of her own self-will, she considers herself the author of her own destiny: "I am free to review my story, to reinvent myself, my world, at any given moment.... No more am I a passive damsel who waits for circumstance to decide her fate; now have I become the scalawag, the swashbuckler, the Heathcliff of my dreams bent on rescuing myself.... No longer am I limited" (201). However, continuing the literary motif, Palahniuk undermines this through the screenplay that supposedly foresees everything that has occurred in the story. Finally, Madison announces, "*I'm not your Jane Eyre. I'm nobody's Catherine Earnshaw. And you? You're certainly no writer. You're not the boss of me; you're just messing with my head. If anybody wrote me it would be Judy Blume or Barbara Cartland. I have confidence and determination and free will—at least, I guess I do*" (236). In *Damned*, besides the allusions to Blume texts, Madison refers to Emily Brontë (62), Alice Walker (74), Jane Austen (140), Mary Shelley (142), and Margaret Mitchell (143). As I mention in *Chuck Palahniuk, Parodist*, Palahniuk likely parodies the Brobdingnagian section in Swift's *Gulliver's Travels* when Madison confronts Psezpolnica (105–06), and this intertextuality—interpreting this text through meaning in the other text—reinforces Madison's status as someone going through the separation-initiation-return cycle.

Hence, Madison starts to identify with heroes from other stories, and this standing on the shoulders of previous characters gives her psychological courage, benefiting from the legacies of her predecessors. The conundrum is they are manifestations of their authors' imaginations—not autonomous individuals. Madison is the only narrator in the two novels other than Leonard who composes several tweets/blogs in *Doomed*, and from a writing as a way of knowing perspective, Madison is empowered through the connections to these other narratives running along the borders of her messages. This form of Bakhtinian dialogism nourishes Madison intellectually, and instead of a spear or sword, she wields Darwin's *The Voyage of the Beagle*. These intertextualities help Madison combat what resembles the grand narrative of her life already composed by Satan. In this way, Madison takes the initiative to rewrite or to revise her destiny. At the end of *Damned*, Madison asserts, "*As the child outlives the father, so must the character bury the author. If you are, in fact, my continuing author, then killing you will end my existence as well. Small loss. Such a life, as your puppet, is not worth living. But if I destroy you and your dreck script, and I still exist ... then my existence will be glorious, for I will become my own master. When I return to Hell, prepare to die by my hand. Or be ready to kill me*" (242). In *Doomed*, Satan continues to espouse his authorial authority when he proclaims her banishment to Earth (14) and then predicts she will commence the "downfall of humanity" (316). Satan's emasculation, symbolically the severing of his heteropatriarchal phallus, ironically by *The Voyage of the Beagle*, is crucial (this might be the only story in which a book was used in this manner). In what could be an illustration of the general structuralist premise that readers control meaning, not the writers, Madison's narrative assumes priority over Satan's master story; therefore, Madison's words empower her to reconfigure the life that Satan and, for that matter, also God have designed for her. In other words, Madison's colloquial anti-authoritative language is a vehicle for her to rebel against the heteropatriarchal ruling ideology that structures hell and purgatory. Importantly, Madison's words are weapons of rebellion.

Just as Madison's language challenges divine agents of power, Palahniuk calls into question readers' expectations of the afterlife. Of course, most readers meet these two novels based on the Judeo-Christian paradigms built upon intertextual relationships between the Bible, the Torah, and other religious doctrine containing stories about heroic patriarchs such as Jesus, Moses, Abraham, and others. In Rabelaisian fashion, Palahniuk undermines those predilections for stable and safe archetypes by proposing, maybe sacrilegiously, that someone as lowly as Madison could influence salvation for all humanity. To cut to the chase, Palahniuk makes fun of everything traditionally sacred in Christian ideology. In *Damned*, one of the most popular teasers put out in publicity combines the secular with the spiritual, as in Palahniuk's hell. As broadcast, Satan could be either Ann Coulter or Big Tobacco (18). Throughout this novel, currency is candy, the best brand-names providing the most purchasing potential. A standard punishment is mandatory viewing of *The English Patient* or *The Piano*, and the two available jobs are Internet pornography and telephone solicitation. The landscape is absurdly blasphemous. Palahniuk constructs thoroughly hideous locations such as Vomit Pond, River of Hot Saliva, Sea of Insects, Dandruff Desert, Great Plains of Broken Glass, Mountain of Toenail Clippings, plus the much more grotesque Shit Lake, Steaming Dog Pile Mountains, Swamp of Rancid Perspiration, and Great Ocean of Wasted Sperm. Madison concedes that her hell is comprised of distasteful "*oceans of scalding-hot barf*" (7), "poop-scented air" (29), and "fat, black houseflies" (29). Likewise, she describes a combination of popular culture and Gehenna, the ancient sewer in Jerusalem:

> Probably any grown-up would pee herself silly, seeing the flying vampire bats and majestic, cascading waterfalls of smelling poop. No doubt the fault is entirely my own, because if I'd ever imagined Hell it was as a fiery version of that classic Hollywood masterpiece *The Breakfast Club*, populated, let's remember, by a hypersocial, pretty cheerleader, a rebel stoner type, a dumb football jock, a brainy geek, and a misanthropic psycho, all locked together in their high school library doing detention on an otherwise ordinary Saturday [7].

Remaining loyal to standard mythological demons in hell, Palahniuk bestows upon Leonard the expertise to identify for Madison creatures such as Ahriman (25), Benoth (49), Dagon (50), Astarte (50), Tartak (50), Mevet (51), Lilith (51), Reshev (51), Azazel (51), Behemoth (51), Cernunnos (81), Mastema (81), Akibel (147), and the Harpies (115). Satirically, Palahniuk includes as demons Robert Mapplethorpe (51) and Charles Darwin (82), as Darwin's book serves as a means of masturbation for Satan in *Doomed*. To add to the irony, Madison comments that Dante did not accurately fictionalize hell, only offering a "generous helping of campy make-believe" (8). An instance of her unreliability, she fails to realize Dante drew on the Catholic tradition and popular mythology plus applied poetic license, and this poke at Dante is emblematic of her trademark sarcasm. Palahniuk could also be self-reflexively pointing a meta-commentary finger at his own composing decisions, which are considered by some reviewers similar to "campy make-believe."

In *Damned*, Palahniuk's descriptions of torture are humorously transgressive. Depictions are akin to 1960s and 1970s cartoons full of violence for comic effect, animated shorts working from the premise children would suspend their disbelief (and not whack brothers or sisters with real hammers, or if they could get them from Acme, real anvils). All things considered, *Damned* and *Doomed* are full of "Do not try this at home" situations. At the same time, these situations do not necessarily seem out of place where they occur. When Madison watches Patterson ripped to shreds by a demon wielding eagle-sharp talons, she compares the procedure to a person tearing apart a steamed crab, describing how Patterson's leg is twisted and popped out of the hip socket, with the tendons breaking free, and then devoured by the dining demon (26). Madison vividly describes the shark-like teeth tearing the flesh from the bone (26). This is indeed horrifying, but it is juxtaposed with physicality that is less conventional and more provocative—much more sexual. Conventionally, demons viciously dissect sinners; this is fairly common knowledge on par with typical depictions of hell.

However, Palahniuk's decision to plant Archer's decapitated head in front of Pszepolnica's clitoris is obviously not standard practice. To increase the sexual comedy, Madison reports that Archer feverishly laps while covered in the god's vaginal lubricants, completely enjoying sexual pleasure from this hyperbolic cunnilingus (77). Palahniuk clearly hopes to evoke reader laughter (spurring memories of Jim Morrison) when Archer shouts, "I AM THE LIZARD KING!" (77). This is accentuated by Madison's not totally processing the sex act that she is viewing. Noteworthy is Madison's comparison of what occurs to Jonathan Swift's Gulliver, who pleasures women sexually in a similar Rabelaisian situation. In Swift's story, the one being pleasured is another gargantuan female with similar amplified sexual organs (73). Connected to Gulliver's excursion in a forest of female pubic hair, the visual image of a gigantic clitoris licked by a punk rocker is transgressively funny. Madison textualizes the sexual by putting it into a literary context that she can grasp. She wants to understand what is really happening with the so-called lizard licker, but she is simply not capable at this juncture to completely identify with the actions. She relies on intertextuality (with the references surprisingly literary canonical) for this action to make sense.

Intuitively, Madison grasps the violence but not so much the sex, as she herself grapples with body image. When she writes to Satan, she admits to having low self-esteem because of her weight, self-shaming herself with pejorative names. From the beginning of *Damned*, Madison bases her physical self-worth through comparisons to Babette, often relying on comic self-deprecatory comments to deflect her self-hatred for not being a skinny blond with voluptuous curves, the mainstream image of feminine beauty. Throughout the narratives, Babette serves as Madison's foil concerning mainstream media-stereotyping of the female body. As self-defensive rationalization, Madison contends girls and boys are intelligent until they begin to mature sexually, basing this premise on what she has seen in Pippi Longstocking, Pollyanna, Tom Sawyer, and Dennis the Menace, grotesquely claiming that first menstruation or first ejaculation signals impending stupidity (12–13). In this novel, she reasons that for both boys and girls hitting adolescence starts something like the "Ice Age of Dumbness" (13). Madison admits she has never experienced an orgasm but knows what one is from reading *The Bridges of Madison County* and *The Color Purple*, mentioning that she understands the cause/effect of clitoris manipulation with Alice Walker's help (74). Madison could conjure up bestial sex scenes for her fictitious diary, but she is unreliable describing actual sexual passion. This increases the comedy when she calls her vagina a "woo-woo" and makes fun of Babette's sexual attributes. In *Damned*, Madison's sexuality is material, designated by commodities, such as when she wears high heels instead of her Bass Weejuns (112). Physical and sexual punishment do not coalesce into masochistic pleasure that someone older and more mature might associate with the two, at least not related to the Marquis de Sade vein of transgression. When she combines the two types of torture, she wishes to possess the sexual physicality of Babette and then be thrown naked into burning lava with River Phoenix, only to thwart his attempts to kiss her. However, this is almost cancelled out by her asking Satan to help her give up this hopeful thinking (20–21).

In *Doomed*, Palahniuk does not provide as much structural campiness or linguistic innuendo, and this might be because of Madison's growth in maturity. There are still comic grotesque scenes that readers do not anticipate as they turn the pages, but Madison is more characteristically shrewd and perspicacious, less surprised by escapades. She is simply more sexually sophisticated after spending eight months in hell, no longer burdened with the guilt that she is in hell because of a marijuana overdose. Death by marijuana adds to the farce, but Palahniuk is again ahead of the curve. As Trevor Hughes, Stephanie Innes, and Jayne O'Donnell report in a December 15, 2019, article in *USA Today*, marijuana is linked to psychosis resulting in death. Madison lets readers know that listening to her parents having intercourse was "an assurance of marital bliss," receiving familial but not sexual comfort from their coital panting and moaning (31). She admits to viewing the wet spots on her parents' sheets as signs of love, signifiers of Antonio and Camille's conjugal emissions (37). She also confesses the stench of cat urine and battery acid associated with the production of methamphetamine reminded her of home (55). Just as playing with reader expectation that no one could really die of smoking marijuana, Palahniuk wants readers to question Madison's interpretations. He allows Madison to spit out what equates to comic one-liners, such as referring to Darwin drinking turtle pee (100), Nana Minnie pulling a tape worm out of Camille's anus (151), or the other scatological quips while at the rest stop (104–10), but when she decides as a last resort to enter the men's restroom, she exposes a different sexual side. As mentioned in the first chapter, Žižek argues transgressive pleasure results from opposing the guilt leveled by the super-ego and going against what Althusserian terms the Ideological State Apparatuses (ISAs) protected by the Repressive State Apparatuses (RSAs). Madison will demonstrate how these can be done.

In *Doomed*, Palahniuk continues to associate Madison's raucousness with ideological rebellion. She becomes intensely excited going into the men's restroom because this rebels against authority (113). Interestingly, her fantasy of being stripped on a pillory and flogged while peasants furtively masturbate to the exhibition (114–15) suggests a sexual maturity not flushed out in *Damned*. Furthermore, when Madison puts her mouth on what is essentially a "glory hole," which she compares to a confessional opening, chiseled out with jagged metal edges, she seems to instinctively yet unconsciously imitate the act of fellatio for which the aperture is intended (116). Nonetheless, Madison's misreading of the penis as an elongated dog turd displays her relapse into innocence. Her description is clearly of a penis inserted through the hole: "What appeared to be a stubby boneless finger now protruded through the snarling mouth hole in the stall partition. This short, this cylinder was mottled brown, fading from a red-brown at the blunt terminus to a soiled beige where it disappeared through the wall. Infinite tiny wrinkles carpeted the finger's spongy surface, and several short, curling hairs clung to it. The finger gave off a sour, not-healthy odor" (118–19). When she closes the penis in the book, and Satan in the form of Papadaddy Ben "wails," the attempt to retrieve the organ results in a bloody mess (123). Madison does not comprehend exactly what has occurred: "As I held fast, gripping my book with the boo-boo-caca shut snugly inside it—me yanking the book on its short tether—the book appeared to vomit. A thin stream of vile sputum jetted from between the pages. This viscous off-white vomitus erupted from the depths of Mr. Darwin's journal" (124). If this were not enough, Palahniuk propels lumps of sperm to land stickily on Madison's shirt, which Nana Minnie smells and then tastes after Madison tries to hide the garment (152). Readers probably notice that the man who told Maddie that she is destined for greatness, to mediate between God and Satan (83), would not condemn her: "You have murdered me, you evil child.... Don't think you won't burn in hell for this!... Forever are you condemned to the unquenchable lake of fire" (131). Concerning the comic grotesque, this certainly rivals the Psezpolnica scene in *Damned*. Significantly, Madison processes all of this differently than she did in the first book.

In *Doomed*, Madison's introduction to Boorism, however, is unlike anything in the first novel. During Bakhtinian carnival, the official language is replaced with the commonplace vernacular, profanities and obscenities are allowed within the context of this temporary hiatus from normal socio-economic hierarchal rules attributed to what is proper and what is appropriate. Palahniuk satirizes official jargon and bureaucratic gobbledygook by condoning vulgarity, even promoting degrees of obscenity. In fact, the language epitomizes Boorism's antithetical approach to standard, traditional, organized religion (68). There are many superb illustrations. Using Ketamine, Special K, to transport into a mystical state to communicate with the dead—as he has seen Marilyn Monroe and Elvis (61)—Crescent City welcomes divinity Madison with a fart and several profanities to set the tenor of the moment (59). As a ghost, he whispers obscenities: "'Piss. Shit. Shit. Fuck. Pussy. Tits. Fucker.... Motherfucker. Butthole. Crap. Crap. Crap" (60). He lets out a series of "Fuck" exclamations (61) before letting Madison know that her parents started what is fundamentally a new ideology. Importantly, Madison considers how religions, or sacred ideologies, are produced by well-intentioned people who do not always anticipate the ramifications of their ideas, even going so far as to fathom Jesus, Buddha, and Mohammed were likely nice, ordinary, and friendly young men (64). She suspects that Boorism is a religion based on profane language and rude behavior (64).

In Rabelaisian fashion, transgressive verbiage in *Doomed* inspires community and advocates citizenship. This is confirmed when Madison observes Crescent City offer a greeting that would possibly result in violence during normal situations: "A merry faggot, cunt, nigger to you, too" (66). In public contexts, people say the opposite of what they would regularly speak. Particularly carnivalesque is Palahniuk's example of the flight attendant's preflight instructions. Madison reports, "I take the window. The flight attendant makes an announcement. 'As we prepare for takeoff, please fasten your fucking seat belts and make sure your cocksucking seat backs are in the full upright and locked position.... The passengers laugh and applaud'" (71). Crescent City explains why this new ideology is working: "No one takes offense. No slur seems to be off-limits. Even the people we drive past, walking on the sidewalks, seated in other cars, they all smile blissfully, as if immune to insults" (68). These pronouncements are obviously what Bakhtin termed billingsgate, coarse communication that is reinvented as carnivalesque language, and they bring people together rather than force them apart, inviting unity and not inciting segregation.

Likewise, Palahniuk applies the comic grotesque to set up his attack against grand narratives and master ideologies. He offers this to combat the false consciousness that people follow through Althusserian ISAs and

Four. "A rude religious revolution" 83

RSAs. Disguised as a limousine driver peddling a script that just happens to be Madison's life, Satan is a likable figure in *Damned*. He tortures fervently those who appear to deserve punishment, operates a fair and equitable hell, giving anyone who has been incorrectly placed a chance for redemption through a salvation test (183). He is nice to Madison, whose letters indicate a pleasant relationship between the two, particularly if Satan is the substitute for God in the *Are You There, God? It's Me, Margaret* parody. This is evident in Madison's constant attempts to eradicate hope. In *Damned*, she writes to Satan, "*Just imagine: me mistaking just some ordinary, nobody-special demon for you. I'm learning something new and interesting all the time from Leonard. On top of that, I've concocted a way-brilliant idea for how to overcome my insidious addiction to hope*" (30). Hope is what drives Madison through the two books, and even though she wants to relinquish what is truly an asset, her ambition makes her hope stronger, giving her an ardent sense of optimism in, of all places, where she should be desolately pessimistic. Madison comments, "My biggest gripe is still hope. In Hell, hope is a really, really bad habit, like smoking cigarettes or fingernail biting. Hope is something really tough and tenacious you have to give up. It's an addiction to break" (20–21).[4] She later states, "My name is Madison, ... and I'm a hope-aholic" (36). Likewise, Madison sees herself as Satan's accomplice:

> There they both are: the H-word [Hope] and the G-word [God], proof of my tenacious addiction to all things upbeat and optimistic. To be honest, all my effort thus far to remain spotless, mind my posture, present myself as perky, affect a cheerful smile, is calculated to endear myself to Satan. In my best-case scenario I see myself assuming a kind of sidekick or comic-relief role, ... so ingrained is my spunky nature that I can't even allow the Prince of Darkness to indulge in the doldrums. I truly am a sort of flesh-and-blood form of Zoloft [38–39].

Of course, hope is an abstraction, a concept, a belief, and, in the Palahniuk fictional universe, it must be tested, verified, and validated.

This occurs in *Damned* when Madison battles traditionally recognized, standard icons of evil. She defeats Hitler (192), Countess Bathory (192), Catherine de Medicis (193), Caligula (195), Vlad the Impaler (196), King Ethelred (197), Thug Behram (197), Bluebeard (197), Hannibal (199), Genghis Khan (199), and Idi Amin (234), gaining confidence after each victory and consequently starting to appreciate her stay in the underworld. Rather vainly, Madison pronounces who she and her parents are by name and declares she possesses a tremendous cache of sweets, persuading all inhabitants in the underworld to bow down to her, at the time, seemingly limitless power (199). Madison never experienced anything comparable in real life, not when she was at the boarding school, not in homes with Goran, only in hell.[5] This eventually leads to Madison's defiance against Satan, which will take her into *Doomed*. On the last two pages of *Damned*, Madison pontificates, "I hope, therefore I am. Thank God for hope," after which she requests to be excused so she can "kick some satanic ass" (246–47).

This may refer to Madison's visit to the séance, to get even with the young women who conjure her spirit, but it probably corresponds to her rebellion against Satan. In *Doomed*, she refers to this point late in the book by reasserting her goal to "kick some satanic ass" for the purpose of proving she exists "beyond Beelzebub's sweaty pedophile fantasy" (318). Madison justifies this by verifying a character could not kill its author, so she cannot simply be a figment of Satan's imagination (318). Honestly, readers are not sure what will finally happen to Madison at the end of the second book. As with life, her fate is uncertain, although she has drastically increased the bets that she is destined for some heroic result, albeit not exactly as Campbell lays out in his paradigm, but perhaps along the same overall pattern. Sometimes, the hero does not return for various reasons to bestow his or her gift, but Palahniuk must have better plans for Madison than for Satan to quash her momentum or for God to implement capriciously an ironic *deus ex machina* ("god from the machine") surprise to show Madison who really is the boss.

Palahniuk generally claims many of his stories are inspired by other texts. In a 2017 interview with *Big Shiny Robot*, Palahniuk admits, "The secret to my best stories is that they're reinterpretations of renowned legends" ("Chuck"). In *Doomed*, Palahniuk nebulously toys with temporality, as Leonard tips off Papadaddy Ben about the climactic showdown on the Pacific Gyre island and, more directly, Archer foreshadows the restroom escapade talking to Madison on the phone (86–87). In these books, everything appears to happen as it should, as it is destined, but admittedly Palahniuk never flushes out the logic operating behind the chronology. Palahniuk relies on Plato's *Dialogues* story related to Solon, a Greek lawmaker who goes to the Egyptian city of Sais to learn from priests the prophecies predicting the end of the world, and he ingeniously locates the progression of apocalypse from outside Los Angeles to Hollywood to Camille's star outside Grauman's Chinese Theater. According to the mythology, the priests tell Plato about Atlantis, which Palahniuk aptly renames Madlantis. Palahniuk lets Leonard predict that a flaming continent with a false messiah will sink eventually into the middle of the Pacific Ocean (95–96). Fortunately, Madison defeats an antichrist spawned from Babette's fellatio of Satan in the opening pages. In a couple succinct statements, Palahniuk offers an ideological aphorism: "Good and evil have always existed. They always will. It's only our stories about them that ever change" (1). In a smart act of ecocritical alliance, opening an avenue to address another ideological theater of controversy, Palahniuk crafts the island out of global waste, the actual growing refuse disaster seen immediately as negative (73). The mythology is promoted by Palahniuk's verification of the prophecy through third-century Zoticus and fifth-century Proclus, both Neoplatonists (223). Following this line of reasoning, Camille assumes the preordained role as birth mother of the savior Madison (234–35).

Of course, Palahniuk knows what he is doing. In *Doomed*, this ideological foundation runs concurrently with as well as counter to Boorism, mixing the sacred with the sacrilegious. Babette takes on the duty of giving life to Madison's doppelgänger during a licentious encounter, and her ringtone of "Barbie Girl" foreshadows the materialism of this competing savior (15). After receiving the prophecies, Madison's parents become New Age, not believing in God or in Christmas (16) but honoring Maya Angelou and celebrating Earth Day (17). Prospering from divine insider information, Antonio and Camille enjoy bourgeois purchasing power, buying Madison high-end products such as Steiff bears, limited-edition Gund giraffes, Häastens mattresses, and sixteen-hundred-thread-count Porthault sheets (23). When Nana Minnie dies, they have the spending power to redesign her body and to mark her love for her daughter through an elaborate tattoo (25). Inconceivably, they command their daughter to ingest an assortment of drugs, which she in turn sloughs off on her pets, joking that these animals would benefit from rehab (54–55). Madison is the outlier, however, not buying into her parents' consumerist ideology. In fact, to aggravate them, in a paramount act of ideological resistance, she blasphemously pretends to date Jesus, even pretending to text him (199–204). This experience with ideological rebellion helps her to assess the daunting news that she has been the chosen one to save the world. Surprisingly, she does not question Babette's information that Madison has been part of a master plan for centuries, revealing that her pseudo-Breakfast Club is comprised of complicit informants who refuse to declare fidelity with either God or Satan (41–42). Eventually in *Doomed*, these friends conspire to pit Madison against the Barbie-Madison who will reign over those seeking immunity from the ISAs and RSAs that ironically promote the bourgeois capitalism that subsidizes their power (239–41).

Hence, Palahniuk deconstructs mainstream master ideologies by exposing the hypocrisy inherently supporting them. Just as in *Fight Club* with Project Mayhem, old ideas must be abolished before they may be replaced with new ones—support groups and fight clubs promote the tearing down and then the rebuilding of ideology. In *Doomed*, a drugged Camille tells Madison that Leonard plans to eradicate other religions and finally to extirpate God. According to Leonard, Boorism would serve as the anti-religion, flipping traditional vices into virtues (253). Camille specifies that Boorist doctrine condemns any offense taken against someone as insignificant, urging people to realize they are not the focus of every earthly action, and promoting humility by not reacting egotistically to affronts or attacks (254). In carnivalesque fashion, people are free to fart as they please, to curse as they want, to act as they like without fear of inciting resentment in others. Significantly, Madison understands why people latch on to this ideology born out of her sarcasm during a random telemarketing call providentially to her parents. In the point in *Doomed*, literally viewing religion from the other side, Madison understands why people embrace paradigms that promise something better than they currently have, and she acknowledges secular humanism only satisfies so far when people yearn for spiritual meaning that provides universal solace (257). Madison knows the perfect belief system is an impossibility, but this enables her to understand why her parents are becoming proselytes of this whacky religion. Comparing herself with Persephone, Madison tells Camille that she has returned to Earth for a greater purpose than her mother could ever imagine (258–60).

Throughout *Doomed*, Boorism, Christianity, and Capitalism intersect without necessarily merging. They remain three separately distinct ideological systems. Although *Damned* contains a transgressive hell that is not horrifying, the precepts related to sin, to punishment, and to redemption are familiar to most readers. Similar to Dante, Palahniuk's inclusion of mythology broadens the scope of the religious, and his references to consumerism expand coverage into the secular. In *Doomed*, Boorism is a vehicle for Palahniuk to hold these other ideologies accountable for their paradoxes and contradictions. Obviously, the language of Boorism is carnivalesque at its most egalitarian. The principle that no one allows another to usurp his or her psychic power through insult, slur, or defamation is the cornerstone of a utopian community (and anticipates similar tenets in *Adjustment Day*, which will be discussed in the ninth chapter). This is complete diversity, total inclusivity, and absolute acceptance. As Crescent City explains, previous rules are abolished, old laws are not enforced, and the apostles of Madlantis enjoy freedom born out of, to return to Marianne Williamson's words to President Trump, the ability to "harness love for political purposes." Crescent City posits, "This is the death of angst. Forget Nietzsche. Forget Sartre. Existentialism is dead. God has been resurrected, and people have a road map for attaining glorious immortality. In Boorism, everyone who'd abandoned religion now has a path by which to return to God, and that feels … great…. It's not the threat of Hell or jail or societal shunning that's brought this bliss. It's the complete assurance of paradise" (70).

In *Doomed*, Madison admits that this seems too good to be true. After passing a mother teaching her baby how to mouth the word "fuck" (177), Madison reflects upon how people devalue profanity, obscenity, and perversity by turning it into the new normative, the new average and, in turn, what is appropriate and not defamatory. By making what was bad into the good, the bad no longer exists; the negative is attributed positive meaning, completely changing signification of the negative. This corresponds to Žižek's premise that people free themselves from the harmful effects of an ideology through anticipation of the harmful influence of that ideology. Just as the narrator in *Fight Club* subsumes his boss's power by hitting himself, people neutralize hurtful language through preemptive expression that neutralizes its potency. As Madison ponders, a world without resentment— aggression as retaliation for intentional as well as unintentional offenses— would be a utopia. Without underlying hatred, envy, jealously, or any other negative feeling harbored by one person toward another, complete acceptance would reign, allowing people to live and to let live (179). The reason Palahniuk selected Darwin's book is clarified when Madison shares apologetically that she has inadvertently messed up the natural scheme of things (179). In effect, she is on her way to debunking the myths sheepishly accepted as truth by generations of humans.

In *Doomed*, this is Madison's moment of ideological discordance, when she is not sure if she should hold herself culpable or consider herself a divine savior, tough choice either way. Madison's heroic helper turns out to be Festus, stereotypically the country bumpkin who gave her a Bible, an angel after his death from, as Madison predicts, farming equipment. His presence confirms for her that God exists, and contextualizing this within popular culture, He is not a celebrity like Warren Beatty (an allusion to the 1943 and 1978 films *Heaven Can Wait*) (275). Palahniuk maintains the comic grotesque, not allowing the tone to stray from the carnivalesque. This is evident in how people perceive the holy face of Madison in the glop of ineradicable spunk on the blue chambray shirt (269), in addition to her parents thinking the blood in the Darwin book was from menstruation that "gushed out of [her] angelic woo-woo" (272) and not from a lacerated penis. When Madison is asked to be a double agent for God (278), readers expecting the conventional good versus evil narrative are prepared for her to give up on Satan and obviously to play for the moral team. This is what any good, ethical, and virtuous young woman would do—what is predictable based on traditional definitions of religious normalcy. Madison is, however, not certain where she wants to claim her allegiance.

Understandably, this is a tremendously major step for her. After Festus informs her that God, not Satan, is the one who tested her inner strength, Madison thinks about her role on His side to get rid of Satan and to return humanity back to the good old days reminiscent of 1950s television situation comedies when morality reigned and sin (as defined by American democracy) was decimated (at least according to shows such as *Father Knows Best*, *Leave It to Beaver*, or *The Ozzie and Harriet Show*) (281). The thought of being God's divine warrior not only to defeat Satan but to get rid of public television and correct other liberal injustices leaves Madison confused (281–82). In perhaps the definitive passage describing the parameters of religious ideology, Madison writes, "God chooses a messenger every few centuries to deliver an updated game plan for righteous living. Moses or Jesus or Mohammad, this person disseminates the newest generation of God's Word 2.0. Noah or Buddha or Joan of Arc, the messenger upgrades our moral software, debugs our ethics, upgrading our values to meet modern spiritual needs. If you believe angel Festus, I am nothing more than the latest version of God's earthly mouthpiece" (283–84). This is not necessarily the dark night of the soul in Campbell's monomyth, but Madison is uncertain which ideology to select. In both cases, she actually loses. Hell did not turn out to be as awful as she expected—she functioned successfully within the framework and did not run into any problems with rule-enforcing demons; heaven does not appear all that attractive, ultra-conservative and anti-transgressive, not very much fun. Madison is literally between a rock and a hard place, albeit on a volcano on a floating plastic island.

The result is not a metaphorical but a literal fight with herself. At the end of *Doomed*, when Madison fights her nemesis Barbie-Madison, she is wrestling with her alter-ego. She notices that her parents love the Barbie simulacrum of her (302), and her duplicate wears the blue shirt, carries the Darwin book, and imitates her features (303). In what she terms as the main event competition between the fittest and the nicest (305), Madison defeats the version of herself that is loyal to, at least in this context, dominant ideology. Through this act, she has symbolically destroyed the undesirable side of herself in effigy, sacrificing qualities of her psyche devoted to making her a diligent, docile, and obedient child, the one who acted out in rebellion but remained, for all intents and purposes, a follower of defined rules. When Madison asserts herself of her own volition, acting from her own free will, taking charge prompted by her inspiration and through her intuition, she becomes liberated to determine her own ideology. To some extent, this imitates the narrator's final battle with Tyler Durden at the end of *Fight Club*. After the narrator recognizes that he is essentially a divided consciousness, he takes back control through self-violence ironically to avoid his complete self-destruction. Plain and simple, Madison faces the same dilemma—her self-annihilation.

Indisputable evidence of this change is in the glances Madison gives to her parents and how she responds to Festus (agent of heaven) and to Satan (agent of hell). In a true act of humility, instead of expressing resentment toward Babette for killing Antonio and Camille while Madlantis is sinking, Madison accepts what has occurred, even using the incident to start a more mature relationship with her parents. In fact, Madison finally moves forward, a relevant point considering the two novels cover a lot of the same temporal terrain. This corresponds to Bakhtin's belief in the tearing down of ideological towers in favor of more pragmatic structures during carnival. Likewise, this relates to Bakhtin's point that degradation lowers the abstract and ideal to the concrete and practical, unifying the spiritual and the earthly into an "indissoluble unity" (*Rabelais* 20).[6] Obviously, Madison is ready to explore philosophical issues about spirituality and politics that she otherwise would not have been able to contemplate with as much courage and confidence. During the Middle Ages, a person who was depressed was considered close to the earth, consequently in tune with the harsh realities of an unforgiving world. Madison achieves the depression that Bakhtin refers to as positive degradation, and she possesses a harmony between body and soul as a result of this final smackdown with her own psychic counterpart on an island that is designed in her own image. Taken further, Madison has quashed her own religion. Satan's throwing down the script that is her life confirms that things have drastically changed (319).

In the last few pages of *Doomed*, however, no one knows what will happen next. Only Palahniuk knows where Madison's journey into paradise, if he imitates Dante's pattern, will take her. Madison comments after her heroic journey, "How could you ever bring yourself to love so deeply if you truly knew how brief a lifetime can be?" (326). The question sounds a lot like something Marianne Williamson would ask. The obvious answer, one Williamson might offer, is predictably: with trust and with faith. This is not hard to surmise since Williamson contends that love defeats forces against love. Applied to Madison, this is definitely the case. Madison concludes that myths are not relegated to the past but can be created in the present and even recreated in the future, and she could volunteer as an archetype for new creations (327). In fact, as Madison weighs her options, neither serving God nor serving Satan is particularly attractive (327). The two representatives of counter ideologies are the RSAs of their respective belief systems. Festus urges, "Return to God" (328); Satan calls, "Abandon yourself" (329). They attempt to hail Madison in the Althusserian sense, to appeal to her super-ego, sense of guilt, her devotion and her dedication to structured belief systems. Madison refuses the interpellation and does not look back. In defiance, Madison proclaims, "Henceforth I will prove my own existence. I will prove that I steer my destiny" (327). With almost having the proverbial angel on one shoulder and a devil on the other, Madison continues forward confidently, a more knowledgeable person, a more experienced person, and one definitely ready to face whatever challenges come her way. During the 2017 interview with *Impulse Gamer*, when asked about readers interpreting his stories, Palahniuk mentions Roland Barthes's structuralist theory that readers subjectively "finish" a text: "I give up and now embrace the idea that the reader will/must complete my work. It's a cop-out, but it's the only realistic position to take" ("Chuck"). Undoubtedly, readers leave this book sequence knowing that Madison will be okay, much better than she has ever been. Williamson seems to be speaking to Madison in this famous passage (frequently mistakenly attributed to Nelson Mandela) from *A Return to Love*:

> Our deepest fear is not that we are inadequate. Our deepest fear is that we are powerful beyond measure. It is our light, not our darkness that most frightens us. We ask ourselves, "Who am I to be brilliant, gorgeous, talented, fabulous?" Actually, who are you not to be? You are a child of God. Your playing small does not serve the world. There is nothing enlightened about shrinking so that other people won't feel insecure around you. We are all meant to shine, as children do. We were born to make manifest the glory of God that is within us. It's not just in some of us; it's in everyone. And as we let our own light shine, we unconsciously give other people permission to do the same. As we are liberated from our own fear, our presence automatically liberates others [165].

Williamson advocated the power of positive thinking to move Hurricane Dorian from its destructive path, tweeting, "The Bahamas, Florida, Georgia and the Carolinas ... may all be in our prayers now.... Millions of us seeing Dorian turn away from land is not a wacky idea; it is a creative use of the power of the mind. Two minutes of prayer, visualization, meditation for those in the way of the storm" (Wu). The hurricane was not as bad as predicted, and maybe the "power of the mind" had some influence. Readers must concur that Madison's ruminations drive much of the action in the two novels.

Palahniuk is no stranger to trust in a higher power, be it a mystical energy or a community of people working toward the same cause. Madison now has a life force within her ready to take her to the next level. Dante was aided by Beatrice, Divine Love, and Madison only has Tigerstripe, which is okay. Williamson's type of love as a psychic force might actually see her through. Or, in a Palahniuk universe, maybe not. Readers will see. Palahniuk respects Campbell's monomyth yet distrusts the possibility that a framework, one reinforced by ideology, could reliably predict outcomes. Campbell's model is the product of studious anthropological research toward what turn out to be formulas to explain how various cultures depict the hero journey. Campbell's archetypal analysis has withstood the test of time, and, as was noted in the second chapter, even postmodernism's assault through the antihero lends credence to the apparent veracity of the monomyth. Palahniuk has many sides, and even though he assumes the public persona as a reactionary, a subversive agitator who certainly gets under the skin of many revered and distinguished academic defenders of American literature, he has a soft side, a sentimental bent aligned with dirty realists whose characters might not live happily ever after but still end up better than when they started, which is just as much a heroic victory. Madison might follow the trajectory of the monomyth, or she might go an entirely different direction. The end of this second novel in a planned trilogy offers optimism that Madison, proving Žižek's theory, will retaliate against what might be the false consciousness of heaven and hell, of God and Satan, as prophesied in dubiously trusted religious texts. Palahniuk loyalists are weary, however, of such neatly anticipated bright endings.

Palahniuk fans are skeptical and cynical, knowing that it is always darkest ... before everything goes totally black. Perhaps beyond his intentions, Palahniuk predicts environmental optimism at the end of *Doomed*. In a *USA Today* article published in October of 2019, Doyle Rice reports an ocean cleanup system is now finally collecting plastic debris among other discarded items in the Great Pacific Garbage Patch, also termed the Pacific trash vortex. Rice mentions that a twenty-five-year-old Dutch inventor—a university dropout—has begun the Ocean Cleanup Project. Of all people, Boyan Slat has designed an apparatus full of buoys and nets that will capture plastic refuge, allowing it to be collected by a ship and then transported to another location. This young person, older than Madison, but only by a few years, may help to save this planet ("Great"). In an earlier article published in March of 2018, Rice claims this mass, first noticed in the early 1990s close to the Pacific Rim, is the largest of five similar collections of plastic in the oceans. More than twice the size of Texas, this body of trash includes about 1.8 trillion pieces of plastic and weighs approximately 88,000 tons, roughly equaling the girth of 500 jumbo jets ("Worlds"). No one has reported the refuge taking the shape of a young woman's face. Fortunately, this project is more about global sustainability than it is related to a holy war. Unbelievably disturbing video broadcast through *USA Today* on December 13, 2019, displays churning pieces of plastic covering a South African beach ("Shocking"). Small shards of plastic are strewn all over an area close to a populated urban city. Palahniuk is not known for addressing many environmental concerns, although one only has to remember the landfill that served as a porn dump in *Survivor* (24–36) or other similar motifs that assume secondary purposes in his plots. Once again, Palahniuk is ahead of the curve concerning key ideological issues. Democratic and Republican presidential candidates will surely continue to spar over global warming and other major environmental issues. Palahniuk has already made his statement about this matter, and readers may expect more along this line in the third book of his trilogy.

Granted, Madison is not Greta Thunberg, the sixteen-year-old environmental activist from Sweden who recently won the distinguished award of *Time* Person of the Year for 2019. Madison has not expressed anything resembling "How dare they" in exasperation over the decisions of those apparently controlling her destiny. Although, Madison does possess some of the anger that President Trump seems to notice in Thunberg. In a *USA Today* piece titled "Trump Attacks Greta Thunberg for being Time's 'Person of the Year,'" David Jackson reports that President Trump tweeted, "So ridiculous, ... Greta must work on her Anger Management problem, then go to a good old fashioned movie with a friend! Chill Greta, Chill!" However, Jackson's coverage of Thunberg's response definitely personifies something Madison would have done: "Thunberg responded swiftly, changing her Twitter profile to read: 'A teenager working on her anger management problem. Currently chilling and watching a good old fashioned movie with a friend.'" That definitely seems like a response Madison would have offered. At the end of *Doomed*, there is hope that Palahniuk is looking forward toward something greater, more beneficial, a happier time. If anything, this is promoted by his main character escaping a horribly grimy death inside the swirling, gurgling, and churning vortex of human waste. Nope, that is not the case this time. Nonetheless, Palahniuk's next adventure for Madison will likely address the question of whether or not an individual is capable of working outside an ideology. Madison brings down one ideology and seems to escape, for the moment, another.

FIVE

"You've become something dangerous: a woman"
The Subversion of Feminism in Beautiful You

On May 13, 2019, Alyssa Milano and Waleisah Wilson proposed a sex strike that in many ways rivaled the one depicted in Aristophanes's *Lysistrata*.[1] In a CNN op-ed piece titled "Why the Time Is Now for a #SexStrike," Milano and Wilson sound a call to all women to react via their physicality to recent state legislative maneuvers that they perceive as threatening the landmark decision of *Roe v. Wade*. Milano and Wilson claim, "We must collectively reject these restrictions on our basic human rights and dignity in every way that we can. This flood of anti-abortion legislation is completely outrageous and an equally bold response is required. And, so, we call on all people whose rights are in danger to participate in a #SexStrike." To defend their position, they point out that "Lysistratic protest is a longstanding, effective and empowering method to fight for change" and provide examples (Iroquois in 1600s, Kenyans in 2009, and Columbians in 2011) to demonstrate how women have withheld sex to men as a means to social, cultural, and political change. To emphasize their purpose, they assert that #SexStrike will force straight and cisgender men to undergo the experience of having their sexual options taken out of their control, and this imposed celibacy would persuade all parties involved toward immediate action against the legislation of reproductive rights. Reporting for *USA Today*, Sara M. Moniuszko, summarizes Milano and Wilson's strategy as simply "women protest controversial new anti-abortion laws by denying men sex."

The #MeToo movement has certainly propelled feminism into a fourth wave. There is no American sex strike, but Milano's "call to arms" suggests that strategies have not completely changed from Aristophanes's 411 BCE to Milano's 2019. As was introduced in the second chapter about *Snuff*—and was broached in the introductory chapters—there remains a paradox in America regarding attitudes toward sexuality. For the most part, there is still the lingering Puritan influence in the mainstream that porn is, for instance, discriminatory toward women because of its prevalent objectification of the female body, not to mention porn's perceived heterosexual aggressiveness toward everything feminine. Behind closed doors, however, porn is consumed abundantly by both males and females, and the assumption that it caters only to straight males is totally antiquated. This is pertinent considering Chuck Palahniuk's choice in *Beautiful You* of going with the sex toy as both female symbol of sovereignty and tool of enslavement. In his 2014 novel, Palahniuk acknowledges the dual signification of sex toys, and, to be fair, in his 2008 novel *Snuff*, he concedes that men also enjoy the manufactured replicas of genitalia, particularly those modeled after their favorite male or female adult stars.

Because of lingering stigma, this is largely an underground pleasure. Most women would not openly declare in a room of strangers that they frequently use blue rabbit dildos, for instance, just as men would not likely admit that they make daily visits to Pornhub, but the sex technology business is currently booming financially. Considering COVID-19 protocol, this activity follows the "safe distance" and "shelter in place" mandates. In a July 17, 2019, article in *USA Today*, Mae Anderson reports that the Consumer Technology Association admitted its mistake in not awarding an innovation award for a "robotic personal massager for women" because of moral standards representative of the organization. This year, the Consumer Electronics Show (visited by over 180,000 people) has started a "sex tech" category as retribution for its discrimination. Valeriya Safronova addresses this debacle in the aptly titled *New York Times* piece "What's So 'Indecent' about Female Pleasure?" by essentially questioning the ideology that influenced the decision that the vibrator was ethically inappropriate. In a *USA Today* article on July 16, Madeline Purdue mentions products available that simulate a lover's heartbeat or a mate's hugs. Targeting women, *Cosmopolitan*, *Glamour*, and other magazines have yearly issues featuring Sex Toy Awards. Women may purchase the best devices from local shops as well as online from Amazon, Walmart, or other major retailers, and as Alison Better, Katie Van Syckle, and Michael Marks and Kassia Wosick contend in various articles, sales are skyrocketing from both male and female purchasers. In the July 2019 *Cosmopolitan* article "The Millennial Sex Recession Is Bullshit," Julie Vadnal shares that her generation utilizes technology to enhance discreetly their sexual relationships as frequently as any other age group. Women are embracing the privilege to explore their sexuality as they want, and retailers are accommodating them with products to satisfy this demand.

Nonetheless, with these new freedoms come additional responsibilities, and with this growing market is a greater risk of exploitation. At the end of *Lysistrata*, after the Athenian and Spartan men have surrendered, Lysistrata scolds the men in front of a nude Lady Reconciliation (usually identified as a beautifully voluptuous woman) for their inane warring instead of devotedly remaining with their wives. Depending upon how the scene is directed, there might be insinuation that the women have not really accomplished anything. The men will capitulate to satisfy their wives, will have sex with them, and will then return to battle. The end of the play includes what amounts to an orgy. In strongly feminist productions, Lysistrata admonishes the men with her famous "I am a woman, but I have a mind" speech (857), and the men display understanding as they obediently comply. In not-so-feminist productions, the men impatiently listen to Lysistrata, trying to conceal their enormous erections, noticeably extending in front of their crotches, ready to dive into the ensuing intercourse after they docilely accept chastisement. How the ending is presented determines the feminist direction and consequently ideological meaning of the play. *Lysistrata* could be either slapstickily funny or dourly bleak, as translators of Aristophanes's play know very well. In this respect, Sarah Ruden offers perhaps the best mediation between the two extremes in her translation of the Greek play.[2]

Many readers do not realize that Palahniuk addresses a similar dilemma in *Beautiful You*. Through the comic grotesque, Palahniuk displays in what appears a rather simplistic plot how seemingly innocuous systems can be malignantly exploitative. During a time when corporations peddle goods that surreptitiously exert tremendous influence on the American economy, Palahniuk chooses products associated with sexual stimulation as the perfect commodities to subjugate the female population. Likewise, Palahniuk calls attention to American ignorance concerning the connection between capitalist consumerism and dominant ideology. He carries this out through a version of the monomyth, a simple framework for a complicated subject, in which his hero, Penny Harrigan, defeats her archenemy, C. Linus Maxwell, who wants nothing less than world domination á la feminine sexual pleasure. Through his line of Beautiful You products, Climax-Well, as he is nicknamed, gives females exactly what many believe they have fought for through waves of feminism, complete sexual autonomy. Blending fantasy and reality, Palahniuk gives all women the power to pleasure themselves on their own terms, so to speak. As mentioned in the previous chapter, Palahniuk respects Joseph Campbell's separation-initiation-return model of the heroic journey, but he, of course, transforms this into a transgressive vehicle to prove his premise about American sociocultural self-deception.

At its core, this fantasy hero story is about rebelling against oppressive ideology. Palahniuk's use of comic grotesque to describe excessive sexual pleasure is blatantly carnivalesque. True, there are currently available estrogen creams and sildenafil citrate tablets to enhance sexual stimulation and performance, but Palahniuk embellishes, to Rabelaisian gargantuan extremes, how often people take advantage of supplements in sexual situations. As has been discussed in previous chapters, Palahniuk questions what is considered normal, but even those addicted to Pornhub (not to diminish the severity of sex addiction) could not physiologically imitate what is presented in this novel. Palahniuk's clinical descriptions of sexuality are certainly more explicit, particularly in the intricate technical minutiae related to orgasm, than in his other novels (*Snuff*, *Survivor*, or even *Choke*, which addresses sex addiction), yet many of these depictions are combined with hilariously satirical innuendoes. Corny Maxwell's cloning of his wife Phoebe is a romantic motif underneath the prevailing one of DataMicroCom's monopoly on everything from shoes to cereal through nanobots infiltrating female bloodstreams. Considering Louis Althusser's premise that ideology is a system full of contradictions disguised through the application of structures (theoretical and practical), Palahniuk hides socioeconomic problems behind the curtain of the traditional battle of the sexes, allowing opposition to heteropatriarchy take attention away from capitalistic corruption. In the novel, Maxwell's power relies on the apparent heteropatriarchal democracy spearheaded by his proxy President Clarissa Hind and enforced by agencies that carry out his ideological agenda. Hind is controlled by Maxwell's sexual technology, and her suicide indicates his complete dominance over her physically as well as psychologically. In addition, Palahniuk engages the Promise Keepers to serve as representative gatekeepers of the moral majority. When women become controlled by Maxwell through his products, they unconsciously ignore interpellation spurred by sociocultural decorum and are loyal to Maxwell's idiosyncratic consumerist ideology. In view of Slavoj Žižek's theory, Penny rebels against this system and initiates change. Through Baba Gray-Beard's tantric principles associated with simple living, Penny is able to reveal to other women the contradictions within the ruling ideology that they serve. Althusser generally believed literature exposes ideological contradiction to an otherwise deceived audience, and Palahniuk definitely discloses the pitfalls of total loyalty, in this case completely to feminism, through *Beautiful You*.

Beautiful You is arguably Palahniuk's most sexually explicit book. To give him credit, the sex scenes are usually scientific and described with plausible accuracy. Regardless, reviews are mostly negative.[3] In a 2016 interview with *Soundcloud*, Palahniuk claims this novel deserves more critical acclaim, but he also notes that the subject of arousal addiction might be "ahead of the curve" in the current cultural climate ("Beaks"). In a 2014 interview in *Hustler*, Palahniuk calls the novel "gonzo erotica" (45), but he states in another 2014 interview with *SLUG* that this is "tongue-in-cheek erotica": "it's not written to be sexually arousing. It's kind of written in a wrong way. It's fantastically sexual content, but it's not arousing. The book wasn't written to excite people; it was written to make them laugh" ("Telling"). Alice Stephens comments whimsically, "If you are squeamish about the subjects of masturbation, sexual arousal, orgasms, and anatomical analyses of female genitalia, then *Beautiful You* is not for you. Even if you are interested in these subjects, this book is likely not for you." Lily Burana asserts, "In a book so heavily invested in the pursuit of the female orgasm, it's hard to resist the criticism that Palahniuk appears to be faking it. *Beautiful You* feels phoned-in, a master satirist's dip in standards." In his review of the novel, Cameron Woodhead writes, "Despite (or perhaps due to) his prolific output, it's been downhill for Chuck Palahniuk, fiction-wise, since *Fight Club*.... Ostensibly a satire on erotic fiction, rape culture and third-wave feminism among other things, Palahniuk's antics seem sneering and inane." Reviewing the novel for *The Oregonian*, after citing Palahniuk's own comments that *Beautiful You* is similar to "something the Marquis de Sade would have written," Angie Jabine remarks, "Don't go looking for any soft-porn pleasures here either.... The effect of Palahniuk's clinical terminology is more alienating than titillating. Which, again, may be exactly the point."

Although, some reviews are distinctly positive. For instance, Carolyn Darr commends Palahniuk's treatment of post-feminism that provides socioeconomic equity between the genders, particularly by portraying a female president: "Palahniuk uses his female characters to magnify the struggle for women's rights.... In its own twisted way, 'Beautiful You' creates a commentary on feminism where the intersection of sexual liberation and dangerous overstimulation is dissected and questioned." Brian Truitt writes, "The novel is full of explicit sex used for narrative and lampooning purposes, and not in an erotic way. Palahniuk wants sex to be uncomfortable and weird. His graphic storytelling is bound to ruffle puritanical feathers, but it's essential to the societal takedown." Peter Petruski mentions, "Casual readers will be hard pressed to find anything else like it on the shelf. Highly recommended for everyone except the prudish or readers of actual romance novels." To counterbalance these positive reviews before analyzing the novel, the most cited review is, however, negative. As mentioned in the second chapter, in her *New York Times* review, Paula Bomer blasts Palahniuk's novel, concluding the overall plot is farfetched and a bit absurd. To reiterate her final opinion from the first chapter, Bomer does not agree Palahniuk's ideas are necessarily good ideas (34).

Palahniuk has admitted the twofold nature of his novel is, on the one hand, not necessarily a substantive story, but, on the other, a treatise advocating personal empowerment.[4] In a 2014 interview in *Fangoria*, reacting to the premise this book functions as a *Fight Club* for women, Palahniuk claims that he "cribbed elements from popular 'chick lit' books and cobbled them together, until the novel's working title was 'Fifty Shades of the Twilight Cave Bear Wears Prada.'" Palahniuk adds, "So, it's a 'slash mash-up' wherein Andrea from The Devil Wears Prada has hot, wet lady-on-lady sex with her elderly boss, Miranda…. Only on the top of Mt. Everest…. And with references to tons of fashion designers." In this interview, Palahniuk reveals that a couple parts of Penny's vagina sound authentically biological but are actually fictitious and named after Palahniuk's friends. When asked about his knowledge of sexual history, Palahniuk confesses that the Chilean magnet stones and two technical names are strictly from his imagination. He concedes that he had planned to auction off imaginary names of female anatomy to raise money for charity, deciding finally to go with variations of his friends' names ("Q&A"). Palahniuk reiterates this in a 2014 interview with *The Talks*. When questioned about the novel's similarity to *Fifty Shades of Grey*, Palahniuk responds, "I'm fascinated by the whole issue of arousal addiction, but to do it in a comic, off-hand way, by depicting it with women, the population least likely to be subjected by it. I also wanted to borrow from all of those kinds of 'chick lit' books and use all of those tropes that are viewed so seriously" ("Chuck"). In a review for *SFGate*, Caroline Leavitt addresses how this novel parodies *Fifty Shades of Grey*.

Another parody, however, might be more interesting. Concerning the comparison between *Fight Club* and *Beautiful You*, Tracy Clark-Flory asserts in *Salon* that females are unlikely to be attracted to this story because "it doesn't address a female desire—even though it is, ostensibly, at least at first, about female pleasure." Clark-Flory claims this novel, comparable to *Fight Club* and other Palahniuk texts, only addresses male neuroses, particularly ones "experienced by supposedly feminized, emasculated men in corporate, capitalist and 'post-feminist' America." Granted, women might not be too hip on seeing the problem of male anxiety solved through the exploitation of female desire through technology. They would possibly detest reading about themselves tricked into feeling as if they have complete autonomy to satisfy their sexual desire independently, divorced whatsoever with men. As was discussed in the chapter about *Snuff*, pornography is now mainstream, and to reiterate, sex tech is a booming industry. If Clark-Flory is right, women would be uninterested reading about the lessening of male anxiety through sexual technology working in men's favor, reinforcing their control, confirming what feminists believe is the purpose underlying porn, dominance over women. This is not the case in *Beautiful You*. Only one man, Climax-Well, appears to be the anxious, feminized, and ultimately emasculated corporate capitalist. He is absolutely not a media-driven representation of traditional manhood, nor would a reader expect such a characterization from Palahniuk. In fact, other male characters in the novel intervene to the widescale sex toy addiction and attempt to eradicate all of the Beautiful You products. In this novel, Palahniuk shows that if males can be addicted to porn, females can reciprocally be addicted to vibrators.

Nonetheless, this comparison between *Fight Club* and *Beautiful You* warrants more attention. Admittedly, *Fight Club* is not a clear-cut model of Bakhtin's theory. The story is dark, satirical, vulgar, but it does not stand out as overtly comic grotesque. In the eighth chapter, an argument will be made defending *Fight Club* as comic grotesque, but the novel is not this in the same way as *Beautiful You*. Of all Palahniuk's work, there is substantially more criticism, commentary, and critique, considerably so, of that first novel than anything else, and no one firmly and exclusively situates that text into the comic grotesque. Granted, Palahniuk satirizes facets of American culture, particularly related to consumerism, and as most who address the novel mention, he exposes socioeconomic disparity through the apparatus of Project Mayhem, but mockery within that plot has a much different emphasis than in *Snuff*, *Damned*, or *Doomed*. Palahniuk's purpose in his first novel is more obviously Marxist—related to socioeconomic inequities—than in those other texts or in *Beautiful You*. With strikingly forceful sentences, surgically cogent in meaning, Palahniuk allows his narrator to reveal simultaneously a fierce antipathy for capitalism and an equally fervent self-loathing. The narrator literally battles himself (through Tyler Durden) as he opposes others (concretely during fight club as well as abstractly through corporate monopolies). Throughout *Fight Club*, there is a strong us versus them, the haves versus the have nots, dichotomy. Cassie Wright and Madison Spencer have their rivals—as in Cassie versus Sheila or Branch; Madison versus the anti–Madison, inhabitants in hell, or Satan—but these are not necessarily based on socioeconomic conflict. Even though *Fight Club* is given to convincingly persuasive gender, queer, and psychoanalytic interpretations, and a plethora of scholarship explores each of these critical areas, the crux of the story is about capitalist ideological exploitation of the masses.

Beautiful You also demonstrates how a Marxist struggle can be veiled behind a tapestry of complex gender issues. Deceptively hidden behind his obvious attacks against facets of feminism, Palahniuk's seditious assault against corporate capitalism is what makes *Beautiful You* in some ways more reactionary than his first novel. Unfortunately, reviewers do not seem to notice how Palahniuk effectively uses the comic grotesque to lighten what could have been a very depressing story about global domination through female enslavement. Just as he does in *Snuff*, *Damned*, and *Doomed* when he portrays highly politicized subjects with hilarious satire, in *Beautiful You*, Palahniuk identifies social and cultural hypocrisies and allows the comic grotesque to amplify their preposterously absurd effects. In this story, Penny does not watch her father and mother electrically melted together, nor does she fight her doppelgänger on an island made of plastic pollutants—she does not physically fight anyone, even though she sexually wrestles with Climax-Well (which in some political circles could be declared sexual assault). Instead, Penny emits a sonic boom from her vagina while a flaming dildo impales her nemesis's crotch. This novel is not *Fight Club*, at least not the initial version of the narrative. Furthermore, this story is not exactly aligned with *Fight Club 2*, although Palahniuk offers similar elements of phallic buffoonery and vaginal tomfoolery, and *Beautiful You* by its nature would become a provocatively interesting graphic text. Similar to *Lysistrata*, production would mean everything. The creation of the images would influence the ideological emphasis on Marxism or feminism.

Initially, Penny appears to be the typical young woman groomed to perform competitively in a heteropatriarchal American society. She has her foot in the door at Broome, Broome, and Brillstein, a highly reputable Manhattan law firm, and although she has failed the bar exam twice, she is encouraged that she will pass the third time. Similar to Madison, Penny lacks self-confidence. Readers notice right away that her primary job is more secretarial or even custodial than jurisprudential. Palahniuk contrasts Penny with sassily self-sufficient Monique and elegantly self-confident Alouette D'Ambrosia. When Tad says "Yo, Hillbilly!" (9), he establishes Penny as the Nebraskan outsider with insufficient cultural capital probably to survive long in this environment. She is destined to fail, fated to return home to a life bereft of attributes identified with feminist success. Similar to Sheila's and Madison's penchant for feminist intellectualism, Penny has a four-year undergraduate degree in gender politics (12). Palahniuk's main character has the requisite book smarts to compete, but when Penny spills coffee in front of her boss and C. Linus Maxwell, she thinks about her physicality, worrying her blouse had become transparent because of the liquid, and relapsing immediately into self-doubt. Albert Brillstein reveals she did not pass the bar a third time, causing her to consider how a "country bumpkin" such as her could dream of a career in law (14–15). As Penny contemplates, "She shouldn't be here. She should be in suburban Omaha. She should be happily married to a pleasant, even-tempered Sigma Chi. They would have two babies and a third on the way. That was her fate. She should be covered in baby spit instead of expensive double-shot espressos" (15).

Prior to this encounter, Palahniuk describes her as not exactly the exemplary or representative feminist. In a lengthy passage, he situates Penny both inside and outside the ideology generally attributed to feminism:

> The truth was, Penelope Anne Harrigan was still being a good daughter—obedient, bright, dutiful—who did as she was told. She'd always deferred to the advice of other, older people. Yet she yearned for something beyond earning the approval of her parents and surrogate parents. With apologies to Simone de Beauvoir, Penny didn't want to be a third-wave *anything*. No offense to Bella Abzug, but neither did she want to be a post-*anything*. She didn't want to replicate the victories of Susan B. Anthony and Helen Gurley Brown. She wanted a choice beyond: Housewife versus lawyer. Madonna versus whore. An option not mired in the lingering detritus of some Victorian era dream. Penny wanted something beyond feminism itself! [5]

Moreover, twenty-five-year-old Penny feels the guilt of not belonging in her seat at the law firm table, albeit not a warm place since she usually gets coffee and finds chairs: "She hadn't found her dream as a well-behaved daughter. Nor had she found it by regurgitating the hidebound ideology of her professors. It comforted her to think that every girl of her generation was facing the same crisis. They'd all inherited a legacy of freedom, and they owed it to the future to forge a new frontier for the next generation of young women. To break new ground" (6). However, Palahniuk prepares Penny for something special, putting her hero story into motion: "She'd never trusted her own natural impulses and instincts. Among her greatest fears was the possibility that she might never discover and develop her deepest talents and intuitions. Her *special* gifts. Her life would be wasted in pursuing the goals set for her by other people. Instead, she wanted to reclaim a power and authority—a primitive, irresistible force—that transcended gender roles. She dreamed of wielding a raw magic that predated civilization itself" (6). This introduction to Penny is crucial concerning her affiliation with third-wave feminism. As such, she does not want to be tied with an ideology but, as is evident in the rest of the novel, she has no compunction about acting on behalf of women's rights when they support what is fair and equitable. Penny is against the arcane labeling and discriminatory pigeonholing, but she believes in what the labeling means concerning human rights.

In some camps of third-wave feminist theory, men and women are at war, and women must take advantage of all their resources if they are to become empowered. In her famous treatise *Intercourse*, Andrea Dworkin writes, "For women, according to the killer/husband, virginity is the highest state, an ideal; and a fall from virginity is a fall into trivialization, into being used as a thing; one dresses up to the thing; one does not have a full humanity but must conform to the rituals and conventions of debasement as a sexual object. But this reduction of humanity into being an object for sex carries with it the power to dominate men because men want the object and the sex" (14). Dworkin contends male "repulsion" of women is manifested through sexual intercourse (8), and she believes women should use this to their advantage: "women manipulate men by manipulating men's sexual desire; these trivial, mediocre things (women) have real power over men through sex.... This dominance of men by women is experienced by the men as real—emotionally real, sexually real, psychologically real; it emerges as the reason for the wrath of the misogynist" (14–15). Dworkin goes so far as to claim that, for women, "murder itself is the sex act or it is sexual climax" (7). In *Toward a Feminist Theory of the State*, after explaining that pornography portrays women as "less than human" (144) thus inciting men to aggress toward them as sexual objects, Catharine A. MacKinnon proposes that "male sexuality is apparently activated by violence against women and expresses itself in violence against women to a significant extent" (145). MacKinnon argues gender should be seen as hierarchal: "perhaps gender must be maintained as a social hierarchy so that man will be able to get erections; or, part of the male interest in keeping women down lies in the fact that it gets men up. Maybe feminists are considered castrating because equality is not sexy" (145). In "It's a Jungle Out There," Camille Paglia understands the male predatory instinct and declares that even if there is not a war between the sexes women should be weary of male intentions: "In our cities, on our campuses far from home, young women are vulnerable and defenseless. Feminism has not prepared them for this. Feminism keeps saying the sexes are the same. It keeps telling women they can do anything, go anywhere, say anything, wear anything. No, they can't. Women will always be in sexual danger" (538–39). To summarize these three contentions, men are naturally predators sexually stimulated by superiority over women that is propagated through assault. This is the indoctrination that Penny has studied but has opted to ignore.

Some third-wave feminists offer, however, options to fight male sexual aggression. For instance, in *Anticlimax*, Sheila Jeffreys writes, "As women and as lesbians our hope lies only in other women. We must work towards the construction of homosexual desire and practice as a most important part of our struggle for liberation. However important heterosexual desire has been in our lives we will all have some experience of its opposite. We will have experience of sexual desire and practice which does not leave us feeling betrayed, a sexual desire and practice which eroticises mutuality and equality" (313). Jeffreys advocates equality through women not having sexual intercourse with men in the conventional sense:

> Our struggle for liberation does not necessarily require chastity, though many women do choose this path and it is an honourable choice. Such a strategy could only cause disbelief in a male-supremacist society in which sex has been made holy. Sex is holy

because of its role as a sacred ritual in the dominant/submissive relationship between men and women. The importance attached to sex defies rationality and can only be explained in this political way. But we can also choose, as many of us have done, to work towards homosexual desire if that suits our lives and relationships. We must remember that homosexual desire will not be recognised as "sex." We do not even possess suitable words to describe it [315].

Jeffreys is not calling for a Lysistratian sex strike comparable to Milano's announcement, but she is requesting people (not just women) perceive sexuality not in terms of an adversarial gender confrontation but as equitable gender alliance, not desire ignited by power but desire nurtured by trust (316). Another example is from *Fire with Fire*, in which Naomi Wolf asserts that women can counteract male sexual aggression by not being "good" girls. Wolf states that the inner child is generally compassionate, but there is also a "mischievous, boisterous, unregenerate twin, the inner *bad girl* lurking in the female psyche" (318). Wolf describes the bad girl as hedonistic, egotistic, and avaricious (318). To succeed, Wolf contends the bad girl must take over the propensity to be the good girl. Wolf writes to female readers:

> Now imagine that you can reach her when you need to. Imagine that you can lay claim to the force of her desire, to her sky-high self-regard, when you are fighting for your rights, negotiating about sex or housework, or putting a price on your labors. Amplify her wishes to adult scope: the respect she wanted on the playground, and in her fantasies of recognition, you want from Capitol Hill. Do not call it "masculine," that will to power in yourself, that desire to transform the world and be *seen*. That is *in* us. It always has been. Use it to walk through this historic door [320].

Of course, others promote various strategies for female empowerment in a heteropatriarchal-dominated capitalistic America that cultivates and subsequently defends ideology that perpetuates male-centered control. Both Jeffreys and Wolf seem to point toward an androgynous label in place of conventional gender identities, but essentially women such as Milano and others affiliated with #MeToo see women banding together (i.e., the national women's marches) toward a common cause. Tarana Burke's motive initially was to raise awareness about sexual abuse and assault, but the movement has evolved into broader initiatives to empower women, extending into a fourth wave.

Palahniuk begins his novel with the assumption heteropatriarchy reigns supreme. In the opening pages, after the remote-controlled rape of Penny while she testifies on the witness stand, Palahniuk flashes back to the beginning, at Penny's workplace. Albert Brillstein is clearly a caricature of old guard male power, particularly wielding dominance as he demeans Penny in front of Maxwell by commanding her to servility, with Penny literally kneeling in subservience to her boss (14–15). Palahniuk is building upon the premise that heteropatriarchy is the controlling ideology, and Althusserian Ideological State Apparatuses (ISAs) and Repressive State Apparatuses (RSAs) are entrenched to maintain compliance, even when there is a female president and other female-oriented agencies that are responsible for the interpellation of violators. Palahniuk's strategy is ingenious. Unquestionably, Penny has been motivated all of her life to confront heteropatriarchy in its various manifestations; she has also tried to succeed exactly by those same heteropatriarchal rules. Standardized tests such as the SAT, ACT, GRE, and others, many operated through the Princeton Educational Testing Services, have been questioned for various cultural biases. Penny's inability to pass the bar is an indication of her failure to meet standards associated with, among other discriminatory matrixes, dominant ideology. Penny is struggling to achieve her goals in a hegemonically man's world, but she also admits that all of her support via feminism is not helping. Penny realizes that there has "never been a better time to be a woman" (4). She understands her ambition to compete "toe-to-toe" with men in the law profession was "radical" (5). She finally questions, in a revealing thought, the "hidebound ideology" of her professors and recognizes that she has failed to trust her own "impulses and instincts" (6). Penny seemingly ignores the Christian ideology infused in the Bibles that her parents send to her each birthday (25). Obviously, Penny is not comfortable with traditional feminist doctrine, nor does she want to be categorized or classified by any abstract ideological markers. In this regard, Penny is a bit naïve. Noteworthy is the nonchalance with which she describes a major Title IX violation that could have been front-page news supporting allegations about fraternity date-rape culture. Thinking Homeland Security is the root reason, Penny is glad she is spared from a violent sexual assault by a Zeta Delta in a basement during Pledge Week. She thinks, "they guarded all Americans. All of the time" (28). At the onset, Penny has been introduced to various ideologies, but she is uncomfortable adopting her own. This reluctance possibly makes her the perfect prey for Climax-Well.

The comic grotesque in this entire novel is fostered by sex technology. If Maxwell embodies masculine anxiety, he does so in a stereotypically nerdy, egg-headed way. He is not the person one would suspect of sexual exploitation, but the point is there is not actually one type. Those who excel at this endeavor are probably not the ones obviously profiled. Penny first notices the shine on his expensive wingtips in addition to other qualities of dress as well as physicality emblematic of the wealthy elite (13). Because of his tantric training, Maxwell is an excellent lover, skilled in extraordinary techniques of the sexual arts. However, his multifaceted intentions are first to create intimate products for women, second to infect women with nanobots for financial gain, and third to finish the reproduction of his first love Phoebe through Penny. After the first impressions of sexual prowess, Penny describes several occasions when Maxwell studies her for sexual experimentation, the subject of hypotheses and results. World domination through female sexual hedonistic addiction sounds farfetched, but it can be plausibly verified through current media. In a fall 2018 article "Stepford Wives Rebooted," Joanna Chiu describes sex robots that have the capability to satisfy any desire. Although this is not nanobot technology, this demonstrates the incredible technology already available. Moreover, Thomas Fox Brewster reports in "'Panty Buster' Toy Left Private Sex Lives of 50,000 Exposed" how Bluetooth insecure access allowed perpetrators to operate remotely the Panty Buster sex toy. Believe it or not, some women lost control of their sex toys (while in operation). Comparable to Maxwell's ability to cause a French actress to writhe in sexual stimulation on stage, these hackers had access to turn on—or turn up—a sex toy outside the visual range of the person enjoying the device. In "Sexed Appeals: Network Marketing Advertising and Adult Home Novelty Parties," Dawn Heinecken states that over a decade ago in 2005 sales of adult toys exceeded $30 billion in America, and she mentions that home sex toy parties "are not only a profitable, but trendy, cultural activity today" (23). Nevertheless, an important facet of the comedy in this novel is hyperbole, the embellishment and exaggeration of feminine indulgence in self-pleasure. True, sexual nanobots are not likely to infiltrate female blood streams, but there is always the possibility that the abuse of sex tech will become more pervasive, and this chance helps bolster the story's verisimilitude. Instead of landline calling of 1-900 numbers for phone sex in the 1980s, one has only to connect via personal computer, smart phone, or easily accessible and purportedly confidential technology. One could only guess how lucrative sex-tech is during COVID-19. During the spring of 2020, Zoom interactive camera technology is extremely popular for a number of purposes, surely including intimate encounters.

A major aspect of carnival is fantasy, and Palahniuk creates such a farcical situation that readers might infer, "That could never happen." They are mistaken. In an April 15, 2019, story in *USA Today*, Aleanna Siacon and Micah Walker describe a case in which a man in Michigan sued his parents for $87,000 for destroying his unbelievably massive porn collection. According to Siacon and Walker, this gentleman lost over 400 VHS tapes, 1,600 DVDs, over 160 CDs, and, pertinent to this subject, seventy sex toys. Not to sound overly facetious, but this person certainly did not seem too self-conscious about drawing attention to his extravagant collection of items for, insinuated in the report, solitary self-pleasure. Moreover, he definitely had a healthy appetite and possibly a high tolerance for sexually enticing technology. Monique's self-isolation during her marathon sex toy sessions in Penny's apartment, noticed after she consistently calls in sick to work (104), do not seem too outrageous compared to this real-life example of sexual hedonism. Furthermore, readers might not question the likelihood of Brenda, the CFO of Allied Chemical Corp., surrendering to her "carnal machinations" as an "unfortunate spectacle" on a street corner, stabbing her exposed vagina furiously with the Instant-Ecstasy Probe (180–81) after learning about this Michigan court case. Again, not to minimize sex addiction—without question a serious medical condition—but people such as Wilt Chamberlin, Warren Beatty, Charlie Sheen, Gene Simmons, Hugh Hefner, and more men who have claimed over 2,000 sex partners, not to forget Messalina mentioned in *Snuff*, have had insatiably gargantuan sexual appetites. However, in reality lawsuits such as the one filed by the Michigan man are anomalous, and this is why they capture national attention when they are publicized.

Palahniuk emphasizes the magnitude of female masturbatory excess by presenting it on a Rabelaisian unbelievably excessive scale. There are women who have notoriously had incredible numbers of sexual partners, but, as a Google search for the identities of these females will verify, sociocultural decorum dictates that it is in bad taste to mention them. The double standard applies, as men are praised for multiple partners and women are blamed as sluts and whores. Traditionally, an insatiable appetite in a female is condemned rather than revered. When Penny begins to intellectualize Maxwell's plan completely, after she internalizes that women are literally "dying from pleasure" (124), Penny relates male arousal addiction to online pornography to the female addiction to Beautiful You products (130). As she contemplates, "It made perfect sense! The constantly changing stimulation was gradually rewiring their female brains.... Once addicted, ladies would binge on pleasure," accurately identifying the source of relentless compulsion and craving (130). Of course, Palahniuk is satirizing what happens when women assert their sexual self-reliance and are capable of assuaging their sexual desire without the assistance of men. Interestingly, *Lysistrata* would be an entirely different play if the women had the technology to motorize their leather dinguses. Continuing this train of thought, perhaps Alyssa Milano is cognizant of all the sexual technology that could replace men if necessary. Palahniuk displays, however, that anyone (no matter the gender) can succumb to sexual hubris.

As I have discussed extensively elsewhere, Palahniuk dilutes any sexual enticement in his descriptions with scientifically sterile and emotionally detached language, yet this objective stance does not make the episodes of lovemaking any less grotesque, maybe even heightening the transgressive effect in many cases. Full of verbal obscenities, the passages are concedingly disgusting to some, yet they are nonetheless carnally comic—especially in terms of the carnivalesque—in their portrayals of the human preoccupation with orgasm, the little death that people go to exorbitant lengths to achieve. In "Chuck Palahniuk's *Beautiful You*, Alfred Kinsey's *Sexual Behavior in the Human Female*, and the Commodification of Female Sexual Desire," I assert this premise about Palahniuk's parodying of Alfred Kinsey:

> Simply put, *Beautiful You* is a transgressive text that is not entirely a transgressive text. To get to Penny's eventual service as Baba Gray-Beard's protégée, Palahniuk parodies the entire enterprise of female sexual stimulation, making it about as scientifically unappealing as reading a college-level Human Sexuality course textbook. The seminal authority in this area is, of course, Alfred Kinsey, and his monumental 1953 report *Sexual Behavior in the Human Female* set the standard in this field. Palahniuk parodies Kinsey and his assistants' descriptions of female genitalia, female stimulation, and ultimately female orgasm, and this enables Palahniuk to develop his hero story with Penny serving as Maxwell's adversary [102].

I continue that Palahniuk depends upon "transgressivity to parody satirically the mechanical presentation of sexuality in *Sexual Behavior in the Human Female*" (105).[5] The parodied material serves to desensitize readers against descriptive dissection of the female anatomy. Penny might reveal that she is excited sexually, and Alouette's squirming on stage makes Maxwell's warnings real, but there is nothing in this novel that functions as content designed to arouse readers sexually. In other words, this is definitely not, no matter the connections insinuated, *Fifty Shades of Grey* romantically depicting Penny's seduction by Maxwell. Regardless of Palahniuk's deceptive claims, this book might take feminists to task for possible hypocrisy concerning female sexual self-sufficiency and girl-power men-bashing run amuck. Truth told, women can be just as sexually gluttonous as men, and most male readers would also find Maxwell morally and ethically despicable.

Actually, Palahniuk is extremely rhetorical in his creation of sex scenes. Just as Maxwell is meticulous in his calculations to achieve the optimum results, Palahniuk crafts his passages to display Maxwell's preoccupation with the physiology of sex, to emphasize his exploitation of technology to manipulate women, or, much more dynamically, to document Penny's moving toward using sex as a weapon for humanitarian and not exclusively feminist reasons. When she and Maxwell are intimate, his mannerisms are "almost clinical," similar to "a doctor or a scientist," with his jotting notes in a book that was "almost an appendage" (45). His words are neither sentimental nor affectionate. He tells her, "Look at yourself. You have a textbook vagina. Your labia majora are exactly symmetrical. Your perianal ridge is magnificent. Your frenulum clitoridis and fourchette.... Biologically speaking, men treasure such uniformity. The proportions of your genitalia are ideal" (48). This is not typical pillow talk. After teaching Penny about her own anatomy, pointing out the purpose, for instance, of her perineal sponge (53), Maxwell maneuvers his entire hand inside Penny, and in a less than romantic interchange, he puts his fingers into her mouth so she can taste some of the ejaculate that she has sprayed in response (54). In scientific jargon he mumbles through the encounter, "The *nervi pelvici splanchnici* branches *here* near your *nervi erigentes*," noting that her coccygeal plexus is dislocated two centimeters yet is "within normal variable parameters" (60). Words such as "vulva," "clitoris," and "urethra" are used, but Maxwell mentions them in conjunction with the Skene's glands (54), not exactly words uttered by a caressing lover. However, while Penny is enjoying—at least at this point in the story—all of Maxwell's douches and accessories, Palahniuk offers what could be sexy vogue: "Whatever the pink fluid consisted of, Maxwell's pumping buttocks and probing cock seemed to force it into her bloodstream. Gradually her legs felt so relaxed she would swear she were floating. The feeling spread to her arms. Her breasts seemed to swell" (50). A few pages later, Penny was "dimly aware that he was still fucking her with the same cadence of long, smooth strokes" (52). All of this occurs during what could be called sexual bingeing, but there is a subtle turn when the narrator states, "There was plenty of sex to come, too much perhaps, but none of it would involve Maxwell's sex organ" (52). Penny is compared with Edison's Menlo Park laboratory and Henry Ford's workshop (60), and Maxwell's language corresponds with the utility of understanding feminine physiology.

Maxwell's exploitation of this knowledge is also suggested by language—or the lack of his particular declarations. Maxwell confides in Penny that his research has made him an expert on female sexuality (80–84), and after Alouette saves her by sucking out the pink magnetic bead through cunnilingus while in a restaurant bathroom stall, Penny begins to recognize Maxwell's full control. The scene in the bathroom is explicit, with descriptions of the pink bead in her vagina working against the black bead in her anus, causing her to become sopping wet with excitement, and her enjoyment riding Alouette's face "as if it were a saddle" (69). Prior to her date with Maxwell, Penny retrieves her diaphragm, wet from being grossly extracted from one of her roommates (24). Readers find out that Penny only had sexual relations in college with men, and there was no sexual experimentation. As Penny admits, she was not a pervert or a slut, nor had she ever had "an *orgas*m-orgasm, not the kind of earth-moving orgasm that made your teeth go numb, the kind she'd always read about in *Cosmopolitan*" (42). The changes in Penny's language mark the development of her conservative to liberal attitudes about sexuality. In other words, her openness with sexual language signifies her relaxed attitude toward the atypical or the taboo.

Considering Bakhtinian heteroglossia, even though readers never find out exactly what she says, Penny brandishes a broad vocabulary of expletives while in the throes of sexual passion. Readers are told that "a torrent of animal gibberish and profanities threatened to boil out of her mouth.... She choked back the howls" (51), and they find out "the filth that had poured from her mouth [that] was totally degrading" (53). The extreme sex language is left to the readers' imagination. To reiterate information mentioned in the second chapter, Bakhtin points out, "The importance of abusive language is essential to the understanding of the literature of the grotesque. Abuse exercises a direct influence on the language and the images of this literature and is closely related to all other forms of 'degradation' and 'down to earth' in grotesque and Renaissance literature. Modern indecent abuse and cursing have retained dead and purely negative remnants of the grotesque concept of the body" (*Rabelais* 27–28). Concerning the slippage of meaning related to "profane," Murray S. Davis explains in *Smut*, "The vocabulary for sex is changing. Lower-class terms like 'prick' are gradually creeping upward while upper-class terms like 'penis' are gradually creeping downward. Scientific terms like 'cotton' are gradually creeping into popular use while popular terms like 'screwing' are gradually creeping into scientific use" (xxv). This is significant because Penny starts to think in terms of profanities, verifying the success of Maxwell's exploitation, or viewed another way, reversing profane into ordinary language. After missing the importance of Erica Jong over Betty Friedan and Gloria Steinem, Penny seems to settle without guilt or without shame, into just eating and mating, "Endlessly. Ziplessly" (56).

Penny's naïveté is finally shaken watching the grotesque deaths of Alouette and Clarissa. With Maxwell, Penny lives in an environment completely foreign to the one in which she typically resides, and she is welcomed into his new normative of sexual gratification. She is ushered into the wealthy high-class world of the sociocultural elite simultaneously while she is not far away from Cassie Wright's world of sexual pragmatism in *Snuff*. In this manner, Penny is assuming a persona in the style of the carnivalesque. She hears Maxwell "selling sex" (61), but she self-deceives herself into believing his intentions are to help women, not to harm them. Penny admits that she was taught materialism leads to happiness, and she wants to be the Cinderella (cast by the media as the Nerd's Cinderella), duping herself to see Maxwell as truly Prince Charming (70). Yet, in her heart, she knows that "love was more than fiddling with nerve endings" (73). After almost overdosing on sex, and her 136 days have expired, Penny gives into using the dragonfly vibrator that transmits the nanobots (92–96). She first witnesses Alouette grotesquely arching her pelvis in the air, humping to meet a "phantom lover" (98), all of her intimate parts exposed for millions to see, consequently to die of an aneurysm (184). If this were not enough, Penny hears the rumor that Alouette acted like "an animal in heat" by "abusing" herself with the Oscar Award (99). After Clarissa tells Penny the truth about Maxwell, Penny feels her nipples get "painfully hard" (115), and in an exemplary section to illustrate how the sexual has now definitely become pathological, the president helps Penny combat Maxwell's technology and tells her about Baba Gray-Beard (114–16). Significantly, the three women are essentially the true feminist alliance in the novel, what Alouette terms "the sisterhood of us" (88). After realizing there is a weapon lurking in her womb that causes something like snakebites (102–03), Penny begins to contrast the hilarious and harmless sexual escapades, such as when the teacher squirts copious emissions all over the elders of the church school (84), to the deaths of two women who were genuinely her sisters in arms.

Penny's alliance with Baba Gray-Beard shifts the focus from sex as feminism to ideology beyond feminism. Baba Gray-Beard's role as a tantric guru emphasizes eco-friendly self-sufficiency that is tied to a transcendental oneness with a higher energy. Maxwell's motivation is egotistical; he wants pleasure, wealth, and love, what most people desire. Even with all of his money, even before the Beautiful You monopoly, Maxwell is spiritually bankrupt. He only believes in the power that is produced through his own ingenuity via science. There is not one instance throughout the novel in which Maxwell expresses any reverence or gratitude to a power supernaturally greater than anything or anyone within his material frame of reference. Penny's matriculation as a future feminist makes her similarly impotent. Not to delve too deeply into the nature versus nurture motif in this novel, as the clone of Phoebe, Penny has the physiological allergy to shellfish and other physical manifestations that link her to Maxwell's 136-day bride. Penny's gift, something Maxwell does not calculate in his formulas precisely because he is devoid of anything similar, is a free will that motivates her toward something higher. Readers are not given enough information to conclude if Phoebe had this motivation, but they can definitely see how Baba Gray-Beard's guidance, comparable to a helping mentor (as she is really the "wise old man" archetype) assisting a hero in the monomyth, causes Penny's apotheosis, spiritual transformation, into someone she would have never been otherwise.

Baba Gray-Beard's instruction of Penny is full of comic grotesque descriptions, but taken in its entirety, Penny's training is built on principles of simplicity. The mentor's philosophy resembles ideas in significant sections of Henry David Thoreau's *Walden*, or, more contemporary, bell hooks' *Where We Stand*. Most know Thoreau's mantra "Simplicity, simplicity, simplicity!" (1018), or some of his other well-known adages such as "Cultivate poverty like a garden herb, like sage" (1141) or "Superfluous

Five. "You've become something dangerous: a woman" 111

wealth can buy superfluities only. Money is not required to buy one necessary of the soul" (1141). hooks offers a version of this by claiming, "Given the reality that the world's resources are swiftly dwindling because of the wastefulness of affluent cultures, the poor everywhere who are content with living simply are best situated to offer a vision of hope to everyone, for the day will come when we will all have to live with less" (129). During the coronavirus pandemic, simplicity is vitally relevant. Some Americans are panicking over shortages in grocery stores of toilet paper while many are dying from COVID-19. Many families around the world are getting back to basics. Baba Gray-Beard is a model of self-sufficiency, given this is a comically eccentric autonomy, especially considering her name is drawn from her long strand of pubic hair, but she functions as the master for Penny's apprenticeship that gives the once vacuous coed the spiritual belief system that is antithetical to Maxwell's maniacal consumer capitalism.

Penny's sexual tutorage with the mystic displays her vast maturity in a relatively short period. In contrast to Maxwell's inserting his hand into Penny, his continuing to take notations while one hand is inserted (60), Baba Gray-Beard draws a finger from her deceased mother from her womb (166), as Penny will eventually keep her mentor's finger in her vagina (217). Penny discovers that all Beautiful You products are adapted from natural resources, bones from previous students (165). When Penny appears, the blind skeleton-thin woman asks profanely, "Do I detect a young, fresh pussy?" (154), and all the information she needs about Penny is extracted with a finger covered in Penny's vaginal wetness (155). There is a clear shift in how sexuality is presented from this part of the book forward. Penny now places no stigma on pleasing another woman because now she understands the spiritual, as opposed to the hedonistic or the scientific, purpose of the interaction. If sex may be used as a weapon, Penny learns that it must be used in moderation (158), and when Maxwell attempts to harm her remotely, the sex witch gives Penny the key to retaliation: "Return the energy to its vile source!" (161). Baba Gray-Beard gives Penny advice that could come right out of a Marianne Williamson book. Warning her not to feel guilty about letting down other women (156), Baba Gray-Beard figuratively knights Penny as the archetypal feminist defender against Maxwell (and symbolically all male sexual aggression) who valiantly gives back in greater force whatever is sent: "The way food drives waste from your body, you must use love to displace the sex magic Max is practicing. Focus on what you love, and you can deflect his erotic spell" (162). Penny finally understands the difference between lust and love, realizing that she could feel the greatest pleasurable ecstasy when sex is combined with caritas, a love for all, the opposite of a self-indulgent or self-centered concupiscence (170). Baba Gray-Beard's last words to Penny are to "rebound his energy. Channel it through yourself and return it with a greater force!" (210). Potentially echoing Williamson, Penny learns what power produces this energy: "Love was paramount" (217). Much earlier in the novel, Penny thought that real love was something "lasting and soulful" (73), not the sex devoid completely of spirituality or a higher energy. In the end of the novel, while thinking about the zipless fuck, Penny correctly attributes the allusion to Erica Jong, and this substantiates her transformation (221).

However, this novel is not just about sexuality or about feminism. Maxwell says earlier in the story that the conflict is not "about boys versus girls. This is about power. We live in an age when women hold the bulk of the power. In government, in consumer purchase decisions, women steer the world, and their longer life spans have left them in control of the greatest wealth" (188). He then clarifies, after reporting that he has implanted 98.7 percent of the female population, "Women are the new masters ... but now I am master of women" (188). Palahniuk's use of brand names establishes the eventual battle between materialism and spiritualism. Social currency corresponds with commercial status, signification attached to consumer merchandise. Early in the novel, the narrator sows the seed that a woman's status depends on her appearance (11), and designer clothing brands are embedded into almost every page. In his 2014 interview with *The Talks*, Palahniuk discusses how people unfortunately form identities through products, and he mentions how some have such strong affiliations with brand names that they have company logos embossed into their tombstones. Palahniuk quips that he could have had the John Deere label engraved into his father's grave marker, and he views the notion of "people living their lives through a series of experiences provided by products" as horribly tragic yet nevertheless frequent occurrences ("Chuck"). Above all, this is consumer materialism.

Palahniuk exposes the extent of this female purchasing power by controlling other desires as well. With a flick of a button, Max can motivate women to purchase a vampire novel (114), clunky shoes (138), soap and dog food (118), or any other product with which his company, DataMicroCom, produces through subsidiaries. Even the names of the sexual products are commercially attractive, and the titles rival the hilarious parodying of commercial film titles presented in *Snuff*. In many countries in which sex toys are banned, the products must imitate forms of rabbits, dolphins, whales, or other devices—just not identifiable as what they really are—calling to mind Cassie Wright's marketing of a shampoo contained in a bottle that was essentially a dildo. The Veggie Play Shaper (80), the Jiggle Whip (174), the Rotating Relaxation Rod (174), the Instant-Ecstasy Probe (127), the Happy Honey Ball (106), the Honeymoon Romance Prod (123), the Love Lizard (85), and the Burst Blaster (83) caused hordes of women to invade private homes in search of coveted batteries, not to forget the long lines of women wasting countless hours waiting for the next improved and updated Beautiful You product. The bottom line is Max controls women, and women control the economy. As Tad points out, women are loyal to brands, and DataMicroCom produces the brands with which they are loyal (118).

This novel's multiple layers coalesce eventually to demonstrate points of Žižek's theory. When Penny is writhing in sexual pain during her testimony, no one comes to her rescue—everyone watches how this scene will play out. Palahniuk infers that her screams, from being remotely "raped" (2), signify the outcry of all sexually assaulted women, and he appropriately labels Maxwell a "rapist" (3). The communal reluctance to assist Penny is indicative of how people take for granted that the trusted systems (political, legal, etc.) will work even while they witness them failing right in front of them. Not a single person steps forward to help Penny. On the one hand, men despise Penny as a potential co-researcher of Beautiful You products, but when they go so far as to threaten to kill her, they are obviously treating her as a scapegoat for the devastation they have allowed to occur. On the other, everyone understands Maxwell's products are behind the impending collapse of American society, and no one seems to step forward besides Penny. In fact, one of the paramedics responds patronizingly that Penny should have married Cornelius Linus Maxwell to become "richer than God" (4). Almost an example of the Genovese syndrome, also called the bystander effect, people watch as poor Penny squirms uncontrollably in, of all places, a courtroom, where she should be protected from harm.

Palahniuk's incorporation of the Promise Keepers as the bearers of the male ideological burden is an appropriate one. Generally, this organization, started by former University of Colorado head football coach Bill McCartney, is not considered a hate group or discriminatory coalition, but it nonetheless has connotations of being a right-wing fundamentally Christian sect strictly adhering to traditionally conservative American ideology. The destruction of sex toys at Yankee Stadium (176) works in tandem with Penny's monumental action to bring down Maxwell, and there is ambiguity whether or not Penny's vaginal blast or a stroke of fate directs the dildo projectile into its symbolic destination, especially if this is taken as one phallic object destroying someone with tremendous (both in terms of Freud and Lacan) phallic power (212). The Promise Keepers could be viewed as the male version of #MeToo, and by having Penny's father as a member, Palahniuk may want readers to sympathize with him as well as not feel antipathy toward her mother for her infidelity with Maxwell when Penny was implanted in her womb. However, just as well-intentioned Christians have burned books that contained information counter to their ideology, the Promise Keepers wait in long lines to destroy Beautiful You products (176).

In the end of the novel. Penny has identified the contradictions within the ideology of feminism. Considering Žižek's theory, Penny becomes the ideology without being exploited by the ideology—she owns the principles; the principles do not own her. To emphasize, Penny is essentially *the* true feminist in the story, and Palahniuk demonstrates that feminist theoretical propaganda does not prepare her for this role, neither does the reification of feminist principles through capitalist consumerism. Penny's final assault on ineffectual ideologies is prompted by the culmination of her experiences *through* those ideologies toward one that works for her. Penny has struggled with ideological discordance, grappling with which principles are true and which are false, on several levels throughout her journey. Penny's exposure to Baba Gray-Beard's version of "living simply" allows her finally to feel confident within her own skin. This is signified by her comfortability with nudity while in the Himalayan cave, able to shed the Yves Saint Laurent pantsuit (and the Vera Wang, the Chanel, or other culturally chic garments) to return to the basics of what is important in life. In the grotesque scene in which Penny tricks Brillstein by assuming the persona of the seductress, probably exactly what the Brooks Brothers-underwear wearing chauvinist fantasized her being, Penny is the one wielding the psychoanalytic phallus, and she uses sex manipulatively to nail down Maxwell's intentions (139–42). Penny tells Monique that she is not at fault for her vibrator addiction, calling her a victim of her own primal obsession (173), a great example of when the ideology controls the one believing in it. Penny yells out to women in the street, simulating Lysistrata's own calls to Athenian and Spartan females, that they must try their best to stop masturbating because Maxwell wants to "enslave all women" (182). Bakhtin mentions that carnival's dominant themes refer to physicality, fertility, and fecundity, not to the cerebral, individual, or egotistical, and they celebrate the vitality of a life actively lived through gratitude for the precious moment, not the dullness of a life sullenly wasted by regret for being granted existence (*Rabelais* 19). In the courtroom, when Penny focuses on her love for Baba Gray-Beard (211), *the* feminist matriarch, the energy expelled through her voice is comparable to all of the profanities that were earlier caught in her throat. Through her powerful empathetic release, the embodiment of all feminine response, Penny is granted what can be deemed serenity.

Palahniuk leaves the door open, however, to suggest that Penny might be susceptible to the lure of tremendous power. In Baba Gray-Beard's cave, she reflects: "This, this was power. She, Penelope Harrigan, would reign over the world, a benevolent lady dictator, awarding well-deserved pleasure to the multitudes. She'd surpassed the power wielded by even her heroes,

Clarissa Hind and Alouette D'Ambrosia. To redeem Max's wicked technology, she would singlehandedly bring about world peace and order. She'd reward good behavior and punish the bad" (220). When Penny decides to use Maxwell's little black box, she succumbs to the same desire to rule as her nemesis. No matter what her intentions, she is corrupted by vanity. By this juncture, she is invincible along the lines of a feminist superhero, and Penny is self-confidently edging toward hubris, being excessively proud of what she has accomplished. Penny's saving grace is the spiritual connection that she has with her higher power, the vision of Baba Gray-Beard. This security is precisely what Maxwell lacked, and even though Penny is not necessarily reverent, never really framing her loyalty and obedience to Baba Gray-Beard through language, her actions demonstrate that she is grounded through her mentor's philosophy. When Penny reiterates with emphasis that this very moment is the perfect time to be a female, she is "intoxicated" with more than just satisfaction (221). Penny has defeated "Evil Max" (204) and is the appointed predecessor to Baba Gray-Beard, ready to teach others variations of precepts inculcated to her: "She, Penelope Anne Harrigan, would accept the torch passed to her by the likes of Baba Gray-Beard and Bella Abzug. She'd liberate women from having to go to men for fulfillment. This legacy—not clothes, not jewelry or practicing law—this was the destiny she had long sought. Hers was a power based on carnal pleasure. Her kingdom a realm beyond interpersonal politics" (216). As Althusser and Žižek infer through their theories, Penny may kid herself, but she can never totally escape ideology—the best she can do is to confront it, as Žižek exemplifies in his commentaries about *Fight Club*, on her own terms. Even when Penny gives women all over the world who were infected by the pink plastic dragonfly the taste of a delicious sweet, the sound of a mellifluous melody, or the smell of an aromatic flower, what is good for one is not necessarily best for all. In other words, some people might not consider Tom Berenger or Richard Thomas (218), or, in her last romantic vision, Ron Howard (222), sexually attractive.

As mentioned in the second chapter, many critics do not understand the complexity of *Beautiful You*. Palahniuk uses sex as a transgressive vehicle but is not writing a sexy novel. Through satire, he follows the tradition of Rabelais (Cervantes, Voltaire, and Swift) to address major social, cultural, and political issues through the comic grotesque. As he does in *Snuff*, *Damned*, and *Doomed*, Palahniuk presents a female character experiencing ideological discordance because the beliefs, values, and attitudes that she once embraced to guide her life no longer seem to work, and just like Sheila and Madison, Penny confronts the false consciousness, in this case feminism as it opposes heteropatriarchy, so she may establish a new way of perceiving the world through a paradigm suitable for her. When he recognizes that Penny has changed, Maxwell states, "You are no longer the weak child whom I tutored in the ways of pleasure.... I sense that under the Baba's tutelage you've become something dangerous: a woman" (189). His hubris in underestimating the power of a woman leads to his own demise. Once again, Palahniuk uses the comic grotesque subversively to expose hypocrisies prevalent in contemporary America. Similar to students refusing to read past the first ten pages of Aristophanes's *Lysistrata* because they believe the play is only about sex, especially if the translation is Sarah Ruden's openly transgressive version, readers reluctant to move past the sex in *Beautiful You* will miss the opportunity to dig into relevant issues about ideology. If nothing else, they will miss a true example of a "dangerous woman," someone who cares deeply for humanity, the type of female who could lead #MeToo against sociocultural inequalities.

Six

"The fringe was the future"

The Future of Dirty Realism in Make Something Up: Stories You Can't Unread

On December 17, 2019, in the *USA Today* article "House Democrats Approve Rules for Debate on Articles of Impeachment," Bart Jansen prepares readers for the impending trial of President Donald Trump. Jansen begins, "Following a day of deliberation, the House Rules Committee voted along party lines to pass rules governing the floor debate about whether to impeach President Donald Trump for abuse of power and obstruction of Congress." After days of deliberation and Democrats and Republicans voting as had been predicted before debate even began, the nation waited as the Judiciary Committee brought the recommendation of impeachment to the full House of Representatives. During a time when Democrats and Republicans could not even agree on whether to call America's leader Donald J. Trump or Donald John Trump, many Americans were experiencing ideological discordance, finding their trust in the democratic political system tested in ways they likely never anticipated.

This was exacerbated by the Commander-in-Chief's open war with House Speaker Nancy Pelosi. In another *USA Today* piece titled "Trump Calls Democrats 'Deranged,' 'Spiteful' in Angry Letter to Pelosi over Impeachment," Courtney Subramanian, John Fritze, and David Jackson report that Trump argued the entire liberal-supported enterprise was an indictment against American democracy: "Trump accused Democrats of 'declaring open war' on democracy with their impeachment drive, in an appearance in the Oval Office, he echoed many of those same points and said he feels 'zero' responsibility for his expected impeachment." The authors cite excerpts from Trump's own infamous missive: "'Any member of Congress who votes in support of impeachment—against every shred of truth, fact, evidence, and legal principle—is showing how deeply they revile the voters and how they detest America's Constitutional order .... More due process was afforded to those accused in the Salem Witch Trials.'"

Americans can see exactly the same sound bite spun two vastly different ways on purportedly objective news programs such as CNN and Fox News. Similar to how a literary critic interprets fiction, political analysts defend liberal or conservative stances from exactly the same set of words, arguing their beliefs of the language's meaning. This does not even take into account fake news passed off on professional-looking websites all over the Internet. Many Americans were anxiously trying to sort out what was true and false, tenuously seeking a middle ground. There was a lot of uncertainty.

In September of 2020, things have gotten both better and worse. In what illuminated partisan political alliances, President Trump survived impeachment. In hind sight, impeachment was not all that big of a problem. At what is hopefully the tail end of the COVID-19 era, America is moving toward perhaps a nostalgic reflection of what is considered mainstream normalcy. If the coronavirus were not enough, America is challenged by social division, first demonstrated through peaceful protest but then manifested in violent riot. Opposition between Democrats and Republications has only intensified, fueled by media allegiances that perpetuate propaganda that undermine any possibility for reconciliation. Palahniuk's Adjustment Day serves almost unbelievably as prophesy. Life imitates art as young people in Portland (Palahniuk's home turf) are acting out the novel's aggression against authority. There is a lot of uncertainty.

Closer to my home, things have gotten both better and worse. On Friday, September 6, 2019, after the threat of natural devastation subsided as Hurricane Dorian turned northwest and headed out to sea, chairperson Angie Stanland sent an email to the entire academic community reporting that a day earlier that president Robert L. Wyatt has resigned from Coker University. The message also mentioned that a search would soon begin for the replacement. For SCNow, a news service including the *Hartsville Messenger* (Coker University is located in Hartsville, South Carolina), Jim Faile provided no new information. Scott Jaschik does not offer any more information in a short blurb about the resignation for *Inside Higher Education*. In "Some Students Left Baffled Following Coker University President's Resignation," Tonya Brown reports that students were surprised about Wyatt's departure, and she quotes several students who praised Wyatt's accomplishments. Regardless, a shock wave hit the usually serene Coker University campus. As of the middle of April of 2020, Coker University is close to hiring a new president. Unfortunately, like many other small private liberal arts schools, Coker has taken a bigger hit from COVID-19. Comparable to other colleges and universities, students vacated dormitories, and in-seat classes moved to online platforms. There is a lot of uncertainty.

One would assume an American university serves as a microcosm of the larger American ideological structure, an institution that both reinforces and questions the larger system in which it resides, particularly those schools relying upon state and federal funding. Louis Althusser contends Ideological State Apparatuses (ISAs), beliefs and values, are enacted through Repressive State Apparatuses (RSAs), those who enforce ISAs. The university president would be the facilitator similar to the national leader, the one who serves as figurehead of the ideology supplying the principles that participants believe in and follow as true. When the leader working the controls of the ideological machine leaves (or is impeached to force an exit), this compromises the entire operation of the mechanism. Slavoj Žižek asserts most people hope for the best, maintaining that the system has checks and balances that will work out the kinks and return any anomalies back into line with what is considered the normative, as things should be and are supposed to be. The burden of correction or remediation never really falls on one person, and if one person feels the stress of this load, he or she has the options of sounding an alarm or just ignoring the problem, assuming someone else will eventually come up with a solution. Granted, although the rationale has been perpetuated that college campuses are microcosms of the "real-world," everyone knows this is not completely accurate. Furthermore, the traditional belief that a student is automatically included in the socioeconomic middle class through matriculation—immersed in values and held to standards associated with that classification—is fallacious, especially in 2019 with the range of "university" options available. If leaders held pristine moral standards previously, then this is not the case now. An example is presented by Sonja Isger in the January 3, 2020, article in *USA Today* titled "Ex-President of Medical College Spent $82,000 in School Funds for Personal Shopping Sprees." There is no guarantee once a student graduates with an astronomical amount of financial debt that he or she will ascend any rungs up the socioeconomic ladder. Higher education no longer ensures a middle-class life, nor happiness, nor prosperity, nor, perhaps most desired, security. When people buy into the American Dream by believing in a person or a system, they are shocked into disenchantment as soon as they are faced with American Reality. Everyone really knows CNN and Fox News are biased and subjective.

Life is simply not a Hallmark Christmas movie, and Palahniuk recognizes this fact all too well. People are either resilient to uncertainty or they are not, and the latter typically causes problems. In a 2017 interview with *MEL*, Palahniuk explains how he was indoctrinated into the American Dream as most people by getting a university degree and then paying off the loans to acquire it, a version of the typical hard work ethic associated with the American myth of success. Eventually, he discovered when he was in his early thirties that this myth is only an ideological illusion, realizing the "good boy stuff" no longer worked and finding out a new plan was necessary: "That's where I was. I was really disillusioned that I'd been given the same roadmap everyone else was given, but that none of us were finding it effective" ("A Conversation"). Once again, Palahniuk verifies what Tom Wolfe predicts in "Hooking Up": in the 2000s, the traditional working-class may have university diplomas, wear white collars, and possess hip things, as in wielding all the popular smart technologies, but they still confront the same challenges as their proletarian predecessors because they remain disenfranchised, bereft of the entitlements enjoyed by those in power, and these privileges are likely more ideological than financial (3).

Palahniuk's best writing is inspired by his reluctance to continue following the typical "roadmap" to American success. His most interesting work demonstrates his refusal to pander to conventional prescriptions affiliated with the middle-class mainstream or to cater to false projections of formulas guaranteeing status-quo prosperity or the attainment of bourgeois bliss. Palahniuk refuses to be pinned down by conventional labels. Early in his career, right after *Fight Club* was published, he seems antagonistic in interviews toward being termed a transgressive writer, but by 2015, when he finished *Make Something Up: Stories You Can't Unread*, he appears resigned to this distinction, perhaps currently the most notorious transgressive author. Although many critics were comfortable calling him a transgressive writer, they failed to broaden their coverage to include him solidly within the literary domain of American dirty realism, a genre revered for its portrayal of those disenchanted and disillusioned with the American Dream. This postmodern skepticism or existential cynicism is often the result of losing faith and relinquishing trust in the promotion of Louis Althusser's Ideological State Apparatuses (ISAs) and the enforcement his Repressive State Apparatuses (RSAs) associated with dominant ideologies. Understanding the effect of controlling systems on his readers, Palahniuk states directly in a 2012 interview for *Feedbooks*, "My books are always about people struggling to gain or maintain power" ("My"). How he depicts his characters' "struggle" sets him apart from his contemporaries, especially during this tumultuous period in American history. No matter how many pep talks (although many are not so peppy) from President Trump and those on his many task forces, many Americans struggle with the negotiation of the American Dream with American Reality, especially during the COVID-19 pandemic. Palahniuk has addressed this dilemma for over a decade. There is a lot of uncertainty.

In the twenty-two stories and one novella in *Make Something Up*, Palahniuk again relies on the comic grotesque to portray ideological discordance in his characters' lives. Although *Adjustment Day* may be Palahniuk's most obvious application of the Bakhtinian carnival and the fantasy of juxtaposing bourgeois and proletarian socioeconomic roles, this collection is unquestionably Palahniuk's most explicit fictional presentation of those marginalized and disenfranchised attempting to reconcile why their obedience to the "roadmap" does not lead them to the American promised land. The strength of this collection is that Palahniuk displays this dilemma through various well-crafted situations, and whereas he relies on fantasy in *Damned*, *Doomed*, and *Beautiful You* to show readers the harmful aftermaths of ideological hypocrisies, in these stories he combines the outlandish with the obvious, just as he does in *Snuff*, to get at the unattractive truths concerning human nature. In numerous interviews, Palahniuk has emphasized that he never sets out intentionally to shock readers into taking stock of their own lives, but readers never believe everything Palahniuk says. No matter how much he dislikes categorization, Palahniuk's strategies make him akin to writers he publicly admires such as Amy Hempel and Denis Johnson but also to Raymond Carver, Richard Ford, Jayne Anne Phillips, Charles Bukowski, Louise Erdrich, and Dorothy Allison, dirty realist and transgressive authors. In many ways, *Make Something Up* introduces the next phase of American dirty realism, although not as multicultural as ZZ Packer or Junot Diaz, Palahniuk depicts working-class scenarios with a sharper narrative cut and a more stinging burnt tongue than his predecessors or contemporaries. Palahniuk has always identified with the working-class, minimizing his journalism degree from the University of Oregon and maximizing a journalistic affinity with Stephen Crane and Jack London. Palahniuk has transported ill people to hospices and worked on diesel engines, participating in grunt work more characteristic of denim than satin or silk.[1] Because of his punk loyalties, Palahniuk is perhaps more aligned with Kathy Acker than Bobbie Ann Mason. Regardless, his personal life has groomed him toward presenting reflections from the dirty realistic prism of experiences.

Palahniuk has certainly not lived the typical American life, but dirty realism questions what is indeed normal. As those familiar with him know, Palahniuk's family has experienced unfortunate and violent deaths. When his father was three, hiding under a bed, he witnessed the self-inflicted suicide of his own father, committed right after he had killed his wife over a sewing machine purchase and an unsuccessful search for his son. Palahniuk's father was murdered by the jealous ex-husband, recently released from jail, of a woman whom he met through a personal advertisement. Palahniuk's mother died from a stroke after suffering from lung cancer. Palahniuk identified his father's body after the shooting, and he took care of his mother during her struggle with cancer. In his introduction to an interview with Palahniuk for *The Guardian*, Ben Beaumont-Thomas writes that Palahniuk faced several personal adversities in 2018, including the deaths of his father-in-law from cancer and his friend Anthony Bourdain from suicide plus the embezzlement of money from his publisher by Darin

Webb. In another *Guardian* article, Alison Floyd reports that Webb stole approximately $3.4 million from the literary agency Donadio & Olson, leaving Palahniuk "close to broke" and propelling the company into bankruptcy. On his fan-supported website *The Cult*, Palahniuk issued a lengthy statement explaining what had happened and confessing that he had paid for many of the provisions for which he is famous during his speaking engagements ("The Big"). Palahniuk is well known for interactive speaking engagements that rely on direct participation; people in the audience are thrown vast amounts of candy and are eligible for elaborate door prizes. In an extremely humble and forgiving reaction, Palahniuk states, "More recently, the trickle of my income stopped. Not that there wasn't always a good excuse. Someone's mother was suffering from Alzheimer's and needed constant looking after. The bank's wire transfer system wasn't secure, and hackers were a new threat. You don't question someone who claims to be the caregiver for a mother with dementia. You let it slide. I let it slide" ("The Big"). Nonetheless, as Mike Harvkey announces in a November 18, 2019, piece in *Publishers Weekly*, Palahniuk has a new agent, a new publisher, and a new book to be released in early January. In a December 19 article in *Publishers Weekly*, Andrew Albanese shares that Webb received a two-year sentence for what in effect financially crippled Donadio & Olson Publishing. Even though he claims in countless interviews that his fiction is the culmination of stories he has collected from diverse sources, many of whom are those attending his speaking engagements, Palahniuk seeds much of his work with the "dangerous writing" resulting from his own painful life experiences. Palahniuk wrote *Lullaby* while processing his father's murder; he composed *Damned* to deal with his mother's death.

Palahniuk credits his mentor Tom Spanbauer with teaching him the benefits of dangerous writing. According to the "Creative Writing" tutorial at *Fandom*, "Dangerous Writing is a brand of minimalism that utilizes many literary techniques pioneered by Spanbauer and other Gordon Lish-influenced writers." The processing of uncomfortable, unsettling, or even traumatic experiences functions as the catalyst to generate dangerous writing, which, for the most part, is expressive narrative prose dealing with transgressive subject matter. Concerning this topic, *Fandom* also defines "burnt tongue," another style connected with Palahniuk, as a writing strategy that causes readers to hesitate by reflecting on the meaning of particular words in the syntax: "A way of saying something, but saying it wrong, twisting it to slow down the reader. Forcing the reader to read close, maybe read twice, not just skim along a surface of abstract images, short-cut adverbs, and clichés." In the 2009 YouTube video "Tom Spanbauer on Dangerous Writing," Spanbauer explains this writing style; in the 2015 YouTube post "Chuck Palahniuk on His Writing Method," Palahniuk explains how this strategy inspired several of the stories in *Make Something Up*, and, during a 2015 interview with Public Radio International titled "Chuck Palahniuk Talks Dangerous Writing," Palahniuk discusses his application of this technique specifically. In a 2014 article in *The Believer*, Spanbauer and others converse with Palahniuk about dangerous writing. When asked about this technique, Palahniuk admits that this form of expression takes the place of costly therapy and substitutes for expensive drugs by inspiring people to articulate their "darkest psychic wounds in a metaphorical way," freeing them to tell the truth about themselves in a public way, almost like making "a confession in church or in a 12-step program" ("A Conversation").

Earlier in the discussion with Spanbauer, after Palahniuk admits his ambivalence being labeled a transgressive author, he points out another dominant theme throughout his fiction, humiliation. The various tactics through which people respond to losing status are prevalent motifs in Palahniuk's stories, especially concerning how young adults react to this problem: "Their worst fear is being publicly humiliated, because that's their only form of power" ("A Conversation"). Addressed more extensively in the first chapter, similar to social satirist Wolfe, Palahniuk portrays how characters subsequently move past the humiliation influenced by the loss of status. Dangerous writing is a means of tapping into the emotions associated with humiliation, and Palahniuk cultivates the resulting emotions, such as alienation and disconnectedness, produced from humiliating experiences. In a 2016 interview with *LEO Weekly*, after he is asked if his own writing sometimes frightens him, Palahniuk claims, "If I'm doing it right ... writing should be a form of therapy, and you should be dealing with the most dangerous, unresolved aspects of yourself" ("A Q&A"). Dangerous writing establishes the purpose underlying Palahniuk's fiction, a more rhetorical agenda than he is given credit. Palahniuk is not trying to shock his readers, especially not just applying the comic grotesque for some vacuous end that temporarily incites a superficial audience response. In the vein of dangerous writing, he is aiming for something much more substantial. Like other dirty realist authors, Palahniuk describes the effects of humiliation in a capitalist culture that values status as a highly desirable commodity.

Concerning *Make Something Up*, there are several positive commentaries. A writer for *Publishers Weekly* notes affirmatively, "The collection is essential for Palahniuk fans and will likely win him some new ones" ("Make"). In a review for *Library Journal*, Brooke Bolton writes, "You either love Palahniuk or hate him. For new readers, this compilation offers a small taste of the author's style. His faithful fans will be entertained, intrigued, and at times a little disgusted, but what else would we expect from Palahniuk?" A critic for *Kirkus Reviews* remarks that Palahniuk returns to his "hard-core" form, noting the collection contains "pathos and panic and penitence from one of the darkest and most singular minds in contemporary American lit" ("Make"). Surprisingly, loyal Palahniuk bloggers are mostly positive with glimpses of negativity. For example, in his review of the anthology, Benoit Lelievre states, "Chuck Palahniuk is the closest thing we have to a literary superstar for the 55 years old and under.... There's some of what he does best in *Make Something Up*, but it overstays its welcome a little bit and start coming off as mechanical at a certain point."

There are also several negative reviews. Cameron Woodhead's claim that Palahniuk's presentation is "immature" represents most short reviews of the collection: "The way Chuck Palahniuk has developed (or not developed) as a writer since *Fight Club* does lend itself to shorter fiction. His puerile imagination is easier to take at a spring, though there are a few stories here that make you want to set fire to each and every page" ("Make"). On the contrary, the stories are maturely complex if one takes into account Palahniuk's application of the comic grotesque. Palahniuk has made it clear that he ignores negative reviews, he is not discouraged by critical reception of his work, and he sloughs off prejudicial commentary from those who consider his writing almost anti-literary. One wonders, however, if the opposition is not born out of a reluctance to acknowledge the accuracy of Palahniuk's satire of trusted ideological systems. For instance, posted on the *Intellectual Freedom Blog*, Ellie Diaz and Kristin Pekoll question Palahniuk's decision to include placenta-eating animals in the story "Liturgy," seeing no reason for the bizarre details. In the story, Palahniuk is parodying the typically bureaucratic approach that leaders of a homeowner association, stereotypically affluent and upstanding inhabitants of the community, take in writing an official letter to solve the extraordinarily gruesome problem. Palahniuk is playing with incompetence of empowered people enacting damage control in a completely absurd circumstance. All too often, reviewers simply do not give Palahniuk credit for how accurately he depicts real-life reactions to surreal occurrences. One only wonders what Palahniuk is planning in response to how people respond to the coronavirus pandemic. Yet, to concede Diaz and Pekoll's contention, the visual image they rebuke is repulsive, which could very clearly substantiate the ridiculous nature of this professional situation.

To return to the second chapter survey of particularly negative commentaries, Sandra Newman's criticism for *The Guardian* is worth reiterating. Generally, Newman rejects Palahniuk as a literary author worthy of serious critical attention, inferring he attracts readers more aligned with flippant popular culture rather than serious literary studies. Newman's criticism is particularly derisive, sarcastic, and unrelenting. She is especially surgical in her slashes of "Expedition," in which the narrator is an undisguised parasitic hack author who makes up vocabulary for sophistic effect.

Newman argues that "Expedition" is composed in a pseudo-Victorian style without any literary or rhetorical purpose, carping that Palahniuk (not the narrator) incorrectly applies words and phrases until meaning is incoherent. Newman wonders why editors did not correct the mistakes, when in all honesty, there *is* a purpose for the neologisms, and Palahniuk nails the persona, who is culpable of the linguistic faux pas, through his approach. To stress, Palahniuk wants readers to scratch their heads while they try to understand his narrator's recollection. Likewise, he inserts malapropisms throughout "Eleanor" for a similar effect (language will be addressed more later in this chapter). Even after so much critical badgering, as mentioned in the second chapter, Newman compliments Palahniuk's combination of the horrific with the absurd, but her criticism is representative of those who fail to recognize the multiple layers of meaning in his fiction.

Palahniuk has claimed *Make Something Up* is his most transgressive book, but contrasted with *Snuff*, *Damned*, *Doomed*, and *Beautiful You*, the reason is more psychological and less physical. Almost bragging, he has stated in interviews that the collection was the most banned book in 2016. In a 2017 interview for *The Beat*, he adds the book was even condemned by the Texas Prison System ("One"). In a 2019 interview for *Big Shiny Robot*, when asked about the transgressivity of *Fight Club 3*, Palahniuk asserts *Bait* or *Make Something Up: Stories You Can't Unread* are more intense: "The latter was the most-banned book in public libraries and schools since the 1960s. It's like if Judy Blume wrote a funny, touching coming-of-age novel about fisting" ("An Interview"). In reality, according to the Office for Intellectual Freedom, the story collection might have gone as high as number eight ("Banned"). In a 2005 interview for *Agony Column*, Palahniuk responds to Rick Kleffel's question about "shock value" by downplaying that his aim is sensationalism for the sake of effect. In this interview, responding mostly to questions about *Haunted*, which contains his notorious "Guts" and the Nightmare Box stories, Palahniuk explains his audience likely feels a little less comfortable in the world after the reading experience. When questioned about creating horror in his work, Palahniuk, who fervently admires Ira Levin (who wrote *Rosemary's Baby* and *The Stepford Wives*), Stephen King, and, of course, Edgar Allan Poe, points toward psychological rather than physical terror manifested in the grotesque. Echoing what he states in the 2014 interview with *The Believer*, Palahniuk holds that there is nothing more horrific in the contemporary world than humiliation, people being stripped of their personal dignity or losing their communal respect and still expecting to exist afterward.

Palahniuk's illustration in this *Agony Column* interview clarifies how this is related to narcotization. He uses an example of people shown the harmful effects of smoking on a mouth to manipulate them to stop.

Palahniuk says that if people see a slightly damaged mouth caused by smoking, they would likely cut down on their smoking. If they view a largely damaged mouth caused by smoking, they would possibly stop smoking to avoid gum disease, tooth loss, and other adverse effects. If they are shown a mouth brutally destroyed by smoking, beyond the scope of repair, then people would probably give up hope that they could ever stop smoking. In this interview with Kleffel, Palahniuk admits that he would hesitate going so far in his depictions of the socioeconomic horrors related to daily living to cause his readers to give up on the opportunity for change. He guarantees this by never killing any of his main characters at the end of a long work. Obviously, Palahniuk has evolved as a writer over the decade since this review in *Agony Column*, but the stories in *Make Something Up* sometimes travel brutally close to the third instance of smoking deterrence. There is the horrific possibility of total humiliation in each of the stories, and, to Palahniuk, this is honestly more profane and obscene than any scene of total annihilation or complete obliteration he could muster. The transgressive shock is proportional to how readers respond to the characters ideological discordance, when they realize what they have held as truth is only falsehood, how they maintain a sense of dignity without capitulating to horrendous humiliation.

Dirty realist authors have been addressing these kinds of subjects for decades, just not to the transgressive degree of Palahniuk. With the exception of Bukowski, most dirty realists do not constantly face his degree of literary discrimination. In a 2015 review of *Make Something Up* in *The Register*, Mark Diston writes that the current social climate prohibits Palahniuk from transgressive statue: "Chuck Palahniuk is probably not well served by the label of 'transgressive' fiction that he has acquired; he is not of that endangered species of writer, who, according to Charles Bukowski, lead lives that are 'more interesting than their books." Diston posits that Palahniuk does not stack up with the Marquis de Sade, William Burroughs, or Bukowski. This critic is not completely correct in his assessment. True, in the plethora of online interviews, most of which are his responses to five or six questions for someone generating publicity for an upcoming speaking engagement, Palahniuk does not assume the aura of a drunken misanthrope reminiscent of Bukowski. Although there are *You Tube* videos of "Roll the Dice" that portray him as the consummate optimist, Bukowski digs deeply into the substance of human despair. Essentially, Bukowski and Palahniuk could be considered rebellious anarchists who zealously defend freedom of speech, particularly in circumstances in which transgressive language pushes against perceptions of the mainstream ideological normative.

Contrary to what Diston thinks, Palahniuk is a dirty realist like

Bukowski. In *Hicks, Tribes, and Dirty Realists*, arguing American fiction has returned to a focus on realistic depictions of human experience, Robert Rebein contends, "Dirty Realism, as I would like to employ the term, refers to an effect in both subject matter and technique that is somewhere between the hard-boiled and the darkly comic. It refers to the impulse in writers to explore dark truths, to descend, as it were, into the darkest holes of society and what used to be called 'the soul of man.' Not the trailer parks and fern bars of minimalism, ... but rather the more intense worlds of war, drug addiction, serious crime, prostitution, prison" (43). This definition differs in degree from what has been considered the industry standard, editor Bill Buford's declaration in the summer 1983 publication of *Granta* concerning a new form of American writing: "a curious, dirty realism about the belly-side of contemporary life, ... so stylized and particularized—so insistently informed by a discomforting and sometimes elusive irony— that it makes the more traditional realistic novels of, say, Updike or Styron seem ornate, even baroque in comparison" (4). Announcing dirty realism as distinctly provincial, Buford explains how this fiction canvasses what he famously describes as "unadorned, unfurnished, low-rent tragedies" (4) about working-class and under-class American experience. Buford introduces a collection of short stories, the preferred genre of this movement, that depict through terse and cogent prose the everyday challenges facing common and ordinary people, those who survive by confronting challenges pragmatically and eclectically, often going against the tenets of conventional morality by promoting the naturalistic doctrine of survival of the fittest, accepting life without grandiose illusions or extravagant dreams (4). A widely cited definition attributed to Buford is from the back cover of the Penguin publication of this renowned eighth issue of *Granta*: "Understated, ironic, sometimes savage, but insistently compassionate, these stories constitute a new voice in fiction." For the most part, although he discounts minimalism, Rebein is identifying how dirty realism has drifted into the purview of transgressive fiction, portraying the "belly-side of contemporary life" as "darkly comic," a counterculture literary form that embodies the vulgar, profane, or obscene.[2]

In *Make Something Up*, Palahniuk's writing falls within the parameters of depicting both Rebein's and Buford's definitions of dirty realism. In a 2016 interview for *STORGY*, Palahniuk explains how Spanbauer promoted minimalism, the writing style favored by dirty realists ("Interview"). In several interviews, such as one for *Nightmare* in 2015 and another for *Lightspeed* in 2012, Palahniuk credits Gordon Lish as teaching Spanbauer this craft at Columbia University, and then Spanbauer taught Palahniuk (á la dangerous writing). The relevance is more significant after remembering Lish was Carver's editor, and Lish is credited for paring down many of Carver's manuscripts into minimalist stories. In the *STORGY* interview, Palahniuk points out that the short, succinct, unadorned minimalistic sentences generate bursts of nervous comic response ("Interview"). This actually describes the reaction evoked by the comic grotesque, when readers are attracted and repulsed simultaneously by the language. In this interview, Palahniuk admits the relevance of tension to move readers through nuances of reactions, beginning with the nervous laugh to an elevated uneasy laugh to varying degrees of laughter until they are hooked ("Interview"). Once the reader is caught, Palahniuk shows no mercy. Referring to his stories "Guts," "The Toad Prince," and "The Facts of Life," Palahniuk says the conciliatory little laugh at the end is the product of his authorial manipulation ("Interview").

Through several interviews, Palahniuk claims an alliance to dirty realism. Generally, his fiction brings to mind an affinity with the work of Mark Richard, Amy Hempel, Denis Johnson, Charles Baxter, and Thom Jones, fellow practitioners of minimalism. In turn, Palahniuk admits following other tenets of dirty realism through his subject matter, calling into question what is considered normalcy. As explained in the second chapter, the meaning of what is normal in a contemporary postmodern world is debatable, a matter of subjective opinion and frame of reference or, significantly, based upon a set of principles constituting an ideology that is revered as true concerning generally shared moral and ethical values, beliefs, and attitudes. As also discussed in the second chapter, the ruling class—those in power—determine through dominant ideology what is, for instance, able-bodied and not able-bodied. Similar to other dirty realists, Palahniuk subversively undermines the controlling ideology by exposing the absurdity of its internal contradictions. As he states in the *STORGY* interview, "Absurdity always, humorously, highlights the ludicrous aspects of so-called normal life" ("Interview"). Palahniuk states that "Loser" is an illustration of revealing this "absurdity," although many of the pieces in *Make Something Up* certainly qualify. Unequivocally, Palahniuk is upgrading dirty realism for millennials, homelanders, or Generation Zers (whatever designation fits) who have been desensitized by media sensationalism of sexuality and violence. In many ways, just as Rebein updated Buford's definition of the movement, Palahniuk is the figurehead for the second wave of the first wave of dirty realist artists.

In his stories, Palahniuk creates characters who behave in politically incorrect ways to drive the "tension" within the absurdity of ordinary existence. As expected, these scenes are entrenched in the comic grotesque. As mentioned in the second chapter, in the "Ideological Fantasy" section of *The Sublime Object of Ideology*, Žižek discusses the cognitive dissonance people feel when they discover what they believe they are "effectively doing" is in reality, to their dismay, not doing anything to benefit their lives (27). As Žižek clarifies, the resolution is an awareness of the "false representation" of the "social reality" (27). In each of the stories in *Make Something Up*, there is a disconnect between what someone thinks is true and what is true. Palahniuk's characters are confronted with the ideological discordance of recognizing the system that they trusted is no longer functioning effectively or efficiently. Just as Americans are grappling with issues related to President Trump, Coker University students are dealing with the loss of President Wyatt, and Palahniuk is recovering from Daniel Webb's embezzlement, not to mention how everyone (since no one is really excluded) is coping with COVID-19 at the moment, characters in these stories wrestle with circumstances that challenge their faith in ideological systems. As works of dirty realism demonstrate, the outcomes are often bleak, dark, and dismal. Many endings in dirty realistic writing predict even more hardship. Palahniuk is true to his word by going this route in *Snuff*, *Damned*, *Doomed*, and *Beautiful You*. Dirty realistic works may simply display characters experiencing subtle epiphanies or gentle revelations, no burning bushes or meteors streaming across skies, that help them to realize their misdirected devotions to flawed frameworks and to endure repercussions of this knowledge the best they can. This outcome is sometimes about as good as it gets, and ending up a little better, or not as bad, at least breaking even, is sometimes just as satisfying as a victory. This is the world of dirty realism, of *Make Something Up*, and of working-class America.

Taken together as a collection, as one complete unit, there is cohesiveness considering the diversity of speakers and heteroglossic discourses. Only the animal parables, providing almost contemporary parodies of *Aesop's Fables*, are interrelated. This book is not a framed narrative like *Haunted* with built-in coherence through a guiding plotline. This said, the theme of ideological discordance helps to establish continuity among the tales. No matter the negative criticism, Palahniuk successfully assumes personas within the contexts of the stories to expose the tension between what is assumed true and what is realized false. In his conversation for *STORGY*, Palahniuk explains his intentions pacing the prose in these stories: "The crutches of spell-checking and grammar-checking software coach everyone into writing correct, clean sentences. But such sentences carry no sense of emotion or authenticity.... The greatest authority comes across in broken, incorrect language" ("Interview"). Palahniuk believes non-standard writing "gives the reader the sense of joy and triumph he or she probably hasn't felt since first learning to read" ("Interview"). Palahniuk also credits punk and new wave rhythms for prose cadences, and he admits employing unconventional wording and punctuation to imitate musical beats that will capture a reader's attention. He reports implementing a series of run-on sentences with repetitions of "even" in "The Facts of Life," tying sentences together with "because" markers in "Cannibal," and utilizing "but," "only," and "except" qualifiers in "Loser" ("Interview"). Palahniuk constructs a dialogical environment in which diverse linguistic registers give various textures to the stories. The manner in which the narrators or the characters speak influences meaning as much, if not more so, than what happens. Readers base their judgments not only on what is said but how it is said, and they unconsciously make assumptions through intertextual references generated through, for a better term, product placement (commodity signification). For example, although Palahniuk does not explicitly name *The Price Is Right* or Burning Man, readers know these are settings, and they prejudge what happens based upon connotations attributed to Britney Spears, Hello Kitty, the Playboy Channel, *National Velvet*, Kardashians and Baldwins, and, of course, *Fight Club*.

In "Eleanor," "Smoke," and "Liturgy," Palahniuk offers illustrations of heteroglossia, and the narrative code-switching draws attention to the stereotypes associated with high and low cultures. "Eleanor" is an exercise in post-structuralism in which readers encounter words as signs that do not make sense on their own yet gain meaning through relationships with other words in contexts. In fact, particularly in this story, the style is more important than the message, which is frankly kind of nebulous. Simply put, the narrator wants to buy a house used in a porn film. Word for word, most of the sentences are incoherent gibberish expressing nonsense. Readers construct meaning by recognizing the embedded conventional structure associated with standard sentences and then decoding, based on their frames of reference, the "correct" words to substitute for clarity. For instance, the narrator states, "He steer south, exacerbating faster and faster the whole way, like a pack of vapid wolfhounds be perusing his Randy ass" (11). Since Randy is driving, he was "accelerating" instead of "exacerbating." Also, the "wolves" would probably be "rabid" rather than "vapid." Another example, one easily deciphered, is this: "Randy, he romanticize her, grilling her steaks and spoiling her fine figure by serving her baked Nebraska for dessert. And, eventually, Gazelle, she subside to marry him" (13). After ironing out the syntax with "romanced her," readers probably will substitute "Alaska" for "Nebraska" and "decide" for "subside." A clue that Palahniuk is playing with linguistically normal patterns is Randy's "Signified!" (17) while trying to retrieve the pit bull.

The next stories also rely on reader extrapolation. Similar to Donald Barthelme's play with language in his famously postmodern story "Sentence," literally a one-sentence tale, "Smoke" is a single paragraph that calls attention to linguistic structure. The story begins, "None of his words just came out anymore. Every syllable had to be weighed and measured. Each was calibrated to trigger laughter or to dominate or to earn him a dollar" (146). Significantly, the narrator questions the traditional ideology explaining the inception of the "word": "He worried that language had come to the Earth and invented people in order to perpetuate itself" (146). He attempts to figure this out through Christian interpretation, the "word" as beginning with God (146). The narrator concludes that the masculine subject would have a similar power: "With his last breath, the sailor would ask, 'Who is he?' and that's all it would take to wreck a paradise" (148). In "Liturgy," Palahniuk displays how people of privilege take advantage of pedantic word play to manipulate those assumed subservient to them. For instance, instead of clearly writing "placenta," the enforcers of policies state: "Under forensic examination, the matter in question proved to be the not-too-recently expelled uterine lining and associated blood-engorged tissue structures resultant from the delivery of a newborn. The superfluous leavings of the human birth process" (178). In each of these three stories, language disguises much larger problems (spousal abuse, inferiority complex, and premature childbirth) that become secondary to the way they are articulated—ambiguity blurs meaning.

The remaining stories may be grouped in levels of comic grotesque based on how a narrator's or a character's motivation is in conflict with the dominant ideology. This clash is caused routinely by something a narrator or a character has done. The story displays the cause/effect reaction resulting from a decision or a choice. Because of the circumstances in the stories, readers might not immediately identify with the narrators or the characters. With a little introspection, readers might empathize or at least sympathize. Referring to information about comedy in the second chapter, most readers would likely feel superior to these characters, and their reactions correspond reciprocally to the degree of connection they feel with the personalities. The first couple of stories in the collection are characterized by readers feeling superior to the miscalculation of the participants. Readers notice the problems whereas those involved are almost completely oblivious to what is occurring. The second grouping is based on the irony of readers clearly perceiving problems while the figures fail to recognize the extent of their circumstances. The third batch include narrators or characters who recognize problems but are unable or are incapable of enacting change. The fourth trio include the supernatural; similarly, the last four are the fables. Through the comic grotesque, Palahniuk offers representations of how people confront contradictions within dominant ideologies. Likewise, he anticipates readers applying their own prejudices to how these fictional personalities respond to ideological discordance. Consequently, Palahniuk also expects readers to acknowledge their own hypocrisies after they reassess their superiority—their own sense of privilege—over these narrators and characters.

In "Knock-Knock" and "Cannibal," Palahniuk depicts apparent resentment and exploitation, and readers perceptibly notice the dysfunction that the participants fail to realize. Palahniuk is very much a performer, and readers undoubtedly benefit from watching him read his stories for intonations and expressions that supplement individual interpretation. In particular, listening to versions of "Guts" as well as "Knock-Knock" are recommended (see bibliography for websites). In planning the arrangement of these stories, Palahniuk admits in a 2015 interview with *Buzz-Feed* that he wanted to start and finish with Christmas tales, but as he explains, "my editor said that the 'Eleanor' story with all of the malapropisms was just too much of a hurdle to start with. So instead, we opened with 'Knock Knock,' which is just filled with racist, sexist, homophobic crap, and is apparently not a hurdle to start with" ("Chuck"). Leading off with "Knock-Knock" is not really easing someone unfamiliar with transgressive writing into this collection. The jokes are all that Palahniuk claims. Beneath the surface of the narrator's telling the jokes, passing them off to an audience whom he mistakes as empathetic, the narrator is struggling with his hatred for his father and the ideology that he promotes—he despises the man as well as his beliefs. The narrator's apology is deceiving: "But, seriously, I'm not doing him justice. It's my fault if this doesn't come across, but my old man is funnier than he sounds. Maybe his sense of humor is a talent I didn't inherit" (2). The tension in the story is increased by each comic-grotesque joke, causing readers to question the speaker's admiration. After the narrator kills his father, the dissonance between love and hate is manifested in the awkwardness with which the narrator tries to portray his father (9).

"Cannibal" is just as unnerving. The narration is almost overly objective, consciously unsentimental. The sexual terms are colloquial, adding a disingenuity toward the severity of the content. Cannibal dives into Marcia Sanders's "jelly hole" (82), Sanders deep throats a "baloney pony" (82), Cannibal eats a "muff pie" (85), and these make the horrific moment when he sucks out a fetus simultaneously terrifying and typical: "bumping between his tongue and the roof of his mouth, right now, is this salt-flavored jelly-bean" (85). If readers are uncertain what happened, a reference to the "smell of your parents' dead grandbaby" (87) provides clarification. The atrocity of this social outcast pleasuring popular young women, taking care of their "mistakes" (86), is emphasized by Cannibal's tasting and afterward farting the pre-birth (86–87). In many ways, this story rivals "Guts" as the most repulsive of Palahniuk's works. This adolescent assumed by what he had read and heard that he was pleasing the young women appropriately according to social standards. This was not his fault, especially since, as the narrator elucidates, his father only watched the Playboy Channel and his mother only followed the 700 Club, so his moral inculcation, thus his ideological matriculation, was a bit suspect if not considerably whacky (82). Looking at this more closely, Cannibal's ideological discordance could be diagnosed as lethal. By all accounts, readers agree these two stories depict self-deceived characters ignorant of their own horrendous dysfunctions.

The next set of stories—"Loser," "Cold Calling," "Romance," "Mister Elegant," and "Zombies"—are less dark because the outcomes are not as catastrophically bleak. There are also Palahniuk readings of these stories available via the Internet. The narration of "Loser" is second-person, but just as in "Knock-Knock," this narrator makes incorrect assumptions about audience perspective. The titled young woman affiliated with Zeta Delta Omega and doing Hello Kitty blotter acid on *The Price Is Right* is at best naïve and at worst an idiot. She refers to the acid as ordinary, tasting like candy (41); when bidding on bread, she thinks of the way her mother finds it "at the farm or wherever bread grows" (42); she bids $8.00 for the loaf; and, concerning potatoes, she describes them as "before they became food, the way they come from the miners" (43). The repetition of "probably" related to "the acid" (46–47) almost verifies her idiocy. In rather callous intertextuality, the cost of Marcia Sanders's abortion is a referent for pricing (47). As comedy, the bid is outrageous: "And on purpose, by accident, you bid a million, trillion, gah-zillion dollars—and ninety-nine cents" (48).

"Cold Calling" and "Romance" deal with the sensitive cultural topics of xenophobia and disability, but the self-deception of the narrators defuses what could be controversial content. In "Cold Calling," the narrator's disclosure that telemarketing customers automatically assume he is Asian offsets Samantha's discriminatory desire for the exotic other. When he is jilted and technically demeans himself, claiming she should stick with Caucasian Christian men (135), he gives into the racist ideology that he is opposing. In "Romance," the narrator is obviously dating a mentally challenged "Britney" (she is never given her real name), but, in the end, he loves her, adores their babies, and accepts the ideological consequences for what they are: "if you keep waiting for somebody perfect you'll never find love, because it's how much you love them is what makes them perfect. And maybe I'm the retarded one because I keep waking up expecting my happiness to run out when I should just enjoy it" (78). In both stories, the major participants are likeable, which causes readers to sympathize with their psychological incapacities to understand their situations. The mother's text that her Zeta Delta Omega daughter is an "asshole!" (48) suggests this privileged young woman is not entirely culpable for her stupidity, and the narrator's chivalric confession about his own limited mental capacity establishes empathy with

Brit (78). Regardless, the major characters in the two stories seem to function, for the most part, blissfully through their ignorance.

In the next two stories, Palahniuk is more direct in his assault against social hypocrisy. In "Mister Elegant," the narrator also appears to convince himself that his circumstances have shaken out for the best, but he may be equally self-deceived. Readers never find out exactly what happened during his epileptic seizure on stage, and the narrator is comfortable with not knowing. He finally seems ready to accept his fate while teaching a "troupe of differently abled exotic dancers" (244) how to strip. His statement toward the story's end suggests he is also ready to accept an ideology that he initially would have discounted: "People will always misunderstand your intentions. People accuse me of exploitation" (244). In particular, this story rebukes ableist misconceptions about the physically challenged. More so than he did in *Invisible Monsters*, Palahniuk provides a remarkable illustration of anti-ableistic literature, much needed during a time of inclusivity and diversity.

Along this same line, "Zombies" is praised for its depiction of unity. Palahniuk states in a 2015 interview in *Men's Health* that "Zombies" is his "anchor story" during live performances because people typically cry, and he admits this response amazes him ("Chuck"). Actually, the narrator's threat to perform a "Push-Button Lobotomy" (32) displays his obvious distrust of the dominant ideology that governs every aspect of his life. He concedes that "words always screw up whatever you're trying to say" (37), and listening to the chorus "If you hurt yourself, you hurt me" (36–38), he creates a community with others just as unsure where "to start" (39). Significantly, Palahniuk anticipates a major cultural movement by having the narrator notice, "And everyone else is nodding, Me Too" (38). In this simultaneous parody and reiteration of #MeToo by offering a truly humanistic application of the principle, Palahniuk inspires compassionate solidarity. On another level, through the Bakhtinian heteroglossic litany of empathetic voices, Palahniuk extends the scope of #MeToo past heteropatriarchy to encompass other sources of anxiety, stress, and frustration felt by young people. Similar to his other clever tropes, selecting defibrillators (a possible substitute for opiates) as the agency through which young people disconnect from reality is perfect. Just a push and a zap, and there is no more worry about life decisions or choices, conscious cognitive freedom from ISAs, RSAs, anything related to ideology. Of course, Palahniuk is not advocating escapism (he promotes action), but he is promoting solidarity against inevitable human hardship. In both stories, Palahniuk describes how individuals fortunately find communities (one of his major motifs) to help them adapt to extreme life challenges.

The next few stories—"Phoenix," "Red Sultan's Big Boy," "The Facts of

Six. "The fringe was the future" 135

Life," "Tunnel of Love," "Torcher," and "Inclinations"—are more complicated. In this list, "The Facts of Life" is the most comic, almost an elongated joke along the lines of "Knock-Knock." This story contains more slapstick with a sudden plot twist than other Palahniuk short fiction. Compared with "Expedition," both rely on patriarchal themes, but this story is definitely more light-hearted, even though the text could be read as representative of rape culture, exhibiting unwanted male assault upon the female body. Unquestionably, there are comic-grotesque descriptions of drive-in movie sex with Troy's mother riding "cowgirl" with "her tits and hair flopping" to an applause of honks, flashes, and "giddyups" (123). The igniting of the hand-sanitizer, tried as an alternative lubricant, with both dad and mom running on fire is at the same time hilarious and disturbing (124–27), with the "sizzling mess" and the "browned meat" (127). The extended joke's payoff resolves the tension between what is both comic and tragic: "That's why you're adopted" (128).

"Tunnel of Love" has a similar resolution. The massage therapist compassionately helps his client with Stage Four cancer die on her own terms, but this occurs after readers learn of her sexual assault and of her assistance in euthanasia (253–54). Both "Facts of Life" and "Tunnel of Love" play off the conventional rules of courtship. Not a drive-in theater, the "tunnel of love" is a drive-through car wash in which the unfortunate woman is unable to escape. As the man proposes, she is blasted, sprayed, and brushed, and to emphasize the force, cut by the belts, and then burned by wax (251–53). As the narrator reports, "The heavy chamois straps descended to start flogging her" (252), and after she accepts the ring, the hot Simonize wax "ran down between her breasts" (252). Apparently, the woman has no animosity toward her beau for planning such an oddly quirky proposal, but readers might react differently with puzzled astonishment. In both stories, Palahniuk reveals how male toxicity is manifested in deceptively affectionate actions. Through dark humor, Palahniuk parodies what could be two wonderfully sentimental occasions. In his universe, however, physical pain accompanies pleasurable relationships.

"Phoenix" and "Red Sultan's Big Boy" also address complex relationship issues, albeit familial ones, through what might be passive-aggressive means. In a 2019 interview for *Big Shiny Robot*, Palahniuk claims that the inspiration for "Phoenix" is "the story of Isaac and Abraham, with God demanding the stabbing of Isaac" ("An Interview"). In this case, daughter April is the sacrifice between competing parents Ted and Rachel. The gross descriptions of cat Belinda Carlisle's diarrhea smeared throughout the house by the robotic vacuum cleaner as well as the cat drinking from the black bidets (103) subtly display the comfortably bourgeois economic position of the household. Likewise, the cerebral dinner conversation about

Toxoplasma gondii in cat feces affirm the family's intellectual status (104), but this is counterbalanced by the raunchy "Pull my hair, Daddy! Fuck me up the ass!" exchanges from the occupants adjacent to Rachel's room (116). As readers digest the details in this story, they notice that Rachel's problem with the cat only masks her resentment toward Ted. In fact, her capitulations through "Nobody can stop anything" and "Nothing will ever be resolved" (119) prepare readers for the ultimate target of her animosity, her husband. She finally informs her daughter indirectly that she has married "a spineless, lazy, stupid man" with whom she is "stuck" for the remainder of her life (120). Although Palahniuk leaves the decision to readers, after Rachel blames Ted (and his cat) for April's blindness, there is malice propelling Ted's hurting his daughter, and there is obvious irony in Rachel's whisper of "Good night" (121). There is nothing good about this resolution.

In "Red Sultan's Big Boy," Palahniuk shows the generation gap between Randall and Lisa. Through media touchstones, the father makes a comparison to Ali McGraw in *Love Story* (59), and the daughter refers to Kim Kardashian and other current celebrities exposed in Internet sex tapes (65). These counterbalance the comic grotesque description of an online video recording a man who eventually dies from a ruptured sigmoid colon caused by coitus with a horse (65). Lisa's uncompassionate response, arguing the bestiality was not unlike "Leda and the Swan" (65) and only a Caucasian male had died (65–66), only amplify her media-produced hyper-insensitivity to the sexual exploitation. Her comment about Mother Nature's retaliation for white patriarchy's treatment of the environment calls attention potentially to liberal ideological indoctrination (66). Blaming media is undermined to some extent by Lisa's greedily setting up photo sessions with this famous stallion (66). The conflict between father and daughter belief systems is stressed at the end of the story. After Randall realizes his daughter had murdered Sour Kraut, he grapples with the "right" reaction to knowledge about the new horse's past. His release of the animal because it is not culpable for its exploitation is juxtaposed against the gun not firing a bullet when he puts it against his temple—both he and the horse are reprieved. As the narrator says, "He'd been forgiven" (69) not by anyone other than himself for creating this entire situation. Just as the students in "Zombie" and the Zeta Delta Omega in "Loser" find ways to avoid the discomfort of ideological discordance, Randall is saved by the pistol's empty chamber.

"Torcher" and "Inclinations" are longer and are therefore more developed stories. The disguised setting of "Torcher" is Burning Man, by its nature carnivalesque. Ludlow Roberts has ditched his family to vacation as Rainbow Bright, Fellowship Facilitator for "three weeks of magic in the middle of nowhere" (162), forgetting his real job as an artist complicit in scams exploiting peoples' fears toward their eventual mortality (170). The practice of shifting identity is apparent when readers find out the two seemingly inept deputies are actually professionals, one a paramedic going to medical school (161), the other a lawyer specializing in entertainment copyright litigation (162). Significantly, neither Ludlow nor the two are comfortable with acknowledging their real-world socioeconomic statuses. Since Burning Man is a major countercultural event, Palahniuk provides details to display how Ludlow tries his best as Rainbow Bright to personify the appropriate ethos for the setting. Different from those in other stories, his ideological discordance is caused by temporality. Embarrassed by his older physique compared to younger naked participants, Ludlow reminisces about previous occasions when he could get "Zombie pussy. Hobbit pussy" (161). The younger women now seemingly have "daddy issues," and he wonders about his own daughter hooking up with someone such as him, a "big-gutted, middle-aged, lowlife predator" (161). In a moment of contemplation, he wonders how the event has changed: "Here was the incubator, the test tube, the petri dish. And he was proud to play a part. The fringe was the future, and what happened next in the world, it happened here first. Fashion. Politics. Music and culture. The next religion would take form, here.... The outside world was a sewer of corruption and discord. It was irredeemable, and the only hope for a cure would come from this band of artists and freethinkers engaged in play" (164).

The transparent allusion to Burning Man gives way to the more serious matter of murder, however. The death of Scooby-Doo, whose few possessions included a copy of *Fight Club* (157), prompts Ludlow's questioning of what he romanticizes as utopian. His wife has outgrown the hippy experience (165), and his vision to change the world, only to have it obfuscated by student debt and other adult obligations, cause him to question his belief system. Ultimately, the practicality of his wife threatening to kill more people forces Ludlow to separate the temporary carnivalesque for permanent reality, and Palahniuk leaves his decision ambiguous. The narrator says Ludlow needs Luminal to go to sleep, but the "excitement" that he feels insinuates that he is not willing to give in to his wife's demands. Just as he helps to trick people into believing they need surgery so they will not die, Ludlow is willing to sacrifice other lives so that he may continue role-playing what he is not. He selects one ideology over another, but he is uncomfortable in both. This position might be inspired by his realization that his once avant-garde life has become capitalistically commercial, and even his own art is manufactured for financial profit, not created as a product of his imagination, something for monetary and not aesthetic consumption.

"Inclinations" is also about self-deception. Kevin Clayton and the other males attempt to manipulate mainstream ideology for capitalistic gain. Similar to Ludlow, they assume personas, but instead of escaping bourgeois capitalism, they exploit prevailing mores concerning sexuality and gender for their own materialistic gain. Mindy Evelyn Taylor-Jackson obviously takes advantage of her parents' conservatively ineffectual belief system. More Porsches do not stop her pregnancies, so they resort to sacrificing her body (an act equally philanthropic and vindictive) to the Commander and his unofficial "Fag Farm" (260). Kevin's using his parents' fear that he is gay is equally manipulative, and his tactic of requesting more Vaseline and additional gerbils and subscribing to *Playgirl* and *Elle Décor* simulate issues concerning sexuality and gender (258). As a gay man, Palahniuk realizes, of course, making Kevin and the other men into "pussy hounds" (264) precipitates the uncomfortable humor that could be considered homophobic. After he understands the duplicity of the Commander's intentions, Kevin realizes the volatility of playing with ideologies. In a revealing passage, Kevin believes in cosmic fortune, his sins offset by the greater ones of others, his moves toward his parents and his community countered by other calculated actions, with God settling everything out in the end (265). The scenes revealing dissections of Betsey are obviously grotesque, as are instances of vomiting and insinuations of necrophilia. Palahniuk tries to pass off this novella as a *bildungsroman* through allusions to other coming-of-age stories such as *The Adventures of Huckleberry Finn* and *Lord of the Flies* (288–89), even *The Great Gatsby* (292) and *The Wizard of Oz* (294), but he only offers these canonical young adult books to substantiate Troublemaker's claim that the homosexual is always the villain (295). In this story, the "dyke" (295) is the hero, albeit Troublemaker has been lobotomized through electrocution and has been impregnated through staff sexual rape. However, Troublemaker still has the potential to come out as the hero of this narrative by reacting instinctively to the Commander's homophobia (309). Although appearing monstrous, Troublemaker has at least taken action against ultra-conservative ideology; she has avenged the abuse enacted upon her lover, Betsey.

The next few stories—"Fetch," "The Toad Prince," and "Expedition"— progress into fantasy, and, concededly, might not seem to pertain as closely to the theme of ideological discordance. In "Fetch," the narrator's jealousy of Hank and objectification of Jenny connect the story to previous ones, but the plot is still fairly conventional with the good Samaritan bestowing the gift of gold to the desperate widow through supernatural guidance of her deceased husband's spirit. As such, the supernatural tennis ball makes for an interesting tale, but there is not much related to the comic grotesque, nor does the story point toward insightful conclusions about ideology. "The Toad Prince" seems to be, however, a transgressive retelling—an extremely provocative parody—of Nathaniel Hawthorne's "Rappaccini's Daughter" in which science is manipulated and, consequently, nature responds destructively. The animalistic grotesque monstrosity that is generated from Ethan's perverted attempt to duplicate native penis "pearling" by infecting himself with various venereal diseases is a profane remake of Hawthorne's tale. Ethan's aim of increasing female sensation during intercourse transforms into a beast taking control of his blood supply and then desiring oral attention from attractive young women. Palahniuk's graphic description parallels with traditional definitions of physical grotesqueness: "The beast expands, nodules blooming from warts, puffing up, ballooning from renegade spurts of inflating flesh. It expands with blood and lymph until all that remains of Ethan is a wadded, shrunken vestige perched midway down the red-dappled, wart-pebbled back of the beast" (143). The story becomes close to a transgressive fairy tale when Mona affectionately offers the entity oral sex (145), making this a postmodern retelling of beauty and the beast, although this is definitely not Walt Disney.

"Expedition" is perhaps the most important ancillary story in the *Fight Club* canon, which is expanding into the author's literary industry, and Palahniuk has discussed the evolving transformation of Tyler Durden in several interviews. In most conversations, Palahniuk announces this story as the prequel to *Fight Club*. Specifically, Palahniuk cites Joseph Campbell's ideas of secondary fathers occupying roles left vacant by primary fathers. For example, in a 2015 interview for *Esquire*, Palahniuk claims Campbell's *Power of Myth* series with Bill Moyers influenced his creation of Tyler Durden and the role of Project Mayhem (or what will evolve into Rize or Die in *Fight Club 2*) ("Chuck"). In a 2015 interview for *The Daily Beast*, when asked if the story reflects aspects of his personal experiences, Palahniuk replies that just like in his own family, every generation of fathers and sons is frustrated, so "Expedition" exposes the "ultimate conspiracy" propagated by a frustrated Tyler Durden ("Fight"). As a prequel to *Fight Club*, this story traces the origin of paternal anger spanning from Felix to Sebastian in *Fight Club 2*, something to be addressed more thoroughly in the eighth chapter. As Palahniuk comments that he was motivated by anger when he was in thirties: "Anger would get me past every humiliation or every time where I felt I was being laughed at and failing. Anger was that little engine that drove me. And that is in Felix big-time, but not in Sebastian. Because Sebastian takes pills" ("Fight"). In a 2015 interview with the *Miami New Times*, when asked if he is constructing a mythology pertaining to fathers and sons, Palahniuk specifies that Tyler is an attractively manipulative figure designed to "destroy people's lives" ("Chuck"). In a 2019 interview with *Big Shiny Robot*, placing Tyler within the context of *Fight Club 2* and *Fight Club 3*, Palahniuk announces his hope that he has created an archetype that will gain traction in contemporary literature. Commenting about Tyler's function as a trope, Palahniuk states, "He's the classic trickster character from world mythology. He's Hermes or Coyote or Loki. I'd be honored to see Tyler become such a universal symbol for our time in history" ("An Interview"). Actually, Tyler is already embedded into the American cultural storehouse of fictional characters whom are referents for cultural signification. Tyler has assumed a transcendence beyond Palahniuk's imagination.

In "Expedition," Palahniuk portrays Felix negatively as a status-seeking posturing artist. Established as an ancestor of the narrator in *Fight Club*, Felix is a pretentiously inept writer who invents words for ostentatious effect. More important, he preys on the unfortunate for interesting content so that the highbrow elite, the culturally tasteful and morally proper, experience schadenfreude (213–15). Palahniuk might intentionally use language in this story to irritate readers (as appears to be the case with critic Newman), but the sentences enrich the diversity of personas in this entire collection. Palahniuk has made his reading of "Expedition" available on a vinyl record (capitalizing on the nostalgic connotation of sound on wax albums), available through the website *Rare Bird*, and a trailer of the reading is offered as a spoken word production through *Vimeo*. As an investigator of the "undeniable proof of divinity" (216), the narrator utters such an esoteric sequence as "A sarcophagied quality characterized the dark. The trickaricious crumbling down of snowflakes. And as the pair trod along, a sepulchrious quiet jellied around them" (220). If this is self-parody, Palahniuk could be using Felix's aim to mask his own:

> The book he was penning, no, it was no mere diary. He expected to attract a vast readership, for not only would it provide valuable lessons regarding perseverance and self-determination, but it would also serve as a balm. A vivid pornography of other people's misery. Such a tone, bound in Moroccan leather, the pages gilt-edged, it could be pored over by someone seated in a velvet armchair beside a snug parlor fire while sipping port. All those suburban pleasures would the unhappiness of this book render more glorious. The folly within those pages would validate the tedious, timorous lives of bank clerks and shopkeepers [215].

The narrator offers what might be the most significant point: "The well-off adored scrutinizing those in poverty" (215). Of all the stories in *Make Something Up*, this one is the most Marxist in terms of philosophy, perhaps looking ahead, as the prequel, to the sharp contrast between the haves and have nots in *Fight Club*. Significantly, this plot portrays a vivid distinction between the ruling class and the servant class.

Within this story, Tyler functions as the archetypal trickster, separating fathers from sons. Palahniuk creates the German setting to promote the gothic atmosphere, and the neologisms intensify the antiquity of the events. In other words, historicity is stressed for effect, and the words might be nonsensical gibberish, but they certainly sound sophisticated and intelligent. For example, when Felix meets Tyler, his sentence constructions imitate those in Victorian texts: "Presenting himself was a rapscallion of the most exuberate sort.... More than a spark of orange mania gleamed in his eyes. To accompany this robust type into the empty night would be sheer folly" (218). Since he is a "connoisseur of the grotesque" (219), Felix is willing to accept the invitation expressed in "faux-cabulary" (218) to meet "something along lines similar to Barnum's Fiji Mermaid," but a lot more hideous and frightening (219). In a play on intertextuality, a self-indulgent dialogism, Palahniuk mimics *Fight Club*: "'Prithee pay heed, the first-most rule regarding the monster is thee must nevermore speak of meeting the monster. The stranger continued to speak thusly in the stilted, archaic parlance of his forebearers a century ere.' The second-most rule regarding the monster is thee must nevermore speak of meeting the monster'" (221). In a section that reflects Palahniuk's admiration for Campbell's theory, the narrator stresses that Felix did not know his father, was punished by "a surrogate father" (a second father), and attributes his rage to being raised primarily by his mother, foreshadowing how his own son will likely experience the same fate if he fails to return (225–26). Indubitably, the monster turns out to be Felix's father, Tyler is named as the prankster, and father and son will remain reunited in darkness (228–29).

One trait in this story stands out from most (if not all) Palahniuk texts: the reference to God. Palahniuk has admitted that he believes in an afterlife, but considering his opposition to master codes, grand narratives, totalizing ideologies, Tyler is surprisingly cast as a divine messenger who secures an endless cycle of absent fathers. In a sense, the qualities of a father not spending time with a son for twenty years is comparable to a working-class or under-class proletarian father forced to be absent because of economic necessity and hardship. However, the father's queries about Felix's forgiveness of both him and of God is uncharacteristic for Palahniuk plots. Furthermore, this is not something usually appearing in a Palahniuk text: "Our salvation lies in not only forgiving one another … but in forgiving God as well" (230). Palahniuk's reason for such conventionality is in the story's conclusion. As Felix and his father continue deeper into the tunnel, in an apparent psychoanalytical metaphor of the unconscious, they will delve into the more abstract causes and conditions underlying their resentments, perhaps getting at the core of their discomfort and discontent. Only after they explore these will they return to "the light and the air" that they "love so well" (231). In this way, they will dig more deeply into the core of their values and beliefs. God might simply take the form of a higher power, a higher consciousness, greater than they are.

The remainder of the stories are interconnected fables.[3] In the 2015 interview with *Esquire*, Palahniuk comments, "I had a lot more of the animal stories and I didn't want to overwhelm the collection with those, so I just chose the four strongest ones. Then some were just thrown by the wayside because when I read them on tour and they didn't get a really strong reaction" ("Chuck"). In "How Monkey Got Married, Bought a House, and Found Happiness in Orlando," Palahniuk attacks mercurial commercialism by showing Monkey's passion for this product "she actually believed in" (25), going so far as to "martyr her dignity for the glory of the cheese" (26). Even though she and Gorilla are what is comparable to being driven out of the store on a rail, there is mutual "understanding" (27) between them about something that had "the worst smell in the world" yet had an "incredible" taste (24). In "Why Coyote Never Had Money for Parking," besides the intertextual tie to Coyote working for Llewellyn Foods, there is a darker and more transgressive irony. Just as in "Knock-Knock," Coyote's resentful discrimination is the flaw that leads to his demise. Coyote exhibits ideological discordance throughout the story by trying to figure out the dynamics of his marriage and his status in the community. After humiliation from his wife, his sarcastic question *"Where's your pussy?"* to transgender Flamingo leads to the unsuspected snapping of his neck (100–01). In "Why Aardvark Never Landed on the Moon," a similar unanticipated conclusion occurs, as Rooster, Aardvark, and Rabbit ironically become exactly what they try to avoid. Specifically, Rooster becomes the bully by destroying Miss Scott's belongings, shouting, "Fucking son-of-a-bitch bullshit stupid little pussy game!" (192). This litany of profanity displays his frustration (as Coyote and Monkey are equally agitated) caused by his egotistical misperception that he could change people, places, and things for his personal benefit. Unfortunately, their past superiority has been replaced literally by a future pipe dream.

In "How a Jew Saved Christmas," the last story, Palahniuk ends on a happy note, as once again expectations fall short of reality. In this case, however, the outcome is optimistic as poor Clara is given the valued diamond bracelet after her coworkers humiliate her. In sequence, they criticize the homemade fudge (assumed to be feces), the macaroni portrait (presumed a mockery), and the hand-knit cap (considered ugly) that Clara spent time, energy, and affection making. As with the other animal fables, this story calls attention to human prejudices and discriminations. Metacritically, Palahniuk could be bashing his detractors in this last tale, as he provides the gifts and the critics offer the condemnation. At least this last story ends with the disenfranchised person being rewarded, and although it is not exactly a Christmas season retelling of O. Henry's "The Gift of the Magi," applauding divine justice, the good are rewarded and the bad are punished. This could sneakily be the author's backhanded swat at opponents. His retaliation might have evolved from his repudiation of Laura Miller's criticism. Most Palahniuk stories do not end this way.

Undoubtedly, Palahniuk's writing is a uniquely idiosyncratic brand of dirty realism, although not many critics link him with that literary genre. This might be because his writing, such as the stories in *Make Something Up*, is much more transgressive than most dirty realistic fiction. Although that may be the case, there are plenty of dirty realistic stories that contain explicit references to sexuality and portray characters expressing Bakhtin's distinctly carnivalesque language. Another chapter (if not another book) could provide comparisons between Palahniuk's stories and writers falling within the parameters of dirty realism. Furthermore, more study could be offered that links Palahniuk's use of the comic grotesque with his dirty realism predecessors. There are striking similarities, for example, between Palahniuk's descriptions of urban marginalization in "Why Coyote Never Had Money for Parking" and comparable details in Denis Johnson's stories in *Jesus' Son*, as both writers certainly address the "belly-side of contemporary life." The depiction of self-centered privilege in "Loser" resembles the lead character's spoiled egotism in "Marita" in Bobbie Ann Mason's *Love Life*. The descriptions of addiction echo those in several of Raymond Carver's *Where I'm Calling From* stories. There is a close connection between how nature is sexualized in both "The Toad Prince" and Charles Bukowski's "Animal Crackers in My Soup" from his *Tales of Ordinary Madness*. Richard Ford's *Rock Springs* contain many stories in which fathers and sons clumsily attempt to communicate and to form relationships. Many of Palahniuk's self-deceived characters resemble the main figure in Dorothy Allison's "Jason Who Would Be Famous." In terms of transgressive presentation of sexuality, Larry Brown's main character believes vagina motivates the penis flasher in "Waiting for the Ladies," and Louise Erdrich's narrator in "Knives" starts a relationship with a stranger who has just raped her. Again, many analogies between Palahniuk's stories and those of recognized dirty realists could be developed to prove Palahniuk's position among this coalition of authors. The point is that the dirty realists often use comic grotesque (extending the legacy of Flannery O'Connor) to expose hypocrisies related to socioeconomic inequalities reinforced by dominant ideologies. Likewise, they subversively use their fiction to incite readers toward taking action against those who attempt to exploit them.

Palahniuk's characters do their best with what they have. In a 2005 interview with *Agony Columns*, Palahniuk clarifies that they desire personal self-actualization rather than the material self-aggrandizement normally attributed to the American Dream ("Chuck"). A decade later, in 2015 when he published this collection of stories, Palahniuk may have revised this goal to include personal self-empowerment toward repressive ideologies propagated as the American Dream. Palahniuk sometimes espouses nihilism as a release from all personal responsibility, as a means for freedom from all master codes, grand narratives, dominant ideologies, any doctrine that attempts to govern human behavior. He also appears existentialist in portraying characters who are alone in the universe, without the help of a god or any higher power, in the naturalistic sense of neither being able to counter any external forces working against them nor understanding any internal forces working within them. Truth be told, Palahniuk believes in an afterlife, and this insinuates that he agrees that there is a divine strategic plan for maintaining checks and balances according to some definition of morality, particularly concerning what is fair and equitable.[4] In her 2015 review of *Make Something Up* for *Pixelated Geek*, Kathryn Adams responds to how Palahniuk is notoriously pessimistic: "Palahniuk likes to play up how ridiculous everything is in life: everything we think is important, everything we're *told* to believe is important, all our motivations and the different ways we talk ourselves down our own path of destruction."[5] Adams is only half right. Palahniuk's characters often escape humiliation by recognizing the ridiculousness in trusting the dominant ideology that tells them what is important. This knowledge is what motivates his characters to talk themselves away from the path of destruction.

In this way, his characters at least accept their plight with as much dignity as they can and keep moving forward. This is Palahniuk's version of Ernest Hemingway's dictum of "grace under pressure." The true marks of fortitude and courage for Palahniuk's characters—as illustrated in almost every one of these stories—is their ability to keep living even when there are reasonable arguments otherwise. In the 2017 interview for *MEL*, when asked about his politics, Palahniuk states, "My politics are about empowering the individual and allowing the individual to make what they see as the best choice" ("A Conversation"). Palahniuk offers his readers models of empowered people. In a 2015 interview for *Sharp*, when questioned if he believes that empowerment leads to happy endings, Palahniuk responds with a laugh, "I just think things are better than they've ever been. People need to recognize that. Our ancestors dealt with much worse shit than we do. We need to recognize the gifts we've been left with, and be a little more grateful. Do a little more with them. Quit whining" ("A Man"). Most of the characters in the stories are not better than when they began, but they are at least not all much worse. Five years ago, Palahniuk could not possibly anticipate COVID-19 and all of its devastating ramifications, but in the scheme of things, putting everything in perspective, things could be worse. Just as those in dirty realistic stories, Palahniuk's characters are not known for sitting on their pity pots and refusing to take steps forward, no matter how small or shaky, because they could be, to apply Palahniuk's words, in "worse shit."

Seven

"To embrace the blackness"
The Irony of Content and Form in Bait and Legacy

In a 2017 health piece for CNN titled "Why Adult Coloring Books Are Good for You," Kelly Fitzpatrick acknowledges that coloring books now attract adults as well as children: "though the first commercially successful adult coloring books were published in 2012 and 2013, the once-niche hobby has now grown into a full-on trend, with everyone from researchers at Johns Hopkins University to editors of *Yoga Journal* suggesting coloring as an alternative to meditation." Fitzpatrick explains that coloring cannot be confused with art therapy (since art therapy demands connection between therapist and client), but she points out that experts in the field contend coloring enables people to "switch off [their] brains," to forget about responsibilities, and to "alleviate free-floating anxiety."

In a story for CBS News, Aimee Picchi reports in October of 2016 that the adult coloring fad might have reached its height of popularity. Picchi states the craze has influenced pencil manufacturer Faber-Castell to pay its workers overtime to meet the demand for color pencils. In fact, Picchi describes a pencil collection (containing 2,500 pencils, a sharpener, and other accessories) called KARLBOX designed by Karl Lagerfeld worth $3,000 sold at the Museum of Modern Art in New York City. Picchi believes the extravagance of this pencil kit reflects a high-culture apex that signals the uppermost appeal of adult coloring. In separate *New York Times* articles published in 2016, Caroline Tell surveys currently popular coloring books for adults seeking "playtime," and Stephanie Rosenbloom claims many upscale hotels and restaurants are supplying adult coloring books for occupants. Rosenbloom asserts, "Coloring books for grown-ups emerged as a fad early last year and by November *Publishers Weekly* had declared, 'It is hard to find a publisher that hasn't entered the adult coloring book market.'"[1]

Chuck Palahniuk's decision to publish *Bait* in 2016 and *Legacy* in 2017 might not have been influenced directly by his concern for his audience's psychological health. Altruistically, he understands, however, his readers need an avenue of escape from the detrimental influences of dominant ideologies, particularly those resembling Althusserian Ideological State Apparatuses (ISAs) that are advanced by Repressive State Apparatuses (RSAs). He knows his readers have the potential to recognize the process through which psychological damage is inflicted and to take action against the systems responsible for its infliction. Those who have attended his public readings or have viewed them through YouTube know that Palahniuk cares about the emotional welfare of his readers. This said, maybe because he literally transported people to support groups (as well as to hospices) and is knowledgeable about recovery doctrine, Palahniuk would not endorse a medium that promises the eradication of "free-floating anxiety" irresponsibly. Nonetheless, Palahniuk surely sees the potential in this art form to open a new front in his combat against social and cultural hypocrisies. Through the avenue of adult coloring, Palahniuk once again subversively uses the comic grotesque to illustrate, literally as well as figuratively, blind allegiance to dominant ideologies. No pun intended, drawing on what is now perceived as a venue for recreational playtimes, Palahniuk offers transgressive stories and a novella that depict problematic predicaments. Through a version of the carnivalesque, Palahniuk enables readers to color without the slightest impunity images that portray traumatically dysfunctional situations. Paradoxically, readers may release stress through coloring scenes that portray characters in tremendously stressful quandaries.[2]

Picchi might have underestimated the appeal of adult coloring, as there are several websites dedicated to the activity, and brick-and-mortar bookstores have rows of merchandise. In 2015, Heather Schwedel reiterates in *The Guardian* that adult coloring books have been broadly praised through vast media for their therapeutic benefits: "Coloring has been said to be able to help you achieve mindfulness, banish anxiety, and even deal with trauma." Schwedel again raises the activity of ordinarily lowbrow coloring to the more attractive highbrow enterprise of "art therapy." In a 2015 contribution to *HuffPost*, Nikki Martinez, a counselor in psychology, explains seven attributes of this pastime by concluding, "Adult coloring books clearly help serve many purposes that are beneficial. They can be so much more than the color by number that people might be thinking they are. They can be focused, therapeutic, relaxing, calming, problem solving, and organizational."

People are cashing into the trend. According to a 2016 article on *ColorIt*, a website marketing coloring merchandise (and this is extensive), benefits range from alleviating stress, anxiety, and pain to disconnecting for a while from technology. This article offers testimony from neuropsychologist Stan Rodski, who states coloring allows people to "switch off" their brains and consequently experience a calming euphoria. Moreover, brain scientist Joel Pearson is cited as contending that the activity "may facilitate the replacement of negative thoughts and images with pleasant ones" (qtd. in "Amazing"). In a 2019 submission in *The Strategist*, the editors point out that the best adult coloring books must help participants "reduce stress" and "calm anxiety." Besides the mass-market availability of coloring books with conventional kinds of gardens, jungles, and forests (a quick Google search verifies this), there are transgressive varieties, such as the interestingly provocative *Make Life Your Bitch: Motivational Adult Coloring Book* (interestingly, published by someone designated only as John T). The promotion blurb on the back cover advocates taking control of the "fucking tough" life with some proactive coloring "ass-kicking." Another stress-reliever is *Love & Pride: Adult Coloring Book* (with a female kissing another female on the cover, this book promotes LBGTAIQ lifestyles). Across the board, adult coloring is promoted as a healthy activity that allows each person to zone out for a while and reconnect with his or her inner child.

Generally, the content of these books is by necessity relaxing and calming, subjects that decrease blood pressure and heart rate, definitely not increase physiological stress. Predictably, Palahniuk's coloring books fall more into shock than the soothe category, and, expectedly, he is more likely parodying this form rather than extending its capabilities. Most likely the case, Palahniuk is taking advantage of coloring to once again subversively camouflage his message beneath the façade of seemingly innocuous black and white images. He wants his readers to think more about "ass-kicking" than "kicking back." This is par for the course considering Palahniuk's propensity to turn a genre back upon itself to produce a provocatively innovative recreation, in this case something advertised as recreational. Palahniuk's own take on coloring revolutionizes its purpose as art therapy or juvenile drawing.

Honestly, not many critics seem concerned with this issue, and there are few in-depth commentaries concerning *Bait* or *Legacy*. The typical review publications announce Palahniuk's combination of fiction and art, emphasizing the component of coloring, but there were few interpretations devoted to the fiction. Most online reviewers pay attention to the aesthetics of the comic-book style drawings. Granted, Palahniuk published these books about the same time as *Fight Club 2*, so many critics address that work with minor references to the others. In fact, *Fight Club 2* is certainly promoted as a more complex, provocative, and serious project than the coloring books. On the contrary, the stories and novella are just as sophisticated as the remake/extension of his most famous novel. Thematically, *Legacy* lays a foundation for Palahniuk's reworking of Joseph

Campbell's theory of the secondary father, just as "Expedition" functions as the identified prequel to *Fight Club*. Representative of the criticism, Will Nevin from the general website *AL* (covering mostly Alabama news) calls *Bait*, to combine a few of his descriptions, confusingly nasty but vulgarly amazing. Nevin continues, stressing the "gross-out" but seeing the poignant: "Disgust is a prevalent theme in his eight short stories, but it's more than a sickness over bodily fluids—'Let's See What Happens' hits the morally-depraved content-creating ethos of hipster culture, while 'Ghostwriter' sadly speaks to the transactional nature of even the most important human relationships." Exemplifying positive criticisms, Syl writes in a blog, "Overall, if you are looking for something different book wise and want to break up the monotony of novels I highly recommend Legacy.... Not only is the coloring potential for the full and half page illustrations endless, but the story is enough to help you relax." For *Entertainment Weekly*, Christian Holub epitomizes those who simply announce the book: "These days, even famous authors are doing their own experiments with the [coloring book] form. *Fight Club* writer Chuck Palahniuk, for instance, released his own adult coloring book last year. *Bait: Off-Color Stories for You to Color* paired several new Palahniuk stories with fascinating illustrations." Writing for *The Los Angeles Times*, Michael Schaub offers a blend of interview and review. After summarizing that Palahniuk's goal in these stories with "dark themes" is to "allow the reader to participate in the story," Schaub quotes the author as stating, "It should be no surprise that the illustrations will deal with adult situations.... That said, they add a child-like quality of innocence to a sometimes brutal story."

There are many available interviews with Palahniuk promoting the two books, and although the obvious aim is to sell copies, the author has expressed his artistic (as opposed to commercial) motivation for publishing his fiction alongside drawings from famous artisans. In a 2016 interview for *STORGY*, Palahniuk claims the mixing of coloring with writing might revitalize the short story and save the publishing industry: "I goaded the artists to depict lurid, outlandish subjects, and they didn't just meet the challenge. They produced images that shocked me.... Perhaps this new model will revive the short story and make it profitable, again" ("Interview"). In another 2016 conversation with *Forces of Geek*, Palahniuk substantiates the appeal as a unique gift book expressing the ethos of the giver: "Still, the glory of *Bait* is that every volume will eventually be unique, and there's no correct, approved way to complete the artwork. To ultimately select 'ideal' executed pictures might dampen the freedom of future readers.... *Bait* becomes a vehicle for the giver to express something to the receiver" ("FOG!"). Granted, the original copies of the books were more plush than later versions (the heat-glued binding does not withstand frequent opening and closing well), but as Michael Kaplan writes in *The New York Post*, *Bait* is "bound in leather ... loaded with typically wild Palahniuk short stories—including one that involves a Web site obsessed with a celebrity's toilet—the book is a treasure for fans of outrageous literature, creepy pictures and, well, coloring." In a 2016 interview with *SLUG*, Palahniuk underscores his claim that the books should have a legacy all their own: "I wanted to produce a book that would be worth keeping and that would be worth the amount of time that the readers put into coloring these things" ("How").

As one would guess, Palahniuk admits that he is seditiously taking advantage of the form. In a 2016 interview for *Paste*, Palahniuk confesses that he found exploiting what was essentially a children's platform "delightfully perverse" and wanted to elevate the importance of the medium: "A coloring book can be like an art book, and it would be worth the time people would put into it" ("Chuck"). In the 2016 interview with *SLUG*, Palahniuk goes further, "*Bait* is kind of a perverted joke because it is such adult material presented in a children's idiom." He repeats that combining a coloring book with short fiction would garner a larger audience, which would sell more books and, more important, make reading attractive ("How"). In a 2016 conversation with *Freak Sugar*, Palahniuk lets slip his subversive agenda underlying the innocent packaging, revealing that he imitated the design of children's books, promoting "people nurturing people," to lure shoppers. He admits playing off mainstream humanistic propaganda of widespread assistance, and then when readers delved into the content, they would be surprised by the transgressively kamikaze and not the tranquilly kumbaya subject matter. As Palahniuk states, "I wanted all these examples of well-meaning assistance—then I wanted to see every good deed go horribly wrong…. Coloring is a window into the psyche. I tried to color well, but I pressed so hard the crayons always broke and ruined the page" ("Chuck").

Palahniuk's word choice of "pressed" is revealing. In his coloring books, coloring is both a relaxing exercise that nurtures only pleasant thoughts and feelings and a repressing action that imitates temporary control over life difficulties and hardships, another mode of escape. In two interviews with Davey Nieves for *The Beat*, Palahniuk talks about facets of this duality. In the October 2016 conversation, Palahniuk reinforces points presented in similar media, but he also emphasizes the convalescent nature of the coloring strategy by referring to a piece published in *The New York Times* in 2015: "a neuroscientist speculated that coloring provides the peaceful mind state of creating art without the anxiety of worrying whether or not the finished piece will be successful. It's creativity minus most of the guesswork. It's tactile and nonverbal. And it frees the creator to engage in conversation" ("Interview"). Conversely, in 2017, Palahniuk discusses the impetus behind the language in *Legacy*, sharing that his creative writing students' propensity to use the cliché "douche" prompted him to design the crude vernacular of his dubious protagonist Vincent Nelson. He adds about the pragmatic purpose of the material: "I fantasize that the father is coloring the book in order to give it to the daughter, someday. Most of the gifts we give are simply bought and presented. I love the idea that 'Bait' and 'Legacy' can be completed as an expression of love, personalized by the giver" ("One"). One might like to be the fly on the wall during a Christmas when a father gives his daughter a fully colored *Bait*, with resplendent pastels showing messy poop and bloody incisions. This might be the good deed that Palahniuk infers goes "horribly wrong."

The images are indeed controversial. In his interview for *Freak Sugar*, as well as in subsequent conversations, Palahniuk mentions that several artists declined to participate because of potential blacklisting—drawing for these two books might jeopardize their standing as artists for children's books ("Chuck"). In a 2017 interview for *Comic Book*, Palahniuk goes into more depth about his motivation to include such provocative content: "I'm attracted to conflict and tension; for instance, upsetting stories told in the form of a coloring book, a pastime normally designed to help people relax.... The absurd never fails to attract me." When asked about his linguistic choices, Palahniuk states, "If anything, I wanted the stories to be a little too language-rich." Comparing "Dad All Over" to *Fight Club*, he points out that he repeated "Dad" and "until" to imitate a rhythm similar to the synthetic drum cadences, particularly the hard-sounding monotonous booms, in 1980s music ("Chuck"). The forceful beat cracks the serene surface of the adult coloring, and this dichotomy between form and content, or practice and theory, signals the irony Palahniuk assuredly wants to generate. No matter what Palahniuk thinks, the packaging does not necessarily hide what is inside. Palahniuk knows all too well that lullabies are songs to coerce children to sleep, but they are also death songs that traditionally have described human atrocities. The artifice of coloring does not necessarily detract from the transgressivity of the fiction.

Although Palahniuk claims he persuaded the artists to depict luridly provocative designs, the graphic images in both *Bait* and *Legacy* are tame compared to what they could be. In *Bait*, the colorless cuts on Squamish in "Salvation," lacking the pools of red they would certainly produce, minimizes the horror of the atrocious transfiguring of the drugged servant's physique (143). The mock crucifixion of Reese in "Mud Slinger" could be more salacious, with the Christ figure perhaps looking up the skirt instead of holding the mirror against her crotch (132). Although there is a nude woman (77) and a sideview of a nipple (78) in "Nonsense," the reach-around of the Woodrow Wilson character could more accurately resemble the graphic sexuality described in words (80). In *Legacy*, the gory portrayal of the violent blood bath in the boardroom serves appropriately as the book's centerfold, and the abundance of viscera, with what appears to be two different angles of shots fired from the table, is surely less offensive without coloring (86–87). To emphasize Palahniuk's assertion that readers interact with the text by finishing the scenes, the stories have the potential to be as transgressive as the colors provided. A blank image in black and white could transform into sublimely grotesque, with varying degrees of vulgarity, with vivid reds, pinks, yellows, and browns corresponding with their physical referents. For instance, the image of Vincent's father could have been much worse. Even though the nose and the ears were supposedly hacked off (126), they are still present in the image. In contrast, the drawing of the dead lawyer "tortured to pieces" without eyes, arms, or a nose is extremely horrific (54). Older readers might remember years ago when cheap paperbacks of classic literature would often have covers with images totally disconnected from the content, as a cover might have a portrait of a blond woman when the heroine is obviously a brunette. The image of Vincent's father could have more closely followed Palahniuk's descriptions (127). Regardless, the image of Yamakawa holding the note "They have my wife" is shockingly disturbing with all of its ghastly implications (65).

This introduces an important point about Palahniuk's transgressive fiction—imagining the content is sometimes more fun than seeing the content. This corresponds with Doubleday Publishing's choice of an actor for Cassie Wright in its videos advertising *Snuff*. Readers have in their minds impressions of characters, and they might not want to see prescribed versions. Readers always have the opportunity to dial up or to dial down the temperature of the transgressive in Palahniuk texts according to their own perceptions, and there is the argument that film versions of his texts lessen the intensity of events choreographed mentally through reading. Just as publishers offer mini-movies on their websites to entice buyers by showing them the plots before they read the stories—enabling readers to engage with the texts passively by visualizing the actors as they read—the images to color might decrease the aesthetic effect of the fiction. This is not to devalue the quality of the art. The artists of *Bait* are excellent: Steve Morris, Lee Bermejo, Kirbi Fagan, Duncan Fegredo, Tony Puryear, Alise Gluškova, Marc Scheff, and Joëlle Jones; as are those of *Legacy*: Morris, Fegredo, and Mike Norton. If the stories in *Bait*, for instance, were compared to those in *Make Something Up*, a consideration might be how the graphic images lead readers toward prescribed responses and therefore scripted interpretations of the fiction.

As will be discussed in the next chapter, images in *Fight Club 2* are much more provocative. Indubitably, the colors in the cartoon panels make the visuals more disturbing. Moreover, the exploding skulls and extensive violent scenes, plus graphics of Tyler and Marla's sexual encounters, accentuate the language associated with the scenes, causing them to be more exciting than the monochromatic images in the two coloring books. To credit Palahniuk, perhaps he simply did not want to push the limits too far for those who purchased the texts for relaxing meditative experiences. Granted, these would be very naïve shoppers. In most occasions, the graphics help to clarify meaning: the drawings either confirm or deny reader response. In *Fight Club 2*, if readers do not understand or cannot follow what is happening in the comic book, such as at the end when Palahniuk changes what occurs, they might simply google the title and read supposedly objective summaries that only lay out the sequence of events and then review what befuddled them in Palahniuk's story. The coloring books work the other way around by offering the words first and the pictures second, and if readers are confused, the drawings help them to understand what they should have received during the initial language interchange. Semiotically, the visuals add signifiers that are not in the texts. Just as a photo offers nuances of meaning differently from language on a page, the visuals supplement meaning. In other words, the images in the coloring books add to but do not control the meaning.

Nonetheless, the stories in *Bait* are just as strong as in the preceding short fiction collection, and *Legacy* is arguably a precursor to *Fight Club 2*. The first story "Dad All Over" has a similar father-child conflict as "Knock-Knock," and the death of the father in this collection is more honorific than in the preceding tale. The rest of the stories in *Bait* include the same dark undertones as those in *Make Something Up*. There are elements of the supernatural combined with the environmental, as "Bait" resembles "The Toad Prince" in the unexpected natural occurrences, and "Ghostwriter" imitates "Eleanor," "Liturgy," and "Smoke" as self-reflexively addressing miscommunication. "Conspiracy" includes shades of "Red Sultan's Big Boy" in terms of the father and daughter relationship. Importantly, similar to *Make Something Up*, Palahniuk uses the comic grotesque to portray nuances of ideological discordance. Perhaps nowhere is this more the case than in "Salvation," in which mutilation is described in concretely exact, unsympathetic language. That story, "Nonsense," and "Let's See What Happens" include situations in which carnivalesque role-switching obviously reflects socioeconomic disparities. Significantly, the shifting of roles is not fluid, as characters are unexpectedly locked into their positions once they decide on the change.

Palahniuk prepares readers in both texts. In the preface to *Bait*, after he offers a couple of examples (his grandfather's drawings and his restaurant doodles) of losing a connection with the past through the absence of significant artifacts, Palahniuk states, "The same goes for coloring books.

They're marketed as a way to create legacy art, but paper being paper" ("A Collaboration" 5), which is a segue into promoting readers to color "something worth keeping" through this text. This lead-in into the collection repeats what Palahniuk says in his interviews, and it echoes all of the reviews advertising the relevance of this new approach to short fiction coupled with adult coloring. In the introduction to *Legacy*, Palahniuk offers a more substantially ideological purpose. Applying a box of buttons accumulated from generations of his ancestors as a metaphor for collecting memories to serve as the family consciousness, the wellspring that replenishes familial identity and reinforces familial community, Palahniuk proposes heritage to combat repression or exploitation. Both Louis Althusser and Slavoj Žižek agree technically no one can escape ideology. However, Žižek also points out people will not want to leave a flawed belief system if it still provides them with a sense of security through its comfortability. Palahniuk views the interaction between readers and his texts as a metaphor displaying how readers can indeed create their own counter-ideologies. They are allowed to regulate meaning based on their coloring, and through the action, they can be comfortable (from coloring) and agitated (from meaning) at the same time. Palahniuk writes, "And that's what this book should become.... Not just an object passed from person to person, but an artifact that demonstrates your creativity and presents some aspect of you to the future. Experiment with whatever coloring method works best. Use paints at your own risk. The same goes for blood" (3).[3]

In "Dad All Over," visuals seem to imitate mental snapshots the narrator will forever hold of his or her (presumably her) deceased father, accompanying a eulogy to the man he or she did not really understand. Palahniuk mentions in the 2016 interview with *SLUG* that this story, originally published in *Playboy*, helped him to resolve issues about his mother, who had died from complications associated with lung cancer ("How"). As noted previously, the repetition of "Dad" in the story, the cadence of that signifier, emphasizes the importance of what that word means to the narrator. On the first page, "Dad" appears in eleven out of 134 words (7). The first sentence sets the tone: "The accident had to look like someone else's Dad" (7). The "accident" (which was intentional) "had to" (for insurance reasons) "look like" the immature, incompetent, and irresponsible work of a person who was not the narrator's father. The next two sentences contrast the "idiot" and "careless" father with "Not our Dad" (7), who was obsessed with the work from which he gained his self-worth. Clearly, the reckless father is not the identity the narrator wants to remember. Yet, the remainder of the story is a deconstruction of this image. Information about cancer is interwoven within masculine gender traits of grinding cylinders and smoking Marlboros, and the "true to form" Dad is almost a Marlboro Man caricature in the drawings. He has a "farmer's tan," gnarled hands, dirty fingernails, and a combat-tattoo (a professional symbol of fidelity), all signifiers of a "man's man," reticent, stoic, and macho (8–9). The references to Isadora Duncan and Tennessee Williams undermine this distinctly male stereotype, but they also verify how someone could die a tragically accidental death. The narrator points how the father would "impress upon you that even smart people die stupid deaths" (12–13). The description of Williams's death by eye-drops cap is complemented by seeing Williams tilt the container to his eye (13) and the father throwing down what appears to be a shot (15). Eventually, readers recognize the father as the unforgiving dictator—the "Dad of no do-overs" (16)—cultivating dysfunction through equal-opportunity demeaning and belittling of every member of the family. Likewise, readers realize the narrator is trying to process the father's selfless act with the resentment for the selfish ones masked behind "Dad." By the end of the story, the repetition of Dad appears to be a defense mechanism to verify his still constant authority, "making his dumb-assed kids mental giants by comparison" (20) to the careless death aptly depicted in the graphic (21). Moreover, the repetition builds to "Dad, redeemed" as the final two words (22).

As a fable, "Conspiracy" is more superficial. The references to Sally Struthers's advocacy for the Christian Children's Fund and to John Holmes's famously long penis suggest an older audience is targeted, but the message of the story is certainly timeless. The reference to Struthers is also pertinent since the father in the preceding tale resembles to some degree Archie Bunker. Sabrina does not appear to be as insensitive as the daughter in "Red Sultan's Big Boy," and even though the boy receiving the bunny "was most likely too busy cutting bunny Sabrina's throat and throwing away her bunny insides" (27), she cares about what happens to the animals. The visual of many rabbits surrounding a gas-masked Sabrina appropriately suggests her naïve detachment with what really is occurring with her gift (26). The visual portraying Sabrina's next birthday, with her holding a bunny countered by flames and markers of death, indicate the girl's changing perspective (29). Palahniuk's repetition of "until" imitates Sabrina's assumptions until they are finally validated as truth (30), and after cable news in addition to the *Today Show* and Bill O'Reilly confirm the meteor strike, Sabrina is finally connected with the "cataclysm," as the impending catastrophe is made real by assigning it to her name (31). In short, instead of hating the meteor, people can hate Sabrina because she "owns" that material object. Ironically, she cared for nature (and by default humanity) earlier in the story. To add another layer to the scapegoating, *Wikipedia* confirms Sabrina is "in cahoots" with the meteor (33), and viewers assume *Wikipedia* is the divine voice of truth. The repetition of "not fair" is also strategic. Rationally, Sabrina has no control over the meteor, and when she thinks "not fair" (35) the second time, she internalizes that "she'd never had a chance" (35). Sabrina's thinking about the sexual debauchery occurring around her while she stays abstinent reflects her strong character (35), and her father's attempts to teach her how life was "brutal and cruel" (36) almost sway her "to embrace the blackness" (37), to give into the cynicism and pessimism. The happily-ever-after ending that is promoted by the two drawings (of her rescue and her watching earth explode), offer an exercise in ideological trust (38–41). As Sabrina watches all the "mean people" die horrendously grotesque deaths, she is actually rewarded with a happy birthday for her relentless optimism.

Not exactly in the same way as *Damned* or *Doomed*, "Let's See What Happens" reacts against spiritual paradigms and religious ideologies. Palahniuk's ploy of only naming the daughter, Heather, and only referring to the two adults through their roles of father and mother, attempts to cast this story possibly as a fable about the fall from grace, but all of the references to popular culture infer this is more so a dirty realistic parody rather than a didactic tale about vanity. The visuals in this story sequentially set up the main order of events: the very secular parents are worried (by mother's side glance and father's hand gestures) about their daughter's interest in participating in a local church (45), the church might not follow conventional (through snake and moonshine) church practices (49), Heather's mom performs what is comparable to a strip show (in bra, panties, and heels) with a snake (51), Heather's father (splashing moonshine in his face) performs his own strip show (57), and Heather dies from venom (snake is beside her) on the floor (69), afterward to ascend into heaven with a menagerie of animals (or this is only hallucination). Heather's claim that she has met her mother's aborted son seems to verify this is a vision (71).

Through verbal slippage, the real problem of marital adultery is insinuated. The father's making fun of Heather's statement that the Holy Ghost "comes" all over the children includes the profanely sarcastic "At least the Holy Spirit knows to pull out in time," which refers to his wife's infidelity (46). The parents begin working under the debunking of a grand narrative: "A child raised with enough self-esteem wouldn't need the crutch of any god's love" (47). They initially question the merit of the dominant religious ideology according to the Temple of the Prophet's Blood, and their profanity and minimizing (47–48) solidify their profound disbelief in this institution, "the perfect church for [Heather's] first and last taste of religion" (49). The mother's and then the father's blasphemous dancing to music from *Cats, Annie, Saturday Night Fever, Magic Mike, Flashdance, Evita,* and *Thriller* comically demonstrates their mockery of the privileged ideology. Reflective of Žižek's point that people believe in whatever provides comfort, the father states, "You heard what you wanted.... Isn't that what religion is all about?" (62–63). Illustrative of Žižek's reasoning, the couple recognize the falsity in the ideology, yet they perform as if they are spiritually inspired. Consequently, they enjoy the experience so intensely that they unconsciously engage in activity actually sanctioned by the ideology they ridicule. Ironically, after the farce of their "Holy Spirit face-off" (67), they experience the true force of a higher power. Palahniuk once again uses repetition, in this case "Now," to emphasize the point that the baby brother was the father's and not Brian's, the "miracle" becoming a harsh lesson in ideological vanity. Highlighted by showing a child coloring, Heather's faith withstands all challenges (61).

In a blend of *Tell-All*, *Snuff*, and "Torcher," "Nonsense" documents a politically incorrect sexual carnival at the Love Club, in which participants pretending to be multicultural historical figures engage in activities that are orchestrated by the signification of their personas. Their personas' placements within dominant socioeconomic ideologies determine the scripts they perform during sex acts. Just as in *Tell-All* when highlighted names, such as Pocahontas or Lillian Hellman, held meaning based on their actual historical antecedents, people costumed as Frederick Douglass, Thomas Jefferson, and Harriet Tubman perform as the personalities whom they emulate.[4] As in Bakhtinian carnival, however, the masquerade leads to role-playing that subverts power relationships, especially in master/slave contexts. Again, pointing toward Žižek's theory, those who select to relive, replay, and reinforce discriminatory relationships may do so, but they are empowered by choosing to humiliate, demean, or degrade themselves or others. Instead of someone inflicting trauma on them, they decide how the trauma will be administered. This corresponds precisely to how violence in *Fight Club* is empowering. In an interview with *The Beat* in October 2016, Palahniuk asserts, "The key is always consent. I'm fascinated by how structured mutual consent allows us to explore our relationships to power. Sexual race play is so popular because it allows people to assume and express the worst racial stereotypes and sexually exhaust the emotion that surrounds them." Likewise, Palahniuk puts forth that the consensual physical violence in *Fight Club* is not all that different from consensual bodily surgery in a hospital. He emphasizes that both inflictions and intrusions upon the body require consent ("Interview").

Ironically, the Woodrow Wilson character consents to his own demise at the hands of what could be perceived as a female predator. In tune with controversial issues, Palahniuk features Race Play Night for this glimpse into Love Club activities, and also maintaining his idiosyncratic rhythm, the story is not necessarily as much about politicized issues concerning race, sexuality, or gender as it is about basic human relationships. Harriet

Tubman is looking for a companion, and everything else is predicated on this goal. As the narrator states, "Not that Harriet couldn't simply order Mr. Woodrow to marry her. But in no way was Race Play Night the real world. Nothing people said here was legally binding. She might hold his life in her hands today, but tomorrow he'd pass her on the street without a glance.... Not that Mr. Woodrow had a wife. Harriet had bribed the window girl for the name off his driver's license, and a web search turned up everything, including the fact he was single" (86). The problem might be how to move from the carnival of make-believe protocols into the reality of ordinary living. Palahniuk refuses to allow the participants to speak out of character (unlike in *Snuff*, real names are divulged), and the man pretending to be Wilson goes willingly—but only after he is brain damaged from strangulation (88).

"Ghostwriter" is also an illustration of carnivalesque role-play, but in this case, the entire story is the speaker's forecasting of a masquerade after her death. In fact, the narrative is an exercise in someone constructing a socially superior and more culturally attractive persona. In truth, Abigail Roster wants to be remembered as someone holding more sociocultural status according to stereotypes of normalcy promoted through dominant ideology. This does not mean, however, that she follows a set of strict moral precepts or adheres to rigid religious principles. Her wish is to be remembered as someone who cultivated an extramarital romance with the proverbial love of her life, someone dedicated to her melodramatically body and soul. Unsurprisingly, Abigail is requesting the services of a romance author, an aspiring one whose work is only available online, but someone with beautiful penmanship and very likely a flare for the sentimental, staples within the ethos of this fictional occupation (90). The ancillary drawing shows covers of the novels and their prices at a meager $0.29 (90). Dying of what is probably cancer, Abigail tells the writer, "Over the course of sixty years I have prepared uncounted meals and washed innumerable dishes. I've dutifully paid my taxes and bills and fulfilled my role in holiday celebrations. I've never resented the day-to-day labor that kept my family well, but I would like to leave my loved ones with the idea that I lived a remarkable hidden life. It's my hope that my awestruck descendants know me as someone who maintained a rich, enduring, unconsummated romance" (91). From what she is requesting, readers learn her husband Walter had a drinking problem, physically assaulted her on occasions, and committed adultery with his secretary (93–94), and her children Renee, Timothy, Travis, and Justine did not live up to her expectations (95). As she instructs the writer, "Even if your work is fiction it can instill in your readers a new, ennobled sense of self" (95). Readers realize that Abigail is looking for this carnivalesque "ennobled sense of self," and although her life is probably successful according to typical American demographic markers, standards that define the normative of what is an average life, she aspires toward a more transgressive version of herself, someone more duplicitous, someone more sexualized. Significantly, these letters manufacture a new version of Abigail that will provide her children with "a legacy," albeit a false consciousness, upon which they continue their lives (97). Amidst all the romantic drawings, Abigail finally asks the writer to reinforce her belief in a spiritual ideology, to remind her that God loves her and is proud of her, that "no misery is without God's generous award" (100). As Žižek theorizes concerning those who are entrenched in ideologies, Abigail wants unconsciously to believe in these falsehoods regardless of her role in designing them, trusting that life can imitate *Wuthering Heights* (100). The "working arrangement" (104) she desires is a reconfiguration of her life, her way of confronting self-disappointment.

"Bait" and "Mud Slinger" are short and not as technically involved as the previous stories. The first sentence of "Bait" anticipates what will occur at the end: "Nothing about tonight was for real, almost" (105). If anything, the images of a dead Senator Gifford Parks (106) and an interview with Nicole Brown's dog Kato (108) are fantastic for coloring. The other drawings in this particular story are also fun because of the fish. Celeste's/Louise's killing of animal whisperer Jellnick fulfilled one goal: "Proved he wasn't a bullshit expert in this world of imitation everything" (116). Jellnick's ability to interpret the goldfish's thoughts just through touch almost resembles Baba Gray-Beard's ability to gain information through vaginal secretions in *Beautiful You*, but this story, with the goldfish shooting a gun at the end, is not as blatantly transgressive.

On the other hand, "Mud Slinger" is about feces, and Palahniuk must have known "Reese's feces" is urban lingo for eating chocolate out of an anus, for defecating Reese's Pieces onto a partner, smearing peanut butter on feces, all evoking grotesque images. When asked about the subject matter during an interview in June 2016 with *The Beat*, Palahniuk comically responds, "The world has long needed a smart story about poop. I mean a really intelligent story about ca ca. Yes, a funny, insightful tale about celebrities and their bowel movements. I've been waiting for Joyce Carol Oates to write it, but I won't live forever" ("Interview"). Speaking with *CBR* in 2016, Palahniuk states (and as depicted in a caption in the article), "Lopez" was a ploy to hide Reese Witherspoon as the likely subject of the story: "Nobody wanted to scotch the reveal, so we used Jennifer Lopez's name on the Hollywood Walk of Stars star.... And, since she roughed up that traffic cop in Atlanta, yes, everyone is afraid of Reese." He defends himself by portraying Witherspoon as "crafty and brilliant ... a gifted manipulator of public opinion." Palahniuk jokes Witherspoon owes him for the caricature ("Palahniuk"). The story itself is not complicated: Someone has leaked online a photo of Reese's feces (the photo is the drawing) (121), and, come to find out, Reese outed herself. Reese reacts against mainstream ideology by exposing herself. Referring to the first two paragraphs in this book, Bella Thorne and Whitney Cummings empathize through their own self-deprecating disclosures. This is clearly an example of Žižek's theory of self-empowerment.

In terms of the comic grotesque, Palahniuk's play with language makes this fairly inane story grotesquely interesting. To describe feces, Palahniuk uses "jumble of noxious, brown bog cloggers" (120), "reeking, jumbled log-jam" (120), "slumped mound of rank butt puppies" (121), "piping-hot bowlful of foul bowel pudding" (121), "glistening school of spineless brown trout" (122), "ripe, ready-to-hatch hoard of hipster eggs" (122), "piped-out smut nuggets" (124), "simmering pot of hole-hurtled gunk chunks" (124), "leprous, bubbling lava" (124), "smelly intestinal tampons" (124), "putrid mud puddle of backside barf" (124), "pushed-out secondhand ham baby" (125), "clay-colored landslide of left-behind former snack foods" (125), "pinched-off pileup of soft-serve monkey tails" (125), "armada of odor-infused brown bananas" (125), "black, slack stacks of gravity-mashed gut mulch" (127), "elephant graveyards of moody, dark thunder bunnies" (128), "phew-scented nest of squat-thrust mush" (128), "collapsed mass of piped-out pulp spatters" (129), "red-brown Bigfoot fingers" (131), and "reeking rectal reamers" (133). Responding to media sensationalism, Palahniuk imitates #MeToo with "#Igo2" (127) of celebrities who refuse to be extorted by the "new sex tape" (128). Palahniuk uses Reese as a mouthpiece to suggest the comic grotesque will "revitalize" faith by "condemning" the act but "rescuing" the image (133). In this way, Palahniuk is advocating rebellion through self-publication (á la Thorne and Cummings). In the context of the story, puns intended, Reese comes out clean by exploiting the media that want to exploit her as dirty, hence turning the tables for her own capitalist gain. Palahniuk's portrayal of communal empathy in the story "Zombies" in *Make Something Up*, with the chorus of "Me too" (38) declarations, is a parodic compliment to "#Igo2" reiterating the importance of solidarity against adversity. For those doubters who question his brilliance as a social commenter, Palahniuk displays humorously how ideology can be turned against itself. Again, as many celebrities recognize, there really is no bad publicity.

The last story is the masterpiece, "Salvation." The tone and diction of this story appropriately underline ruling-class audacious hubris to transform a working-class servant from a male into a female, all under the pretense of noblesse oblige, saving the servant from drowning. The narrator makes several misogynistic assumptions as he brutally disfigures

Squamish, who passively allows the mutilation to occur. The transformation of Squamish might be considered grotesquely monstrous, but more revolting could be the psychological nonchalance with which the operation is conducted. As in "Expedition," the language is stilted and pedantic. To introduce the scene, the narrator refers to the sinking of what appears to be the *Titanic*, "The result being that this once-seaworthy enterprise is rapidly losing buoyancy. Hereafter, every chandelier crystal and watch fob and dangling tassel hangs skewed at an increasingly catawampus angle" (135). The responsibility of the wealthy elite is expressed conceitedly: "Servants, a valet in particular, restrict one to one's best behavior at all times. Not that one seeks approval from the lower orders as much as one must retain their respect, and one hopes to model a superior manner of conduct" (136). The speaker both objectifies and commodifies Squamish, claiming, "Domestic servants amount to one's personal responsibility" (136), and this sense of entitlement excuses the narrator's decision to change the man into a "lady," which luckily is helped by his effeminate physique (137), promoted in the drawing on the following page (138). From this point onward, there is more grotesqueness than there is comedy—quite unlike what happens in the preceding stories. The most graphic scene is, as expected, the amputation and castration of the genitals. The descriptions are not overly melodramatic, but the implications make the details unsettling. The laudanum, cocaine, and brandy immobilize Squamish, who was surprisingly docile from the beginning of this project. The drawing of a passive man having his chest sliced open so bills may be smuggled out as female breasts is sinisterly disconcerting (144). Palahniuk's objectively clinical approach, deftly slicing with the razor, rivals the writing of his friend Bret Easton Ellis (142). This is accentuated by the narrator's acceptance that he is successfully creating a woman, even persuading the servant that women menstruate, so the blood is associated with "her" gender (142). He self-deceptively believes that Squamish has become a "natural beauty" (144), an "angel" (145). In short, the narrator is just as unreliable as one of Poe's narrators in his grotesque or arabesque stories, and just as Poe's narrators appear more sane as they descend deeper into insanity, this narrator's final act of what he considers devotion, compassion, and sacrifice is to go down with the ship, ceremoniously and romantically bidding adieu in a lifeboat to what readers would guess as a reluctant victim of extreme sexual assault. Importantly, Squamish's passivity dialectically calls attention to the narrator's aggressiveness, drawing a sharp distinction between bourgeois and proletariat socioeconomic roles.

Perhaps the most emotionally jarring drawing in both coloring books, and one that is emblematic of the effect of the comic grotesque on readers, appears on the very last page of *Bait*. Across the page, the narrator unknowingly exposes the bourgeois callousness through the privileged women commiserating with Squamish because he/she is menstruating on top of the ship sinking and the inconveniences such a catastrophe causes them. Granted, this is the narrator's unreliable point of view, but through his eyes, women are merely accessories, elegant consorts (141), and the drawing of Squamish against what appears to be stained glass, which resembles that within a church as well as what could have been in the *Titanic*, elevates the servant to hyperreal status—the female version replicates the actual man. Compared to the mother sexually gyrating with a snake around her neck—with an audience that resembles those in a strip club as much as in the church, particularly with the preacher smiling a corrupt televangelist lustful expression (51)—Squamish is more the vision of Madonna than whore, and although nude, the servant is not sexualized as the naked Harriet Tubman (77) or with Woodrow Wilson in back of a pitchforked dildo (87). The nude drawing of Squamish is likely the narrator's fetishized projection, and contrasted with the last image, the facial expression in the glass is not of ecstasy but of relaxed compliance, almost the pose of comfortable rapture, succumbing to the assault. The position of Squamish's body in the last image corresponds to stereotypical feminine Victorian posturing. The gloved hands rest in the lap, the back is straight, the ostentatious hat tilts over coiffed hair, and the eyes look directly toward the reader with an anguished yet resigned gaze. As the ship goes down in the background, readers must assume the speaker will perish with the "emigrating unfortunates" (146) who are trapped in the bottom decks. Squamish's forlorn expression communicates despair and is a distressing end to the collection. Squamish has capitulated wholeheartedly to the dictates of the ideology that determines his place in the world, and he has given up all hope of fighting against the control those principles have on his existence. His face broadcasts the effect of that resignation.

Metaphorically, Squamish has been tortured so he may be saved, just as people abide by ideologies that are flawed but still operative. These people follow the precepts even though they realize the hypocrisy of the allegiance. Squamish's expression captures this resignation, and his/her self-knowledge is both a detriment and a gift. The other passengers on the lifeboat are turned away, and to expand the scope of the scene, this is reminiscent of Plato's "The Allegory of the Cave" with Squamish serving as the one who has discovered the truth associated with the manufactured light producing what is considered reality upon the wall. This realization is both fortunate and unfortunate—similar to the Quixotic question of whether or not living happily through insanity is a burden or a boon—and Palahniuk strategically ends *Bait* with this enigmatic visual, leaving the reader to ponder the fate of someone both saved and sacrificed. Squamish has a similar experience as those who have seen what is inside Palahniuk's Nightmare Box. Viewers are off balance because of the configuration of the apparatus, and only fate or circumstance determines when the shutter will open to allow a few to glimpse into the darkness that ultimately yields truth. Readers wonder how this newly transgendered person will deal with his own glimpse into the darkness. The narrator assumes that he is graciously improving Squamish's life, and he likely would not understand why someone would not want to transcend class and upgrade to what is traditionally designated as an easier life. He claims, "As a female of the gentry, hers will be a world of lap dogs and cucumber sandwiches. Parasols and canary birds. Blessed, blissful leisure. Hours stretching forward, unfilled. Striving always toward a vast idleness" (146). The narrator is obviously self-deceived into believing that happiness is ensured as long as one is granted ruling status within the framework of a dominant ideology. In other words, form (structure) is more important than content (meaning) in the ideological illusion of personal prosperity. Squamish's exterior has changed, but internally he (or she) is still the marginalized working-class person, to draw an analogy with *Fight Club*, ripe for recruitment into Project Mayhem. The frightening aspect of the drawing is the corruption of Squamish's self-identity. Palahniuk wants readers to be appalled by the somber look, albeit in black and white, in Squamish's eyes.

Legacy anticipates many of the ideas presented in *Fight Club 2*. Observant colorers will notice Rize or Die stenciled on the dumpster when Baccarat sets herself on fire (43)—as they will also catch Donald Trump's *The Art of the Deal* underneath Vincent's underwear when his apartment is ransacked (51). Palahniuk has admitted that this story is a retelling of myth. During a 2017 interview with *Big Shiny Robot*, in response to a question asking about the inspiration of the story, Palahniuk answers, "Don't laugh, but I wanted to reinterpret the story of the Buddha meditating beneath the Bodhi tree. Only in my version the tree is tiny, and the mystic seeking insight is a big, sexist, misogynistic coke head" ("Chuck"). In an interview with *Read It Forward*, Palahniuk summarizes *Bait* as a collection of stories about "parents and children" that have "redemptive endings" and *Legacy* as a novella about an "amoral investment banker who receives an inheritance promising immortality," clarifying that both combine "high culture anthropology" with the "low culture world of coloring" ("8"). In a 2017 interview for *Hollywood SOAPBOX*, Palahniuk reiterates that his inspiration for *Legacy* is myth: "The goal was to write about a completely unspiritual, self-centered douche bag devoted to his own neurosis and pleasure because he had no idea of his place in history. I've given this klutz something helpless that forces him to live beyond his own selfish desires." Palahniuk compares this story's plot to *Breakfast at Tiffany's* and *Three Men and a Baby*

("Interview"). Honestly, Palahniuk might be trying too hard in this story to revitalize myth. To jump to the payoff in this tale, Vincent learns compassion through the enterprise: "He's awoken under [the tree's] tiny shade. Enlightened, somehow. How he'd given up his pride and his comfort in order to provide it with wind and rain. By caring for it he'd forgotten about his own misery. In worrying about its possible death, he'd lost track of his own. The little tree, so helpless but so immortal, it had been his father and his son. Like the Earth it had belonged to him and he'd preserved it so that it might belong to someone in the future" (138). This is indeed a moment of keen introspection, but Palahniuk makes strong points through the comic grotesque to help readers understand this catharsis.

Nonetheless, Palahniuk hits his mark about heritage. Although Vincent is intentionally created to be a schmuck, the character is actually quite ordinary, especially if compared to the narrator in *Fight Club* when he describes his nascent consumerism. Similar to that character, Vincent is philosophically empty and spiritually bankrupt, embodying the Marxian dictum of participating according to ideological principles without realizing that he is even doing so—he is simply caught up in the capitalism that motivates his decisions. Case in point, Vincent immediately assumes that his inheritance, his legacy, will translate into expensive commodities representing high social status (the drawing of the jet and car indicate this) (8–9). The bonsai is not what he anticipated. Instead of welcoming the gift as an artifact loved by his father that he in turn could cherish, he egotistically worries about his colleagues chastising him for not receiving anything worthy according to their materialistic value system (7). Vincent's comparison of the plant to a fifth of Seagram's reveals the shallowness of his inner soul (9). Later, he drinks Hennessy's while surfing interracial amputee porn online (31). Simply put, Vincent is ruled by his phallus, not according to power but to instinct, motivated by sex—he is a "hard dick" (76). Moreover, his decision to travel straight to a strip club—subsequently scolding the dancer, "Your bush almost busted off my tree?" (15)—suggests something about his priorities. The comic grotesque description that follows coincides with the tone initiated by Vincent's actions: "In actuality her crotch was shaved smooth, glossy with a layer of oil. As her labia touched the crown of the tree, they looked like the lips of a feeding giraffe. When she stood, several leaves clung to the oil, and with them plastered between her legs she looked like some ancient something from a museum" (16). The drawing of the giraffe eating leaves while flanked by nude strippers supplements this tone, and the phallic shape of one ear is particularly hilarious (16). This "stripper bitch" (17) ironically turns out to be the young woman who, out of pride and vanity, ate the peach pit blessed from Moloch with the gift (or the curse) of remaining eternally twenty-three (117–19). Coincidentally,

Baccarat is an archeology student at Sarah Lawrence, the school where former mythology guru Joseph Campbell taught.

The references to all of the popular materialistic items stress Vincent's and Baccarat's capitalistic and opportunistic motivation. In an interview with *The Beat* in 2017, Palahniuk offers the reason for Baccarat's name: "People tell me that exotic dancers almost always choose stage names comprised of the names of luxury goods. Thus 'Lexus Diamond' or 'Cristal Porsche' making themselves objects, but objects of value and high status. Maybe Baccarat was inspired by the character of 'Miriam Blaylock' in the film 'The Hunger'" ("One"). For examples of merchandise, Vincent keeps the bonsai in a Gucci baby carriage (21), and the contents of his domicile include Berber carpet, a Phillipe Patel watch, as well as a Rolex (53). Before Baccarat goes ablaze, she jokes about her things, telling Vincent that her coat is Hermès, her scarf is Fendi, but her purse is from Penney's, declaring "it's got all my shit in it" (40–41). Of course, Baccarat is gorgeous, but her physicality (highlighted in all of the drawings) coupled with the status-symbol objects cause Vincent to achieve erections when he is with her. Not only does this pyro exhibition prove that she is immortal, but Baccarat points out that she sets herself on fire if she wants to make more money stripping (44–45). The abandoned train tunnel in Grand Central Station allows Palahniuk to compare the materialism in his story with an historical antecedent, Andy Warhol's birthday party, and the complicated drawing, with a myriad of small objects, provides a great canvas to color as well as details hinging on the grotesque. The deteriorating cake and other festive items are simply gross, not transgressively repulsive (120–25). The piñata laying on its side with its bottom ripped out, showing candy ready to be eaten by a rat, as another rat peers from the object's backside, is disgusting (129), but, if one wants to dissect this scene, one would assume rats would have scouted out this abandoned 1965 ceremony many years prior to Vincent's meeting with his mother and introduction to Arturo at this location.

Vincent's ideological discordance is essentially a conflict between American consumer capitalism and ancient mythological transcendence. Pointing toward *Fight Club 2*, Vincent has been disconnected from his father, yet his mother Alice, a civil court judge who was destined to be on the Supreme Court (48), had apparently raised her junior bond trader son well. Her portrait displays her strength (12), as does the "not a snowflake" thought bubble and her image of withstanding torturous flaying (63). Victor's knowledge that he "had never been alone" (106) changes his entire point of view. After Baccarat informs him that his real father had saved him during several key incidents and gives him the name Brach Hubbard, plus that he selected Alice because of her apparent strength (104–10), Vincent combines this heritage with the potential bloodline to Leif Erikson and everything associated with that Nordic ancestry (110). This is emphasized in the juxtaposition of Erikson and Vincent (111). However, the positive heritage is then contrasted by Baccarat's sexualized history of heteropatriarchal abuse, as Vincent's male ancestors had consistently assaulted her. In political terms, she plays the victim card. Baccarat tells Vincent the story about Arturo impaling the knife into her chest (possible phallic image), only to ask for the return of this knife without questioning its effect (32–39). She also demonstrates through the scrapbook how all of the males, generations of grandfathers, shot her, stabbed her, and committed other "tricks" because of her immortality (70–79). She guilts Vincent into subservience by manipulating him into redeeming "their sacrifice by accepting their gift of eternal life" (78). The story about the anchoress also generates sympathy (114–15). Visuals supplement Baccarat's scheme. To add to potential misogyny, Alice appears weak (in text and in drawing) in her dealing with her son's behaviors (90–93). The narrator states concerning Vincent's thoughts about the anchoress, "Okay, it takes a few hundred years, but she's a forever-hot girl, and she begins to worry she made a bad bargain" (119). He equates this to creation myths: "Meanwhile, our temple virgin's true story? Word gets out. After a few millennia it becomes the basis for Chinese mythology and the eternal apple of the Nordics" (119).

At the end of the novella, the duality comes together, although Vincent does not really seem to learn all that much from the experience. Turning things around—in a carnivalesque manner—Baccarat is revealed as the villain, and Arturo is acknowledged as the protector. Although unclear, when Arturo comments that his nemesis tricks a new man every thousand years to eat the peach, thereby relinquishing his soul, he remarks, "Ask Leif Erikson!" (135). This appears self-reflective, indicating that Arturo is Leif Erikson. If true, then Vincent's decision to travel with Arturo/Leif on a private jet to an exclusive island in the Bahamas undermines all of the serious moral and ethical education Vincent has supposedly received throughout the novella (139). Comically, Alice's quip that she will be the antagonistic thorn in Baccarat's side for the next millennium certainly dismantles the heteropatriarchal authority of Vincent's bloodline. However, since Vincent is still mortal, just like his father, he is consequently doomed to a potentially uneventful life comparable to the one preceding news of the heirloom that was deemed his legacy. Technically, the message "To my child and the child of my child" and so on is only a farce, a false prophesy pronounced by "the million-year-old stripper archeologist-slash-temple-virgin-slash-serial-killer-slash-serial-liar" (138), even though she ensures that the priceless tree is "safe" (138), and the two men confidently posture as males would in a situation-comedy relying on gender stereotypes after the overbearing women leave the scene: "The two men stood without speaking as the noise of the battling women faded into the distance. After a beat, Arturo turned and gave Vincent a winking leer of supreme douche bigness" (138–39). Vincent might have learned compassion. Or, perhaps more likely, he did not learn anything at all.

Maybe Vincent ultimately sees himself as a part of something bigger than himself. This does not need to be a monumental higher power but simply something larger than just his individual self. This is the beginning of developing humility. The main characters in *Bait* as well as *Legacy* all seem to depict this same grappling with truth about themselves, who they really are and where they fit within the universal scheme of things. In a 2016 piece in *Mashable*, Jonathan Keshishoglou quotes Palahniuk as saying, "Readers will agonize over choosing the ideal color for Prometheus' liver and how suntanned to make Tennessee Williams at the moment of his death" ("Morbidly"). Hopefully, readers will therapeutically color while they sort through all the dysfunction, not getting stressed over tints and shades. In a way, coloring books might serve as the ideal medium for Palahniuk's fiction. The physical act of coloring helps to decrease the psychological pressure (remember Palahniuk's comment about his breaking crayons) caused by the process of reader connection with what happens in the texts. Some people interact with what they read through marginal comments or writing words directly in printed sentences. Others react through journal responses, or what is timelier, blog posts or chat comments. Coloring is a fairly safe strategy to take charge of feelings generated from getting too involved in a story.

Snowflakes fall in many of the panels throughout *Legacy*. In one scene, they fall all around Vincent and Baccarat as this seductress enticingly leads him down an alley with a super-sexy glance (28). Vincent thinks, "This is bullshit. Snow was bullshit" (30). In *Fight Club*, Tyler Durden tells recruits that they are not snowflakes (134), meaning they are neither special nor unique. President Trump has applied snowflake to those whom he considers weak, but this started with Kellyanne Conway's calling Trump's adversaries snowflakes (Lo Dico). There is a general perception that those born during the second decade of the 2000s are within the "Snowflake Generation," easily susceptible to having their delicate and sensitive psyches hurt. In a 2017 interview in *MEL*, Palahniuk points out "snowflake" really refers to empathy, asserting people are actually more alike than they are different. They are not unique snowflakes but are included within a community of snowflakes ("A Conversation"). Needless to say, Palahniuk depicts characters who feel ideological discordance while situating themselves into the broader world. Almost all of them are indeed snowflakes, uniquely individual yet a part of a communal humanity. Palahniuk does this once again through the coloring books *Bait* and *Legacy*.

Eight

"Human beings don't cultivate ideas"
Subverting Fight Club *Ideology* through Fight Club 2 *Mythology*

In the farce "Fight Club for Kids," easily available online through YouTube, Chuck Palahniuk says after introducing himself by name, "I'm the author of ... [hesitation] really just *Fight Club*." He has obviously published other works, but most, truth be told, only recognize him as the author of that book. Undoubtedly, *Fight Club* is Palahniuk's most famous work, and that novel is tremendously pervasive in American culture. Most people recognize references to "fight club." Even though the first rule of fight club is not to talk about fight club, people have certainly talked about fight club. If they have not read Chuck Palahniuk's 1996 novel, they have seen David Fincher's 1999 film, which is broadcast frequently, maybe too often. Cable networks like to broadcast the sanitized version of the film.

In the Coker University library, at the school where I teach, copies of the movie *Fight Club* are often not returned, stolen by students who probably pay more for the library copies than they would if they purchased the DVDs through Amazon or bought them at Walmart. When I attempt to check out the film for one of my classes, I am baffled when I discover through the electronic library holdings catalog that *Fight Club* is once again "Lost," what I have been told is library code for the item was not returned, or once again stolen. What is happening at my school occurs all over. People really like this movie. In my school's library, students steal the film, but they never take the actual book. This is not surprising, but they do not realize what a wonderful experience they are missing. They should steal the book instead of the movie.

Unquestionably, there is more commentary published academically about *Fight Club* than any other Palahniuk work. Most experts in gender and feminist studies who teach this novel in upper-level undergraduate courses and esoteric graduate classes have no inclinations to crack the covers of Palahniuk's other books. Generally, in blogs and other media about

Palahniuk, *Fight Club* is the standard by which every other Palahniuk text is compared. To concede, this novel rivals "Guts" in several circles, but, for the most part, *Fight Club* is the literary instrument by which most Palahniuk's fictional works are measured. So far, *Fight Club* has been mentioned in every chapter in this book. *Fight Club* is mainstream.

People enjoy talking about *Fight Club*. In 2020, there is still an underground following. The book still has popular culture currency. The story still resonates with audiences. Just as *Die Hard* is making progress rivaling *It's A Wonderful Life* and *A Christmas Story* as "the" Christmas film, *Fight Club* the film compares with *The Big Lebowski*, *The Rocky Horror Picture Show*, and *Animal House* as a cult classic. The novel *Fight Club* is in the same category with *Slaughterhouse-Five*, *On the Road*, and *Fear and Loathing in Las Vegas* as counter-culture masterworks. People readily recite memorized quotes from the film and the book versions of *Fight Club*. Palahniuk might someday compete with graphic text authors Neil Gaiman, Marjorie Liu, Alison Bechdel, and Art Spiegelman.

Fight Club parodies confirm just how entrenched this book is in American culture. Adult Swim broadcasts a commercial around Christmas that mocks *Fight Club*. There are numerous mainstream television parodies. *Law & Order: Special Victims Unit*'s 2011 episode "Pop" has detectives investigate a clandestine fight club after a young man dies from injuries. Much less serious, *Family Guy*'s 2017 episode "Crimes and Meg's Demeanor" includes a segment in which Stewie participates in a Jewish fight club, which does not include much fighting. In April of 2019, Joshua Rotter announces in the *San Francisco Examiner* that Peaches Christ, an infamous "drag queen" performer, and Raja, a recent winner in *RuPaul's Drag Race*, star in the performance *The First Wives Fight Club*. In movie reviews published in October of 2019, Adi Robertson for *The Verge* and David Ehrlich for *IndieWire* make direct comparisons between *Joker* and *Fight Club*. Halsey's music video for "Nightmare," released in May of 2019, displays an all-female version of fight club in an urban street, with bystanding females yelling from building fire escapes. Three incredibly funny *Fight Club* parodies available on YouTube are "Cuddle Club" (fist fighting is replaced with pillow fighting), "Write Club" (combatants literally write instead of fight), and "Nap Club" (fighting is replaced by napping). A witty combination of *Fight Club* and *Pride and Prejudice* is "Jane Austen's Fight Club." This video is linked on the Core Curriculum subpage of the Columbia College (in Columbia University) website, and as Keith Staskiewicz's interview with its creator in *Entertainment Weekly* verifies, Palahniuk's story is becoming a staple in feminist studies in addition to other scholastic venues. Again, there just is not as much buzz about Palahniuk's other works (*Snuff* and *Beautiful You* are obvious options, especially in Women's Studies courses).

Over the course of 2019, there were unfortunately many reports of real fight clubs that are not in the least humorous. In a February 6 article for *US News Online*, Jim Salter covers a St. Louis criminal case in which charges were dropped against two children's day care workers who allegedly held a "fight club" with toddlers. The notoriously leaked video of the "toddler fight club" was posted all over the Internet (in short and long versions), and major news networks and sensational news services followed the controversial accusations and indictments. In a March 12 report, the Associated Press claims a teacher in Cloverdale, California, was suspended for refereeing a fight club in his classroom that led to several students' injuries ("High"). In an April 1 release, Conor Morris describes how students at Hocking College were disciplined for creating a video titled "Put the Gloves On! Hocking College Edition" that depicts physical violence in the school's dorms (11). In a July 30 post, the Associated Press reports that Tatiana Patten, an assistant principal at Montville High School in Norwich, Connecticut, was charged for not reporting a fight club that consisted of a substitute teacher organizing slap-boxing bouts ("Administrator"). Robert Gearty shares in an October 14 article that three workers were arrested at an assisted-living and memory-care facility in Winston-Salem, North Carolina, for pitting elderly patients against each other in a geriatric fight club. In a less atrocious example, in an August 15 article, Nate Ulrich writes that Cleveland Browns coach Freddie Kitchens motivated his players to "to stand up for themselves" in what resembled a fight club during a preseason football scrimmage against the Indianapolis Colts. These *imitations* of *Fight Club* contrast starkly with *parodies* of *Fight Club*.

Many commentators acknowledge the prevalent cultural status of *Fight Club*. Over five years ago, in an October 9, 2014, article in *Esquire*, Garin Pirnia argues in "Why *Fight Club* Matters More Than Ever," speaking more about the film than the novel, "*Fight Club* quickly spiraled into a lost generation of men seeking something more than nihilism.... [The film] may be about men coming together for shared experiences, but the themes about experiencing real pain and release are universal." In a March 17 article in *Medium* titled "The 20th Anniversary of *Fight Club* and *The Matrix*: Two Futures All Around Us in 2019," Barry Vacker contends, "More than mere entertainment, *Fight Club* and *The Matrix* remain intellectual touchstones in contemporary culture." Addressing only *Fight Club*, Vacker remarks, "the book and film offer clever and trenchant commentary about corporate life, consumer society, and evolving/devolving visions of masculinity. That much is obvious and has received ample commentary. No need to repeat all that, especially given the [fucked] up 'manliness' still on display everywhere, with advanced primates thumping their chests and claiming to make Russia and America great again." In a July 2019 article for *BBC*, David

Eight. "Human beings don't cultivate ideas" 171

Barnett discusses how largely misunderstood Tyler Durden has transformed into a major masculine icon, mentioning Palahniuk will not declare if this apotheosis is positive or negative: "So it's perhaps unsurprising that that ultimate aggrieved macho fantasy figure Tyler Durden has become something of an unironic poster boy for Men's Rights Activism. The men's rights movement has been around for decades as a riposte to feminism, but really found its feet in the internet age—and if you tune into conversations between its followers on the news aggregator and discussion forum Reddit, you can see Fight Club, and Durden, are two of its clear obsessions." In a typical response, truly representative of many readers' feelings, Benoit Lelievre states, "Chuck Palahniuk's 1996 *Fight Club* is the most important book I've ever read.... I'm sure there are others who think of Palahniuk's novel with the same reverence. It's perfect in its imperfection."

Lelievre expresses this opinion in his 2016 review of *Fight Club 2*, the sequel to Palahniuk's eponymous novel that grew from a seven-page story (later the sixth chapter) into an iconoclastic text that struck a rebellious nerve with a diverse range of readers at the end of the twentieth century. Understood as an ideological treatise, *Fight Club* reflects how people respond to inequalities within American sociocultural relationships. Consequently, *Fight Club 2* undermines the stability of this treatise, as Palahniuk questions the authority of his own master narrative, dismantling the counter-culture philosophy he built as formidable structure in his 1996 text. Through a revision of the major principles presented in *Fight Club*, Palahniuk applies the comic grotesque to address the differences between ideology and mythology, splitting elements of his story that have been generally perceived as a unified belief system. At the end of the sixth chapter in *Fight Club 2*, after he has already told Sebastian that Tyler is an infection contaminating countless generations (153), Dr. Wrong exclaims, "Human beings don't cultivate ideas" (159). A page later, as he and Sebastian prepare to meet Junior, Dr. Wrong finishes this thought, "Ideas control us" (160). This concept is reiterated by a cartoon version of Palahniuk before Tyler executes him to ensure the birth of Tyler's son: "Those beliefs aren't yours. You belong to them.... Ideas are real. We are not" (259). During a 2016 interview with *SuicideGirls*, asked if he really believes this, Palahniuk replies, "I kind of do. I really wonder if the ideas are the things that exist across time and that we ourselves die, and, in a way, we are just the vehicles that extend the lifespan of these ideas ... [thought of this way,] the ideas seem much more important than we ourselves" ("Interview"). In the Bakhtinian tradition of carnival, Palahniuk presents in *Fight Club 2* a parody of *Fight Club*, deconstructing his initial story to contrast ideology and mythology. Readers who see the fighting as literal focus on the ideology of *Fight Club*; those who perceive the fighting as metaphorical tap into the mythology of *Fight*

Club. Many people miss this very important differentiation, and perhaps Palahniuk is satirizing the misappropriation that inevitably is the result.

The medium Palahniuk selects for his sequel illustrates the carnivalesque nature of his project. The graphic novel is extremely popular, and no one can say loudly in a room full of millennials or Generation Zers that this genre is less than or scholarly diminutive of the honored and revered form of the literary novel without expecting a passionate argument. Many academics are loyal to this medium, which demonstrates the converging of highbrow and lowbrow into the common ground of popular culture. There are several sources advocating the graphic novel as a serious form, so there is no need in this chapter to diverge into a history or to digress into an analysis of graphic novels.[1] Without question, the graphic novel deserves sincere respect. There is the argument that readers achieve similar goals finishing an animated text of *Moby-Dick* as they would sloughing through Melville's prose *Moby-Dick*. A point of concession might be, however, that Melville's particular stylistic bursts of incredible literary acumen, such as the language in the famous "Whiteness of the Whale" sentences in Chapter 42, cannot be captured identically in a graphic text. Melville's linguistic word play through the signification of "white" (151–57) might not be reproduced for the same interpretative effect in a comic text version. Palahniuk's publisher for *Fight Club 2*, Dark Horse, released a graphic version of *Moby-Dick* illustrated by Christophe Chaboute in 2017 that is certainly impressive, but even though this version (and there are several "illustrated" renditions) is very innovative, meaning is lost linguistically in one sense as it is gained visually in another. The black and white (not color) text of Dark Horse's *Moby-Dick* resembles Palahniuk's coloring book pages. There is no "Whiteness of the Whale" chapter, but in "The Chase—First Day" and "The Chase—Second Day" chapters, the white whale drawn is terrifyingly sublime. The same premise about prose eliciting a more imaginative response (conjuring the image rather than seeing it) could be made about *Fight Club* and *Fight Club 2*.

In the criticism, there is little bias expressed that one is better because of the format. Nonetheless, a more interesting position is to assert first that *Fight Club* follows, at least in theory, conventional narrative structure. Although stylistically minimalistic and affiliated with dirty realism (both are touched on in previous chapters), *Fight Club* lends itself to graphic depiction, which is why the film is such an effective adaptation of the novel. *Fight Club 2* offers animated characters that are merely costumed farces of who they were in the original story. Through the graphic reconfiguration of the original plot in addition to moving ten years past its conclusion, Palahniuk provides an elaborate masquerade of the seminal characters. In graphic panels, propelled by a myriad of voices—expressed in speech balloons and text boxes—Palahniuk can imitate the conventional imaginative descriptions, narrative dialogues, and typical paragraphs presented in any novel. Importantly, the graphic text by its nature functions as the carnivalesque counterpart of the prose novel. Not in any way to diminish the importance of a graphic text, in terms of high and low art, the novel is traditionally superior. As the literary canon is evolving, becoming more inclusive and diverse, this might surely change (many people are pushing for this currently). Notwithstanding, by choosing the graphic form, Palahniuk plays with transgressive depictions and heteroglossic voices in what is already a carnivalesque medium.

In several interviews, Palahniuk has discussed his rationale for the comic sequel. In a 2014 article in *Publishers Weekly*, Rich Shivener comments many contemporary authors such as George R.R. Martin, Quentin Tarantino, and Joss Whedon are being lured into writing graphic texts. Shivener claims Palahniuk was eventually persuaded to participate by Dark Horse editor-in-chief Scott Allie, who working through Palahniuk's friends, eventually secured the project (8). In a 2016 piece also in *Publishers Weekly*, Heidi MacDonald reiterates the appeal of graphic texts: "Since the graphic novel boom began over a decade ago, many well-known authors have dabbled in writing comics—or adapting their works to comics. Recently authors Margaret Atwood, Chuck Palahniuk, and William Gibson have all written (or announced) original comics projects in the hope of gaining new fans—and sales" (5). In general Palahniuk folklore, the impetus of *Fight Club* is attributed to a horrendous black eye he received after asking a neighbor to turn down his music during a vacation camping trip. Palahniuk explains in a 2009 article in *The Times*: "It all started with a punch: the sock heard round the world." With vivid description, Palahniuk goes on to say none of his co-workers would even slightly acknowledge his monstrously deformed face ("Duel"). Palahniuk was fascinated that none of his fellow workers would say anything about the mutilation, choosing to ignore the obvious result of violent exchange. This inspired what later became chapter six combined with two other short pieces, one about support groups. In a 2015 conversation with *UPROXX*, Palahniuk offers his particular reasons to create the sequel: he was rejuvenated after completing *Make Something Up*, he was ready to explore the genre of the graphic novel, and he acquiesced into accepting *Fight Club* would be his literary legacy, a staple of American transgressive fiction. Moreover, Palahniuk knew that he simply could do more at less expense through comics. As he continues in the *UPROXX* interview, "movies could never make the images in *Fight Club 2* literal enough to record on film. Come on, dying children? Comic spousal abuse?… Comics, however, give the audience enough wiggle room to accept the potentially overwhelming elements of an extreme story" ("Chuck").

In other conversations, Palahniuk explains the graphic form provided him with opportunities to expand the ideological dimensions of *Fight Club* into the mythical realm of the archetypal collective unconscious. In a 2015 interview with *The 1st Class Lifestyle*, Palahniuk stresses the cyclical nature of his story, insisting readers will notice in the comic text that the "original story was a small limited part of a cycle that's taken place over and over for most of human history. Sebastian is just one person who's been dominated by Tyler. Tyler has been around for a long, long time and his plan is about to finally come to completion" ("How"). Responding in 2015 to *DCist*, Palahniuk comments that he would like *Fight Club* to achieve similar mythic status to George Lucas's *Star Wars* stories: "I didn't realize that people were going to be asking me about *Fight Club* for the rest of my life, and that the story would have such legs ... [the plot had to be told through] a brand new medium, and a graphic novel couldn't be compared directly to either of the predecessors" ("Interview"). Speaking in 2015 to *Men's Health*, Palahniuk holds that concision was a priority: "No one wants to read a comic book that's just a page full of words. It's a more visual medium, so the action needs to be clean and clear and precise and the dialogue needs to be really spare" ("Chuck"). In a 2015 interview in *Esquire*, Palahniuk describes the difficulty associated with conjuring the exactly right physical move in each frame, "Unpacking every physical action and gesture into really specific beats, because each panel can only show a gesture of starting or completing and you can't show a combination of gestures" ("Chuck"). In the 2015 discussion with *UPROXX*, Palahniuk mentions how he adjusted by breaking the physicality into segments that would simulate the progression of time, and he believes that he got better at this technique as he completed each of the separate issues of the comic ("Chuck"). During a 2016 interview with *SuicideGirls*, after confirming his first novel's influence on American culture, Palahniuk reiterates reasons offered in *UPROXX* for going with the graphic version at this juncture in his career: he needed to process his relationship with his father, he wanted to experiment with the format of the graphic novel, and he had a strong support system to complete both tasks ("Interview"). Thus, Palahniuk almost felt like continuing Fight Club was his personal destiny, if not his cultural obligation. Cervantes wrote the second book of *Don Quixote* after he discovered his story had assumed a life of its own. As he expresses in interviews, Palahniuk had similar motivation.

In other conversations, Palahniuk digs more deeply into the thematic purpose of the sequel, explaining why the comic form more adequately allowed him to delve into the mythology of *Fight Club*. In a 2016 interview with the *HuffPost*, when asked how his first novel addresses current American political differences, Palahniuk exclaims that the central point of his first novel was "the empowerment of the individual through small, escalating challenges." He divides these into liberal actions taken against institutions and conservative actions taken against agents of authority, synthesized into one battle against a dominant father figure. Queried about the male toxicity propagated through masculine violence, Palahniuk stresses that even though he does not condone violence, the consensual fighting is therapeutic and restorative, so the male-on-male pugilism is empowering: "It's a mutually agreed-upon thing which people can discover their ability to sustain violence or survive violence as well as their ability to inflict it" ("Fight"). In a 2018 conversation in *GEN*, Palahniuk shares an anecdote to verify how *Fight Club* resonates with women as well as men, justifying the appeal of a sequel to both genders. On his sofa, he has a pillow bearing the inscription "The things you own end up owning you," knitted for him by one of his female fans ("Fight").

Although Palahniuk might claim to explore new media by continuing a story about empowerment through community, he narrows this focus to the paternal father/son relationship. For example, in an interview with *Bustle*, a website with a largely young female audience, Palahniuk returns to the comparison between *The Great Gatsby* and *Fight Club*—explored thoroughly in Suzanne Del Gizzo's scholarly article about the similarities—claiming the sequel is possibly inspired by his reverence of F. Scott Fitzgerald's 1925 novel: "In *Fight Club 2* I wanted to revisit the characters 10 years later. To see them making exactly the same mistakes, and assuming the same kind of social roles, becoming the same failures, that they condemned their parents for being" ("On"). Palahniuk announces this connection to Fitzgerald in the 2005 Afterword to *Fight Club*, spurring discussions relating the two books (215–16). In a 2016 discussion with *CBR*, however, Palahniuk reveals the more likely rationale for this 1996 book: "I was kind of conducting this ongoing journalist field study of all my male friends, saying, 'What do you wish your father had taught you? What are you dissatisfied about?' It was a kind of form of journalism" ("Palahniuk").

In several interviews, Palahniuk reiterates the paternal theme in *Fight Club 2*, but he bases the impetus upon the significant anthropological work of Joseph Campbell. For the most part, commentators appear to trust Palahniuk's explanation in the Afterword. Case in point, Del Gizzo begins her study of *The Great Gatsby* and *Fight Club* by referring to Palahniuk's "playful and good-humored" (69) position that he updated *The Great Gatsby* for a contemporary readership. Palahniuk's Cacophony Society and Suicide Club backgrounds plus a whimsically sarcastic demeanor masked by soft, slow speech might raise doubt about his honesty, but readers can take for granted that Campbell's discussion with Moyers in *The Power of Myth* is the impetus for the mythological potentiality of *Fight Club*. In the Afterword, Palahniuk writes that after he suffered his infamous black eye, he watched a television broadcast showing how street gangs became surrogate families for young men without fathers, training them to become men by imposing structure, what "a coach or drill sergeant would do" (214). Although Palahniuk does not mention Campbell, he is almost certainly referring to the famous conversation between the anthropologist (although he was a Renaissance man with expertise in many areas) and journalist Bill Moyers aired first in 1988 but then reshown countless times through the Public Broadcast Service (PBS), often as a staple during fund-raising telethons during the 1990s and 2000s. Immediately after mentioning the Moyers program, Palahniuk shares what establishes the novel's position as a male-specific text, specifying that bookstores only catered to female clientele: "*The Joy Luck Club* and *The Divine Secrets of the Ya-Ya Sisterhood* and *How to Make an American Quilt*. These were all novels that presented a social model for women to be together.... But there was no novel that presented a new social model for men to share their lives" (214). Henceforth, *Fight Club* has been literary fodder predominately for critical interpretations from those interested in gender theory and queer theory. Of course, Marxist and cultural theorists have responded to the obvious anti-capitalist theme. Unbelievably, the book has been generally neglected concerning a Campbell-based archetypal or mythological interpretation.

Palahniuk's own statements call for this reading of *Fight Club*.[2] Palahniuk has said repeatedly that he got the idea of "secondary father" from watching Campbell. Based on the section in the Afterword and considering Campbell's ideas were not dispersed as broadly on the Internet in 1995 when he composed his novel, Palahniuk must have viewed Campbell's chatting with Moyers during the eight-hour presentation spread out over several nights and replayed numerous times on PBS. Campbell does not state "secondary father" explicitly, and a scan of indexes in Campbell's many books and a Google search combining "Campbell" and "secondary fathers" only yields references to Palahniuk's own attribution of the "secondary father" to the anthropologist. However, Campbell discusses how the "hero" is separated from his father and is then taught by a wise and experienced mentor or "old man" figure who functions as a "second" father. Likewise, there are incidences in various media of Campbell citing contemporary gangs as surrogate families or home communities for young people in the late twentieth century.[3]

Palahniuk must have surely seen these episodes and extrapolated upon what he viewed. In a 2015 interview in *Sharp*, when asked if he continued to address the "absence of male role models" in *Fight Club 2*, Palahniuk responds by saying Campbell talked about someone who supplements the work of the biological father, "a teacher or a clergyman or a drill sergeant or a coach, some secondary father who wasn't related to the son, who could discipline the son to adulthood." He concedes, however, currently priests and teachers no longer maintain their roles as mentors or models, leaving young males not many places to turn for guidance. As he comments in many forums, Palahniuk mentions that *Fight Club* is one of the few works that address male issues ("In"). In the 2015 interview in *Esquire*, Palahniuk attributes Campbell as the major inspiration for his first novel. After admitting that he had seen the conversation between Campbell and Moyers on PBS, Palahniuk insists Campbell revealed the concept of secondary father as someone who cultivated in young people (both males and females) abilities that would improve their self-confidence and thereby increase their social status. Palahniuk reiterates that this secondary father is comparable to a coach, a teacher, or a drill sergeant, and this mentor displays a strong affection while maintaining strict authority ("Chuck"). In a 2015 interview for *MTVNews*, Palahniuk warns that Campbell's secondary father—once again designated as an instructor, a preacher, a sergeant, or a coach—becomes misidentified as a predator or abuser, eventually relinquishes his role, and consequently creates a void ("Author"). In a 2015 interview with *The Verge*, Palahniuk admits his sequel illustrates how someone not as close to the child as a parent—again, a "mentor, a teacher, a reverend, a minister, a drill sergeant, a sports coach"—drives performance, and he reiterates that absence of the secondary father reciprocally promotes the cultivation of gangs, "which have always acted as a secondary father for certain groups" ("Interview"). Consistently, Palahniuk bases his meaning of secondary father on Campbell's principles broadcast in *The Power of Myth*, and he typecasts Tyler in this surrogate parent role.

Of course, Palahniuk also refers to Tyler as the trickster archetype in many of his interviews. This reference is not necessarily from Campbell's dialogue with Moyers but more likely the product of Palahniuk's reconfiguring his character to fit comfortably within a larger framework, a broader mythological paradigm that identifies Tyler with a principle or a concept rather than as either the manifestation of the narrator's insecurities or as a projection of his aspirations. This also sustains the fluidity of Tyler's signification, allowing him to slip into various meanings. In the context of *Fight Club* as a mythology, Tyler ensures the progression of the familial cycle that includes the secondary father, so he must constantly facilitate the ongoing separation of fathers from sons. When asked in the 2015 interview with *The 1st Class Lifestyle* about his preparation, Palahniuk replies that much of *Fight Club 2* continues research completed for the first novel (and left out of that book), notably looking at the work of Campbell, Victor Turner, and other sociologists who study the father/child relationships ("Interview"). Through his sequel, Palahniuk is constructing the mythology that replaces the ideology in *Fight Club*. In other words, Palahniuk is replacing the philosophical foundation of his first novel. Viewed this way, Palahniuk deconstructs what he manufactured in 1996, and he carries this out through the comic grotesque, ironically satirizing his own principles. In a 2017 interview with *The Beast*, Palahniuk reflects, "When I was writing *Fight Club*, I did not know a single man my same age that felt prepared for adulthood. They all felt that their fathers had failed them in teaching them whatever they needed to know" ("Fight"). Importantly, when there is no strong father, lured away by trickster Tyler, there is the surrogate mentor Tyler. Palahniuk's most famous character has a different archetypal function depending upon the context.

This is the crucial point in Palahniuk *Fight Club* sequencing. In a 2015 interview for *Sharp*, Palahniuk states that Tyler Durden is the product of a spiritual or mystical "vacuum": "Tyler is pretty much the universal trickster character. In Norse mythology that was Odin, in Greco-Roman mythology it was Hermes, in Native American culture it was Coyote. Every culture has a kind of trickster character that comes in and stirs the shit and upsets people, but also brings them enlightenment" ("So"). In a 2015 interview with the *Miami New Times*, Palahniuk describes Tyler as "a thing that is reoccurring, as a kind of evil genie across time whose purpose is to destroy people's lives in a specific way.... Tyler has been working to estrange fathers and sons and even daughters and fathers so that eventually they'll all follow Tyler" ("Chuck"). In a 2019 conversation published in *Big Shiny Robot*, Palahniuk clarifies that Tyler is the classic trickster, again comparing him to Hermes, Coyote, and Loki, going so far as to foresee him as "a universal symbol for our time in history" ("Interview"). In the 2015 interview for *UPROXX*, Palahniuk calls Tyler a "child-stealer" who has been devastating families for centuries, noting that as parenting skills continue to deteriorate, Tyler "becomes the only remaining figure of parental authority for a final generation" ("Chuck"). In a 2015 interview in *The Beast*, Palahniuk classifies the psyches of his two male figures in *Fight Club 2*: Tyler is the "fully-expressed person," assertive and self-confident; Sebastian is the "fully-suppressed person," passive and self-deprecatory ("Fight").

Comparable to the critical reception of *Bait* and *Legacy*, most of the media reaction to *Fight Club 2* is presented in interviews that resemble more advertisements than reviews or in announcements that acknowledge Palahniuk's newest creation. In a review for *The Guardian*, Alison Flood offers the typical introduction: "The unnamed narrator of Chuck Palahniuk's Fight Club is back, dragging a dependence on prescription drugs, a bored wife and a destructive son along with him.... It shows the character 10 years on, knocking back prescription drugs ... and disavowing everything about his former existence." Several reviews, however, seem to refer to *Fight Club* as a novel about fathers and sons. For instance, in a post for

UPI Entertainment, Annie Martin states that sequel remains focused on Palahniuk's "tirade against fathers." Significantly, she adds that the graphic novel is self-reflexive parody: "The author says the continuation is 'as much a meta-fictional comment on the cultural response to *Fight Club* as it is a sequel.'" Reed Tucker summarizes for *The New York Post* the important meeting that initiated the project: "Chuck Palahniuk says he read horror comics growing up in the 1970s but never considered working in the medium until a friend threw a dinner party attended by Portland, Ore., comic stars Brian Bendis ('The Avengers'), Matt Fraction ('Sex Criminals') and Kelly Sue DeConnick ('Captain Marvel')." In a short article for *USA Today*, Brian Truitt quotes Palahniuk as saying that Tyler Durden will resurface as a mystical figure who "has been around for centuries," adding that the sequel allows him to explore more deeply resentments against his father (and what he heard others report about their fathers): "Now to find myself at the age that my father was when I was trashing him made me want to revisit it from the father's perspective." In totality, reviews confirm the graphic form lends itself to Palahniuk's innovative recasting of *Fight Club*.

As most familiar with him acknowledge, Palahniuk is definitely not the reticent literary recluse who refuses to engage in interpretations of his own creations. He likes publicity, and he is very good at assuming his own distinctive persona. This said, Palahniuk has contributed vastly to the dispersion of *Fight Club* ideology that has saturated the American cultural landscape. In *Fight Club 2*, Palahniuk revitalizes what he has sown. He is not totally destroying what exists, but he certainly makes noticeable changes to its components. Implementing Campbell's theory more explicitly allows him to fertilize what is already flourishing. Honestly, if Palahniuk is now the face of American transgressive fiction, Campbell was likewise the guru of American archetypal criticism. To return to Sandra Newman's claim that Palahniuk writes for people who do not necessarily read often, Campbell was known as the kind, affable, dedicated teacher who simplified mythology for a general audience not particularly interested in the technical aspects of anthropology. Campbell's famous "Follow your bliss" was a mantra for the pursuit of happiness in the 1980s, and his template to demonstrate that myths are essentially variations of a single epic master story revolutionized how initiation narratives are interpreted. Developing the partnership with Campbell reinforces Palahniuk's ethical credibility in portraying Tyler as a trickster responsible for fatherly dysfunction and masculine alienation.

In *The Hero's Journey*, a collection of his interviews, Campbell offers a way of looking at life that corresponds to many of Palahniuk's commentaries about his own beliefs. During a panel honoring the release of *The Hero's Journey* film in 1987, after asked if the view of the earth from the moon has become a major mythology, Campbell points out that seeing an image is not enough: "A mythology doesn't come from the head; a mythology comes from the heart ... how do you *feel* about people? Not how do you think about people. But what is the feeling system? A mythology comes from the feeling and an experience—not from thinking. The difference between an ideology and a mythology is the difference between the ego and the self: ideology comes from the thinking system and mythology comes from the *being*" (266). Palahniuk wants his readers to indeed *feel* what they are reading, to internalize the message articulated through his comic grotesque presentation of reality. His negative critics fail to recognize how the Rabelaisian descriptions evoke visceral responses that are grounded within the consciousness. Not many critics read Palahniuk's work to ruminate over eternal philosophical conundrums or to contemplate humanity within some grand cosmic plan. People read Palahniuk for the experience, and the gifts are, admittedly, entertainment first and knowledge second. Astute readers move past the entertainment into Palahniuk's themes. One of Campbell's standard points is a Buddhist dictum that life is difficult, a proposition consistently crystalized in Palahniuk's fiction and in dirty realism. Campbell's instructions are not passively to accept this inevitability but to fight it as hard and as long as possible. He declares in the same interview, "Now there's a wonderful saying in the Buddhist world: 'Life is joyful participation in the sorrows of the world.' All life is sorrowful. You are not going to change that. It's all right for everyone else to be sorrowful, but what about you being sorrowful? Well, participate" (267). This profound point must be stressed: Palahniuk believes adamantly in participation—to act is to fight.

In "Myth and the Modern World," the first chapter in the edited version of *The Power of Myth* interviews, there is a section that is likely the source for Palahniuk's "secondary father" theory. In their discussion of marriage, Moyers questions Campbell about the function of marriage in mythology. Campbell explains that "marriage is a relationship" but "not a simple love affair," and he clarifies the first stage motivates the couple to bear children, and the second stage determines the couple's personal bond to one another (7). Campbell mentions two alternative results of these stages. If there is a true commitment, then the effect is "beautifully realized" (7); if there is not, Campbell predicts the father leaving: "Daddy will fall in love with some little nubile girl and run off, and Mother will be left with an empty house and heart, and will have to work it out on her own, in her own way" (7). After he ruminates over the deterioration of the marriage ritual, Moyers asks, "What happens when a society no longer embraces a powerful myth?" Campbell responds, "What we've got on our hands [in 1987]. If you want to find out what it means to have a society without any rituals, read *The New York Times*" (8).

Moyers asks the question to which Palahniuk refers in his Afterword to *Fight Club*. In "Myth and the Modern World," after an interchange, Moyer poses, "where do these kids get their myths today?" In an extremely relevant passage, Campbell responds, "They make them up themselves. This is why we have graffiti all over the city. These kids have their own gangs and their own initiations and their own morality, and they're doing the best they can. But they're dangerous because their own laws are not those of the city. They have not been initiated into our society" (8). Campbell links the increase in violence to a lack of a collective American ethos (8), and he warns that law, distinct from an ethos, maintains order among diverse communities (9). In "The First Storytellers," also in *The Power of Myth*, continuing on this topic, Campbell remarks, "A ritual is an enactment of a myth. By participating in a ritual, you are participating in a myth" (103). Moyers asks, "We have none of those rites today, do we?" To which, Campbell replies, "I'm afraid we don't. So the youngsters invent them themselves, and you have these raiding gangs, and so forth—that is self-rendered initiation" (103). In all likelihood, Palahniuk refers to these comments by Campbell in the Afterword. Moreover, he is probably considering Campbell's description of a mentor as a "second father." If Campbell speaks about this point directly, he does so outside his major writings.

Regardless, in the hero's journey, the mentor definitely assumes a parental role. In *The Hero with a Thousand Faces*, Campbell introduces this figure as a primary helper: "For those who have not refused the call, the first encounter of the hero-journey is with the protective figure (often a little old crone or old man) who provides the adventurer with amulets against the dragon forces he is about to pass" (69). He next describes the mentor as someone who in contemporary positions could be a drill sergeant or a sports coach (to apply Palahniuk's comparisons): "Not infrequently, the supernatural helper is masculine in form. In fairy lore it may be some little fellow of the wood, some wizard, hermit, shepherd, or smith, who appears, to supply the amulets and advice that the hero will require. The higher mythologies develop the role in the great figure of the guide, the teacher, the ferryman, the conductor of souls to the underworld" (72). Campbell claims that this mentor teaches the hero to *participate*: "Herewith the world-discrediting insight of the monk, 'All life is sorrowful,' is combined with the world-begetting affirmative of the father: 'Life must be!' In full awareness of the life anguish of the creatures of his hand, in full consciousness of the roaring wilderness of pains, the brain-splitting fires of the deluded, self-ravaging, lustful, angry universe of his creation, this divinity acquiesces in the deed of supplying life to life" (146). Generally, Campbell likes to use Obi-Wan Kenobi from *Star Wars* as the exemplary mentor, praising George Lucas's film as creating a contemporary monomyth. Expanding the circumference of helpers from "secondary father" to those within a community, Campbell asserts that these figures can assume a number of identities, human or otherwise (326). Consequently, he anticipates the problematic reunion between father and son, and this is precisely the dilemma Palahniuk presents in *Fight Club 2*. In Campbell's monomyth, the son is revitalized through the father's atonement: "The problem of the hero going to meet the father is to open his soul beyond terror to such a degree that he will be ripe to understand how the sickening and insane tragedies of this vast and ruthless cosmos are completely validated in the majesty of Being. The hero transcends life with its peculiar blind spot and for a moment rises to a glimpse of the source. He beholds the face of the father, understand—and the two are atoned" (147).

Of course, Tyler is not the father (even though at the end of *Fight Club 2* he is prepared to accept this role). In a 2015 interview with *BuzzFeed*, Palahniuk explains his motivation behind "Expedition." If this story is the prequel to *Fight Club*, Palahniuk needed to apply a different speech register in the dialogue to establish his trickster's idiosyncratic demeanor. Palahniuk tells the interviewers that he channeled H.P. Lovecraft, Edgar Allan Poe, and Nathaniel Hawthorne the previous summer in Spain "to unlearn all of the minimalism" so he could "expand on the Tyler Durden mythology." His goal was to take the story forward as well as backward chronologically, stretching the parameters of *Fight Club* so that it did not seem only about one character within a restricted place in time, to increase the universality of the tale ("Chuck"). As was mentioned in the previous chapter, and not to rehash the same information in this section, "Expedition" contains a lampoon of the pedantic and egotistical narrator whom readers like to see get his comeuppance as an exploitative investigative reporter. The stilted Victorian language provides a temporal reference. True to form, the story drips with Lovecraft's ostentatiously gothic stylistic influence. The fairly standard sequence for these types of mystery plots is anticipated, as Tyler tricks the self-deceived narrator into a darkness that psychoanalytically turns out to be emblematic of the mystical dark space in which fathers are separated from their sons and later sons are returned to their fathers. Therefore, Tyler tricks the narrator, presumably the narrator in *Fight Club*'s grandfather, into the pitch blackness to confront a monster that is both other and himself. As the father leads his son deeper into the paternal unconscious, readers could consider this both positive and negative. During the same incident, to apply Campbell's ideas, there are actions affecting two generations, the father/son separation and the father's atonement. As the trickster, Tyler is putting into motion the impetus of a son's resentment for his father while concurrently assuaging that damage through a son's empathic forgiveness for his father's neglect. Palahniuk is correct that this story helps to generate the myth (setting up the protocol) of Tyler as trickster. Furthermore, the parodic content and style of "Expedition" imitates Palahniuk's strategy in *Fight Club 2*.

Campbell bases his archetypes on the seminal work of Carl Jung, who has written extensively on the trickster figure. Pertinent to this study, Jung positions this character in the context of Bakhtinian carnival. In "On the Psychology of the Trickster-Figure," referring to comparisons Paul Radin made between Native American trickster mythology and medieval instances of carnival, particularly the reversals within the power hierarchy (135), Jung categorizes this figure as both demonic and redemptive (136). Noteworthy in his definition is that the trickster "fights" himself, of course a major component of *Fight Club*: "He is a forerunner of the savior, and, like him, God, man, and animal at once. He is both subhuman and superhuman, a bestial and divine being, whose chief and most alarming characteristic is his unconsciousness. Because of it he is deserted by his (evidently human) companions. He is so unconscious of himself that his body is not a unity, and his two hands fight each other" (143).

Jung believes that the civilized person has neglected the trickster, but he asserts that when people "get together in masses and submerge the individual, the shadow is mobilized," thus liberating the trickster "shadow" habitating in the psyche of each person but realized through the crowd, a community (147). Jung argues that a person "looks to the State for salvation" from the negative effects of this entity (147). In a crucial point pertinent to *Fight Club*, Jung asserts that this presence, the "expression of the polaristic structure of the psyche" (149), causes a break in consciousness. He describes this split in terms of a consciousness and its reflection, which becomes an autonomous entity (149–50). Applying this theory to Palahniuk's narratives, Jung theoretically predicts the creation of Tyler as the split personality who functions as the trickster figure in the *Fight Club* mythology.[4] Palahniuk's trickster is definitely affiliated with Friedrich Nietzsche's Dionysian chaos (inclined to violence) rather than Apollonian order (apt to rationalize). On the other hand, the wise old man is paradoxically Apollonian.

An extremely important point, one not yet addressed fully by those who study *Fight Club*, is that Palahniuk puts Campbell's theory of "fight" as an initiation ritual into practice. Moreover, no one has addressed in any depth how *Fight Club* ideology becomes actualized through *Fight Club* mythology. In "On Becoming an Adult," Campbell describes rituals in which fighting is a vital component to masculine maturation. He explains that in simple societies boys are inculcated to fear the masks that men wear in rituals. The masks represent the gods, or what he calls the "personifications [of] the powers [that] structure societies." During the rite of initiation, boys are forced to confront the men donning masks. Using New Guinea culture as an illustration, Campbell explains how the boy must fight the man wearing the mask, in effect battling a god. The man eventually allows the boy to win, places the ritualistic mask on the boy, and passes along the responsibility of promoting the myth. As Campbell emphasizes, the boy has "broken past the image as fact and understands the image as metaphor," and the boy now represents "what the metaphor stands for." Through this process, Campbell claims the "infantile ego" has died. Therefore, the boy is freed from the "psychological bondage" of subservience to parents (asking for approval or reproof) and has been liberated into the "mature ego of authority." For those who think Palahniuk condones random violence (i.e., fight club is merely fighting), Campbell provides a plausible explanation for the activity as ritual. Combined with his commentary about secondary fathers, Palahniuk's fight pushes the combatant past the infantile ego into the mature ego of authority. Tyler as trickster is the catalyst for this ritual by separating the person from parental-type oppressive agencies, hence moving the person toward literally standing alone to engage with societal and cultural masks that provide the definitions of normative masculinity (and femininity). The fight initiates the youth into adulthood, taking on all of the responsibilities that this entails.

In *Fight Club 2*, Palahniuk reverses the hierarchal structure in *Fight Club* by redefining the major characters' roles, consequently reconfiguring their personas, into hyperreal versions of themselves. Significantly, the thoroughly postmodern Palahniuk, one skeptical of totalizing principles and cynical of grand narratives, calls into question his own ideological constructions. Fight club and Project Mayhem are governed by rules that support the ideological structure. Those who do not follow the rules are exiled; those who do are praised and rewarded. Ironically, all of this imitates the process through which people embrace ideologies even though they intuitively recognize the internal contradictions beneath the façade of stability. In the transcribed version of *The Power of Myth*, Moyers asks Campbell, "What happens when people become legends? Can you say, for example, that John Wayne has become a myth?" Campbell responds, "When a person becomes a model for other people's lives, he has moved into the sphere of being mythologized" (20). In other words, Wayne becomes hyperreal. Palahniuk's characters transform into something similar. To those in fight club and Project Mayhem, Tyler is hyperreal, known by what he represents rather than what he is.

Before demonstrating how Palahniuk does all of this in *Fight Club* and *Fight Club 2*, Žižek's reading of *Fight Club* needs to be revisited. In his review of Sophie Fiennes's film about Žižek titled *The Pervert's Guide to Ideology*, Yosef Brody reaffirms Žižek's contention that the "hidden universal framework of ideology must be unmasked in order for liberating political change to be given a chance." Once people expose an ideology, they can dismantle it. Brody acknowledges the ensuing contradiction: "Paradoxically, it hurts to step outside of it and examine it critically; by default we tend to resist seeing the world from any angle other than the one fed to us." Palahniuk refers explicitly in *Fight Club 2* to this paradox. One only needs to think of Poe's placement of the infamous epistle right out in the open, the last place to look, in "The Purloined Letter." Palahniuk reveals the influence of Campbell's theory through the comic grotesque without much subterfuge. When Sebastian attempts to infiltrate Project Chaos occupying the dilapidated Paper Street house, in the first frame, the head of recruitment observes, looking out over all of the men waiting the three full days to prove their dedication for acceptance, "Textbook Joseph Campbell" (63). In adjoining text boxes, the narrator claims, "The way Campbell explained it, young men need a secondary father to finish raising them. Beyond their biological father, they need a surrogate, traditionally a minister or a coach or a military officer" (63). Echoing both Palahniuk and Campbell, the recruiter elucidates this is why "street gangs are so appealing," and he points out that "**traditional** mentors" (Palahniuk's emphasis) have forgotten the importance of their roles (63). On the next page, Palahniuk offers speech balloons with comments that religious leaders, sports coaches, and military leaders have failed in their jobs as mentors, corresponding directly to what he expressed in multiple interviews. Early in *Fight Club 2*, Palahniuk clearly identifies what he wants readers to see as the dominant theme in *Fight Club* mythology. Importantly, the narrator is telling his story about Tyler after the experience, but even as he reports what he knows, he seems confused about Tyler's true identity. He seems to "resist seeing the world" as it is, still unclear about what really has occurred.

Not too far into *Fight Club 2*, Palahniuk offers references to Christian ideology. There are two panels showing Moses wandering long enough, as the text boxes indicate, to eradicate the generation that held onto principles attached to slavery ideology (66–67). Without gutters separating the panels, Sebastian speaks to Marla while holding the Holy Bible, and Junior reads from what might be the same book (54). This is offset later with five panels having pale blue backdrops (not the typical beige) with Sebastian taking the Bible away from Junior because he is "way too young" to understand the content (75). On the next page, there are three panels illustrating verbatim Genesis 6: 11–13, which is also tattooed on the bartender's neck when Sebastian wants a drink (19) and is again tattooed on the Project Chaos disciple when Sebastian first arrives at the house (68). In this manner, Palahniuk validates *Fight Club* mythology through its alliance with Christianity, as the tenets of this ideology are laid out on the page. All of the words from the Bible are not visible, but the passage includes these verses from the New Revised Standard Version of the Holy Bible: "11 Now the earth was corrupt in God's sight, and the earth was filled with violence. 12 And God saw that the earth was corrupt; for all flesh had corrupted its ways upon the earth. 13 And God said to Noah, 'I have determined to make an end of all flesh, for the earth is filled with violence because of them; now I am going to destroy them along with the earth.'" By literally equating Project Chaos's agenda with God's prophesy, as expressed through the Old Testament, Palahniuk creates a carnivalesque parody, an imitation of the sacred word of authority, hence elevating Tyler's role as the master trickster, Satan.

In the Palahniuk oeuvre, this is consistent with Satan as trickster per divine scriptwriter in *Damned* and *Doomed*, although Satan in those texts is vastly different from Tyler in these stories. Lampooning the cerebral occupation of psychotherapy, Palahniuk has Dr. Wrong proclaim to Sebastian, "He's an **archetype** [Palahniuk's emphasis]. Tyler works like a superstition or a prejudice. He becomes part of the lens through which you see the world" (152). To emphasize the plausibility of a text influencing a vast array of readers, Palahniuk offers an intertextual reference to mass suicides known as Werther Fever, caused by the main character's suicide in Johann Wolfgang von Goethe's *The Sorrows of Young Werther* published in 1774 (169-70). Dr. Wrong's comment is actually correct when he informs Sebastian about the transcendence of fictional characters as models of behaviors (170). Through this sequence of references, Palahniuk makes his recasting of *Fight Club* transparent. He offers examples of texts that provide principles that people trust as true and follow no matter their initial reluctance. These principles comprise the ideology that determines mainstream normalcy. According to this standard, those who are "corrupt" and filled with "violence" will be vanquished.

Before it can be reversed, the ideology must be created, and *Fight Club* might not actually represent all that Palahniuk claims. Furthermore, *Fight Club* might not transition smoothly from its prequel "Exhibition." Considering how he advertises Campbell's theory of secondary fathers, Palahniuk might be projecting what he thinks his first novel promotes. At the end of the first chapter of *Fight Club*, the narrator reveals Tyler's "real target" is the national museum, the repository of American artifacts (14). Campbell warns in *The Hero with a Thousand Faces*, "Wherever the poetry of myth is interpreted as biography, history, or science, it is killed. The living images become only remote facts of a distant time or sky. Furthermore, it is never difficult to demonstrate that as science and history mythology is absurd. When a civilization begins to reinterpret its mythology in this way, the life goes out of it, temples become museums, and the link between the two perspectives is dissolved" (249). Tyler's goal is not only to demolish the iconic structures of capitalist consumerism but to destroy the museum in which mythology is housed as ideology. The narrator admits, "I don't want Marla, and Tyler doesn't want me around, not any more. This isn't about *love* as in *caring*. This is about *property* as in *ownership*" (14). As such, he acknowledges the destruction of the ideology over the mythology. Significantly, the narrator looks forward to this obliteration as the precursor to mythologization: "Maybe we would become a legend, maybe not. No, I say, but wait. Where would Jesus be if no one had written the gospels" (15). In the last chapter, at least in the beginning, the narrator appears to have died, in his "father's house" as if he were experiencing an afterlife. This could suggest atonement with his father, as in a deity, since he names the location as "heaven" (206) and has what appears psychotherapy with God. When God asks if he realized people are snowflakes, "manifestations of love," he replies nihilistically: "We are not special. We are not crap or trash, either. We just are. We just are, and what happens just happens" (207). This is rejected by God, potentially providing an optimistic ending. Obviously affiliated with Project Mayhem, calling him "Mr. Durden" and saying, "We look forward to getting you back" (208), the orderly anticipates *Fight Club 2*. Prophetically, the narrator could foresee all of this in the first chapter: "You don't understand any of it, and then you just die" (12).

Working through both novels helps readers to understand, however, the enigmatic ending. As I state elsewhere, in two submitted manuscripts (see the second endnote), *Fight Club* begins with chapters two and four advocating recovery ideology. In particular, after the narrator is advised by his physician to witness "real pain" suffered by those afflicted with brain parasites, bone diseases, brain dysfunctions, and various cancers, he describes meetings with two major figures, Chloe and Bob (19). Often capitalized as "Narrator" or called "Joe" because of the self-reflexive statements—such as "I am Joe's Clenching Bowels" (62)—the speaker repeats in the third chapter how he is almost an automaton traveling in his position as a recall campaign coordinator, and perceptive readers will detect that Tyler, in his job as projectionist, is a manifestation of his own psyche. Two clues are the repetition of "I know this because Tyler knows this" and the back-and-forth descriptions of the narrator and Tyler, as in "You wake up at SeaTac, again. You're a projectionist and you're tired and angry" (29). In the sixth chapter, when asked about injuries, the narrator correctly responds, "I did this to myself" (48). There are two points, incidentally, that many readers might overlook but that foreshadow future events in the novel. After the narrator mentions that he first met Tyler on a nude beach, he comments, almost as an aside, "Tyler had been around a long time before we met" (32). If Tyler is a conceptual archetype, the reference to "long time" infers his generational presence as trickster who separates fathers from sons. A more plausible hypothesis is, considering Jung's theory, Tyler has been buried in the narrator's subconscious and has been waiting for the optimum moment to cross over from the darkness into the light. Moreover, the narrator consciously states, "I had to know what Tyler was doing while I was asleep. If I could wake up in a different place, at a different time, could I wake up as a different person?" (33). In the introduction and in the conclusion, the narrator emphasizes that he remembers everything that occurred, substantiating his credibility, but readers obviously recognize his unreliability. There is not any extensive background concerning his family, no mention of his separation from his father. However, the psychotic episodes infer something from the narrator's past are causing his current situation.

The prequel and sequel to *Fight Club* explain why Tyler exists. Following Palahniuk's prompting, readers can take for granted that what happened to the father in "Expedition" is the root reason to the narrator's psychosis. In *Fight Club*, the narrator mentions that his father was incapable of giving him meaningful advice about life, such as when the father recommends that he simply get married (51). Later, the narrator sarcastically comments there was no advice from his parents that he would "embroider on a cushion" (66). Suggestively, in a fit of self-pity, the narrator says that he was "dumped" by his father, inferring abandonment, physical or psychological (134). If the prequel is believed, the narrator's father must have been duped into exile and then experienced a reunion with his own absent father. Nonetheless, people in the support groups function as secondary fathers. The narrator's attention to Chloe and Bob illustrate their significance as helpers, although neither offers the significant guidance affiliated with a mentor. The support communities—people who not only deal with discomfort but also recover from affliction—provide the lifelines for the narrator, as those participants intervene to save him on top of the Parker-Morris Building. Tyler's role is a mixture of trickster and mentor, and Palahniuk reinforces Tyler's mystical presence simply through his spectrality. Considering Campbell's words, Tyler is metaphorical, an imaginative construction, and once he is cast as a flesh-and-blood entity, he loses his mythological dimensions. Tyler's goal is not at this juncture to lure the narrator into the darkness only to pursue, fueled by resentment, the monster-as-father. Conversely, he is more the parental super-ego who affirms, since he is a part of the narrator's psyche, an empowerment strategy born from support groups but transformed into fight club and revitalized into Project Mayhem. In *Fight Club*, Tyler as mentor may take the solution to the problem of masculine empowerment too far. He advocates anarchy propelled by the Paper Street Soap Company, he enacts minor proletariat retaliation against the bourgeois, and he promotes major anti-capitalist aggression toward corporations. Later, in *Fight Club 2*, Tyler separates Junior from Sebastian. In this second novel, there is evidence that Tyler existed before the narrator claims and, as trickster, instigated the death of Sebastian's (and the narrator's) father and mother through two separate fires (39–40). With the help of Tyler, Junior attempts to kill Sebastian and Marla through a well-planned house fire (32–33). Outside the boundaries of a panel, Sebastian bears the stigmata from the red-hot doorknob, with the text box stating, "Whatever he calls himself, his destiny has come home to roost" (33). This must be emphasized: in *Fight Club*, Tyler is the mentor; in *Fight Club 2*, Tyler is the trickster.

Essentially, fight club is a carnival, with men assuming personas in the early Sunday morning hours that are different from who they are in their commonplace lives. Considering this, Tyler's duel function is not surprising. The purpose of fight club is to establish community, in much the same way as through support groups. Anonymity is sacrosanct, and identity is only revealed in fight club and later Project Mayhem when a member has died. The arena of fight club is a microcosm of the larger rule-governed social order, and Project Mayhem organizes that structure into a militaristic machine. Undoubtedly, Palahniuk is grotesque (not so comic) in his descriptions of the physical aftermath following fights, paying attention to bruises, blood, and other features. The narrator is explicit about this carnivalesque world: "Who guys are in fight club is not who they are in the real world. Even if you told the kid in the copy center that he had a good fight, you wouldn't be talking to the same man. Who I am in fight club is not someone my boss knows. After a night in fight club, everything in the real world gets the volume turned down. Nothing can piss you off. Your word is law, and if other people break that law or question you, even that doesn't piss you off" (49). When the narrator has his first fight with Tyler (actually himself), he reacts against everything that aggravates him: "Instead of Tyler, I felt finally I could get my hands on everything in the world that didn't work" (53).

When he queries Tyler about what or whom he was fighting, really posing this question to his alter ego about himself, he is surprised by the answer. Literally, the narrator is fighting others like himself who enjoy the temporary control this carnival provides. Psychologically, fight club provides much more than this. Tyler's response is that the narrator is fighting his father (53). The narrator retorts, "Maybe we didn't need a father to complete ourselves" (54). Later in *Fight Club*, Tyler tells the narrator, "You weren't really fighting me…. You said so yourself. You were fighting everything you hate in your life" (167). The narrator's self-talk with his persona is very important. Even though he realizes that Tyler is a "projection," a "disassociative personality disorder," a "psychogenic fugue state," finally a "hallucination" (168), the narrator still admits: "I love everything about Tyler Durden, his courage and his smarts. His nerve. Tyler is funny and charming and forceful and independent, and men look up to him and expect him to change their world. Tyler is capable and free, and I am not" (174). Tyler allows the narrator to role-play the idealized projection of true manhood, and Marla's lust for Tyler in *Fight Club 2* validates the desirability of this version of masculinity. The sexualized Marla wants a masculine Tyler over an effeminate Sebastian who controls his psychosis, as a rational person would do, through medication. Tyler is not inhibited by rules, but Sebastian allows his life to be dictated by them.

The relationship between the narrator and Marla in *Fight Club* is obviously dysfunctional. Granted, the marriage between Sebastian and Marla is not strong in the beginning of *Fight Club 2*, with Marla cuckolding her husband for wild unrestrained sex with Tyler (and Cameron Stewart's sexual scenes in vivid colors illustrate the carnal intensity of her attraction to Tyler). Frankly, Marla in *Fight Club* is for the most part neurotic before she is redeemed during the conclusion. When she tries to attract him in the kitchen, as she literally performs a sexually enticing strip tease, the narrator is oblivious to her intentions (67). Even though he instinctively feels as he has been having sex with Marla all night (56), and Marla discouragingly admits that she cannot maintain his attention (68), the narrator seems to want a relationship with his competitor for prime support group gatherings. At any rate, he perceives Marla as a femme fatale for Tyler's affections. If he notices hints of Tyler's true identity, he appears to ignore them concerning Marla, not realizing that the three of them are never in the same room (70) or wondering why Tyler is so adamant about his not being mentioned to Marla (72). There is no foreshadowing that the narrator and Marla will spawn a son, and this is strengthened by Marla's apparent abhorrence for motherhood. In the famous line (also in *Fight Club 2*), the narrator declares that Marla considered becoming pregnant only for the opportunity to abort Tyler's progeny (59). Different from her counterpart in *Fight Club 2*, Marla is self-destructive and self-loathing. She regularly attempts suicide at the Regent Hotel (58), she tricks her mother into sending her liposuctioned fat (93), she burns herself with cigarettes sitting in the kitchen (61), and when saved from coming too close to dying, Marla demeans herself to rescuers (61). A change occurs when Marla finds her second lump, and she and the narrator are able to communicate meaningfully (102). Even though the narrator gave her a black eye, Marla genuinely cares for him, and the progression of "like" (197) to "love" (199)—rationalizing that if Tyler loves her then he must love her (198)—anticipates the relationship in *Fight Club 2* that will produce Junior.

In *Fight Club*, if his relationship with Marla helps him to love, his interaction with Chloe and Bob teach him to feel compassion. In the support groups, the narrator seems to feel sympathy for Chloe at the Above and Beyond meeting. He introduces her with obvious pity: "The little skeleton of a woman named Chloe with the seat of pants hanging down and sad and empty, Chloe tells me the worst thing about her brain parasites was no one would have sex with her. Here she was, so close to death that her life insurance policy had paid off with seventy-five thousand bucks, and all Chloe wanted was to get laid for the last time. Not intimacy, sex.... Our Chloe, however, is a skeleton dipped in yellow wax. Chloe looking the way she is, I am nothing" (19–20). Before going too far into her situation, the narrator reports that her sister Glenda verified that Chloe had died (35), so readers know this before they actually get details of her appearance. The narrator portrays Chloe as grotesque: "Picture Chloe's popular skeleton the size of an insect, running through the vaults and galleries of her innards at two in the morning.... At night, Chloe ran around the maze of her own collapsing veins and burst tubes spraying hot lymph. Nerves surface as trip wires in the tissue. Abscesses swell in the tissue around her as hot white pearls.... Chloe's splashing through the ankle-deep backup of renal fluid from her failed kidneys" (36). He completes this section with a countdown to Chloe's death juxtaposed with a condemnation of Marla's masquerading as a victim (37). The narrator's comments about Bob are not as warm but still sympathetic. The narrator points out that Big Bob was once a famous body builder but is currently known as a steroid "juicer" with gynecomastic "bitch tits" (21) who has emotional "jerking sobs" (17). Bob is the central figure at the Remaining Men Together meeting, but he is later recognized for his fidelity to Project Mayhem. When he is killed by police who mistake his cordless drill for a firearm, he is given a hero's wake. The narrator repeats what is yelled at every fight club after the incident: "His name is Robert Paulsen and he is forty-eight years old" (177). Big Bob, the "big cheesebread" (39) is granted legendary status.

Up front, Palahniuk warns his audience in *Fight Club 2* against elevating *Fight Club* to the level of doctrine. He seems to be keeping in mind Campbell's assertion that ideology is intellectual (understood through thought) and mythology is feeling (internalized through action). By creating a mythology around *Fight Club*, literally enclosing it within "Expedition" as the prequel and *Fight Club 2* as the sequel, Palahniuk is seditiously debunking his own paradigm. This is pure Palahniuk irony. As an event, fight club is a ritual in which there is an initiation (as first timers must fight) of men into a community that collectively provides mentoring into manhood. Just as Campbell claims children fight adults to earn the privilege of wearing the masks, men fight to transcend themselves as individuals toward inclusion within a higher consciousness of masculinity. This is the myth that *Fight*

Club promotes. As an ideology, giving concepts and precepts structure that is, in Althusserian terms, documented, categorized, and then enforced, fight club is perverted into Project Mayhem and Project Chaos, systems that distort the meaning by reifying the spiritual into the political. A major component of fight club is personal sacrifice for the benefit of the community. There are constant references to "hitting bottom" as the opportunity for spiritual transcendence. In a famous quotation from *Fight Club* already mentioned in the first chapter of this study, Tyler philosophizes, "It's only after you've lost everything ... that you're free to do anything" (70). Through the support groups, the narrator learns that "Losing all hope was freedom" (22), and through his interactions with those like him, he reflects on his family, particularly his father: "I knew my dad for about six years, but I don't remember anything. My dad, he starts a new family in a new town about every six years. This isn't so much a family as it's like he sets up a franchise. What you see at fight club is a generation of men raised by women" (50). Project Mayhem does not officially take shape until the sixteenth chapter of *Fight Club*, and Tyler's aim is unmistakably political. The narrator contends the ultimate goal of Project Mayhem is the complete obliteration of civilization (125), causing the entire "world to hit bottom" (123).

To carry this out, Palahniuk refuses to take himself too seriously. Through the graphic novel form of *Fight Club 2*, he tears down his own ideology. Even in his first novel, Palahniuk calls attention to the distortion of support groups into "Organized Chaos. The Bureaucracy of Anarchy" (119). The exploitation of fight club is illustrated by popular media stereotyping the action as pugilistic pummeling for the sake of satisfying peoples' primal urges to inflict pain, in many ways reinforcing preconceptions that everything about fight club cultivates toxic masculinity. Fight club is not about getting two toddlers to hit one another, not about sparing two demented geriatric patients, not about simply hitting, punching, and whatever else occurs during face-to-face physical assault. Those who are truly disciples of the novel know this; those who only know the novel through the media propaganda do not. Fighting is the action associated with the ritual, and the ritual is what allows the participants to connect with a higher consciousness. In *Fight Club*, Chloe's leading support group people through mediations, having them slide on ice with their power animals (2), a memorable scene in Fincher's film, is an example of such a transcendent action. Palahniuk mocks his own ideology by exposing its hypocrisy. In *Fight Club 2*, Palahniuk's allusions to the Bible, references to Campbell, and intrusions into the text, all within his use of the comic grotesque, allow him to succeed in his enterprise. Conversely, fight club as an ideology, digested piecemeal when the consumption is beneficial, is no different from any other political agenda that Palahniuk has satirized in his many texts.

Eight. "Human beings don't cultivate ideas" 193

There are many intertextual links between *Fight Club* and *Fight Club 2*. Not far into the story, Marla begins infiltrating support groups as she had done previously. Sebastian does not, and even though he follows Marla to the progeria group, he only observes Marla's unloading reasons for her self-pity to those that, unlike the support groups in *Fight Club*, she clearly does not resemble in any manner—the short, elderly-looking, large-headed, thin-bodied young-yet-old participants are very different from thirty-five-year-old Marla looking like a well-groomed young professional female (13). Palahniuk's mastermind thirteen-year-old Brandon Whittier suffered from progeria—turning this manipulatively to his advantage—in *Haunted*. In *Fight Club 2*, this Marla who speaks about being "fucked back to life" (14) contrasts with her predecessor who seems to participate in sex in her mid-twenties with much less enthusiasm. There are references to Sebastian's father marrying many times (48), as mentioned in *Fight Club*. The bartender whom Sebastian encounters who calls him "Mr. Durden" (19) resembles the bartender whom he meets in *Fight Club* who offers the salutation "Welcome back, sir" (158). The reference in *Fight Club 2* to "mass-produced Ikea ideologies" (20) corresponds with the previous text's criticism of material status-symbol possessions (43–45). Sebastian's first return fight in *Fight Club 2* is with a grotesquely mutilated ten-year-older Angel Face (102), the handsome young man designated as "angel face" (128) after the narrator defeats him on the night Tyler created Project Mayhem (122) in *Fight Club*.

Of course, in *Fight Club 2*, the rules of fight club and its terrorist offshoot are identical. The term "snowflake" is given comparable significance in both stories. A contrast is Tyler's killing of the college student Raul Seymour (81) and the directed murder of Human Sacrifice Number 3683— (78–90) to the narrator's letting Korner Mart clerk Raymond K. Hessel live as long as Hessel follows his dream of becoming a veterinarian (151–55) in *Fight Club*. Project Mayhem's "blazing demon mask on the Hein Tower" in the first novel (121) is shown in a radiant Stewart visual in the second (73). The composition of substance abusers (77) in *Fight Club 2*'s Project Chaos and their sabotaging couches with used needles (68–69) corresponds with the addicts in *Fight Club*'s Project Mayhem (137) whom the narrator says could have been just as likely at an NA meeting as in the house on Paper Street (139). In *Fight Club 2*, the ploy to destroy all the famous art that Tyler does not like by severing arteries and spraying the objects with blood relates to the incident in *Fight Club* during which the narrator's abduction via a Cadillac serves as a test of his devotion to the cause. This sequence in *Fight Club 2* provides vividly grotesque panels, with vibrant redness oozing over the gutters and splashing onto the pages, making one full page completely obfuscated (124–35). In the companion section in *Fight Club*, the mechanic driving the car wants God and everyone to recognize their names after they set fire to the Louvre and vandalize the *Mona Lisa* (141). In *Fight Club 2*, two important panels (one almost touched by random spermatozoa crossing gutters) depict the new Marla remembering herself as the punk-looking old Marla exploring her "root chakra" (204–05) during therapeutic meditation. The first novel includes several more sympathetic portrayals of these support group sessions. There are, of course, other similarities between the books, but these examples help to verify that *Fight Club 2* is a parody of *Fight Club*.

Many of the scenes that display the comic grotesque pertain to Sebastian and Marla's relationship. If Marla tried to persuade the narrator in *Fight Club* that they shared a compassionate intimacy, in this version, she obviously has a licentious flame burning for Tyler. Granted, at the end of *Fight Club* Marla appears to have finally figured out what is going on with the narrator—that the one whom she thought was Tyler is indeed the narrator. However, Stewart's illustrations in *Fight Club 2* show a highly sexualized Marla who yearns for Tyler. For instance, Marla whispers into Sebastian's ear, "Tyler.... Deliver me from this bland, boring life" (24). This is followed by an explosion of love-making—accented by "barks" per doggy position, vibrant reds and oranges with a Zeppelin exploding and trains colliding in flames—exhibiting her and Tyler having passionate intercourse (25). This is prior to Tyler's attempted rape of Marla, only going so far as cunnilingus (84–85). A sensualized Marla is seen in her post-coitus afterglow, with the text box "Marla looks like she's died and gone to heaven" (26). Wanting to find where Junior was taken, Marla, in camisole and panties, for a moment reminisces about sex with Tyler, remembering the ecstasy with a characteristic cigarette in her hand (51). Marking the contrast, she then smashes Sebastian with the toilet tank cover (55–57).

Marla seeks out creator Palahniuk to find her son, not necessarily to help Sebastian. Tracking Palahniuk through "Bite Club," "Pint Club," "Raw Fuck Club," and "Film Club," with the text box stating "Fun Fact—The real-life clubs cited here all have names inspired by the original fight club" (86–87), as all of these are also cited in the Afterword (211–12), Marla finally demands in "Write Club" to know the location of her son (89).[5] Palahniuk's asking her not to bother him and his cadre of fellow writers is almost an intermission in the story to call attention to the apparent farce. Humorously, at "Quilt Club," where Marla asks the babysitter Tracy if she has seen Junior, Marla notices she has lost a nail as one of the women gets "marching orders" through Rize or Die to go to Mogadishu as a mercenary (92–93). Before Palahniuk's head is vividly blown off (in variegated colors), Marla is shown going to an abortion clinic, which refers to Marla's *Fight Club* declaration that she wants to have Tyler's abortion (260). Worth mentioning is that in *Fight Club* the narrator genuinely cares for Marla when she finds the second lump in her breast and discovers the hardening of lymph glands, but, in *Fight Club 2*, the changes in Marla's breasts only verify her pregnancy with Tyler's child (268). The graphics accentuate both the comedy and emphasize the grotesqueness of all these scenes.

Palahniuk takes many more liberties with comic grotesque descriptions of Chloe and Bob, reincarnated from the dead to function as conventional cartoon characters. They are definitely not their realistic personalities in *Fight Club*. Palahniuk afflicts Chloe with a different disease, at least when she is first presented, so he can lampoon the Make-A-Wish Foundation via the Magic Wand Foundation, which grants Chloe's request to send her and others to current political hot spots all over the world. Moreover, by giving a Space Monkey named Marshall the order of ISIS suicide bomber (98), Palahniuk sets boundaries in this pro–American "cleansing myth" (222) pitting "good" Chloe, Marla, and the support-group commandoes versus "evil" Tyler and everyone connected with Project Chaos. About the same time Marshall finds out his mission is related to ISIS, one of Chloe's crew learns he is going to Angola, with his adding, "Don't forget my AK-47" (98). While they are bonding during combat, Chloe confesses she is "OLD AND DECREPIT!" like Marla, and Stewart appropriately captures mid-thirties Marla's chagrin in the panel showing her response (113). The truth that Chloe was an imposter similar to Marla and Sebastian, not really having cancer but going to support groups to receive "love" (113–14), completely reinvents her character in *Fight Club*. Marla and Chloe's embracing demonstrates their total empathy (116), vastly different from their positions previously.

Undoubtedly, this is not the same Chloe portrayed in *Fight Club*. Palahniuk focuses on the travesty of Chloe admitting that she has been "fake dying" (146). However, right after expressing that she has a "malignancy," Chloe reveals that she adores black men (147), and then she and Marla discuss why Marla married Sebastian over delicacies catered through an air drop from Magic Wand (154–55). The situation becomes more hyperbolically impractical when Magic Wand provides an armada of planes to allow Chloe and her friends to parachute over Tyler's mansion and replicate a Special Forces attack—even though they are all supposedly disabled (189–95). The full-page illustration of these figures, one yelling, "Banzai!" (191) while another is in a wheelchair, another with a combat knife in his/her mouth, is hilariously absurd in its lampoon against ableism. The section devoted to Operation Inferno is equally outlandish in its portrayal of these unlikely soldiers. Tyler as a viral trickster, infecting generations of Sebastian's paternal bloodline—mapped out in a family tree (201)—and his caricature as the serpent in the Garden of Eden (218) offset the depictions of invasion. Sipping champagne with the Magic Wand organizer, Chloe turns out to be an incredibly strong and capable ally to make sure the bad people are punished (244).

Bob does not enjoy the same rejuvenation in *Fight Club 2*. He functions solely as a monster, with half a skull, swinging breasts, and hulk-like intensity. Bob makes his first appearance in a panel with Marla and Chloe leaving Palahniuk and his female colleague's writing group. Palahniuk has reported in interviews that he is loyal, most of the time, to his group, and these are cartoon versions of his real-life friends (91). In his next appearance, Bob saves Marla and Chloe as they are chatting, not paying attention to potential mortar fire on their location. No frontal view of Bob is displayed, only a side or back view of his hideously distorted features. One full page is dedicated (seven panels) to Big Bob's attack on the Rize or Die mortar unit. As he runs forward, there is a speech balloon that says "Gynecomastia," and the mortar spotter asks, "Bitch tits?" (115). Stewart's illustrations embellish the swinging female-like breasts, with one panel offering a close-up of a hairy nipple (116). A later panel shows Tracy (Junior's babysitter) and her comrade have been killed (145). After this, Angel Face attempts to save Sebastian in the salt cavern (232), but Bob moves the boulder obstructing the escape, supernaturally creating a gigantic diamond (253), which Sebastian later gives to Marla as an anniversary present (257). Following the routine, the group chants, "His name was Robert Paulson" (253) to summon what is now a creature. The past verb tense is interesting compared to *Fight Club* because Big Bob is now dead in *Fight Club 2*, serving as a magical helper who shows up at the right time to help the good people. Palahniuk decided to make this superhuman character a gentle giant who, unlike his role in *Fight Club*, is not someone who requires hugs and physical closeness for comfort. This Bob is only functional, seemingly ruled more by instinct than rational faculties.

The comic grotesque is also promoted in the two endings of *Fight Club 2*. Dr. Wrong establishes that Tyler has "bred" Sebastian and Marla "like farm animals" (158) for the purpose of creating "a vehicle for himself" (159). Palahniuk uses Dr. Wrong to construct the myth of Tyler that is not in *Fight Club*, and the psychiatrist's attempt to exorcize Tyler from Sebastian exemplifies how Tyler can supernaturally occupy more than one body (220). The dismantling of fight club ideology takes place during the surprise ending when only the bad guys are killed and Palahniuk is allowed the privilege to gloat that he "tricked the trickster" (245), egotistically to garner praise from his caricatured associates. In metacommentary, however, Palahniuk questions his literary decisions as a belligerent mob complains uniformly that they do not like the ending. Likewise, these fictitious readers assert that they actually like Tyler, even considering him an optimist

(248). A frustrated Palahniuk—during an innovative depiction of authorial self-criticism—retorts, "In the book the ending was different" (248), only to hear the ironically comic return, "Wait—There was a book?" (249). This one scene identifies Palahniuk not as the sarcastically pedantic author but as the self-deprecating postmodern artist. As one might guess, Palahniuk conjures Big Bob (253), saves the major players (254–55), and even depicts Tyler trying to seduce Lidia, with libidinous Tyler commanding Palahniuk to "write Lidia and me a sex scene" (255). The "We H8 Tyler" (257) happy ending is predictably undercut with images of Palahniuk shot in the head, presented in clumps and blotches of reds and yellows, with bone, teeth, and glasses being shattered outward from the blast (261). This is the appropriate ending for those who follow the *Fight Club* ideology, who intellectualize the plot, expecting a totalizing paradigm that neatly resolves with a traditional denouement. On face value, Palahniuk offers a cartoon conclusion, a transgressive replica of the usual fate of Wile E. Coyote when he fails to outwit the Roadrunner. Palahniuk then provides a more contemplative or philosophical ending, more consistent with *Fight Club* mythology.

Basically, the second ending is more plausible and less farcical. Palahniuk titles this "Fight Club Ending Redux: The End of the Original Novel, Revisited." In *Fight Club*, the narrator realizes that he "used to be such a nice person" (98), and this is repeated in the second *Fight Club 2* ending (265). Palahniuk actually offers a synopsis of several major events, with the narrator visiting his bombed apartment, attending support groups, confronting antagonistic Marla, and fighting multiple combatants (265–72). The sequential panels showing first Tyler aiming a pistol at Sebastian but second Sebastian holding the pistol inside his own mouth portray the realistic psychological conflict within this one man. Sebastian is now metaphorically "fighting" for his health, and Marla's compassion and the medical attention are authentic for someone in his condition. Significantly, the secondary father consists of the support community willing to help Sebastian any way possible (275). There are no animated versions of Chloe and Bob. The prequel "Expedition" has no bearing on this ending, and all the commentary about Campbell theory about tricksters or mentors is irrelevant. Notwithstanding, the second ending is loyal to the original premise of *Fight Club*.

The issue then becomes where the extra information works within this second ending. As mentioned, Palahniuk adds to this ending Marla's pregnancy, not treating her lump as potential breast cancer (266). In *Fight Club 2*, an eleven-panel montage illustrates Tyler pulling Sebastian nude out of a grave in what could be metaphorically interpreted as Sebastian's resurrection (273–74). In a panel showing the perception of Tyler aiming the pistol in Sebastian's mouth, preceding the actual scene of Sebastian performing the action solo, Tyler states poignantly, something that indeed reflects Campbell's principles, "You need to die a **Hero's** Death" (Palahniuk's emphasis) (275). This might refer to his impending martyrdom, to die and to be resurrected as a postmodern deity, a representative savior for contemporary readers. This action is entrenched inside the realm of mythology.

To test Palahniuk's mockery of his first novel, a return to Slavoj Žižek is necessary. Late in *Fight Club*, the narrator declares, "If you're male, and you're Christian and living in America, your father is your model for God. And sometimes you find your father in your career" (186). This occurs right after he discovers his boss has been executed. To return to an idea introduced in the second chapter of this study, in "The Violence of the Fantasy," Žižek believes the scene in which the narrator hits himself (Tyler does something similar with his boss) illustrates how one takes action against ideological repression. Žižek argues that this anticipation of force within the master/slave dynamic empowers the slave over the master (286). The apparent rationale for the narrator's self-abuse is that the narrator has "nothing" (114) but the bosses have "everything" (115), and the narrator inflicts violence upon himself to preemptively take that power from his boss. Figuratively, Palahniuk is accomplishing something similar in *Fight Club 2* by tearing down the ideological structure that he constructed. By doing so, Palahniuk takes power away from all of the misrepresentations and misappropriations of the *Fight Club* narrative for various purposes, pernicious as well as innocuous. Through literary self-deprecation, Palahniuk actually reclaims deferred power by reconstructing a deeper meaning through forging a bond between Tyler as trickster and the concept of second father. As a matter of fact, he mocks himself better than anyone could mock him, and then he, in carnivalesque fashion, revitalizes the old by adding something new through the parody. The entire enterprise of *Fight Club 2* is Palahniuk putting Zizek's theory into literary practice. Even though *Fight Club* might be his professional destiny, with which he will always be identified, Palahniuk is neither ruled nor enslaved by its tremendous popularity. In fact, he not only hit himself in the head. Palahiuk allowed the spawn of his creative imagination to shoot him in the head.

Palahniuk will continue this story. As mentioned in the first paragraph, he has already released "Fight Club for Kids," a fake advertisement of a children's version of *Fight Club*. In the approximately three-minute video, the atmosphere (visual and auditory) is disguised as a children's program. The story of the "Horsing Around Club" refers to a marginalized child trying to fit into the mainstream. Palahniuk's "accidental" indiscretions while reading, humorously full of *Fight Club* reverberations such as "Start a fight" and "You are not your khakis," point toward the original text, and there is the same set of rules that make fight club so famous. *Fight Club*

3 has already been published in separate comic books. Dark Horse Comics offers this summary of the first comic book serialization: "Marla, her first son, and her husband—the unnamed narrator in the novel, who now goes by Balthazar [form] ... a ruthless and deviant plan to fine-tune mankind, leading Balthazar to forge an unlikely alliance ... with Tyler Durden" (*"Fight Club 3"*). There are also plans for a *Fight Club* musical. In a 2015 interview for *Buzzfeed*, Palahniuk lets out that David Fincher is working with Trent Reznor on what would be this decade's signature rock opera, rivaling *Tommy* and *The Wall* ("Chuck"). Once again, Palahniuk moves forward by replenishing his narrative, not backward by repackaging the plot.

Time will tell if Palahniuk remains loyal to the mythology or if he gives in to the ideology. As the two endings in *Fight Club 2* suggest, Palahniuk can go either way. The ideology might appeal to most readers, but the mythology is what lasts. Palahniuk surely believes this to be true, no matter how skeptical or cynical that he might be. Of course, Palahniuk advocates feeling through the heart over thinking through the intellect. Fortunately, loyal Palahniuk fans know the difference. In her 2019 article titled "Everyone Misunderstands the Point of *Fight Club*," Rebecca Renner shares what she believes to be the story's lasting message: "The real lesson, regardless, isn't about how to be a hypermasculine bro or Übermensch hero. It's that the world doesn't owe you shit. So stop listening to gods, fathers, and advertising agencies; be yourself, and you'll be free. Fuck the rules." Palahniuk would surely agree. The point is that simple.

NINE

Toward "a structure for communion"
Ideological Carnival in Adjustment Day

Events prompting California Democratic congresswoman Katie Hill's resignation in late October of 2019 include many of the elements that Chuck Palahniuk satirizes in *Adjustment Day*. The media have been all over Hill's situation. For *Rolling Stone*, Peter Wade writes that thirty-two-year-old freshman representative Hill, who is openly bisexual, is going through a "contentious" divorce from Kenny Helsep, her husband who allegedly released the two provocative photos that have gone viral, one showing a nude Hill with an Iron Cross tattoo on her inside hip and holding a bong, and another displaying a nude Hill brushing fully-clothed Morgan Desjardins's hair. On October 23, in a *USA Today* article, Jeanine Santucci describes the start of an ethics investigation; on October 27, in the same publication, Jordan Culver announces Hill's resignation. For *BuzzFeed*, Kate Nocera states the website *RedState* published incriminating text messages and nude photos substantiating claims that Hill had a consensual sexual relationship with a female staffer, Desjardins. For *Salon*, Igor Derysh claims a declared Republican supporter told CNN that he had 700 provocative photos of Hill. For *The Washington Examiner*, Madison Dibble reveals Hill and her husband uploaded a nude photo of the congresswoman on a wife-swapping website to the thread "WouldYouFuckMyWife." For *UPROXX*, Stacey Ritzen notes the outrage over Hill's "Nazi tattoo" as a hate symbol.

Then there are repercussions. *Time* correspondent Charlotte Alter extends Hill's indiscretions to other millennials, saying Hill's nude photos documenting her "throuple" relationship with her husband and Desjardins is matter of course for her generation: "Since millennials live most of their lives online, it's only natural that their sex lives have gone digital as well, and Hill was no exception." Alter contends "revenge porn"—also called "electronic assault" and "digital exploitation"—can be "easily weaponized by disgruntled exes or abusers." Alter also argues Hill will not be the last millennial in politics to fall because of leaked images. A writer for *Mag-AMedia* notices the irony concerning the harassment, with Hill identifying herself with #MeToo as a victim of heteropatriarchal double-standards, and Desjardins also claiming #MeToo status, especially after Hill demanded Desjardins rub suntan lotion on her body after the relationship had concluded (Small Town Andrew). For the *HuffPost*, Jennifer Bendery analyzes Hill's "cease and desist" letter to the *Daily Mail* for continuing to post the nude images. Jackie Salo in *The New York Post* reports other photos show Hill and Desjardin "canoodling during a vacation in Alaska."

Not all reports are negative. Madison Pauly for *Mother Jones* and Makena Kelly for *The Verge* both state Hill is preparing to fight revenge porn publicly and to reach out to help other victims. In a *USA Today* article, Savannah Behrmann reiterates that Hill is trying to spin a negative situation into something positive. In *Elle*, Madison Feller commends Hill for her diligent work on the House Oversight Committee. All of this is, however, very different from honorific publicity such as Trudy Ring's 2018 praise for Hill in *The Advocate* as one of the few LBGTQAI people in Congress and Dana Goodyear's calling Hill a "new kind of Democrat" in a 2018 article in *The New Yorker*. Alia E. Dastagir writes in a *USA Today* piece, "The allegations Hill had sexual relationships with two of her staffers have led to debate on both sides of the political aisle around the double standards female elected officials face. They also have ignited conversations around revenge porn, biphobia … [and] domestic violence in the digital age."

Hill's situation acknowledges many contemporary issues thus far addressed in Palahniuk's subject matter. Many responses on websites featuring articles about Hill's situation request directions to online sites that actually show Hill's nipples and pubic area (the photos blur these areas), and Hill has even mentioned that she is offended by how thousands of online viewers "use" those images. In her farewell speech, Hill declares, "I am leaving because of a misogynistic culture that gleefully consumed my naked pictures, capitalized on my sexuality and enabled my abusive ex to continue that abuse, this time with the entire country watching" (qtd. in Jessica Bennett). Paradoxically, there is a lowbrow desire to see more of Hill simultaneously as there is a highbrow condemnation of her behavior.

Through his fiction, Palahniuk chronicles how the world is indeed changing. Bella Thorne and Whitney Cummings (as well as Tasha Reign, Lisa Ann, and other mainstream adult-film personalities) could testify that the uploading of nude breasts or naked torsos (i.e., Hill's images only as nudes) is really no big deal. Moreover, Hill's gender and sexuality do not add sensational value to the nude images to make them a big deal. A significant factor that makes them relevant is Hill's status as an elected official, someone with political power. Furthermore, as in the cases of Thorne and Cummings, the implication of how the nude images are manipulated as revenge porn or for financial extortion is certainly controversial. In the fall of 2019, in an extremely divided American political climate, people weighed in on both sides of Hill's situation, declaring their positions for or against the congresswoman's decisions. Those who never heard of Hill before the third week in October expressed their opinions about the politician's sexy selfies, bisexual trysts, provocative tattoo, and drug choices. As Jessica Bennett says in her *New York Times* article, this is a complicated situation, especially after considering President Trump's confirmed affair with porn star Stormy Daniels and the endless proliferation of salacious content related to politicians on the Internet (e.g., the Bigfoot allegation mentioned at the beginning of the second chapter). Even a commentator borrowing the iconic moniker Tyler Durden, using the Brad Pitt movie face as the avatar, offered opinions on the Hill scandal for the website *ZeroHedge*.

In *Adjustment Day*, Palahniuk addresses sexuality, race, and politics through the comic grotesque, using fiction to confront real-world issues. This novel could not have been published during a more opportune time. Palahniuk does not hit global pandemic, but he touches on about everything else. America is separated by a range of ideologies affiliated with Republicans and Democrats, pro-Trumps and anti-Trumps, conservatives and liberals, plus a myriad of subcultures delineated by principles which define, classify, categorize, and, consequently, separate. Mentioned in the previous chapter, in *Fight Club 2*, Dr. Wrong, the representative pseudo-intellectual, points out that ideas propagate people—people do not propagate ideas (159–60). Intruding into the graphic novel, Palahniuk propounds that ideas, not people, generate reality (259). People identify with ideas, they personify the concepts, they embody the precepts, and they are willing to defend abstractions as they would defend loved ones. By literally becoming the principles, like ideological magnets, they are attracted and repulsed by political impulses. People respond to the ideas. Case in point, Katie Hill signifies several meanings: values held by Southern California liberals and anti-Trump Democrats, in addition to identifying as female, bisexual, and millennial. Likewise, her web photos and posts suggest meanings associated with sexual appetite, recreational drug use, and racial loyalties. Hill is doubtful a closet white supremacist, but the Iron Cross may certainly be interpreted according to white supremacist ideology. One only has to consider the controversy in early October of 2019, as Adrianna Rodriguez reports in her *USA Today* article, when a Universal Studios amusement park worker costumed as Gru from *Despicable Me* held the "OK" sign on the shoulder of a child of color, technically flashing a now recognized symbol of hate. The Iron Cross next to Hill's genitalia could be read similarly. There are also the connotations related to #MeToo and to pornography (and their interrelations to feminism) in current American popular culture. In fact, Katie Hill's situation could be viewed as a media exercise in semiotic interpretation.

The American climate provides others just as fruitful. In early November of 2019, Elizabeth Warren began closing the gap on Joe Biden as the Democratic presidential frontrunner. In 2012, Garance Franke-Ruta questioned in an article for *The Atlantic* if Warren were actually, as she self-identified in her law school application and elsewhere, Native American. After Warren retracted her identification as Native American, media pounced. In 2019 articles, Aaron Feis writes in *The New York Post* that Warren deleted information about a DNA test, Thomas Kaplan comments in *The New York Times* that Warren apologized for the controversy during a Native American forum, Nick Martin announces in *The New Republic* that Warren's apologies are not enough, Michael Brendan Dougherty argues in the *National Review* that Warren's "Native American" problem is not going away, and the Associated Press shares that Warren apologizes for any harm she had caused ("Elizabeth"). Charles Pierce repudiates President Trump's derogatory "Pocahontas" in a report for *Esquire*, and Tina Nguyen contends in *Vanity Fair* that this nomenclature exposes his racism. During the summer of 2019, President Trump's labeling of "the Squad" spurred immediate censure, as indicated by Christal Hayes in "House Resolution Will Condemn Trump's 'Disgusting' Attacks on AOC, Tlaib, Omar and Pressley." Sophia A. Nelson notices the problem within the Democratic party in "Alexandria Ocasio-Cortez is Right, Speaker Nancy Pelosi Has a Women of Color Problem." In two *USA Today* articles, William Cummings summarizes the controversy of President Trump calling for the congresswomen to return to their designated homelands in "'This is What Racism Looks Like': Congresswomen React to Trump's 'Go Back' Tweetstorm" and "Trump Tells Congresswomen to 'Go Back' to the 'Crime Infested Places from Which They Came.'" All of this only confirms America is becoming more separated into ideological factions.

In *Adjustment Day*, Palahniuk seems to draw on the old adage "Be careful what you wish for because you might receive it." Considering American allegiances to ethnographic subcultures, Palahniuk gives many readers what they want: American jurisdictions based on sexuality and race, identity politics. As expected, this is dangerously sensitive territory to cover, so Palahniuk projects his utopia/dystopia into the near future, not that far from today, which he repeatedly refers to as "Before Times." Through the camouflage of social parable, Palahniuk reverses the American power hierarchy based upon capitalist privilege and status entitlement by allowing the traditional have nots swap places with the typical haves, replacing the old structure with a new one not based on political affiliation but on race and sexuality, two demographics that are more personal, more sensitive, and, as everyone knows, much more volatile. Palahniuk once again applies the comic grotesque to expose the hypocrisies that underlie allegiances to the false consciousnesses that comprise ideologies. Through a range of different kinds of characters, Palahniuk portrays how easily people can be motivated to trust precise ideologies that serve their own exact political agendas, even though they believe their zealous attachments are solely based on the purest of humanitarian intentions.

One only has to think about the recent strictly partisan votes concerning presidential impeachment. Representatives voted according to political ideologies, not necessarily moral or ethical beliefs. Drawing on conventional stereotypes, Palahniuk displays how an ideology can be constructed, communicated, and enforced to exploit prevailing prejudices and discriminations. Palahniuk shares the process through which pithy soundbites disguised as trusted axioms substantiate ideologies, ones that are defended through violence and fostered through segregation. Publishing this story at just the right time, when Americans appear openly divisive and prone to stratification, Palahniuk synthesizes many of his previous themes. In this 2018 satire, Palahniuk investigates what happens when separatist propaganda undermines dominant ideology created to unify the variety of disparate American belief systems. Speaking through Talbott Reynolds, he manufactures an alternative ideology that is deceptively repressive, exclusionary, and demeaning. Of course, Palahniuk could not have anticipated COVID-19, but if a coronavirus had been added, this book would have included most of the components causing Americans nervous distress moving into the first few decades of the 2000s.

In interviews, Palahniuk downplays *Adjustment Day* as his response to the American political climate.[1] In a 2018 interview for *Vice*, after he is asked if the 2016 presidential election inspired his novel, in his characteristically sarcastic wit, Palahniuk first responds glibly that Pornhub has consumed most of his time, so he was unaware there was an election. More serious, alluding to Michel Foucault's "repressive hypothesis" (49) mentioned in *The History of Sexuality*, Palahniuk snaps that talk about protest and resistance only energizes Trump's power. When asked if *Adjustment Day* is an "inverted *Fight Club*," Palahniuk replies that his first novel "was about empowering the individual and setting him on a path toward his personal vision. And that requires destroying the existent powerless person. *Adjustment Day* is about presenting a pattern for gathering men together. My books are always about the individual. The triumph of the individual man or woman." When queried if organizations were sanctifying his writing to defend their beliefs, Palahniuk scoffs that "snowflake" has substituted "faggot" as a major term of deprecation ("Chuck"). To continue this thread, in a 2018 interview with *The Beat*, Palahniuk confesses his research for *Adjustment Day* included surveying online separatist websites: "The civil war and ethnic nationalist fantasies I follow on the web seem split between Keith Ellison's proposal for a black nation state, now echoed by the Black Panthers. That, and the quest for a white nation, as advocated by Jared Taylor" ("Interview").

Palahniuk seems to defend this book more than previous ones. Speaking in 2018 with *NW Book Lovers*, Palahniuk notes that one misconception readers have about *Fight Club* is that the community is valued over the individual, clarifying the entire purpose of the community is to cultivate each individual's potential toward personal empowerment. When asked directly if he is satirizing the Trump political environment, Palahniuk points out that he only addresses how humans love to politicize, and he is tired of American novels portraying problems without offering viable solutions. He insists *Adjustment Day* provides a serious solution tinged with comedy, and this novel warns against identity politics that privileges the community over the individual ("Shelf"). Along these lines, speaking with *Big Shiny Robot* in 2018, Palahniuk claims his novel confronts his audience's potential "separatist fantasies and civil war fantasies" by showing how disastrously complex life would become if there were "nation states based entirely on identity politics" ("An Interview"). In a 2018 interview for *The Good Men Project*, Palahniuk reiterates that his inspiration came from a range of sources, from ultra-conservative alt-right advocates to racial separatists, piecing together "militant fantasies" of nations "built on identity politics." All in all, Palahniuk agrees *Adjustment Day* is a cautionary tale against alliances valuing the group over the individual.

In several interviews, Palahniuk compares *Adjustment Day* to John Steinbeck's *The Grapes of Wrath*, F. Scott Fitzgerald's *The Great Gatsby*, and Ayn Rand's *The Fountainhead*. Previously cited, Dr. Wrong proclaims in *Fight Club 2* that fictional personalities outlive their readers (170), and Palahniuk understands this all too well. In the interviews already mentioned with *NW Book Lovers*, *The Beat*, and *Vice*, Palahniuk offers (with hilariously colorful language) what he wished would have happened in Steinbeck's and Fitzgerald's novels. He would have liked the Joads to have stopped dumping bodies and to have cooked meth, peddled moonshine, or made anthrax to get wealthy, just as most Americans become rich. Likewise, he would have liked Nick to find the guts to tell off Tom and Daisy using an assortment of profanities, and he wanted Gatsby to rise from the pool so he could shoot Tom, not letting Tom get away with being such a jerk. Not surprising, thinking about his stance toward personal empowerment, Palahniuk says he admired Rand's propensity to develop unlikeable characters into strongly assertive individuals who steadfastly maintain their convictions and stalwartly finish what they start. Palahniuk frames his profanely irreverent comments about sacrosanct American authors and novels within his vilification of so-called classics that pander to the status quo and surrender to defeatism. Although he makes fun of Steinbeck and Fitzgerald (praising Rand), he is reprimanding their literary approaches to prove his assertion ("Shelf").

These thoughts likely contributed to Palahniuk's plan that *Adjustment Day* would set up the causes and conditions for the next American civil war. In the interview with *The Good Men Project*, Palahniuk admits that he was wondering how Rand would have composed *Gone with the Wind* ("Exclusive"). In a 2019 interview for *The Millions*, Palahniuk continues about the influence of Margaret Mitchell's novel: "Once you recognize the myth you're retelling, then you're truly free to cleave unto it or to violate the myth. So many groups are calling for civil war, or self-segregating, it seemed like a new American civil war novel was needed" ("Does"). In the interview with *The Beat*, he confesses Civil War–era author Harriett Beecher Stowe, whom President Abraham Lincoln labeled as one of the primary Northern agitators, was the model for Talbott Reynolds ("Interview"). As will be discussed later in this chapter, Palahniuk certainly parodies Mitchell's novel for sections related to Blacktopia. One flaw in Palahniuk's depiction is the bifurcation of this particular region. On the one hand, Blacktopia is a rendition of Mitchell's South. On the other, the landscape is utterly spectacular, unlike any moment in American history.

Reviewers obviously notice the relationship between current national affairs and Palahniuk's story. A writer for *Kirkus Reviews* indirectly calls attention to the similarity to *Fight Club*: "A caustic fantasy about emasculated men, power reversals, proletariat revolution, and extreme violence. Sound familiar?" ("Palahniuk"). For *Library Journal*, Robert E. Brown offers this verdict: "Palahniuk is an acquired taste; those who have it will devour this, for others, it might be the place to start." A critic reviewing the novel for *Publishers Weekly* concludes, "The over-the-top premise is classic Palahniuk, but he stumbles in its delivery, focusing more on the farcical aspects of these societies rather than on the characters living in them, resulting in a thin story" ("Adjustment"). Writing for *Nerdist*, Rosie Knight reports in a neutral criticism that Palahniuk started his novel after getting a distorted view of American news through the Internet while he visited Spain. According to Knight, this motivated Palahniuk to rewrite "*Gone with the Wind* with the civil war resulting in 'multiple identity-based nations.'" In representative reviews that target the novel's structure, Tyler Wolter in *Open Letters Review* and Ben Arzate in *Cultured Vultures* notice that the storylines merge together and sometimes lag, and Jordan Blum comments in *Pop Matters* that this is not Palahniuk at his best. In *Coachella Review*,

D.M. Olsen shares that the hardcopy of *Adjustment Day* without the dust jacket actually *is* Talbott Reynolds's book.

Several reviewers argue Palahniuk is only trying to shock readers. In a review for *NPR*, Jason Sheehan sees this novel as pure Palahniuk provocation: "before you get offended, throw the book down, walk away from it for good. He wants to see how thin of a tightrope he can walk between satire and slur, provocation and revulsion." Sheehan concludes, "And I gotta tell you, watching him try it? It's fun," but he later couches this in a schadenfreude context. In a scathing review that could have been included alongside Alexander Larman's blistering 2018 *Guardian* assault on this novel (discussed in the first chapter), Jake Kerridge of the *Daily Telegraph* states that Palahniuk has written about "the beleaguered American male" with a "genuine anger" that has infused an "energy" into his satires. In his well-articulated negative dissection of *Adjustment Day*, Kerridge identifies the comic grotesque in not only the slicing of ears as prized status tokens but also in various descriptions of discontent in one of the three regions generated from misdirected political correctness, what he perceives as "a cleverly economical way of insulting as many people as possible [that] ... betrays a juvenile desire to shock." Continuing this train of thought, he accuses Palahniuk of teasing readers with "glimpses" of meaningful prose but then seeming just not to care about the rest of the story. Kerridge concludes that readers should tackle this novel when they are disgruntled about the state of humanity, when they want a little weeding out of the human race.

Palahniuk expresses this intention in various conversations. In the interview with *The Good Men Project*, Palahniuk admits his story is in response to current ideological systems not working, especially for young men. He calls the novel a "cathartic narrative" that might help young males establish more productive strategies than ones affiliated with violence and destruction. Moreover, Palahniuk calls Talbott an "evil mentor," but he also specifies that Talbott creates pragmatic writing tasks that are based on qualities of tough love, many of which Palahniuk was taught ("Exclusive"). In his interview for *The Millions*, Palahniuk describes Talbott as an archetypal mentor (as was discussed in the previous chapter) instead of a deranged egomaniac who only wants to pass his wisdom to his heir apparent. Not surprisingly, Palahniuk compares Talbott with Tyler Durden (as mentor as opposed to trickster) in that both might be "wrong-headed" yet neither is "malicious" thus not psychopathic ("Does"). In his interview with *The Beat*, Palahniuk expands upon the *Fight Club* and *Adjustment Day* comparison, even repeating words verbatim from *Adjustment Day* (157) in his response: "*Fight Club* depicted a process for coaching individuals to discover their greater potential. Once they'd reached this awareness, the members were expected to spin off and pursue a personal quest: To build a house, to paint a self-portrait, to write a book" ("Interview"). Palahniuk envisions the combination of *Fight Club* and *Adjustment Day* as pairing with Ayn Rand's *The Fountainhead* and *Atlas Shrugged* ("Interview"). This book is definitely a parody of popular texts, many of which have served as ideologies and even mythologies to guide people's lives.

Perhaps Palahniuk's intention is to demonstrate the absurdity of assuming one work could motivate individuals to form groups that would rebel against dominant ideologies. Throughout history, other books have appeared to serve this purpose. Palahniuk might be questioning, however, if this could happen in the twenty-first century. He might be challenging the notion that a counter-ideology outlined in one book could eliminate sexism, racism, ableism, and other varieties of prejudice, discrimination, and harassment. *Adjustment Day* proves there are no simple solutions such as lists, aphorisms, or realignments to extremely complex ideological problems affecting human interactions. Through this novel, Palahniuk displays the hubristic folly that drives people to commit malicious atrocities all for the sake of political correctness based on ideas.[2] He undertakes an extremely noble enterprise, a gargantuan political task, all through the comic grotesque. In this one book, Palahniuk takes on the national ideology that is advertised as democracy and defended by legislators, but he also goes after partisan ideologies, such as feminism (which he addresses in *Snuff* and *Beautiful You*) in addition to a host of other principles related to liberal subcultures. Palahniuk is stretching his satire perhaps farther than he ever has previously, and the tone is farcically didactic, which dubiously makes it an attractive ideology.

Palahniuk knows what he is doing. Without the dust jacket, in the blue-black coloring with gold type, *Adjustment Day* looks like the *Alcoholics Anonymous* (AA) Big Book. The early avant-garde proliferation of Palahniuk's fictional movement imitates the underground word-of-mouth that eventually connected recovering alcoholics and consequently established a mainstream recovery network. Commented upon in the first chapter of this study, Palahniuk knows all about support groups and fringe alliances. The kidnapping of Talbott Reynolds and the circumstances leading to the dictations to Walter are vastly different from Bill Wilson's meeting Dr. Bob Smith and the creation of the AA bible, but an unpredictable chain of events certainly motivated Talbott and Wilson to accomplish unprecedented results. There are similarities concerning the curt truisms in Talbott's text and that of AA, which has "Easy Does It," "First Things First," "Let Go and Let God," "Keep It Simple," in addition to the parsing of "ego" into "edging God out" and "fear" into "false evidence appearing real." As mentioned in *Adjustment Day*, the popularity of Talbott's book, as it was not sold anywhere, is also similar to AA. The narrator compares the work to the Quran, the *Book of Mormon*, and *The Communist Manifesto* (68). There have been books that have orchestrated once-thought unimaginable sociocultural change, so *Adjustment Day* could be this next book. This text could provide the panacea of all sociocultural ills plaguing America.

Palahniuk has built his reputation on this kind of effort. As Ben Beaumont-Thomas writes in his summary of an interview with Palahniuk, "Fight Club Author Chuck Palahniuk on His Book Becoming a Bible for the Incel Movement," Palahniuk writes stories that stimulate productive argument, introducing subjects that, in the writer's words, are "going to be in the culture forever," because "in creative work, resolution is death." Unfortunately, some extreme right-wing groups are claiming *Fight Club* as their Big Book, as their blue-black treatises espousing their ideological tenets.[3] As discussed in the preceding chapter, they misinterpret Palahniuk's message, or, more specifically, they confuse the ideology with the mythology (although Palahniuk is the first to admit that his fiction is open to reader interpretation). There are more characters in this narrative than in his other books, where there are distinctly delineated subtexts, and the transition between his subplots becomes a little fuzzy and are a bit bumpy, but Palahniuk, as he always does, likes to take narrative chances. The apposition of Walter creating the book *Adjustment Day*, following the progress of the book as it is composed, with sections depicting events that occur chronologically after the book has been released is not difficult to follow. In *Beautiful You* and *Tell-All*, for instance, Palahniuk starts the beginning with the ending, and this is also easy to understand. Considering pagination, *Invisible Monsters Remix* goes back and forth, and *Survivor* goes backwards. To concede what Palahniuk's critics see as flaws, Palahniuk may attempt to synthesize all of his narrators for the sake of equity, not giving attention to one particular group, although Blacktopia prospers while the other territories flounder.

As mentioned in previous chapters, Palahniuk likes to parody established mythology, claiming little of what he creates is original and mostly imitates previous narratives. As a postmodern author, Palahniuk refashions mythology according to John Barth's extremely influential proclamation in his 1967 essay titled "The Literature of Exhaustion," perhaps the manifesto of postmodern literature. Barth argues writers reproduce old ideas into new ones (73). In his 1980 article "The Literature of Replenishment," Barth adjusts his stance by claiming parody enables authors to generate new meanings from previous ones (206). In the 2011 essay "Do I Repeat Myself? The Problem of the Already Said," Barth asserts, "Originality, after all, includes not only saying something for the first time, but re-saying (in a worthy new way) the already said: rearranging an old tune in a different key, to a different rhythm, perhaps on a different instrument."[4] Barth's statements legitimized parody, in its contemporary application, as a distinctly postmodern genre.

Through Talbott Reynolds's plot, Palahniuk contemporizes the Judgement of Paris that is credited in Greek and Roman mythology with initiating the Trojan War. As the story goes, Zeus realized he could not directly decrease the human population through his own devices, as many of the gods and goddesses on Mount Olympus held attachments with various mortals, so he had to devise a plan to coerce others to carry out his intentions. Zeus held a wedding ceremony for Peleus and Thetis, the parents of Achilles, without inviting Eris, the Goddess of Discord. As anticipated, Eris threw the Golden Apple bearing the inscription "For the Fairest" into the party, and Hera (Zeus's wife), Athena (his daughter), and Aphrodite (another daughter) all claimed possession. Zeus deferred the decision of the winner to Paris, a shepherd but also, unknown to him, a prince of Troy. Aphrodite promised Paris the most beautiful mortal woman, Helen. A Trojan prince, Paris kidnapped Helen from her husband in Sparta, and the Greeks launched their thousand ships to get Helen back. Zeus succeeded in his plan to cull the population. Likewise, although not godlike, capitalist Talbott persuades Walter Baines, although not a prince, to create the website with The List and to recruit acolytes through Narcotics Anonymous meetings to start his own culling of the American population. Talbott's strategy avoids the nuclear blasts that will decrease the youth bulge (12)—an actual sociodemographic theory—of too many males through, comparable to Zeus, exploiting the vanities of his audience. Talbott realizes separating factions based on identity politics will lead to corruptible governments. War will eventually occur based upon loyalties to ideas. As the omnipotent fictional godhead, Palahniuk projects what would occur if those associated with liberalism actually got what they wanted, the illusion of genuine equity. Similar to the Judgement of Paris, the result is mass genocide, not enforced by the ruling entity but implemented by factions believing in their rightful and justifiable causes. Talbott claims his fantasy was never supposed to happen, but he presents an enigmatically pompous stance at the end of this novel. Times change, but the result of discord remains the same.

Of course, Palahniuk realizes how controversial speaking about political correctness is now. If he did overtly express an opinion, Fox News and CNN would predictably present the story from politically partisan "objective" reporting. Thus, Palahniuk relies on the comic grotesque. As the situation with Katie Hill demonstrates, issues related to race and to sexuality are extremely sensitive. Notwithstanding, Hill's bisexuality (as a millennial female) coupled with the nude photo displaying her tattoo (as a potential hate symbol) plus her election to Congress (one of the recently famous first-term females) provides a lucrative amalgam of anti-heteropatriarchal content for media to sensationalize. Moreover, this situation draws the attention of many leaders all too ready to espouse venomous diatribe against opposition to the ideas that they fiercely defend. The alleged victimization of Katie Hill based on all sorts of politically incorrect reasons illustrates the timeliness of Palahniuk's contemporary "judgment" story.

Just as Dr. Wrong served as the representative academic in *Fight Club 2*, Dr. Emmitt Brolly functions in this capacity in *Adjustment Day*. Palahniuk allows Brolly to pontificate about the reversal of the power hierarchy before he is executed by two disinterested young men. After claiming there have always been "lists," Brolly describes with enthusiasm "power-reversal rituals!" through comparisons to Halloween and Christmas rituals (49–50), but then he foreshadows "Fasching," German for "final carnal indulgence," about to occur. He gives his killers a lesson about the temporary hierarchal position switching during carnival. He instructs them about the significance of the profane and the grotesque, and he also inculcates them about the relevance of sexuality and physicality. For the most part, Palahniuk uses Brolly as a mouthpiece to explain many of Bakhtin's tenets about this social, cultural, and political enterprise (51). After Brolly summarizes how the rebellion that led to the Reformation began during carnival, he admits the problem of not allowing the working-class and under-class to purge themselves temporarily of animosity toward the empowered: "That was a fatal flaw of this great country, he surmised. It never allowed the weakest, the poorest and the most disenfranchised to enjoy even an hour of ritualized power" (51). Significantly, Brolly predicts the impending catastrophe resulting from no American carnival (51). He offers this ironically before his assassination. As the remainder of the novel shows, for a little over a year—as Esteban calculates from 374 scratches on the toilet stall (287)—the disenfranchised fringe and the ruling mainstream reverse places. Palahniuk's entire novel portrays the temporary appropriation of power integral to carnival. In this manner, Palahniuk provides a contemporary reformation.

Although, Palahniuk's application of the comic grotesque is a little different from his treatments in *Snuff*, *Damned*, *Doomed*, and *Beautiful You*. References to sex in *Snuff* and *Beautiful You* lend themselves to the physicality usually associated with transgressivity. Cassie's quest for 600 sex acts and Penny's crusade against sex products must obviously portray graphic descriptions including what are considered profanities and vulgarities. These books are about overtly sexual experiences, so they should include representative illustrations that appear realistic. Although *Damned* and *Doomed* pertain to the afterlife, Palahniuk must, reflective of his creative modus operandi, sexualize inhabitants and accouterments in his version of hell. As discussed in previous chapters in this study, ideology is important, as two of the novels are clearly fostered by feminism and the other two deal with issues concerning free will versus determinism. Admittedly, *Adjustment Day* is much more political, so the comic grotesque scenes typically support an agenda tied to a cause. This does not mean the other four Palahniuk novels were not political—as they surely were—but the ideology was not so transparently linked with political stances. Louis Althusser's Ideological State Apparatuses (ISAs) and Repressive State Apparatuses (RSAs) were not so obvious or as visible within the plots.

Nonetheless, Palahniuk undergirds his presentations with his characteristic transgression. There are plenty of depictions that are unquestionably gross. In the opening section, Walter's viewing the mound of bloody body parts (3) makes more sense after readers discover later that he is trying to stop Adjustment Day. The graphic details of Brolly's bloody head, with gore spewed behind him (52), might remind readers of similar images drawn in vibrant colors in *Fight Club 2*. The scene in which Terrence's mother rips the catheter out of her son's penis, with urine, blood, and bacon splattered all over the room, not to forget the blood gushing from her nose, broken by the force of Talbott's book smashed into it, is humorously disgusting (74–75). Equally repulsive is the lump of fat spouting from Talbott "like so much ketchup-colored jizz" (115) as Walter tries to extract a non-existent transmitter. Details about the deterioration of Gregory Piper's body eaten by maggots is just as repugnant but necessary as a metaphor for impending change (175–76).

There are also scenes of the sexually transgressive. Two in particular are definitely Rabelaisian. Palahniuk does not offer many shocking or vulgar scenes in this novel, but when he does, they are whoppers. Palahniuk sets up his scene with Charm by pointing out that female genitalia, "exposed pussies" (210), was demonized in mythology (a detail Palahniuk interestingly omits from *Damned*). As the narrator states, "Neither Satan nor any evil could endure the sight of the female sex organs" (210). Charm's counterattack against the men's varsity lacrosse team by exposing her vulva is pure comic grotesque: "Weaned on the tame hairless vaginas of pornography, the young men had recoiled in terror. As a charging army of hairy vaginas had spooked the winged stallion Pegasus, Charm's hirsute sexual center had shocked those would-be suitors. As their jeering had fallen silent, she'd clenched her buttocks, thrusting her sex at them like a deadly saber" (210). Similar to his descriptions in *Snuff*, Palahniuk is utilitarian in how he allows Charm to weaponize her sexuality. Just as when one reads *Gargantua and Pantagruel*, a reader can only imagine how this scene plays out in all of its incredible transgressivity. No media presentation could compete against the burlesque bawdiness this scene evokes in the imagination.

Just as hilarious is Shasta pulling off Charlie's penis, which is reminiscent of Madison's similar penis extraction in *Doomed*. After secretly inflicting the multiple bites from brown recluse spiders on Charlie's genitals, Shasta falls backward after yanking off the penis. After his obvious reaction, full of emblematic medieval gibberish, Shasta replies to Charlie's speech, "Dude, stop with the Renn Faire-speak, already!" (306). The passage that follows humorously pokes fun at Charlie's corruption of power:

> Without pause did she fling the wilted meat stick against a bed chamber casement of highly colored glass, through which it exploded in a shower of reds and golds and plummeted a goodly distance, wriggling down from the cloudless sky, to where it flopped, bouncing damply at the feet of many filed wives who recognized the item instantly as it thudded among the row of Swill chard and zucchini. There in the dust did it come to rest and was the relic immediately seized upon by hungry, devouring ants [307].

His reaction exhibits his powerlessness, "Ye shall burn for this vile, beldame!" (307). Charlie's speech, as well as Miss Josephine's fake dialect, promote heteroglossia in this novel, but this is nowhere near what Palahniuk creates in *Snuff*, with clearly demarcated voices infusing the textual atmosphere. Charlie's "Ye," "beldame," and other antiquated verbal markers are less about dialogical variety and more about linguistic historical identity. Charlie and Josephine use speech to situate themselves artificially into a sociocultural past. Regardless of the slapstick humor in these scenes, most of the comic grotesque passages reinforce a political message.

Even though Palahniuk does not identify one major character, Walter seems to assume center stage. His actions provide the bookends serving as the introduction and the conclusion, and his kidnapping of Talbott and the creation of The List via the website set into motion what becomes Adjustment Day. Walter is the boyfriend of Shasta, and he is the one who seems to change the most throughout the events in the story. His character does not exhibit the degree of ideological discordance as other Palahniuk personalities, but of all the characters in this novel, his vision of a better life is challenged, and he pays the price for his choices. The narrator even credits *Adjustment Day* (the book readers are perusing) to Walter: "Before everything you've read so far in this book … before this book was a book, it was the dream of Walter Baines" (26). Moreover, the narrator addresses readers directly to give Walter's vision a context: "Back in the world you still know … back in Before Times, here's how Walter had always dreamed of doing it" (26).

Without Walter, *Adjustment Day* would be a vastly different novel. Not to belabor this point, but the entire story could be Walter's fantasy, a figment of Walter's imagination. There are enough examples, however, such as Talbott's phone call to Nick searching for Walter (6–7), to disprove this premise, but Walter definitely is the catalyst that leads to the carnivalesque hierarchal reversal. As a product of the proletariat, Walter is groomed to equate happiness with money (33). Idiosyncratic to his personality, he fantasizes about serial killers' lists of victims, and he considers strangling Shasta with a garrote as a viable alibi (29). He really likes Internet pornography, and the narrator compares porn's fortifying effect on him to what spinach does to Popeye (55).[5] His scheme to achieve socioeconomic power includes abducting a second father, a rich mentor comparable to what Palahniuk discusses in several interviews concerning *Fight Club 2*. Walter rationalizes that there is no reason why he could not adopt a father, and this person might as well be wealthy, and he ends this thought by projecting a rich father could change him from redneck to respectable (57). After he abducts Talbott, Walter refers to him point blank as his new father, and Talbott unbelievably agrees to teach him all of his tricks to wealth, starting with transcribing a new ideological doctrine, the Declaration of Interdependence (119).

Walter's relationship with Talbott puts in motion Adjustment Day. Without Walter, Talbott would not have had the same opportunity to express his beliefs. Ironically, Talbott devises the mechanism that kills many materialistic capitalists just like himself. Granted, Talbott would have been privy to the attitudes influenced by Gunner Heinsohn's "bulge" theory (12), and he likely would have had access to statistics concerning crime attributed to millennial males (22). Talbott would have felt the fierce resentment of the serving class against the ruling class, and he would have predicted the resulting discontent and dissatisfaction (38). However, nothing could really happen until his abduction. If Walter had not kidnapped Talbott, World War III would have decreased the youth bulge, and Talbott would only be a mentor with a student, a second father without a son. As the architect of Adjustment Day, Talbott understands what Tyler Durden knows: violent revolutionary change occurs after those who are frustrated, angry, and resentful form a community guided by a set of rules. A book was necessary to include those principles, some type of manifesto, and Talbott considers *The Communist Manifesto*, the Bible, the Quran, and *The Feminine Mystique* (93) as models.

Walter filters Talbott's rhetoric. A connoisseur of licentious material, Walter believes Talbott's book "read like pornography. What his new old man had dictated to him amounted to a pornography of power" (269). Moreover, Walter knows the most effective approach to marketing, drawing upon the success of children and young adult fiction that rely on the miraculous hero transformations of workers over their oppressive bosses (270).

First, Walter relies upon chivalry, getting men to see themselves as knights rising up against the evil tormentors so they may establish their own rightful places in the world, so he advertises Talbott's book as a romance illustrating how good defeats evil (270). Second, Walter counts on competition, persuading men to see retaliation as a sporting event, knowing full well men almost value winning as much as they do sexual satisfaction, so he advertises Talbott's book as a guide to competitive success (270). Perhaps without his realizing, Walter indirectly identifies Talbott's actual purpose in creating the book, unadulterated spite, not related to chivalry or to competition. As Walter's second father, Talbott is educating his apprentice about the difference between ideological community and mythological communion, the variance between ideas being intellectualized in the mind and ideas being internalized in the heart. Talbott's antipathy for totalizing ideology might be his true incentive for reciting *Adjustment Day* to Walter. His disdain for the American power hierarchy drives his carnivalesque reversal of social roles. Walter's comparison to pornography is relevant. Talbott knows power tempts, pleases, and corrupts every person. No one is safe from power's enticing effects.

The start of the plan was not elaborate. Talbott begins simply by building the website with The List (131), and after sixty days, the list would be removed, points would be fixed, and everything would be set for "adjustment" (62). Only those who sacrificed for "the cause" by harvesting ears would assume power (113). Not surprisingly, politicians, academics, and journalists comprised most of "America's Least Wanted" (156). Those who enforced the current ideologies were the ones most disliked. Walter listens as his newly designated father figure (156) pontificates that democracy was only an experiment, and American tradition had always rewarded men who seized power and took control (157). Those associated with creating, teaching, and spreading ideology were predictably targeted, as they were the ones affiliated with the intellectualization of ideas. Theoretically, those who were connected with feeling, internalizing ideas through their bodies, into their souls, would be the new leaders. Incidentally, Talbott appears misogynistic, as no women are ever referred to as leaders, although lesbians appear just as empowered as gays in Gaysia. In Caucasia, women subversively take the phallic power away (literally as well as figuratively) from Charlie. In the end, women rule.

As occurs in *Fight Club 2*, Talbott mines recovery groups for the disciples who will spread his doctrine. As mentioned in previous chapters in this study, Palahniuk argues support communities have replaced traditional churches, and Talbott makes the same assertion, considering churches are now only places to flaunt status and legislate morality, sanctums of hypocrisy: "A true church had to serve as a place where people went in safety to risk confessing their worst selves. Not to boast and display their pride. Those who attended recovery groups, they arrived defeated. They told the story of their failure. Their sins and shortcomings. To admit their culpability, and in doing so they receive a communion with their flawed peers" (220). Talbott requires Walter to conscript those afflicted with what is now termed addictive personality disorder, namely addicts and alcoholics, who understand the nature of self-destruction (220). Through a new "communion," Talbott wants the "learned helpless" (221) to distribute his call for revolution. He advises Walter to tell homosexuals that they will have their own isolated community, to inform Caucasians they will be likewise segregated, and to share with African Americans that they will no longer "kowtow to any other race" in their own sanctuary (220–21). Walter follows a script when he recruits members, and although not stated, this strategy of word of mouth eventually attracts Jamal, Charlie, and Garrett. Several of the first followers are heroin addicts, whom Talbott confides in as Walter wears a phone speaker (229). Although there is no indication that the "first rule of adjustment day is not to talk about adjustment day," the clandestine spreading of the plan to those included in the working-classes and under-classes, the disengaged and the disenchanted, just as in *Fight Club*, is necessary for the coup to be effective. Similar to *Fight Club*, word of mouth activates the plan, even if the plan is secretive.

Regardless what Palahniuk says in interviews about his character, Talbott might be a psychopath performing as a pragmatist. Walter admires Talbott as a mentor, and Talbott certainly nurtures this trust by appearing ethically credible. He knows about "youth bulges" (158–59) and explains how blacks, whites, and gays have all secretly prepared for eventual conflict (189). Revealing his own prejudices, Talbott views the three groups as "opioid-addled, NASCAR rubes," "the grill-grinning, thuggish blacks," and "sex-crazed queers" ready for inevitable violence (190). Not listening to his conscience, Walter's desire for wealth overrides the thought that Shasta would question the philosophy (269–70). Late in the narrative, however, Talbott's vision is seemingly validated, and, significantly, Palahniuk casts this in terms of ideology. Talbott demeans Communism, Fascism, Christianity, even Capitalism (all capitalized proper noun entities), and he calls the destruction of these systems a tremendous human accomplishment, sounding a lot like a quintessential postmodernist opposed to all totalizing paradigms (275). Echoing Palahniuk, the narrator offers a rational explanation to defend Talbott's position. Males want communion, and geographical closeness provided this in the past, but the instability of jobs and irrelevancy of churches impede this opportunity. Therefore, as Talbott contends, "race and sexual preference had to become the last bastion for community. As all the grand uniting narratives foundered ... when all the tenuous, external circumstances failed us, we'd be forced to form our ranks based on our most basic elements: skin color and sexual desire" (275–76). He also declares that consumption would serve as self-expression; status would be marked by consumption (276). The narrator reflects that because the media had not predicted the bloody reversal of status (39–45), to differentiate truth from false, it would thereafter verify truth by the capacity to shock, titillate, and evoke (89).

Although Talbott might be considered unstable and hence unreliable, as anyone willing to withstand hundreds of cuts over several months could not be altogether sane, his calculations appear to be accurate. His primary premise for the three territories is that civilization is simply consuming itself: "That had been his explanation for why Western civilizations were dwindling. Citizens of the white Diaspora were consuming themselves with drugs. Blacks with violence. Homosexuals with disease" (276). He also realizes humans will continue destructive behavior well after they get the separation and autonomy they desire. And Adjustment Day seems to happen just before grouse season opens, as inferenced three separate times: first, after the bloody massacre in the Senate (102); second, when Walter calls Senator Daniels about World War III (231); and third, at the very end of the book, when the next American civil war is about to commence (316). Actually, just like Tyler in *Fight Club* texts, Talbott is both the trickster and the mentor. On the one hand, as a second father, he pushes Walter toward achieving leadership abilities that he never would have realized otherwise. Walter had his romantic pipe dream of prosperity with Shasta, but without Talbott's help, he would have never actually taken any real action. On the other, as a maniacal capitalist, Talbott finally has all the pieces necessary to enact his master plan of genocide. Clearly a sadist, Talbott is just as manipulatively charismatic as Hitler, Manson, or any other psychopath who persuades others to do the dirty work. Palahniuk might tilt the scale toward mentor, but an argument could be made either way.

In the previous chapter, attention was given to both of the mentor and the trickster archetypes. In *A Handbook to Critical Approaches to Literature*, Wilfred L. Guerin and other editors devote a chapter to the mythological and archetype approach to literary criticism, considered passé by many contemporary academics (like Brolly). In this guide, the wise old man is referred to as a potential savior, redeemer, and guru, and he (masculine only) is recognized for goodwill, morality, and wisdom (163). These are all qualities Talbott possesses as Walter's surrogate father. Inversely, the trickster is perceived as a joker and a prankster: "The trickster appears to be the opposite of the wise old man ... [but] he has a positive side and may even serve a healing function through his transformative influence" (164). Comparable to Tyler Durden, Talbott Reynolds could be interpreted as either archetype depending upon the particular reading of the story, especially how a reader interprets the conclusion. Before the final pages, Gaysia overruns the Blacktopia embassy and declares war against both Caucasia and Blacktopia (276–77). Tensions escalate over the sluggishly slow exchanging of children between homosexual and heterosexual territories. By this time, Gaysia, Caucasia, and Blacktopia are established, and those with Asian genetics have left for Asia, the Jews have traveled to Israel, and Mexicans (Hispanics included) have migrated to Mexico (256).

In an extremely important moment in the story, everything that has happened is called into question. The rug is pulled out from under the meticulous details setting up the three territories, calling into question everything—not the least of which are the arranged killings of countless victims—predicated on Talbott's words. When he sees the title of the book as *Adjustment Day*, Talbott immediately explodes, "That's not what I said!" and after calling Walter an idiot, screams, "Stop the presses!" (278). At this crucial juncture, Talbott confesses, "I told you to call the book *A Judgement Day*!" and the narrator critically adds, "God only knew what else Walter had misheard" (278). As a trickster, Talbott realizes that he has set in motion his own Judgement of Paris, culling the population through human violence (not natural agencies). Conversely, as a mentor, he has tried to teach Walter that humans (although he specifies "men") are ruled by self-propagation, generating ideas: "constant dissemination of self" (303). In terms of carnival, even though he had the financial power to influence national security, Talbott assumes a different persona with Walter, appearing to welcome the chance to play, ironically, a professorial role. Estaban praises *Adjustment Day* as a treatise containing principles to empower him and others to retake control of their lives, and from this viewpoint, Talbott is undoubtedly a wise old man (286–87). Talbott calls the book a "fantasy," and he bases his concepts on the suppositions that blacks shoot each other, gays kill each other with disease, and whites decimate themselves with opiates (303). His miscalling Walter by the name "Warner" is extremely important, indicating both men are unreliable (304). Functioning as mentor, Talbott confides in "Warner": "You're as close as I will ever have to a son. You, you're the apprentice every man dreams of teaching. You will carry my lifetime's wisdom into the future so that mankind will benefit!... The world wants a unified field theory.... A thing, one something that explains everything—give it to them!" (304). This could be the final rant of a madman or solemn wisdom imparted by a prophet. Regardless, Walter's ideological discordance as a result of this revelation returns readers to the first chapter and Walter's execution. Incidentally, at the end, Talbott walks away.

All things considered, readers surely perceive the resulting America as a dystopia. In the grand plan, the tri-partisan states with outlier districts potentially would encompass a utopia. If one thinks about it, Katie Hill would still be in ideological no-woman's land. As a Caucasian bisexual millennial female, her home would be Caucasia—ironically California, her jurisdiction, is Gaysia (120). Palahniuk makes certain to offer sections that show Adjustment Day does not produce a perfect America cleansed of all prejudices contaminating the smooth operation of political correctness. Undeniably, violent rebellion does not change basic human behavior. For instance, Nick just wants to get high. He realizes that there is a shortage of food, water, energy, let alone wild animals attacking people, but all that he wants is hydrocodone, Vicodin, anything to get him through what he considers misery (137). Gavyn notices fascism enforced by teachers obligated to read Talbott's text aloud (as Piper's narrative is constantly broadcast through all media) and by students who record each other so they may report deviant anti-social unconformity, ensuring retribution against those who do not express allegiance to the social order (165). In Gaysia, Delicious (Susan) must perform as a lesbian so she and Gentry (Brian) can remain in the same territory. Delicious knows that if a woman looks at a man provocatively, she risks losing everything she has—her job, her home, and her children—and would likely be designated immediately for repatriation to another location (170). Satirically, Palahniuk plays with reverse discrimination in that the couple must hide out as "closeted heterosexuals" (177).

Perhaps the best example of dystopia is Maryhill, Charlie's fabrication of a medieval society when, in his mind, females were only relevant for breeding and working. Blending his vision of medieval culture with American antebellum values, Charlie establishes a plantation society based on agrarianism (249). Charlie's egotism is manifested in his obsession to return to monarchal rule that is based more on his imagination than historical reality, and this is why Charlie will never be satisfied. This is substantiated by the narrator's contention that Charlie can wear "tabards and brigandines, quilted gambesons, jerkins, and houppelandes," and he can institute the "Revival of Proper Culture" charged with promoting chivalry and implementing "White-Speak," and he can bring back homage to Odin and Thor within a cathedral "complete with a flying buttress and naves," but he will never be completely happy (173). He is trying to recapture something that never existed. As a trickster, Talbott might have anticipated this exploitation of power, understanding humans are motivated by their hedonistic appetites. Shasta's duplicitous emasculation of her lord demarcates a clearly feminist motif in a text that is extremely testosterone driven. Charlie's treatment of women is definitely chauvinistic, and his retribution at the hands (literally) of Shasta would make Camille Paglia, Andrea Dworkin, and other feminists proud.

Palahniuk's emphasis on stereotyping also demonstrates Talbott's inclination to be judged more as a trickster, shaking things up prior to impending national chaos, than a mentor, providing a viable alternative to inevitable national self-destruction. Bing expresses the mantra of Gaysians to control more than their territory: "We will prove our queer power and earn the right to control the nation ... that controls the world!" (94). Garrett espouses the apparent discrimination against homosexuals who are ruled by identity politics, which he believes has reduced both those who are gay and lesbian in addition to African Americans to only caricatures of their "dignified" selves (95). Likewise, Palahniuk sees whites being reduced to the most hideous "one monstrous stereotype" (95), a bunch of "goose-stepping Nazi NASCAR storm troopers" (96). On the contrary, he equally blasts all three groups.

Palahniuk attributes sexual improprieties with, one might guess, the Gaysians, who are defined by their sexuality. For instance, when Gentry and Delicious sneak off to the restroom, while performing cunnilingus on his heterosexual wife, Gentry gives Delicious "pussy farts" while giggling into her vagina. This occurs as Delicious tells her lesbian date not to "be racist" by checking on her (184). While worrying her stepson (from her pseudo-lesbian relationship) is giving away his apparent heterosexuality, Delicious thinks to herself that he should be listening to Gloria Gaynor songs and exhibiting other stereotypically gay mannerisms, ogling men not women (235). Delicious realizes that one slip would lead first to detainment and then exportation. Joking with Felix, she sarcastically asks if he has a circle jerk in which to participate, and, in comic grotesque irony, he responds that he already deposited during a school sperm drive (235). When Delicious hangs out at the porno den of iniquity to hook up with Gentry, she discovers he is carnally spent because of donating repeatedly to a sperm drive at his office (238). These drives were designed to produce children that could be eventually swapped for homosexuals detained in Caucasia and Blacktopia. Frustrated, Delicious glances at a vintage gay film and thinks, while watching the two men swap sperm facials, "What a waste!" (239). Palahniuk emphasizes the obviously repressive treatment inhabitants fear under what seems a totalitarian regime in this region. If anyone is suspected of not being homosexual, the reprisals are severe and the repercussions widespread, apparently without fair and equitable consideration for all of those affected. This is exacerbated by Palahniuk not giving equal sovereignty to blended families, mixing various ethnicities.

Blacktopia is by far the most advanced and most assimilated of the three regions. Critics have compared this location to the fantastic Wakanda in the film *Black Panther*, and the heritage of this population resembles a lost civilization well beyond the curve of current technology. Palahniuk mentions the link to *Black Panther* in a 2018 interview in *The Matador*

Review ("Heaven"). Most of the characters given attention, however, are not affiliated with anything supernatural. When Adjustment Day begins, Jamal is comfortable with the killing, and Bing and Garrett appear to enjoy it, so these three characters from the onset harbor resentment against the mainstream ruling-class that impose its ideology upon African American "human colonies" under "cultural imperialism" (85–86). Jamal realizes that power is freedom from ideological repression, ruminating that once those of his generation no longer conform to "one-size-fits-all" white heteropatriarchal European standards, they will acquire self-authority by breaking the cycle of being socially manufactured automatons (87–88). In this way, Jamal represents the disenfranchised minority American who rebukes societal conformity and resents cultural hegemony. To concede, readers discover Jamal is of mixed race, the last living Peabody male heir (300), yet he is the representative African American in most of the story. Contrary to Spike Lee's Magical Negro whose special abilities help whites—Palahniuk makes this the "so-called magic negro" (201)—inhabitants of Blacktopia eschew from helping those who enslave them, and this cuts off their oppressors from enjoying tremendous scientific innovations. Besides the unfathomable flying pyramids (188), advanced robots (251), and regenerating animal food supplies (253), African Americans possess unbelievable capabilities as the bearers of the cosmic mystery and universal truth (201). As the narrator states, they returned to the fluid vernacular that remained silent for centuries, resurrecting speech that had remained stifled through adversity and hardship, overshadowed only by the tremendous gift of mental telepathy (201). The narrator continues that black inhabitants reclaim in this paradise a destiny taken from them by white rulers (202). Noteworthy, similar to how heterosexuals are caught in Gaysia, whites impersonating blacks betray themselves by trying to imitate complicated handshakes, sagging pants, and other stereotypical behaviors. The black-faced pretenders are betrayed by their idiocy (203). As revenge, blacks tell gullible whites drinking urine cures cancer (203), and Charm's mother is seen drinking urine (226).

Jamal's homesteading at the Peabody mansion contrasts with what might appear to be a black utopia. Miss Josephine Peabody is the most obvious caricature in the novel, representing the Southern white belle devoted to the family estate, personifying its white dedication to the principle of *noblesse oblige*. Her histrionic imitation, especially in speech, of a house slave displays the other side of this ruler/ruled dynamic. In this rewriting of *Gone with the Wind*. Arabella is the devoted black servant, and her transformation from being obligated to serve an elderly white matriarch to freely choosing to help a geriatric woman in need is astonishing. If there is a proactive realistic change, Arabella embodies this socioeconomic improvement as she is empowered, moving from a "hunchbacked old frump" to a beautifully revitalized African American woman (272). Miss Jo's black face via Methoxsalen is, of course, a major social faux pas in 2020, as many politicians and celebrities are trying to account for their previous blackface indiscretions. Miss Jo's attempts to mimic African American behaviors based upon the grossest of stereotypes only amplifies her attempts to pass as Barnabas, long-time worker at the estate. Her own transformation displays compassion and sympathy. As the narrator states, Josephine can no longer bear the burden of her ancestors, and she is willing to relinquish this responsibility. The narrator attributes Miss Jo with "white fatigue," bearing the burden of representing her ancestors, functioning as the remaining signifier of everything antebellum Southern, and she is thoroughly exhausted trying to withstand the sociocultural assaults on her antiquated way of life (294). Josephine counterbalances Charlie by donning a linguistic mask to validate her social position. For instance, her initial words to Jamal about his intentions are cast in stereotypical dialect: "Ah ah-soom yah'll wanz tah ee-rad-ah-kate Mizz Jo's fambly play-s?" (254). This contrasts considerably with the sentence structure in Charlie's section: "His courtier arrayed him in capes of lime green faux sable and fringed gauntlets of pleather studded with costly ersatz pearls. Thusly adorned he mounted the battlements of Maryhill to survey the rich plantings of sugar beets and sweet onions, the arabesque bedding schemes of acorn squash and endive, the wealth of his kingdom" (218).

The burning of Peabody Manse resembles Southern gothic straight out of a William Faulkner novel, and the signification corresponds to the blending of the past with the present and the heaviness of history upon those now living. After Jamal reveals his secret, there appears to be total resolution, as Jamal's recommendation to act completely opposite to the Joad's in *The Grapes of Wrath* suggests positive change (302–03). To highlight the Edenic portrayal of Blacktopia, the narrator describes the setting in almost supernatural terms. Whereas Caucasia had escaped into the country, Blacktopia settled as a beautifully progressive city with elegant domes and stylish spires, gracefully accommodating form and function, synthesizing technology with humanity. More significant, Blacktopia allowed Mother Earth to replenish and to revitalize, to assume sanctuary surrogate status as Mother Africa joined with Atlantis (250). Palahniuk emphasizes the now freely applied "pyro-spiritual and electron-expressive technologies" (250) had been secretly withheld from the white oppressors. In contrast to Charlie and Josephine, who must wear languages to represent the socioeconomic levels in which they desire inclusion, residents in Blacktopia only publicize what has been hidden from the long-standing dominant race. Arabella is free to communicate as she wants, unrestrained by ideological expectations. Josephine's decision to work as Barnabas for Jamal exemplifies a blind allegiance to an ideology out of apathetic acquiescence.

If whites enjoyed power historically, Palahniuk diminishes their influence in this story. From the beginning, when Piper is hired to read script, whites are characterized as having callused hands, smelling like sweat, and drinking cans of beer (15). They wear plaid flannel shirts and wife-beater T-shirts, and, if LaManly is emblematic, they are connected with white supremacists. Instead of an Iron Cross like Katie Hill, LaManly has a swastika tattooed on the side of his thick neck (16). Palahniuk promotes the misconception that whites are against cultural diversity. Case in point, after Frankie's fire marshal father sprays accelerant at the posters displaying smiling children holding hands under a rainbow bearing the caption "Love Comes in Every Color" (24), he declares, "Eat it, cultural Marxism!" and "Get fucked, vibrant ethnic diversity" (25) as he ignites the flames. Dr. Ramantha Steiger-DeSoto, a senior professor in Gender Studies, interprets the pyromania as psychoanalytically sexual, comparing the spraying of accelerant to spraying sperm and diagnosing the arsonist as someone influenced by toxic masculinity, probably a member of an extremist men's group (34). Ironically, Garrett lets Ramantha survive because she finally exhibits empathy and compassion (albeit she is unaware he initially left her stranded to be killed by wolves) (244). Blatant references to white negative stereotypes refer to food. Given the duty of selecting Charlie's brides, Brach owned diners that served Nazi penne pasta, Klan burger, and Hitler veggie taco salad (179). When Xavier and Esteban eat, their choices are the Lester Maddox Chicken Salad and Paula Deens while country-western music plays (222). When Garrett and Ramantha dine, they choose from Grand Dragon or Grand Wizard (large or small) portions of Eva Braun White Cheddar Mac 'n' Cheese, Woodrow Wilson Egg Salad Sandwiches, or Lothrop Stoddard Vanilla Sundaes, while the server chews Juicy Fruit gum (245). White academics signify privilege and entitlement. Dr. Brolly's office—with its marble, leather, and rosewood features—is like the Peabody Manse full of Victorian ostentatiousness, elitist elegance, and privileged poshness (46).

The sections dedicated to Charlie are perhaps the most antagonistic to an identity marker. Charlie is zealously patriotic, believing he is on, to apply the sports metaphor—since, of course, stereotypically white men follow sports—the winning team (64). One can hear the echo "USA!" or "Make America great again!" in the background for the world leader. He and Garrett represent the white working-class, and similar to Jamal and his crew, they benefit greatly from the socioeconomic upheaval (65). They both saw themselves as just plain folk completing the simple jobs put before them (66), yet after the slaughter of those mostly associated with the ruling-class leadership, they felt obligated to reestablish a connection with the ideology created by their ancestors (66). At Maryhill, Charlie recreates the white heteropatriarchal rule that was the target of all multicultural scorn and derision. Nevertheless, Charlie is incapable of understanding that having power is not the same as pretending to have power and living in a castle does not make a man a king (67). More than any other character, Charlie fails to grasp the difference between ideology and mythology, assuming that the proclamation of rules and the subsequent enforcement of them will give him complete authority. Charlie sees Adjustment Day as a chance to return to the good old days of white power, but Palahniuk does not cast him as an intentional bigot or chauvinist. Charlie recollects that all of his life white heteropatriarchy had been blamed for all of the evils in the world (109).

The speech in Charlie's sections is ostentatiously convoluted and superficially ornate to imitate his preference for the gentility that he attaches to medieval life (or, as Shasta claims, to Renaissance Fairs). His speech choices suggest his preference for appearance over substance. Women of Caucasia are required to cover their heads in public, and Charlie's reasoning is that mandatory hats ensure ethnic solidarity (227). Shasta's ridiculously bulky headdress of candles to imitate a crown of thorns became an exercise in dexterity as well as a symbol of Caucasia ethnic lunacy (185). The reference to Shasta's genetic test embodying Caucasia xenophobic intolerance as her Hispanic ethnicity is the negative kind, not the positive type Eurocentrically associated with Spain (186). In a derogatively profound and bigotly discriminatory (on several levels) passage, Charlie ruminates,

> If white people could slack off ... and maybe just nail some pussy, then civilization would have a chance. Not that white women were much help. No, they were only just getting their feet wet with inventing X-rays and eBay, and they obviously did not savor the idea of giving up public accolades and putting their legs in the air. That's why Adjustment Day had gone down. It would give the few remaining alpha studs the chance to boost white numbers. It would remove the temptation of Women's Studies degrees and other horseshit that baited ladies to let their precious Aryan eggs dry up [194].

Palahniuk offers stereotypes such as these to enhance comedy within his satire, knowing how sensitive political correctness is during the first two decades of the twenty-first century, pushing the envelope as only he does. He backs off before he goes too far. In the 2018 interview with *The Good Men Project*, Palahniuk reveals that Charlie is his favorite character because he screws up his chance at positive change, unfortunately illustrating the Peter Principle. Palahniuk is correct that Charlie misses his opportunity, but the cause is more his zealous attachment to false ideas after he is promoted up the ranks than his incompetence. Indirectly, Charlie is perhaps the best example in the novel of someone buying completely into the false consciousness promoted through dominant ideology.

Palahniuk does not disguise his intentions. Talbott's manuscript maps out principles of governance through the Declaration of Interdependence. The primary ISAs that promote the preexisting principles are populated by politicians, professors, and reporters, those in government, in academia, and in the media. After those people are extirpated, people are free to experiment with Talbott's plan, presumably based on Keith Ellison's ethnic divisions (119). After the dominate ISAs have been eradicated, the precepts of the new ideology in Talbott's *Adjustment Day* can be implemented with new political leaders assigned in Gaysia, Blacktopia, and Caucasia. Out with the old, and in with the new. Those with guns assist with the transition. Interestingly, when Ramantha describes the attack in which many of the adjunct faculty were killed, focusing attention on a graduate student almost finished with his dissertation and supposedly targeted because he required students to read something by bell hooks, she mentions that almost every student pulled a weapon from either a Hello Kitty or a G.I. Joe backpack (195). The new structure replaces the old structure, and according to Shasta, people welcomed the change, rather passively, because no recently applied solutions worked any way (119). This is substantiated by Jamal's perceptions that people would not oppose rebellion since there were really no alternatives. People had long since lost faith in religion, in education, and in government (160–61).

According to Althusserian theory, ISAs allow the ruling class to dominate through means other than force, and then the RSAs apply the force. Those who distributed Talbott's book and, more important, created The List and supported the website, promoted the new ideology. Unfortunate yet predictable, as everyone in *Adjustment Day* discovers, the new ruling class is as flawed as the previous one. Power does not guarantee effective leadership. The first violent overthrow of the government, the schools, and the media enforced the installation of the new principles, but the upcoming civil war will determine how strongly they will be implemented. According to Gavyn, the Declaration of Interdependence generated respect for all diversity just as long as the diverse groups remain separated, kind of like relationships that function better as long as participants are apart (163). Ironically, a relationship is for the most part erased or dissolved if separation is a feature of its composition. Simply put, if people are apart, they are not together. Evidently, the principles of the new doctrine will soon be tested through a war that, at least on the surface, Adjustment Day tried to avoid.

What happens is exactly what Slavoj Žižek theorizes would occur. Even though the new ideology appears to be just as ineffective, people trust that it will nonetheless be okay. The narrator reports that workers fear retaliation or retribution through votes on The List. Even though that instrument is supposedly gone, the threat of a new version is enough to inflict fear in the entire American population. As Michel Foucault predicts in his famous analogy, the mass media resemble the prison panopticon that ensures obedience because prisoners fear an ongoing and constant threat of being observed ("Panopticsm" 195–98). The possibility that The List returns online is a similar deterrent, and people fear they might be cited for what could be construed as misbehaviors. This is, however, an acceptable tradeoff for a new ideology to follow. The narrator comments, "As per the Talbott book people were kept confused, living on the brink of chaos for so long that they'd be grateful to accept the terms of any new governing body. The word *grateful* falls short. Absent the constant threat of death, they were gleeful, joyous with relief. Willing to pledge allegiance to any new order so long as it kept the peace" (123). Like sheep, people will obediently follow the bad rules because they are better than the previous bad ones.

Calling attention to his own ideological treatise, Palahniuk has Walter ask Talbott if his book is like *Fight Club*. After clarifying if his apprentice meant the film or the novel, as there are different endings, Talbott explains that *Fight Club* illustrates the process through which each man completes steps toward self-empowerment through the guidance of mentors within a community (157). In obvious self-deprecatory parody, Palahniuk allows Talbott to refute this message by inferring Palahniuk only writes about castration or abortion (157), poking fun at his own rhetoric. Talbott's differentiation between his work and *Fight Club* essentially brings to mind Žižek's theory, as discussed in several preceding chapters, to the narrator's hitting himself in his boss's office—taking action against himself so his boss has less control. Talbott's proclamations concerning Adjustment Day enact a large-scale replica of this scene. Americans hurt themselves through these factions via identity politics instead of allowing the traditional government (with the standard ISAs and RSAs) inflict the pain upon them. In Talbott's distorted vision, people become empowered through self-abuse rather than withstanding the exploitation, repression, or discrimination imposed by traditional political control (157). This illustrates Žižek's point about taking initiative against an unfair and unjust ideology.

As pessimistic as this might sound, as abuse is pejorative no matter how it is spun, there is still optimism. Talbott's next comment in this passage relates to Palahniuk's premise in *Fight Club* and more obviously presented in *Fight Club 2*: "What men want … is a structure for communion" (157). This corresponds directly with Palahniuk's argument that the intellectualization of ideology is not the same as the internalization of the mythology, and men (and women) want the spiritual transcendence only available through ritualistic communion that provides the connection to a higher power, something beyond the individual. Later, echoing Palahniuk, the narrator mentions that humiliation is an inevitable but passing phase (198). People accommodate resiliently to humiliation. More directly, people are likely to endure humiliation while they accept the nascent ideology promoted and enforced by new leaders as long as their basic needs were met and they were generally content. In other words, at the end of Adjustment Day, people accept complacently that the past is the past, and they will docilely follow the status quo since things will simply work out in the long run any way (199).

Undoubtedly, this novel is Palahniuk's own carnivalesque parody of several texts. In the story, *The Great Gatsby* and *Gone with the Wind* are referred to as including suicide and murder with someone escaping to pass along what happened, a sequence that American readers tend to expect (117). Of course, there is the meta-reference in *Adjustment Day* to *Fight Club* as a story that presents various archetypal meanings (118). Readers might not agree the narrator is "self-aware" in that novel's conclusion, yet *Adjustment Day* imitates the end of *The Grapes of Wrath*. Charlie's child is birthed by a washerwoman and nurse, and readers find out Terrence was lied to by his mother, the washerwoman, because she wanted him "to believe in a father and by extension a God…. Life's just easier that way" (314). The president makes an appearance out of nowhere, and Talbott walks away (315–16), an interesting shift of leadership. Especially in 2020, the significance of *Adjustment Day* is not looking backward toward *The Grapes of Wrath*, *The Great Gatsby*, or *The Fountainhead*, all fantastic American novels. Palahniuk's work needs to be validated in the present as accurately displaying the extreme fracturing in this country. Hopefully, Americans are not complacently okay with broken belief systems just because life seems to be "easier" by ignoring the ideological discordance. One wonders.

There were many examples in 2019 to substantiate what Palahniuk addresses in his novel. Nicquel Terry Ellis and Charisse Jones state in the October 14 piece "Banning Ethnic Hairstyles 'Upholds This Notion of White Supremacy.' States Pass Laws to Stop Natural Hair Discrimination" that several minority people believe they are discriminated against because of their natural hairstyles. In the November 13 article "Florida Student Body President Faces Impeachment for Donald Trump Jr.'s $50K Campus Visit," Joshua Bote writes, "[President Michael] Murphy not only endangered students marginalized by the speakers' white nationalist supporters … but also abused his power to advance a particular political party at the expense of the students he should represent." Shelby Fleig reports on November 14 in "Pastor Accused of Being 'Practicing Homosexual' Takes Leave of Absence" that self-identified lesbian Pastor Anna Blaedel asserts, "There is this whole generation that is seeking deeper belonging, community, ritual and spiritual practices to sustain social justice work.... It makes me so sad to see this church that I have loved kind of killing itself by its refusal to focus on what really matters." This is just a handful of stories illustrating how systems are broken.

Art certainly imitates life (or vice versa). Adrianna Rodriguez explains in a November 27, 2019, *USA Today* article titled "Florida Man Tries to Recruit IS for Terrorist Attack on Deans after Getting Kicked Out" how a student tried to contract the Islamic State to "commit a crime of violence," preferably using explosive devices, against deans at Miami-Dade College and Broward College, where he was suspended and expelled. Without a doubt, if The List had been available, Salman Rashid would have posted the names of those two deans and lobbied for "adjustment" against their perceived unfair abuse of power. Rodriguez mentions that the FBI had been investigating Rashid since 2018 after several of his Facebook posts called for "an overthrow of democracy and the establishment of Islamic law." In the December 5, 2019, article in *USA Today* titled "Divided We Fall? Americans See Our Angry Political Debate as a 'Big Problem,'" Susan Page begins, "Americans are united on this: They are sick and tired of being so divided." Many Americans are driven zealously by alliances with traditional political and religious factions, but they are also aligned with others affiliated with economic, sexual, and ethnic populations. For better or for worse, Palahniuk addresses all of these issues satirically through the comic grotesque in *Adjustment Day*.

TEN

Toward a Palahniuk Aesthetic of Comic Grotesque

In "The Biggest Social Media Operation You've Never Heard of Is Run Out of Cyprus by Russians," Lisa Kaplan reports that *Smart Banana*, operated by TheSoul Publishing, is spreading fake news through a lovable character named Mr. Banana. Kaplan offers these two convincing examples from a history lesson about the Soviet Union: Josef Stalin is depicted as a modern-day Robin Hood, taking from the rich and giving to the poor, and Nikita Khrushchev is credited with gifting Alaska to the United States in 1957, not that the territory was sold to America in 1867. In this December 18, 2019, article posted on the website *Lawfare*, Kaplan notes that this Russian-operated company based in Cyprus has New York offices, and its funding comes from lucrative ad revenues from YouTube, Google, and Facebook. Point blank, Kaplan states, "Measured in terms of views and subscribers, [TheSoul Publishing] had the third-largest reach of any group of entertainment channels on YouTube in November—outranked only by Disney and WarnerMedia."

American viewers might believe what they hear Mr. Banana tell them. The website looks trustworthy, with videos about how to fix things, to eat healthily, and to live happily. Mr. Banana does not admit some of what he says strays from the truth, and *Smart Banana* does not offer disclaimers that the information may be false. Essentially, Mr. Banana is rewriting history, and in so doing, he is establishing principles that manipulate how viewers (targeted Americans) perceive communism. After watching the history lessons, viewers take away that Lenin and Khrushchev were nice, generous, altruistic leaders. By extension, Soviet Communism must have promoted equality and fairness. Communism must be a good ideology.

Twentieth-century German playwright Bertolt Brecht did not want spectators watching his plays to escape the reality of their lives. He did not want them caught up in tropes, devices, and other techniques to transport themselves imaginatively away from real-world experiences. Through "epic theatre"—characters speaking with those in the audience, characters assuming more than one role, and other innovative strategies—Brecht deliberately deterred viewers from buying into the illusion produced through the art. Influenced by Walter Benjamin, who understood the capabilities of mass-produced media, Brecht wanted people to understand that artistic performance is a vehicle through which the bourgeois exploited the proletariat.[1] Brecht tried to demonstrate how passive compliance with principles presented through artistic mediums would not lead to improved lifestyles. He wanted his audience to understand the persuasive agency of media to manipulate, to indoctrinate, and to exploit. Undoubtedly, Brecht would not want viewers in the least falling for Mr. Banana's propaganda.

In *One-Dimensional Man*, published in 1964, Herbert Marcuse argues most people are incapable of reacting even after they understand how media dupe them into believing principles affiliated with ideologies.[2] Marcuse agrees that art communicated through media functions as a mechanism to spread ideology. Contrasting ruling-class self-affirmation with counter-culture revolution, Marcuse remarks:

> While this bourgeois order found its rich—and even affirmative—representation in art and literature ... it remained an order which was over-shadowed, broken, refuted by another dimension which was irreconcilably antagonistic ... represented not by the religious, spiritual, moral heroes ... but rather by such disruptive characters as the artist, the prostitute, the adulteress, the great criminal and outcast, the warrior, the rebel-poet, the devil, the fool—those who don't earn a living, at least not in an orderly and normal way [62].

Marcuse anticipates fictional characters replacing representatives of the bourgeoisie, figures that Brecht feared readily seduced those of the proletariat into passive compliance. Marcuse describes these "not normal" types: "The vamp, the national hero, the beatnik, the neurotic housewife, the gangster, the star, the charismatic tycoon perform a function very different from and even contrary to that of their cultural predecessors. They are no longer images of another way of life but rather freaks or types of the same life, serving as an affirmation rather than negation of the established order" (62). Marcuse also understands the range of Mr. Banana's effect, and he too would warn viewers against falling for his kitschy misinformation.

Palahniuk recognizes how media coercively spread information that supports dominant ideologies. He knows likeable, attractive, and charismatic characters have the power to influence audiences. Like Brecht, Palahniuk warns readers against unknowingly becoming complicit in the propagation of exploitative ideologies, and he also uses his own medium to shake his readers from their self-deceptive allegiances to principles, precepts, and tenets spread through what appear innocuous and harmless outlets. Palahniuk answers Marcuse's call for a reactionary art, one that expresses not the values, beliefs, and attitudes of the ruling class or whomever controls mainstream concepts of normalcy, but one that represents the "freaks" on the margins, the disenfranchised, the disenchanted, the disengaged, those on the fringe that will eventually take over the future. Palahniuk's characters reflect the counter-culture Marcuse describes. Through the comic grotesque, Palahniuk attempts to show readers how ideologies affect their lives. In turn, this might motivate them to examine their own lives. They notice how Palahniuk's characters confront ideological discordance, and perhaps, using them as models, they decide to work through their own anxieties, frustrations, and discomforts toward resolutions that enable them to take ownership of their life decisions. Palahniuk just wants each individual to regain his or her personal integrity, sense of self, and feeling of serenity. He acknowledges the importance of the group or the community to facilitate individual growth, but the ultimate goal is personal transcendence, no longer restricted by any domineering system—complete empowerment.

To reiterate what was thoroughly covered in the first and second chapters, the theory of Mikhail Bakhtin serves as the basis for Palahniuk's brand of the comic grotesque. Specifically, Palahniuk takes advantage of Bakhtin's carnival as the opportunity for the reversal of socioeconomic roles comprising the political frameworks in which dominant ideologies function. Palahniuk parodies traditional power structures, thereby calling attention to the inner contradictions inside the false presentations that people take for granted as stable and beneficial. Just as Rabelais applies profanities in bawdy situations associated with the physical transgressivity of low life in *Gargantua and Pantagruel*, Palahniuk draws on the experiences of the ordinary populations, portraying their commonplace struggles, with just as much decadent vulgarity. Palahniuk's reliance on comedy tinged by grotesqueness reflects the carnivalesque inversion of power roles. Those identified as defining what constitutes the normative and then enforcing it as mainstream are mocked because of the power they hold. Palahniuk's characters stand in for those who are not necessarily normal as determined by controlling ideologies. Palahniuk's readers probably identify more with the Rabelaisian type of character than the "religious, spiritual, and moral heroes" whom Marcuse attributes to the ruling class. Applications of Louis Althusser's and Slavoj Žižek's theories help to explain how Palahniuk exposes ideological structures.

Palahniuk has spoken about this directly in a 2008 interview with Josh Jackson in *Paste*. Hesitantly, Jackson eases into a question about the revolutionary effect of his writing by asking Palahniuk if he considers how his characters could serve as models to be imitated. Palahniuk responds first by acknowledging the compliment underlying the imitation, but then he explains how readers typically copy in short spans of simulacra what they do not initially understand, hence breaking down pieces of the original into smaller bites. Palahniuk admits, "So I think one of the highest compliments is to see your work reduced to one-liners on *The Simpsons* or *Jon Stewart*.... Because that is [a] really good sign that the culture is still breaking this thing down and digesting it." Palahniuk also recognizes the effect this has on readers to "try on these new ways of being as a sort of costume," wearing aspects of meaning as they would slip on various pieces of clothing, discovering what works and finding out what does not ("Catching"). Palahniuk's phrasing related to performance calls attention to carnivalesque role reversal, allowing readers to emulate the ideas as long as they wish. Just as the Bakhtinian shift is temporary, Palahniuk infers this role-playing is indefinite. He might be acknowledging that a right fit could involve self-actualization, when readers would gain something productive through the identification with the characters.

In a 2014 interview with *Huck*, Palahniuk expounds upon how he facilitates this process. Responding to why his fiction is "carnal," Palahniuk reflects that many books that he was forced to read during the process of his education lacked this tenor. Palahniuk remarks, "I think in Western culture, maybe all culture, we think of stories that engage us physically as being low-culture—pornography, or horror, that if we feel something within us then it is low culture and so we kind of stay away from that visceral quality in high-culture things" ("Chuck"). The comic grotesque allows Palahniuk to communicate with his readers on a "physically sympathetic level." In this *Huck* interview, Palahniuk clarifies what he means by his mantra that the "fringe is the future" ("Foreword" 9). After speaking about British anthropologist Victor Turner and his quest for the completely status-free community (e.g., Burning Man, essentially the carnival), Palahniuk points out that cultures are constantly shifting, the next dominant culture improving upon the one it succeeds and surpasses ("Chuck"). As has been demonstrated throughout this study, and as the Mr. Banana example illustrates in this chapter, Palahniuk is essentially chronicling how the so-called lowbrow fringe is making its way into the highbrow mainstream, toward Marcuse's bourgeois normal, creeping closer to the center Yeats identifies in his "The Second Coming."

Palahniuk believes individuals are responsible for making this move happen. In a 2017 interview with *MEL*, Palahniuk describes his then twenty-two-year-old father scaring him by threatening to cut off his finger after telling him to stop playing with a metal washer because he would surely get one stuck, which eventually happened. His father threw the axe blade about an inch from his finger. Palahniuk confesses that the incident taught him to take responsibility for the things that occur in his life, and he was to take ownership of what happened ("A Conversation"). This position of taking personal control is at the heart of most Palahniuk texts. In a 2005 article in *Rolling Stone*, Erik Hedegaard quotes Palahniuk as offering this reason for shaving his head: "It's a way of acknowledging that nothing is so sacred that it can't be made better. Suddenly that precious person who you've primped and worked so carefully to make look good, there's no saving that person. That person is fucked. He's lost his ego. He's lost his identity. He's been humiliated." Palahniuk sees this action as freeing.

Palahniuk takes advantage of his writing to express these attitudes. In a 2011 interview in *Lemuria*, Palahniuk shares that writing is "a sort-of therapy that allows you to vent demons in your life, using the mask of an invented character." He believes others will have similar demons, and they will benefit from what they read ("*Lemuria*"). Palahniuk wants his writing to be pragmatic, not like the highbrow books that he chastises. This is the reason, as he shares in a 2018 interview with Michael Bailey, his characters are "based on actual people" ("Ah-Ha"). Palahniuk applies the comic grotesque to allow others to face their ideological demons. Readers might be shocked, but they will later try to figure out the causes for their reactions.

The Palahniuk literary aesthetic was born in his first novel. Jake Arnott agrees in his review of *Adjustment Day* for *The Guardian*, writing that *Fight Club* "hit a zeitgeist moment in the dying years of the 20th century, channeling the spirit of exhausted consumerism and disaffected masculinity. A wry satire on self-help groups and slacker culture, it was a gloriously acerbic swansong for that fin de siècle spawn we called Generation X." Palahniuk created an extended metaphor in *Fight Club*, using the trope fight club as a carnivalesque role-play to depict the vicious struggle a person must endure, often overcoming humiliation, to achieve serenity, the feeling of peace that transcends intellectual understanding. This novel lays out the basic premise that reappears in almost every Palahniuk fiction thereafter, and there could be an argument that Palahniuk self-parodies this first novel continuously throughout his oeuvre. Palahniuk usually portrays a character struggling with ideological discordance, slightly different from cognitive dissonance, the acute anxiety caused when someone realizes the principles that have been trusted as true are false. When the character goes through this revelation, understanding firmly held beliefs are only fabrications created to manipulate, he or she must "fight" by relying on his or her own intuition and instinct, finding strength and reinforcement through rituals initiated through community, and ultimately act independently based on his or her own desires. In every work addressed in this book, characters have followed this pattern in one way or another.

Palahniuk will continue to irritate critics. In an interview with *Paste*, sharing the space with fellow writer Chelsea Cain, Palahniuk confesses that he is working on a coloring book (maybe of *Lullaby*) and a collection of short stories ("Fainting"). In January of 2020, Palahniuk published *Consider This: Moments in My Writing Life After Which Everything Was Different*. In *USA Today*, Barbara VanDenburgh calls the book about writing the "'hottest new book release' of the year." Palahniuk is also receiving critical acclaim in many reviews for *The Invention of Sound*, released in September of 2020. Expectedly, Palahniuk published *Fight Club 3* in April of 2020. Other Palahniuk projects include Andy Mingo's film version of *Lullaby*, James Franco's planned production of *Rant*, and there is still hope for either a mini-series or a big-screen adaption of *Snuff*. There is a proposed television series of *Invisible Monsters*. Of course, there will likely be the next graphic novel *Fight Club 4* and the musical version of *Fight Club*.

Palahniuk will continue to advocate on behalf of those who seek support against forces that they do not understand and over which they have no control. Palahniuk is not afraid to expose these forces for what they are, and he is willing to satirize and to parody them through comic grotesque to make them less frightening and less terrifying. After people are able to laugh at what they fear and find horrific, they are better suited to address them directly, to fight them, and to relinquish them. In the second chapter, Palahniuk's infamous Nightmare Box was described as a vehicle displaying what could be understood as ideological reality. Exposure to the truth is unpredictable and brief, sporadic and quick, and, in the cases presented, progressively debilitating to the viewers. This insight should be, however, beneficial instead of detrimental. Palahniuk is the defender of the counter-faith. In a November 20, 2019, article in *USA Today* titled "Puppies, Phones and Porn: How Model Legislation Affects Consumers' Lives," Kristian Hernández and Pratheek Rebala, both members of the Center for Public Integrity, share this information: "Model bills have tried to mold the debate around moral flash points. A model resolution, written by the National Center on Sexual Exploitation, declares pornography a public health crisis," with porn seen as harmful as smoking. Tying this book's conclusion all the way back to its introduction, noting Bella Thorne's sexual selfies and *Her & Him* direction, this claim that porn is a health risk is exactly the kind of bureaucratic ideology that Palahniuk attacks as ludicrous in the first quarter of the twenty-first century. This is precisely what Palahniuk satirizes through the comic grotesque, exposing the absurdity that underpins such a precept and revealing the hypocrisy that fosters it. Readers are fortunate he does. In the introduction to the *MEL* interview, John McDermott jibes that Tyler Durden would probably wear a Make America Great Again cap and attend President Trump rallies ("A Conversation"). Indeed, no other writer in contemporary American literature does this better than Chuck Palahniuk. And, he is needed.

Chapter Notes

Chapter One

1. For more information about *Fight Club* as a proletarian text, please consult my article "Chuck Palahniuk's *Fight Club* as a Working-Class Novel." Discussed later in this book, in *One-Dimensional Man*, Herbert Marcuse is noted for recognizing that those in the middle class are not all that much different from those in what was traditionally considered the working class, as both are exploited by capitalism. In *Fight Club*, although the narrator is employed in a white-collar position as "a recall campaign coordinator in a shirt and tie" (49), a bureaucratic job that causes him to travel extensively and provides him with the earning capacity to purchase "the things you used to own, now they own you" (44), popular commodities attached to cultural prestige, he is confronted with similar problems associated with blue-collar lifestyles.

2. Conceding the point that Wolfe did not write fantasy along the lines of many of Palahniuk's fiction, much of Wolfe's stories could be considered allegorical. In *I Am Charlotte Simmons*, there is the basketball jock, the frat predator, the nerdy intellectual, the privileged coed, and other stereotypes. However, in "Stalking the Billion-Footed Beast," Wolfe advocates for a new type of realism in contemporary literature, going so far as to claim "non-fiction fiction" is better than pure fiction and to argue journalists would surpass artists in creative depictions of American life (166). Wolfe declares this adamantly in "My Three Stooges" when he posits that "the American novel is dying, not of obsolescence, but of anorexia. It needs ... food. It needs novelists with huge appetites and mighty, unslaked thirsts for ... America ... as she is right now" (170–71). Wolfe asserts that the direction of American writing must not be determined by "isms" but by a commitment to portraying real life unadorned by ideological subjectivity. He reiterates these ideas forcefully through eloquent sarcasm in his essay "In the Land of the Rococo Marxists." Palahniuk could be the writer answering Wolfe's call.

3. Through this line of reasoning, Palahniuk contends that strong literature is, to apply Roland Barthes's terms in *S/Z*, what are called "writerly" instead of "readerly" narratives. According to Barthes and demonstrated through his interpretation of Honoré de Balzac's story "Sarrasine," a readerly text offers almost a passive experience for the reader to understand meaning, whereas a writerly text demands active engagement from the reader to interpret meaning. Palahniuk does not say this explicitly, but he is talking about how readers' expectations change as they mature, and they return to texts with frames of reference that allow them greater opportunities to fully experience texts.

4. In "Teaching Postmodern Parody through Stephen King, Chuck Palahniuk, and *Fight Club*," I thoroughly analyze "The Fringe is the Future" and "The Power of Persisting." In *Chuck Palahniuk, Parodist*, I devote several pages in the first chapter to a discussion of Palahniuk's philosophy, acknowledging Palahniuk's perhaps disingenuous allegiances to romanticism and critics' impulsive propensity to classify him a nihilist, finally placing Palahniuk's ideas somewhere between pragmatism and existentialism (11–15).

Chapter Two

1. I discuss Laura Miller's and Lucy Ellmann's reviews in *Chuck Palahniuk, Parodist* (15–16). I also mention that Miller's criticism is unfortunately what those who access *Wikipedia* as the collective storehouse of all existing knowledge will consider as representative Palahniuk commentary. Concerning information about Palahniuk, these are the trusted book-length publications: Douglas Keesey's *Understanding Chuck Palahniuk* (the best source for general information about Palahniuk pre-2016); Francisco Collado-Rodriguez's *Chuck Palahniuk: Fight Club, Invisible Monsters, Choke*; Cynthia Kuhn and Lance Rubin's *Reading Chuck Palahniuk: American Monsters and Literary Mayhem*; Jeffrey Sartain's *Sacred and Immoral: On the Writings of Chuck Palahniuk*; and Read Mercer Schuchardt's *You Do Not Talk About Fight Club: I Am Jack's Completely Unauthorized Essay Collection*. In the remaining chapters, I do not include information from the many theses and dissertations about Palahniuk and his work. Please note that I am leaving titles as they appear in the original documents. For instance, if an author does not italicize *Fight Club*, I keep "Fight Club" or Fight Club as the item appears in the originally published source.

2. Stallybrass and White write, "We have chosen therefore to consider carnival as one instance of a generalized economy of transgression and of the recoding of high/low relations across the whole social structure. The symbolic categories of grotesque realism in which Bakhtin located can be rediscovered as a governing dynamic of the body, the household, the city, the nation-state—indeed a vast range of interconnected domains" (19). Concerning the body, they state, "To complete the image of grotesque realism one must add that it is always in process, it is always *becoming*, it is a mobile and hybrid creature, disproportionate, exorbitant, outgrowing all limits, obscenely decentred and off-balance, a figural and symbolic resource for parodic exaggeration and inversion" (9). This is specified as "ritual inversion" in which "Status degradation through exposure of the grotesque aspects of the body and exorbitant exaggeration of its features" (183). The top of the body infers the spiritual; the bottom part of the body refers to the rational. I mention many of the definitions of transgression in the first chapter of *Chuck Palahniuk, Parodist* to a summary of transgressive writing (11–12).

3. Specifically, Frye states:
The conception of irony meets us in Aristotle's *Ethics*, where the *eiron* is the man who deprecates himself, as opposed to the *alazon*. Such a man makes himself invulnerable, and, though Aristotle disapproves of him, there is no question that he is a predestined artist, just as the *alazon* is one of his predestined victims. The term irony, then, indicates a technique of appearing to be less than one is, which in literature becomes most commonly a technique of saying as little and meaning as much as possible, or, in a more general way, a pattern of words that turns away from direct statement of its own obvious meaning. (I am not using the word ironic itself in any unfamiliar sense, though I am exploring some of its implications) [40].

4. In his preface, after noting the pejorative meanings of "disability," Goodley comments, "*Disability* might be understood as an identity position, often a negative, marked and stigmatized social position. But, as we flesh out the narrative and seek its characters and plot lines, we might find disability is a potentiality: a moment, an event, a calling and an encounter" (xi). Campbell includes those with disabilities within the category of "stigmatized people," viewing ableism as synonymous with racism, sexism, and homophobia (22–23). Nevertheless, considering optimism over pessimism, she asserts that disability could be perceived as a strength rather than a weakness. After stating that those with disabilities are initially viewed as freak show participants (28), Campbell explains, "The second image is of disabled people engaged in guerrilla activity—rejecting the promises of liberalism and looking elsewhere, daring to think in *alternative ways* about impairment" (29). She contends that realistic "disability success stories," ones celebrating abnormality, contradict romantically idealistic narratives advocating disablism/ableism: "Normally these stories are often based on the notion of 'success *in spite of*

impairment' which is profoundly different to stories that embrace impairment and are based on the notion of 'success *because of* disability' or stories about living with ableism" (29). The meaning of Other in this context is not unlike its signification in postcolonial studies (see Edward W. Said's *Orientalism* or Gayatri Chakravorty Spivak's "Can the Subaltern Speak?").

5. In his lectures about the abnormal, Foucault calls attention to this point: "When I say these are grotesque texts I use the word *grotesque*, if not in an absolutely strict sense, at least in a somewhat restricted and serious sense. I am calling 'grotesque' the fact that, by virtue of their status, a discourse or an individual can have effects of power that their intrinsic qualities should disqualify them from having" (11). He later claims,

> We leave it to others, then, to pose the question of the effects of truth that may be produced in discourse by the subject who is supposed to know. As for myself, I would rather study the effects of power produced in reality by a discourse that is at the same time both statutory and discredited. Clearly, we could pursue this analysis in different directions. We could try to identify the ideology behind the discourse I have illustrated with examples. We could also start from their institutional support, from judicial and medical institutions, in order to see how they arose.... Rather than attempt an ideological or "institutional" analysis, I will try to identify and analyze the technology of power that utilizes those discourses and tries to put them to work [14].

A helpful source to understand Foucault's ideas is David Couzens Hoy's *Foucault: A Critical Reader*.

6. In his famous letter to Franz Mehring, Engels writes that "ideology is a process accomplished by the so-called thinker consciously, indeed, but with a false consciousness. The real motives impelling him remain unknown to him, otherwise it would not be an ideological process at all. Hence he imagines false or apparent motives." In *History and Class Consciousness*, Lukács states,

> It might look as though by dissolving the dilemma in this manner we were denying consciousness any decisive role in the process of history. It is true that the conscious reflexes of the different stages of economic growth remain historical facts of great importance; it is true that while dialectical materialism is itself the product of this process, it does not deny that men perform their historical deeds themselves and that they do so consciously. But as Engels emphasises in a letter to Mehring, this consciousness is false. However, the dialectical method does not permit us simply to proclaim the "falseness" of this consciousness and to persist in an inflexible confrontation of true and false. On the contrary, it requires us to investigate this "false consciousness" concretely as an aspect of the historical totality and as a stage in the historical process.

7. These scholars are undoubtedly the authorities on the grotesque, and for my purpose here, there is no need to summarize their extremely influential commentary on this subject. For historical, social, and cultural information about the grotesque, these books are highly recommended: Wolfgang Kayser's *The Grotesque in Art and Literature* (perhaps the most influential work), Geoffrey Galt Harpham's *On the Grotesque*, Bernard McElroy's *Fiction of the Modern Grotesque*, Dieter Meindl's *American Fiction and the Metaphysics of the Grotesque*, James Goodwin's *Modern American Grotesque*, and Philip Thomson's *The Grotesque*. Also worth perusing is the collection of essays in Blake Hobby's *The Grotesque* as well as Irving Howe's famous "The Book of the Grotesque" (included in Hobby's book).

8. Dunne also addresses this subject in "Beyond Grotesqueness in *Winesburg, Ohio*" and "The Book of the Grotesque: Textual Theory and the Editing of *Winesburg, Ohio*." I apply Dunne's criticism in my article "Sherwood Anderson's Grotesques in Thomas Boyd's *Points of Honor*" submitted to *ANQ: A Quarterly Journal of Short Articles, Notes, and Reviews*.

9. The narrator explains the underlying theory of the old man's stories: "That in the beginning when the world was young there were a great many thoughts but no such thing as a truth. Man made the truths himself and each truth was a composite of

a great many vague thoughts. All about in the world were the truths and they were all beautiful" (4–5). After categorizing varieties of truths, the old man establishes a protocol, prefacing that "it was the truths that made the people grotesques" (5). The narrator then clarifies, "It was his notion that the moment one of the people took one of the truths to himself, called it his truth, and tried to live his life by it, he became a grotesque and the truth he embraced became a falsehood" (5).

10. Besides the mentioned criticisms by Dentith, Renfrew, and Holquist, these sources provide helpful commentary about Bakhtin's concepts: Richard M. Berrong's *Rabelais and Bakhtin: Popular Culture in Gargantua and Pantagruel*, Don Bialostosky's *Mikhail Bakhtin: Rhetoric, Poetics, Dialogics, Rhetoricality*, M. Keith Booker's *Techniques of Subversion in Modern Literature: Transgression, Abjection, and the Carnivalesque*, Deborah J. Haynes's *Bakhtin Reframed*, Michael Holquist's *Dialogism: Bakhtin and His World*, Cheryl Emerson's *Critical Essays on Mikhail Bakhtin*, David Lodge's *After Bakhtin: Essays on Fiction and Criticism*, Pam Morris's *The Bakhtin Reader: Selected Writings of Bakhtin, Medvedev and Voloshinov*, Graham Pechey's *Mikhail Bakhtin: The Word in the World*, Katrina Clark and Michael Holquist's *Mikhail Bakhtin*, Ken Hirschkop and David Shepherd's *Bakhtin and Cultural Theory*, and Barry A. Brown, Christopher Conway, Rhett Gambol, Susan Kalter, Laura E. Ruberto, Tomás F. Taraborrelli, and Donald Wesling's *Bakhtin and the Nation*. Another useful source is Craig Brandist's entry "The Bakhtin Circle" in the *Internet Encyclopedia of Philosophy*. Julia Kristeva's theory of intertextuality—in which all texts are interconnected, past ideas intertwined linguistically with present ideas, similar to T. S. Eliot's main premise in "Tradition and the Individual Talent" and proposed in John Barth's "The Literature of Exhaustion"—is usually compared to Bakhtin's heteroglossia or dialogism. Please refer to Kristeva's "Word, Dialogue, and Novel."

11. Renfrew asserts that the union of "degradation and renewal, death and rebirth" subordinates the official importance of language while it simultaneously elevates the diversity of linguistic expression (144).

12. Significantly, Bakhtin continues by pointing out "degradation" and "debasement" are related with the lower body or lower stratum, connected with "the life of the belly and the reproductive organs," consequently associated with "defecation and copulation," facets of grotesque realism (21).

13. These sources are also beneficial for understanding more about Althusser's theory: William C. Dowling's *Jameson, Althusser, Marx: An Introduction to The Political Unconscious*, Gregory Elliott's *Althusser: A Critical Reader*, William S. Lewis's *Louis Althusser and the Traditions of French Marxism*, Warren Montag's *Louis Althusser*, and Robert Paul Resch's *Althusser and the Renewal of Marxist Social Theory*. Worth accessing for a general overview of "ideology," comparable to Edwards and Graulund's coverage of "grotesque," is James Decker's *Ideology*. A recent publication also worth perusing is *Allegory and Ideology* by Fredric Jameson, author of *The Political Unconscious* and countless other publications on this subject. Althusser also articulates his theory in *For Marx* and *Philosophy of the Encounter*. Althusser's disciple Pierre Macherey in *A Theory of Literary Production* proposes that "the speech of the book comes from a certain silence, a matter which it endows with form, a ground on which it traces a figure. Thus, the book is not self-sufficient; it is necessarily accompanied by a *certain absence*, without which it would not exist. A knowledge of the book must include a consideration of this absence" (85). This means that criticism exposes the ideological "unconscious" beneath the surface of literary text, precisely the goal of my interpretation of Palahniuk's fiction.

14. Althusser's description of ISAs is beneficial. Althusser insists the following are obvious institutions promoting ideologies [his formatting is maintained in this quotation]:

the religious ISA (the system of the different churches),
the educational ISA (the system of the different public and private "schools"),
the family ISA,
the legal ISA,
the political ISA (the political system, including the different parties),
the trade-union ISA,

the communications ISA (press, radio and television, etc.), the cultural ISA (literature, the arts, sports, etc.) [96].

Althusser contends two premises about ideology: ideology signifies the imagined connection between people and reality (109), and ideology is expressed through materialism (112). People believe in ideology to guide their practical lives, and they trust the forces that impose that ideology. Althusser's conclusion is worth reading verbatim, although per copyright, it cannot be quoted in its entirety here. Significantly, Althusser argues ideologies are not created out of ISAs but from socioeconomic factions in class battle. The ramifications of the struggle initiate the ideology (26). RSAs are designated as the "muscle" behind ISAs, enforcing through physical and perceptible means the intellectual and imperceptible ISAs.

15. These sources are also beneficial for learning more about Žižek's theory: Rex Butler's *Slavoj Žižek: Live Theory*, Sarah Kay's *Žižek: A Critical Introduction*, Tony Meyers's *Slavoj Žižek*, Ian Parker's *Slavoj Žižek: A Critical Introduction*, Matthew Sharpe's *Slavoj Žižek: A Little Piece of the Real*, and Marko Zlomislić's *Žižek: Paper Revolutionary: A Franciscan Response*. Another useful source is Matthew Sharpe's entry "Slavoj Žižek" in the *Internet Encyclopedia of Philosophy*. Žižek is essentially Lacanian in how he formulates his psychoanalytical theory. See Jacques Lacan's *Écrits* for an explanation of psychic developmental stages of the Imaginary, the Symbolic, and the Real.

16. Žižek provides this commentary concerning Sloterdijk's theory of kynicism:

We must distinguish this cynical position strictly from what Sloterdijk calls *kynicism*. Kynicism represents the popular, plebeian rejection of the official culture by means of irony and sarcasm: the classical kynical procedure is to confront the pathetic phrases of the ruling official ideology—its solemn, grave tonality—with everyday banality and to hold them up to ridicule, thus exposing behind the sublime *noblesse* of the ideological phrases the egotistical interest, the violence, the brutal claims to power. This procedure, then, is more pragmatic than argumentative: it subverts the official proposition by confronting it with the situation of its enunciation; it proceeds *ad hominem* (for example when a politician preaches the duty of patriotic sacrifice, kynicism exposes the personal gain he is making from the sacrifice of others [26].

Significantly, Gilles Deleuze and Félix Guattari in *Anti-Oedipus* contend the domination of Freudian psychoanalytic theory deters people from this "confrontation." Moreover, in *A Thousand Plateaus*, they argue that humans as "desiring machines" are repressed by societal agencies and capitalistic consumerism. They believe that authority is the nemesis of desire, and only "nomadism" successfully rebels against authority because it claims no tie to it (*Thousand* 382). Their rhizome theory could be applied to the anonymous ideological systems discussed, but that is perhaps the subject of an entire chapter, perhaps another book.

17. Noteworthy is Marko Zlomislić's refutation of this theory in *Žižek: Paper Revolutionary: A Franciscan Response*:

Žižek's answer to fight the system is given in his analysis of *Fight Club*. When Ed Norton's character beats himself up in front of his boss, Žižek says, "the fact of beating up oneself renders clear the simple fact that the master is superfluous." For Žižek, beating oneself up is "the first act of liberation." It is of course funny to realize that Ed Norton's character never beat himself up at all. It was all an act. No real blood was shed. Žižek would have us believe, "the same strategy is used in political demonstrations ... the way to bring about a shocking reversal of the situation is for individuals in the crowd to starting beating each other." This is idiotic. Of course, since the proof is always in the pudding, I don't recall Žižek beating himself up when the Yugo-Serbian Army attacked Slovenia. He was, of course, hidden from real danger watching films and pretending that he had an answer to the stain of the Real flooding in the streets of Ljubljana [114].

Žižek repeats his argument about *Fight Club*, almost verbatim in sections, in three different texts: "The Violence of the Fantasy," "Redemptive Violence," and "An

Ethical Plea for Lies and Masochism." He mentions his argument briefly in *Violence: Six Sideways Reflections* (126). Olivia Burgess refers to Žižek's critique of *Fight Club* in "Revolutionary Bodies in Chuck Palahniuk's *Fight Club*." Burgess's article is highly recommended reading.

Chapter Three

1. Granted, these statistics and others cited in tabloid news services are from *Paint Bottle (paintbottle.com)*, a now defunct porn site. I offer these statistics not as valid polling information but to show the prevailing trend in how popular news services (not necessarily first-tier trusted services) spin the information.

2. As I mention in the chapter about *Snuff* in *Chuck Palahniuk. Parodist*, many of the references to Hollywood celebrities are sexual. I mention how Palahniuk offers factoids pertaining to Rock Hudson, Gene Kelly, Oliver Reed, Lorne Greene, Marlene Dietrich, Tallulah Bankhead, Lauren Bacall, Barbara Stanwyck, Dolores del Rio, Rita Hayworth, Betty Grable, Jeff Chandler, Eric Fleming, Richard Burton, and, of course, Marilyn Monroe (42–43).

3. Sheila states specifically about the importance of Grace Quek in gaining a feminist foothold in the porn industry:
You could cite Annabel Chong—real name: Grace Quek—who fucked that first world's record of 251 losers because, for once, she wanted a woman to be "the stud." Because she loved sex and was sick of feminist theory portraying female porn performers as either idiots or victims. In the early 1970s, Linda Lovelace was delivering exactly the same philosophical reasons behind her work in *Deep Throat*. The last thing today comes down to is personal growth. Do you respect someone's right to seek challenges and discover their true potential? How is a gang bang any different than risking your life to climb Mount Everest? And do you accept sex as a form of viable emotional therapy? It only came out later, about Linda Lovelace being held hostage and brutalized. Or how, before becoming a porn star, Grace Quek had been raped in London by four men and a twelve-year-old boy [24].

4. In the manuscript "Cassie Wright, Stormy Daniels, and #MeToo: Teaching Chuck Palahniuk's *Snuff* as a Response to Heteropatriarchy," soon to appear in Eyal Handelsman and Chris Burlingame's *Chuck Palahniuk: The Treasures of Trash and Transgression* by Palgrave Publishing, I offer a feminist interpretation (or explain the protocol for one such reading). I comment about Cassie's ultimate empowerment: "instead of Cassie Wright's death—the purpose of a snuff' film—she experiences something comparable to a feminist apotheosis, a spiritual rebirth, which refutes [Andrea] Dworkin's claim that the sexual climax is death. In *Snuff*, *la petite mort* takes on new meaning. I wanted students to see Cassie Wright as gaining complete redemption at the end of *Snuff*."

5. In *Chuck Palahniuk. Parodist*, I point out how Palahniuk plays with Jean Baudrillard's theory of simulacra in this novel. If time and space would permit, investigation of all the film parodies might lead to interesting and provocative conclusions. This might lend itself to a structuralist reading that would analyze the relationships between signifiers in the Hollywood versions, the porn versions, and corresponding connections between various actors. I mention in my previous book that there is real-life progression of *The Wizard of Oz* to the porn *Not The Wizard of Oz XXX* released in 2013, starring porn legend Nina Hartley, who seems to fit the fictional Cassie Wright profile (51). I also comment that a film version of *Snuff* starring Darryl Hannah as Cassie, Tom Sizemore as Branch, and Thora Birch as Sheila was planned. By the way, Birch is the daughter of porn legend Carol Connors, adding a level of simulacra to the production (51–52).

Chapter Four

1. The website dedicated to *A Course in Miracles* is sponsored by the Foundation for Inner Peace: https://acim.org/acim/. This website contains links to various components comprising this spiritual ideology. *A Course in Miracles* is the definitive treatise for this master narrative, and its tenets are often expressed along the lines of Christian gospel. One might think of other texts that

identify plans toward enlightenment, such as *Alcoholics Anonymous*, which explains twelve-step recovery protocols and contains testimonies from those whom benefitted from following the dictums of the master code. As Helen Schucman was supposedly divinely inspired, some think Bill W. and Dr. Bob had divine guidance in formulating the twelve steps.

2. In *Chuck Palahniuk, Parodist*, I address Palahniuk's imitation of Blume's book in the chapter entitled "*Damned* as Parody of Dante's *Inferno*" (90–109). I state about the Blume/Dante/Palahniuk connection: "In effect, by imitating Dante's elaborately mapped out literary geography of hell and taking content from Blume's depictions of the hellish experiences associated with the feminine rite of passage into tweendom, Palahniuk offers a postmodern parody that merges high culture and popular culture" (92). Madison is actually thirteen, but Margaret starts out as eleven and has her twelfth birthday in Blume's novel.

3. Situating Madison within parodies of Dante and of Blume, I trace in *Chuck Palahniuk, Parodist* how Palahniuk draws indirectly from his Italian predecessor but cribs more directly from the young adult author. I explain how Madison models the "every person" archetype in Dante's journey story traveling through hell, purgatory, and paradise. I also contend Madison's ultimate goal is personal empowerment fostered by a nurturing community. Her transformation from nerd to leader would not have happened if she had not been helped by the other characters in the story, which, in her case, is the hellish process associated with puberty (92–93).

4. Referring to sinners who can relinquish all hope, almost wishing she too could do something similar, Madison shares how she could hear those brutally tortured in cells next to hers, surmising that they have given up all hope, and, in turn, envying their ability to do so (25). Madison starts to believe she is addicted to hope in much the same manner as she was addicted to Xanax (23), comparing hope to a drug from which she is incapable of craving (33).

5. Granted, Madison begins feeling empowered when she tricks her parents (later readers find out they knew her plan) so she can stay at the boarding school over Christmas break. In bad-girl mode, she rejects decorum, convention, everything connected to authority. Walking naked outside the dormitory, thinking about campus security and enjoying the falling ice crystals, Madison exclaims in bad-girl vocabulary: "All of me felt the thrill of being touched at that same instant. You see, I wanted to be discovered. I wanted to be seen at the very height of my prepubescent power, my tits-out, bare-fanny, legally off-limits kiddie-porn Lolita power" (67). In hell, as she gains control, Madison replaces her desire to just fit in, which was what she initially wanted, with much more authority: "Yes, now it's power I want. Not affection. I don't want that kind of pointless, impotent power, as earlier discussed" (195). At this juncture of the story, she plans to take full advantage of all the opportunities death provides.

6. Bakhtin explains "degradation" (mentioned in first chapter) within the boundaries of the body and lower stratum stomach and genitalia (*Rabelais* 21).

Chapter Five

1. I took advantage of this same event to introduce my feminist approach to *Snuff* in "Cassie Wright, Stormy Daniels, and #MeToo: Teaching Chuck Palahniuk's *Snuff* as a Response to Heteropatriarchy" in *Chuck Palahniuk: The Treasures of Trash and Transgression*, edited by Eyal Handelsman and Chris Burlingame (forthcoming through Palgrave). I apply similar wording in both paragraphs.

2. Please refer to my article entitled "'Just hear that potty mouth!': An Argument of Sarah Ruden's Translation of *Lysistrata*" published in a 2018 issue of *Neohelicon* for more information about the various approaches to translating *Lysistrata*.

3. I offer a similar review of criticism about *Beautiful You* in my article entitled "Chuck Palahniuk's *Beautiful You*, Alfred Kinsey's *Sexual Behavior in the Human Female*, and the Commodification of Female Sexual Desire" (119–20). The point in both the article and this chapter is critics largely ignore Palahniuk's application of the comic grotesque to demonstrate his points about American ideology. This novel definitely deserves more attention.

4. A variation of this section also appears in my article about *Beautiful You* (104).

5. In my article about *Beautiful You*, I also explain how Palahniuk taps into twenty-first century tropes relying on sexist jokes and misogynist fantasies that are crudely transgressive yet communicate, nonetheless, relevant meanings about gender relationships (118).

Chapter Six

1. Douglas Keesey's *Understanding Chuck Palahniuk* is currently the standard for background information including biography. Keesey's first chapter (1–14) offers a concise yet thorough overview of Palahniuk's life. Other interesting biographical articles are Erik Hedegaard's "Chuck Palahniuk: A Heart Breaking Life of Staggering Weirdness" in *Rolling Stone* and Joshua Chaplinsky's "Strange But True: A Short Biography of Chuck Palahniuk" in *The Cult*. Additional sources about the alleged embezzlement is Sadye Scott-Hainchek's "Chuck Palahniuk 'Close to Broke' After Alleged Embezzlement" and Michael Schaub's "'Fight Club' Author Chuck Palahniuk Says He's 'Close to Broke' after Agent's Accountant Charged with Embezzlement."

2. I provide a similar explanation of dirty realism in "The Dunning-Kruger Effect in Dirty Realism: Dorothy Allison's 'Jason Who Will Be Famous,' Larry Brown's 'Waiting for the Ladies,' and Chuck Palahniuk's 'Romance'" forthcoming in the *Journal of the Short Story in English*. I also summarize these two seminal definitions of dirty realism as Note #2 in the manuscript "Cassie Wright, Stormy Daniels, and #MeToo: Teaching Chuck Palahniuk's *Snuff* as a Response to Heteropatriarchy" forthcoming in *Chuck Palahniuk: The Treasures of Trash and Transgression*. In his influential dissertation *Towards a Definition of Dirty Realism*, Tamas Dobozy addresses the contradiction between expectations and results, or what he terms the "aesthetic of hypocrisy," distinguishing dirty realism from other genres (62). In the article "In the Country of Contradiction the Hypocrite is King: Defining Dirty Realism in Charles Bukowski's *Factotum*," Dobozy defines the "hypocrisy aesthetic" in terms of production: "Dirty realism finds itself in a culture crying out for a 'countercultural' program at the same time that the culture feeds off such countercultural forms" (44). Referring to this article, Alice Whitmore clarifies, "Dirty realist narratives, Dobozy argues, tend towards paradox and self-contradiction as a kind of passive-aggressive reflection of postmodernity, simultaneously confusing and undermining traditional representations of imaginings of society." Seen through the lens of this study, what is deemed as counter-cultural in dirty realism might actually be what is now becoming the mainstream in most of America, confirming Palahniuk's prediction that the marginalized are replacing those in the power middle. Dirty realistic writing illustrates this move.

3. Concerning Palahniuk's application of animals in parables, Benjamin Judge writes that Palahniuk is "at his best, our Aesop," and he refers to *Fight Club* as Palahniuk's most famous example.

4. Noteworthy are two quotes from Palahniuk. Speaking about his drawing from Campbell's archetypes, Palahniuk exclaims in a 2004 interview in *The Guardian*, "In almost all my work, I try to re-invent Christian images and stories and themes. You'd be amazed by the letters I get from young Christians who recognise this and enjoy it" ("It's"). In a 2005 *Three Monkeys Online* interview, Andrew Lawless quotes Palahniuk elaborating on this point, reiterating that he offers alternatives to religions and other totalizing systems: "We used to go to church to confess our worst behavior, to be heard and forgiven, then to be redeemed and accepted.... In most of my books, people achieve this same reunion with their peers, but through the new 'religious' forums of 12-step groups, support groups, and [writing groups]."

5. Adams contends "Torcher" would develop into an interesting novel, and most readers might agree. They probably would. Compared to all of the other stories, Palahniuk subversively uses the comic grotesque through what is clearly a version of Bakhtinian carnival to display ideological power oppositions working at the various levels of mainstream culture versus

counter-culture, older generation versus current generation, and masculine versus feminine (portrayed generally but also within Ludlow's marriage).

Chapter Seven

1. As visual and graphic artists attest, there is of course aesthetic theory supporting coloring books. Since this analysis is more literary than artistic, there will not be additional summary devoted to the coloring medium. I realize there is indeed a tradition that precludes Palahniuk's application of the coloring book, yet my aim does not necessarily demand a survey of thought and practice that informs what is provided in *Bait* and in *Legacy*.

2. Palahniuk published *Fight Club 2* in 2015, preceding the publications of *Bait* and *Legacy*. However, attention will be given to the coloring books before the comic book primarily because Palahniuk's stories and novella correspond to those in *Make Something Up* (2015) and secondarily because the violence, particularly the characters' reactions against repressive ideologies, in the sequel to *Fight Club* is similar to what occurs in *Adjustment Day* (2018). Palahniuk definitely plays with form and content in *Fight Club 2*, but he accomplishes this through a strategy that anticipates points in his last novel. The stories and novella refer to what Palahniuk did so masterfully well in *Make Something Up*.

3. The significance of familial "blood" will be explained in the next chapter about *Fight Club 2*. As a hint, after ingesting blood thinner, members of Rize or Die spray precious art that Tyler does not like with their blood. Palahniuk is comparing blood metaphorically and literally to paint.

4. An interesting study of Palahniuk's choices of historical personalities would reap several significant results. Just as the names of real as well as fictional personalities in *Tell-All* becomes a play of signifiers pointing toward various meanings, and thus packing each paragraph chocked full of semiotic denotations and connotations leading to fruitful interpretations, Palahniuk appears to choose his characters based upon inferences to white supremacy, racism, and heteropatriarchy. An article has yet to be written that digs into all of the structural ramifications of Palahniuk's choices.

Chapter Eight

1. The purpose of this chapter is not to analyze *Fight Club 2* as a graphic novel or to compare and contrast that text with its prose counterpart. Perhaps the most academic treatment of this genre is Hillary Chute's groundbreaking "Comics as Literature? Reading Graphic Literature" published in 2008 in the well-respected journal *PMLA*, the publication of the Modern Language Association. Chute introduces her study: "The field hasn't yet grasped its object or properly posed its project. To explore today's comics we need to go beyond preestablished rubrics: we have to reexamine the categories of fiction, narrative, and historicity. Scholarship on comics—and specifically on what I will call graphic narrative—is gaining traction in the humanities.... Throughout this essay, I treat comics as a medium—not as a lowbrow genre, which is how it is usually understood" (452). An entire chapter could address the subtleties and nuances of such an analysis. For additional information about graphic texts, please consult these excellent sources: Francisca Goldsmith's *The Reader's Advisory Guide to Graphic Novels*, Scott McCloud's *Understanding Comics: The Invisible Art*, his *Reinventing Comics*, Matthew Miller's *Class, Please Open Your Comics: Essays on Teaching with Graphic Narratives*, Stephen E. Tabachnick's *Teaching the Graphic Novel*, Joseph Michael Sommers's *Critical Insights: The American Comic Book*, Gary Hoppenstand's *Critical Insights: The Graphic Novel*, Keith M. Booker's *"May Contain Graphic Material": Comic Books, Graphic Novels, and Film*, Greg Garrett's *Holy Superheroes!: Exploring the Sacred in Comics, Graphic Novels, and Film*, Andrew Dale's *Graphic Novels: Essential Literary Genres*, Karin Kukkonen's *Studying Comics and Graphic Novels*, Jake Jakaitis and James F. Wurtz's *Crossing Boundaries in Graphic Narrative: Essays on Forms, Series, and Genres*, and Daniel Stein and Jan-Noël Thon's *From Comic Strips to Graphic Novels: Contributions to the Theory and History of Graphic Narrative*. A simple guide to writing about

graphic texts is available through the Duke University writing center. Refer to "Writing about Comics and Graphic Novels" in the bibliography.

2. In other articles, I address *Fight Club* as a recovery text by applying the second and the fourth chapters to ideological principles laid out in *What is the Oxford Group?*, *Alcoholics Anonymous*, and *Twelve Steps and Twelve Traditions*. My article "Disability Studies Simulacra in Chuck Palahniuk's *Fight Club(s)*" is forthcoming in the spring issue of *The Midwest Quarterly*. I have submitted a much shorter piece in which I only explain how the two chapters promote recovery ideas in "The Importance of the Support Group Chapters in Chuck Palahniuk's *Fight Club*" to *The Explicator*. There are many publications about *Fight Club* (novel and film), and the girth of this paragraph demonstrates the attention the story has received. The following is a selective list—there are many more online sources—of recommended criticism about Palahniuk's most famous book: Robert Bennett's "The Death of Sisyphus, Existentialist Literature, and the Cultural Logic of Chuck Palahniuk's *Fight Club*," Kevin Alexander Boon's "Men and Nostalgia for Violence: Culture and Culpability in Chuck Palahniuk's *Fight Club*," Olivia Burgess's "Revolutionary Bodies in Chuck Palahniuk's *Fight Club*," Jeremy De Chavez's "The Political Subject Is a Lover Not a Fighter: Reading Chuck Palahniuk's Fight Club as a Love Story," Jason J. Dodge's "Spaces of Resistance: Heterotopia and Transgression in Chuck Palahniuk's *Fight Club*," Justin Garrison's "'God's Middle Children' Metaphysical Rebellion in Chuck Palahniuk's Fight Club," Henry A. Giroux's "Private Satisfactions and Public Disorders: Fight Club, Patriarchy, and the Politics of Masculine Violence," Starling Hunter and Saba Singh's "A Network Text Analysis of Fight Club," Melissa Iocco's "Addicted to Affliction: Masculinity and Perversity in *Crash* and *Fight Club*," Matt Jordan's "Marxism, Not Manhood: Accommodation and Impasse in Seamus Heaney's *Beowulf* and Chuck Palahniuk's *Fight Club*," Jesse Kavadlo's "The Fiction of Self-Destruction: Chuck Palahniuk, Closet Moralist," Elizabeth Kinder and Patricia Pender's "'A Copy of a Copy of a Copy': Framing the Double in *Fight Club*," Simon Lindgren's "A Copy of a Copy of a Copy: Exploring Masculinity under Transformation in *Fight Club*," Peter Mathews's "Diagnosing Chuck Palahniuk's *Fight Club*," Mary W. McCampbell's "'Paradigms Are Dissolving Left and Right': Baudrillard's Anti-Apocalypse and Chuck Palahniuk's *Survivor*," Andrew Hock Soon's "Muscular Existentialism in Chuck Palahniuk's *Fight Club*," Alexandra Reuber's "Identity Crisis and Personality Disorders in Edgar Allan Poe's 'William Wilson' (1839), David Fincher's *Fight Club* (1999), and James Mangold's *Identity* (2003)," Read Mercer Schuchardt's "'A Copy of a Copy of a Copy': *The Matrix*, *American Beauty*, and *Fight Club* as Retellings of Pink Floyd's *The Wall*," Robert T. Schultz's "White Guys Who Prefer Not To: From Passive Resistance ('Bartleby') To Terrorist Acts (*Fight Club*)," Ana Sobral's "'Hitting Bottom': Deviance in Chuck Palahniuk's *Fight Club*," Markus Oliver Spitz's "Plot, Psychosis and Protest in Chuck Palahniuk's Fight Club," Christina Wald's "Second Selves, Second Stories: Unreliable Narration and the Circularity of Reading in Ford Madox Ford's *The Good Soldier* and Chuck Palahniuk's/David Fincher's *Fight Club*," and Stacy Weida's "Review of Becoming the New Man in Post-Post Modernist Fiction: Portrayals of Masculinities in David Foster Wallace's *Infinite Jest* and Chuck Palahniuk's *Fight Club*."

3. To support the argument that Palahniuk probably equates "secondary fathers" with "mentors" or "old man" archetypes, this additional information might help. In *Writing Speculative Fiction*, Eugen Bacon summaries Christopher Vogler's famous replication of Campbell's ideas for drama in *The Writer's Journey*. Explaining that Campbell borrowed from Carl Jung's theory, Bacon claims that Campbell's "myths are the masks of God through which persons seek to relate themselves to the wonders of existence" (43). Besides the mentor helper, Bacon accounts for other archetypes that comprise the category of "second father": threshold guardians (the gatekeepers), heralds (the messengers), shapeshifters (the schemers), shadows (the opponents), allies (the comrades), and tricksters (the mischief-makers) (43–44). In his work, Vogler offers the following introduction to the category of mentors:

"Like heroes, Mentors may be willing or unwilling. Sometimes they teach in spite of themselves. In other cases they teach by their bad example. The downfall of a weakened, tragically flawed Mentor can show the hero pitfalls to avoid. As with heroes, dark or negative sides may be expressed through this archetype" (44). Vogler then subdivides mentors into "dark mentors" (44), "fallen mentors" (44–45), "continuing mentors" (45), "multiple mentors" (45), and "comic mentors" (45), adding "mentor as shaman" (46). In a clear and succinct summary from the adult-learning site *ThoughtCo.*, Deb Peterson explains the role of "mentor": "The mentor is the wise old man or woman every hero meets fairly early in the most satisfying stories." She offers examples of Dumbledore (*Harry Potter*), Q (*James Bond*), Gandalf (*Lord of the Rings*), Yoda (*Star Wars*), Merlin (*King Arthur*), Alfred (*Batman*), and ends with Mary Poppins. Peterson explains mentors function as mediators between various factions, and she points out mentors are not always humans, as objects and experiences serve in this capacity as well.

4. In a significant section of this essay, Jung proposes that the trickster waits in the psyche for the opportune time to break out. Jung predicts the "shadow" anticipates the perfect occasion to materialize as a "projection" (146–47). This is exactly what Tyler does in *Fight Club 2*. With the help of Marla, Tyler is released from Sebastian's psyche.

5. In the Afterword, Palahniuk discusses the widespread proliferation of *Fight Club* in Americana through a series of "Before ..." lead-ins. For instance, he writes, "Before *Saturday Night Live* featured 'Fight-Like-A-Girl-Club' ..." (211). In this list, which surveys the transcendence of *Fight Club* throughout American culture, Palahniuk includes "Fuck Club" and "Bite Club" (212). Worth mentioning is Brad Pitt's admitting participation in AA. In a September 2019 article in *USA Today*, Maeve McDermott shares Pitt's confession: "I had taken things as far as I could take it, so I removed my drinking privileges, ... men sitting around being open and honest in a way I have never heard. It was this safe space where there was little judgment, and therefore little judgment of yourself." Anonymity fosters this honesty.

Chapter Nine

1. Palahniuk provides extensive online commentary about *Adjustment Day*, and even though what he shares adds to this analysis, the content is mostly ancillary. In the *NW Book Lovers* interview, Palahniuk says his inspiration for his 2018 novel was Ayn Rand novels because he wanted to show many different people working together toward beneficial social change ("Shelf"). In his interview with *The Beat*, Palahniuk compares the attractiveness of superficially vacuous websites on the Internet to minimally talented bands getting a significant following after their flashy videos saw airtime on *Music Television* ("Interview").

2. Noteworthy is the 2014 article "Proposed Title for Chuck Palahniuk's Next Book: 'There Isn't Enough Entertainment for Men Club.'" In this piece for *The Mary Sue*, Jill Pantozzi accuses Palahniuk of inferring the collective "males who read" is a marginalized subculture. Pantozzi suggests Palahniuk ignores real marginalized groups and is only tapping into the male audience for consumerist exploitation. She cites as evidence Palahniuk's off-the-cuff remarks that women like to read while men are interested in media. Pantozzi spins Palahniuk's comments that publishers are trying to attract this "marginalized" male clientele as minimalizing genuine disenfranchised populations. Palahniuk is only advocating that more male writers focus on male readers, especially since many young male artists have recently committed suicide: "If male writers could better serve that readership, it would explode. We're only marginalized if we accept that status" ("Proposed"). Regardless, Palahniuk certainly understands how patriarchy has been liberally tagged as the root for many social, cultural, and political problems.

3. Incel and Alt-right affection for *Fight Club* illustrates how that novel has been absorbed into American popular culture and appropriated to serve various ideologies. Beaumont-Thomas cites Palahniuk as saying that men do not have many positive metaphors to model or protocols to follow in popular media since most contemporary literature targets women. Beaumont-Thomas reports Palahniuk as

concluding *Fight Club* is one of the few novels written toward a male audience ("Fight"). In a 2019 article in *Esquire* that compares *Fight Club* to *Joker*, Olivia Ovenden claims the film version of Palahniuk's novel is still associated with radical movements, with "snowflake" becoming a popular insult and Brad Pitt's Tyler becoming a status symbol: "At 20, the legacy of *Fight Club* is more complicated than ever, with the film now often described as a 'Bible for incels' due to how men's rights activists have taken to quoting it on online forums ... toxic masculinity was always the target of *Fight Club*." Ovenden adds that *Fight Club*'s director David Fincher predicted females would notice the comic grotesque more quickly than men because they would cut through the male aggressive as only male posturing.

4. In *Chuck Palahniuk, Parodist*, I address this thoroughly in the first chapter. In particular, I spend substantial attention on how Barth's theory of imitation ushers in postmodern parody (8). The scope of the current project does not necessitate a revisiting of Linda Hutcheon's seminal theory in her highly recommended works *Irony's Edge: The Theory and Politics of Irony*, *Narcissistic Narrative: The Metafictional Paradox*, *A Poetics of Postmodernism*, *The Politics of Postmodernism*, and *Theory of Parody: The Teachings of Twentieth-Century Art Forms*.

5. Walter's descriptive imagination also seems to set him apart from the other characters. For instance, he thinks about Shasta in a well-articulated passage describing with vivid language packed with strong adjectives and adverbs her sexual physicality. Palahniuk compares the tactility of her mouth with a Hostess fruit pie infused with corn syrup and flaking like the skin of a baby snake (28–29). This is a particularly detailed narrative passage.

Chapter Ten

1. Through *Verfremdungseffekt*, or the "estrangement effect," discussed in his 1936 essay "Alienation Effects in Chinese Acting," Brecht displayed for his audiences how the ruling class deceptively exploited the working class through its largely undetectable and mostly unrecognizable proliferation of ideology. For more information about Brecht's theory, please consult these sources: Martin Esslin's *Bertolt Brecht*, Frederic Ewen's *Bertolt Brecht*, John Fuegi's *Bertolt Brecht*, Willy Haas's *Bert Brecht*, and Peter Demetz's *Brecht*.

2. Specifically, Marcuse writes, "One-dimensional thought is systematically promoted by the makers of politics and their purveyors of mass information. Their universe of discourse is populated by self-validating hypotheses which, incessantly and monopolistically repeated, become hypnotic definitions or dictations" (16).

Works Cited

Adams, Kathryn. "Review: Make Something Up—Stories You Can't Unread." Review of *Make Something Up : Stories You Can't Unread*, by Chuck Palahniuk. *Pixelated Geek*, 30 June 2015, pixelatedgeek.com/2015/06/review-make-something-up-stories-you-cant-unread/. Accessed 2 Oct. 2019.

"Adjustment Day." Review of *Adjustment Day*, by Chuck Palahniuk. *Publishers Weekly*, vol. 265, no. 12, Mar. 2018, p. 48. *EBSCOhost*, search.ebscohost.com/login.aspx?direct=true&db=lfh&AN=128558610&site=eds-live&scope=site. Accessed 31 Oct. 2019.

Albanese, Andrew. "Bookkeeper Gets Two Year Sentence for Scheme That Destroyed Donadio & Olson." *Publishers Weekly*, 17 Dec. 2019, www.publishersweekly.com/pw/by-topic/industry-news/publisher-news/article/78860-darin-webb-gets-two-years-in-prison-for-embezzlement-scheme-that-destroyed-donadio-olson.html. Accessed 21 Dec. 2019.

Alcoholics Anonymous: The Story of How Many Thousands of Men and Women Have Recovered from Alcoholism. 1939. 3rd ed., Alcoholics Anonymous World Services, 1976.

"All Chucked Up." *NY Press*, 11 Nov. 2014, www.nypress.com/news/all-chucked-up-EVNP1020080924309249995. Accessed 17 Oct. 2019.

Allen, Brendan M. "The Sequel to the Sequel That You Didn't Know You Needed: *Fight Club 3* #1." *Comicon*, 4 February 2019, www.comicon.com/2019/02/04/the-sequel-to-the-sequel-you-didnt-know-you-needed-fight-club-3-1/. Accessed 16 Mar. 2019.

Allison, Dorothy. "Jason Who Will Be Famous." *Tin House*, vol. 10, no. 4, 2009, pp. 249–58.

Alter, Charlotte. "Katie Hill Is the First Millennial Lawmaker to Resign Because of Nudes. She Won't Be the Last." *Time*, 29 Oct. 2019 (updated 30 Oct. 2019), time.com/5712395/katie-hill-resigns-nude-photos/. Accessed 4 Nov. 2019.

Althusser, Louis. *For Marx*. 1965. Translated by Ben Brewster, Verso, 1990.

———. "Ideology and the Ideological State Apparatus (Notes Towards an Investigation)." 1970. *Lenin and Philosophy and Other Essays*. 1971. Translated by Ben Brewster, Monthly Review, 2001, pp. 85–126.

———. *Philosophy of the Encounter: Later Writings, 1978–87*. 1993. Edited by François Matheron and Oliver Corpet, translated by G. M. Goshgarian, Verso, 2006.

"Amazing Benefits of Coloring for Adults." *ColorIt*, 5 Feb. 2016, www.colorit.com/blogs/news/85320388-amazing-benefits-of-coloring-for-adults. Accessed 6 Oct. 2019.

Anderson, Mae. "Sex Tech Is In, Skimpy Outfits Are Out as CES Addresses Diversity." *USA Today*, 16 July 2019, www.usatoday.com/story/tech/2019/07/16/consumer-technology-associations-ces-introduces-sex-tech/1750101001/. Accessed 6 Sept. 2019.

Anderson, Sherwood. *Winesburg, Ohio*. 1919. Bantam, 1995.

Aristophanes. *Lysistrata*. Translated by Sarah Ruden. *The Norton Anthology of World Literature*, edited by Martin Puchner et al., 3rd ed., vol. A, Norton, 2012, pp. 823–62.

Arnott, Jake. "Adjustment Day by Chuck Palahniuk Review—Blood and Guts, but No Heart." Review of *Adjustment Day*, by Chuck Palahniuk. *Guardian*, 9 Aug. 2018, www.theguardian.com/books/2018/aug/09/adjustment-day-chuck-palahniuk-review-millenials. Accessed 14 Nov. 2019.

Works Cited

Arzate, Ben. "Adjustment Day by Chuck Palahniuk Review." Review of *Adjustment Day,* by Chuck Palahniuk. *Cultured Vultures,* 9 Oct. 2018, culturedvultures.com/adjustment-day-by-chuck-palahniuk-review/. Accessed 31 Oct. 2019.
Askew, Robin. "Annabel Chong: Sex: The Annabel Chong Story." *Spike,* 1 Oct. 2000, spikemagazine.com/1000annabelchong/. Accessed 13 Dec. 2019.
Associated Press. "Administrator in 'Fight Club' Case Seeks Accelerated Rehab." *AP Regional State Report—Connecticut,* Associated Press DBA Press Association, 30 July 2019. *EBSCOhost,* warehouser.coker.edu/login?url=http://search.ebscohost.com/login.aspx?direct=true&db=n5h&AN=AP20be15bf8e914ce0a55a974338387061&site=ehost-live. Accessed 10 Oct. 2019.
_____. "Elizabeth Warren at Native American Forum: 'I Am Sorry for the Harm I Have Caused.'" *Los Angeles Times,* 19 Aug. 2019, www.latimes.com/politics/story/2019-08-19/elizabeth-warren-native-american-dna-apology. Accessed 4 Nov. 2019.
_____. "Former Disney Kid Bella Thorne is Now a Director—of Porn Film 'Her & Him.'" *USA Today,* 27 June 2019, www.usatoday.com/story/entertainment/movies/2019/08/13/former-disney-kid-bella-thorne-directs-porn-film-her-him/2004457001/. Accessed 14 Aug. 2019.
_____. "High School Teacher Allegedly Allowed Classroom 'Fight Club.'" *AP Regional State Report—California,* 12 Mar. 2019. *EBSCOhost,* warehouser.coker.edu/login?url=http://search.ebscohost.com/login.aspx?direct=true&db=n5h&AN=AP05d1d9febe4f4da1b66131ff333bb229&site=ehost-live. Accessed 10 Oct. 2019.
_____. "Rapinoe Stands by Statement about Not Going to White House." *USA Today,* 27 June 2019, www.usatoday.com/story/sports/soccer/2019/06/27/rapinoe-stands-by-statement-about-not-going-to-white-house/39629899/. Accessed 17 July 2019.
Bacon, Eugen. *Writing Speculative Fiction: Creative and Critical Approaches.* Red Globe, 2019.
Bakhtin, Mikhail. *Problems of Dostoevsky's Poetics.* 1963. Edited and translated by Caryl Emerson, U of Minnesota P, 1984. Theory and History of Literature.
_____. *Rabelais and His World.* 1965. Translated by Hélène Iswolsky, Indiana UP, 1984.
"Banned and Challenged Books." *ALA Office for Intellectual Freedom,* 2019, www.ala.org/advocacy/bbooks/frequentlychallengedbooks/top10#2016. Accessed 19 Sept. 2019.
Barnett, David. "Is Fight Club's Tyler Durden Film's Most Misunderstood Man?" *BBC,* 23 July 2019, www.bbc.com/culture/story/20190717-is-fight-clubs-tyler-durden-films-most-misunderstood-man. Accessed 17 Oct. 2019.
Barth, John. "Do I Repeat Myself? The Problem of Already Said." *The Atlantic,* 5 July 2011, www.theatlantic.com/magazine/archive/2011/08/do-i-repeat-myself/308572/. Accessed Nov. 2019.
_____. "Literature of Exhaustion." 1967. *The Friday Book: Essays and Other Nonfiction,* Putnam, 1984, pp. 62–76.
_____. "Literature of Replenishment: Postmodernist Fiction." 1980. *The Friday Book: Essays and Other Nonfiction,* Putnam, 1984, pp. 193–206.
Barthelme, Donald. "Sentence." 1970. *Postmodern American Fiction: A Norton Anthology.* Edited by Paula Geyh, Fred G. Leebron, and Andrew Levy, Norton, 1998, pp. 33–37.
Barthes, Roland. "The Death of the Author." 1967. *Image-Music-Text.* Translated by Stephen Heath. Fontana, 1977, pp. 142–48.
_____. *S/Z: An Essay.* 1970. Translated by Richard Miller, Macmillan, 1974.
Barton, Chris. "'Damned' by Chuck Palahniuk." Review of *Damned,* by Chuck Palahniuk. *Los Angeles Times,* 29 Nov. 2011, www.latimes.com/books/la-xpm-2011-nov-29-la-et-book-20111129-story.html. Accessed 11 Aug. 2019.
Baudrillard, Jean. *Simulacra and Simulation.* 1981. Translated by Sheila Faria Glaser, U of Michigan P, 1994.
Beaumont-Thomas, Ben. "Fight Club Author Chuck Palahniuk on His Book Becoming a Bible for the Incel Movement." *Guardian,* 20 July 2018, www.theguardian.com/books/2018/jul/20/chuck-palahniuk-interview-adjustment-day-black-ethno-state-gay-parenting-incel-movement. Accessed 25 Sept. 2019.
Behrmann, Savannah. "Rep. Katie Hill's Last Day in Congress Will Be Friday Following Resignation Amid Ethics Investigation." *USA Today,* 30 Oct. 2019 (updated 31 Oct. 2019),

www.usatoday.com/story/news/politics/2019/10/30/katie-hill-california-congresswoman-last-day-friday/4105196002/. Accessed 4 Nov. 2019.
Bendery, Jennifer. "Katie Hill Sends Cease and Desist Letter to Daily Mail Website Over Nude Photos." *HuffPost*, 24 Oct. 2019, www.huffpost.com/entry/katie-hill-cease-and-desist-nude-photos-daily-mail_n_5db21ac7e4b0bc7f96fe62bf?ncid=engmodushpmg00000006. Accessed 4 Nov. 2019.
Bennett, Jessica. "The Complicated Case of Katie Hill." *New York Times*, 1 Nov. 2019, www.nytimes.com/2019/11/01/us/katie-hill-photos-relationship.html. Accessed 4 Nov. 2019.
Bennett, Robert. "The Death of Sisyphus, Existentialist Literature, and the Cultural Logic of Chuck Palahniuk's *Fight Club*." *Stirrings Still: The International Journal of Existential Literature*, vol. 2, no. 2, 2005, pp. 70–88.
Berrong, Richard M. *Rabelais and Bakhtin: Popular Culture in* Gargantua and Pantagruel. U of Nebraska P, 1986.
"The Best Pop Culture-Themed Hotels and Rentals of 2019: Barbie, Harry Potter, Lisa Frank, More." *USA Today*, 10 Dec. 2019, www.usatoday.com/picture-gallery/travel/hotels/2019/12/10/barbie-twilight-2019-best-pop-culture-themed-hotels-rentals/4259931002/. Accessed 11 Dec. 2019.
Better, Alison. "Vibrator Nation: How Feminist Sex-Toy Stores Changed the Business of Pleasure." *American Journal of Sociology*, vol. 124, no. 3, 2018, pp. 938–40.
Bialostosky, Don. *Mikhail Bakhtin: Rhetoric, Poetics, Dialogics, Rhetoricality*. Parlor, 2016.
Blume, Jordan. "I Know This Because Talbott Knows This: Chuck Palahniuk's 'Adjustment Day.'" Review of *Adjustment Day*, by Chuck Palahniuk. *PopMatters*, 3 May 2019, www.popmatters.com/adjustment-day-chuck-palahniuk-2636107818.html?rebelltitem=1#rebelltitem1. Accessed 31 Oct. 2019.
Blume, Judy. *Are You There God? It's Me, Margaret.* 1970. Atheneum Books for Young Readers, 2001.
Blush Design. *Love & Pride: Adult Coloring Book.* Blush Design, 2019.
Bolton, Brooke. "Doomed." Review of *Doomed*, by Chuck Palahniuk. *Library Journal*, vol. 138, no. 14, 2013, p. 101.
―――. "Make Something Up: Stories You Can't Unread." Review of *Make Something Up: Stories You Can't Unread*, by Chuck Palahniuk. *Library Journal*, vol. 140, no. 9, 2015, p. 79.
Bomer, Paula. "Beautiful You." Review of *Beautiful You*, by Chuck Palahniuk. *New York Times*, 24 Oct. 2014, www.nytimes.com /2014/10/26/books/review/chuck-palahniuks-beautiful-you-and-more.html. Accessed 10 July 2019.
Bonner, Mehera. "Inside the Greatest 'Outlander' Sex Scenes." *Marie Claire*, 18 Oct. 2017, www.marieclaire.com/culture/a13027952/the-making-of-outlander-sex-scenes/. Accessed 31 July 2019.
Booker, M. Keith. "*May Contain Graphic Material*": *Comic Books, Graphic Novels, and Film.* Praeger, 2007.
―――. *Techniques of Subversion in Modern Literature: Transgression, Abjection, and the Carnivalesque.* U of Florida P, 1991.
Boon, Kevin Alexander. "Men and Nostalgia for Violence: Culture and Culpability in Chuck Palahniuk's *Fight Club*." *Journal of Men's Studies: A Scholarly Journal about Men and Masculinities*, vol. 11, no. 3, 2003, pp. 267–76.
Bote, Joshua. "Florida Student Body President Faces Impeachment for Donald Trump, Jr.'s $50K Campus Visit." *USA Today*, 13 Nov. 2019, www.usatoday.com/story/news/education/2019/11/13/florida-student-president-may-impeached-trump-jr-event/4179852002/. Accessed 13 Nov. 2019.
Brandist, Craig. "The Bakhtin Circle." *IEP*, Internet Encyclopedia of Philosophy, www.iep.utm.edu/bakhtin/. Accessed 23 July 2019.
Brecht, Bertolt. "Alienation Effects in Chinese Acting." 1936. *Brecht on Theatre: The Development of an Aesthetic*, edited and translated by John Willett, Hill and Wang, 1964, pp. 91–99. whatistheatrereally.files.wordpress.com/2015/04/brecht-alienation-effects-in-chinese-acting.pdf. Accessed 18 Nov. 2019.
Brewster, Thomas Fox. "'Panty Buster' Toy Left Private Sex Lives of 50,000 Exposed." *Forbes*,

1 Feb. 2018, www.forbes.com/sites/thomasbrewster/2018/02/01/vibratissimo-panty-buster-sex-toy-multiple-vulnerabilities/#20478d2b5a94. Accessed 6 Sept. 2019.

Brody, Yosef. "How Ideology Seduces Us—and How We Can (Try to) Escape It." Review of *The Pervert's Guide to Ideology*, by Sophie Fiennes. *Truthout*, 28 Nov. 2012, truthout.org/articles/the-perverts-guide-to-ideology-how-ideology-seduces-us-and-how-we-can-try-to-escape-it/. Accessed 23 Oct. 2019.

Brown, Barry A., Christopher Conway, Rhett Gambol, Susan Kalter, Laura E. Ruberto, Tomás F. Taraborrelli, and Donald Wesling, editors. *Bakhtin and the Nation*. Bucknell UP, 2000.

Brown, Larry. "Waiting for the Ladies." *Big Bad Love*, Vintage, 1990, pp. 79–89.

Brown, Robert E. "Adjustment Day." Review of *Adjustment Day*, by Chuck Palahniuk. *Library Journal*, vol. 143, no. 7, 2018, pp. 65–66. *EBSCOhost*, search.ebscohost.com/login.aspx?direct=true&db=lfh&AN=128931035&site=eds-live&scope=site. Accessed 31 Oct. 2019.

Brown, Tonya. "Some Students Left Baffled Following Coker University President's Resignation." *WPDE*, Sinclair Broadcast Group, 9 Sept. 2019, wpde.com/news/local/some-students-left-baffled-following-coker-university-presidents-resignation. Accessed 28 Sept. 2019.

Buford, Bill. Editorial. "Dirty Realism: New Writing from America." *Granta: Dirty Realism: New Writing from America 8*, Penguin, 1983, pp. 4–5.

Bukowski, Charles. "Animal Crackers in My Soup." *General Tales of Ordinary Madness*, 1983, Virgin, 2009, pp. 197–209.

———. "Roll the Dice." *YouTube*, uploaded by SpokenVerse, 12 Feb. 2012, www.youtube.com/watch?v=36CYMdFmDeQ. Accessed 5 Aug. 2019.

Bunn, Austin. "Open Book." Review of *Snuff*, by Chuck Palahniuk. *The Advocate*, 21 May 2008, www.advocate.com/news/2008/05/21/open-book. Accessed 13 Dec. 2019.

Burana, Lily. "In New Book, 'Fight Club' Author Meets His Match." Review of *Beautiful You*, by Chuck Palahniuk. *The Washington Post*, 23 Oct. 2014, www.washingtonpost.com/entertainment/books/book-world-beautiful-you-by-chuck-palahniuk/2014/10/23/c473e908-54a0-11e4-892e-602188e70e9c_story.html?noredirect=on. Accessed 4 Sept. 2019.

Burgess, Olivia. "Revolutionary Bodies in Chuck Palahniuk's *Fight Club*." *Utopian Studies*, vol. 23, no. 1, 2012, pp. 263–80.

Butler, Rex. *Slavoj Žižek: Live Theory*. Continuum, 2004.

Campbell, Fiona Kumari. *Contours of Ableism: The Production of Disability and Ableness*. Palgrave Macmillan, 2009.

Campbell, Joseph. *The Hero with a Thousand Faces*. 1949. U of Princeton P, 1972.

———. *The Hero's Journey: Joseph Campbell on His Life and Work*. New World Library, 2003.

———. "Joseph Campbell on Becoming an Adult." *YouTube*, uploaded by CampbellFoundation, 1July 2010, www.youtube.com/watch?v=aGx4IlppSgU. Accessed 17 Oct. 2019.

———. "Myth and the Modern World." *The Power of Myth*. 1988. Interview by Bill Moyers. Edited by Betty Sue Flowers, Anchor, 1991, pp. 3–43.

Carstensen, Melinda. "This Is What Porn Does to Your Brain." *New York Post*, nypost.com/2017/02/16/is-watching-porn-harmful-to-your-health/. Accessed 30 July 2019.

Carver, Raymond. *Where I'm Calling From*. Vintage, 1989.

CassieWrightLives: Chuck Palahniuk *Snuff* Advertisement. *Myspace*, myspace.com/cassiewrightlives. Accessed 1 Aug. 2019.

Chaplinsky, Joshua. "Strange But True: A Short Biography of Chuck Palahniuk." *The Cult, Chuck Palahniuk Fan Website*, chuckpalahniuk.net/author/strange-but-true-a-short-biography-of-chuck-palahniuk. Accessed 30 Sept. 2019.

"Chitty Chitty Gang Bang." *Ad Age*, Crain Communications, 4 June 2008, creativity-online.com/work/snuff-chitty-chitty-gang-bang/1251. Accessed 1 Aug. 2019.

"Chuck Palahniuk." *Wikipedia: The Free Encyclopedia*, Wikimedia Foundation, 12 July 2019, 8:40 pm, en.wikipedia.org/wiki/Chuck_Palahniuk. Accessed 15 July 2019.

"Chuck Palahniuk Interviews Cassie Wright-Part 1." *YouTube*, uploaded by Doubleday Publishing, 14 Apr. 2008, www.youtube.com/watch?v=jJFl9qrFxLE. Accessed 1 Aug. 2019.

"Chuck Palahniuk Interviews Cassie Wright-Part 2." *YouTube*, uploaded by Doubleday

Publishing, 17 Apr. 2008, www.youtube.com/watch?v=ptdbl5stHmM. Accessed 1 Aug. 2019.
"Chuck Palahniuk Interviews Cassie Wright-Part 3." *YouTube*, uploaded by Doubleday Publishing, 29 Apr. 2008, www.youtube.com/watch?v=gxNeAco5iBU. Accessed 1 Aug. 2019.
"Chuck Palahniuk on His Writing Method." *YouTube*, uploaded by DJAnon 1981, 15 Jan. 2015, www.youtube.com/watch?v=cKE3KCMwyhc. Accessed 30 Sept. 2019.
"Chuck Palahniuk Reading Knock-Knock." *YouTube*, uploaded by l7r41n, 24 May 2010, www.youtube.com/watch?time_continue=3&v=_jbp5R3nw3o. Accessed 25 Sept. 2019.
"Chuck Palahniuk Talks Dangerous Writing." *PRI*, Public Radio International, 31 May 2015, www.pri.org/stories/2015-05-31/chuck-palahniuk-talks-dangerous-writing. Accessed 30 Sept. 2019.
Chui, Joanna. "Stepford Wives Rebooted." *Herizons*, vol. 32, no. 3, 2018, p. 41.
Chun, Rene. "Naked Lunch and Dinner." *New York Times*, 23 Apr. 1995, pp. 49, 52.
Chute, Hillary. "Comics as Literature? Reading Graphic Narrative." *PMLA*, vol. 123, no. 2, 2008, pp. 452–65.
Clark, J. Michael. "Faludi, *Fight Club*, and Phallic Masculinity: Exploring the Emasculating Economics of Patriarchy." *Journal of Men's Health*, vol. 11, no. 1, 2002, pp. 65–76.
Clark, Katerina, and Michael Holquist. *Mikhail Bakhtin*. Belknap, 1984.
Clark-Flory, Tracy. "'A billion husbands are about to be replaced': Imagining the Wildly Effective Vibrators of the Future." Review of *Beautiful You*, by Chuck Palahniuk. *Salon*, 27 Oct. 2014, www.salon.com/2014/10/27/a_billion_husbands_are_about_to_be_replaced_imagining_the_wildly_effective_vibrators_of_the_future/. Accessed 4 Sept. 2019.
Collado-Rodriguez, Francisco, editor. *Chuck Palahniuk: Fight Club, Invisible Monsters, Choke*. Bloomsbury, 2013.
Comella, Lynn. "Why Pornography Deserves Its Own Academic Journal." *Pacific Standard*, 17 May 2013, psmag.com/social-justice/why-pornography-deserves-its-own-academic-journal-57816. Accessed 30 July 2019.
Corpora, Lisa Ann. "Lisa Ann Talks with Captain Jack." Interview by Captain Jack. *AdultDVDTalk*, 20 May 2018, interviews.adultdvdtalk.com /lisa-ann/. Accessed 31 July 2019.
Costello, Carol. "Want To Learn About Consent? Ask a Porn Star." *CNN*, 8 Oct. 2018, www.cnn.com/2018/10/05/opinions/porn-star-teaches-consent-opinion-costello/index.html. Accessed 24 Sept. 2019.
A Course in Miracles. Foundation for Inner Peace, 2019, acim.org/acim/. Accessed 6 Aug. 2019.
"Crimes and Meg's Demeanor." *Family Guy*, directed by Greg Colton, season 16, episode 8, Fox Broadcasting Company, 3 Dec. 2017.
"Cuddle Club." *YouTube*, uploaded by Noah Baron, 24 May 2011, www.youtube.com/watch?v=66W4xPPEwXU. Accessed 5 Aug. 2019.
Culver, Jordan. "Democratic Rep. Katie Hill Announces Resignation Amid Allegations of Relationship with Staff Member." *USA Today*, 27 Oct. 2019 (updated 28 Oct. 2019), usatoday.com/story/news/politics/2019/10/27/katie-hill-california-congresswoman-resigns-amid-ethics-probe/2481703001/. Accessed 4 Nov. 2019.
Cummings, Judith. "Disabled Model Defies Sexual Stereotypes." *New York Times*, 8 June 1987, p. C12.
Cummings, William. "How Politics Led to an 8,000 Percent Surge in 'Bigfoot Erotica' Searches on *Pornhub*." *USA Today*, 1 Aug. 2018, www.usatoday.com/story/news/politics/onpolitics/2018/08/01/bigfoot-erotica-searches-pornhub-leslie-cockburn-denver-riggleman/882183002/. Accessed 29 July 2019.
———. "'This Is What Racism Looks Like': Congresswomen React to Trump's 'Go Back' Tweetstorm." *USA Today*, 14 July 2019 (updated 15 July 2019), www.usatoday.com/story/news/politics/2019/07/14/ocasio-cortez-omar-pressley-tlaib-respond-trump-tweet/1729018001/. Accessed 4 Nov. 2019.
———. "Trump Tells Congresswomen to 'Go Back' to the 'Crime Infested Places from Which They Came.'" *USA Today*, 14 July 2019, usatoday.com/story/news/politics/arizona/2019/07/14/president-donald-trump-tells-democratic-congresswomen-go-back/1728525001/. Accessed 4 Nov. 2019.

Dale, Andrew. *Graphic Novels: Essential Literary Genres*. Abdo, 2017.
"Dangerous Writing." *Fandom,* creativewriting.fandom.com/wiki/Dangerous_Writing. Accessed 30 Sept. 2019.
Dante Alighieri. *The Divine Comedy: Hell, Purgatory, Paradise.* 1320. Translated by Henry Wadsworth Longfellow, 1867, Chartwell, 2008.
Darr, Carolyn. "Daily Book Review: 'Beautiful You.'" Review of *Beautiful You*, by Chuck Palahniuk. *UWIRE Text*, 14 Jan. 2015, p. 1. *Academic OneFile*, link.gale.com/apps/doc/A397563030/AONE?u=cokercoll&sid= AONE&xid=2db591ea. Accessed 4 Sept. 2019.
Dastagir, Alia E. "Katie Hill's Resignation is About Much More Than an Alleged Affair and Explicit Photos." *USA Today*, 28 Oct. 2019 (updated 29 Oct. 2019), www.usatoday.com/story/news/nation/2019/10/28/katie-hill-photos-congress-resigns-revenge-porn-husband-kenny-heslep/2486073001/. Accessed 4 Nov. 2019.
Davis, Murray S. *Smut: Erotic Reality/Obscene Ideology.* U of Chicago P, 1983.
De Chavez, Jeremy. "The Political Subject Is a Lover Not a Fighter: Reading Chuck Palahniuk's *Fight Club* as a Love Story." *ANQ: A Quarterly Journal of Short Articles, Notes, and Reviews*, vol. 31, no. 2, 2018, pp. 123–31.
Decker, James. *Ideology*. Palgrave, 2004. Transitions.
Deleuze, Gilles, and Félix Guattari. *Anti-Oedipus: Capitalism and Schizophrenia.* 1972. Translated by Robert Hurley, Mark Seem, and Helen R. Lane, Penguin, 2009.
———. *A Thousand Plateaus: Capitalism and Schizophrenia.* 1980. Translated by Brian Massumi, U of Minnesota P, 1987.
Del Gizzo, Suzanne. "The American Dream Unhinged: Romance and Reality in *The Great Gatsby* and *Fight Club*." *The F. Scott Fitzgerald Review*, vol. 6, no. 1, 2008, pp. 69–94.
Demetz, Peter, editor. *Brecht: A Collection of Critical Essays.* Prentice-Hall, 1962. Twentieth Century Views.
Dentith, Simon. *Bakhtinian Thought: An Introductory Reader.* Routledge, 1995. Critical Readers in Theory and Practice.
Derysh, Igor. "Katie Hill Vows to Fight Revenge Porn as GOP Operative Reveals he has 700 Images of Lawmaker." *Salon*, 29 Oct. 2019, www.salon.com/2019/10/29/katie-hill-speaks-out-gop-operative-reveals-he-has-700-revenge-porn-images/. Accessed 4 Nov. 2019.
Desblaches, Claudia. "Death and Dying as Literary Devices in Brite's *Exquisite Corpse* and Palahniuk's *Damned*." *The Final Crossing: Death and Dying in Literature*, edited by John J. Han and C. Clark Triplett, Peter Lang, 2015, pp. 155–70.
Diaz, Ellie, and Kristin Pekoll. "Spotlight on Censorship: 'Make Something Up.'" *Intellectual Freedom Blog*, American Library Association, 12 Apr. 2017, www.oif.ala.org/oif/?p=9273. Accessed 28 Sept. 2019.
Dibble, Madison. "Rep. Katie Hill Used Wife-Swapping Website to Post Naked Photo of Herself Smoking Bong." *Washington Examiner*, 24 Oct. 2019, www.washingtonexaminer.com/news/additional-nude-photos-of-katie-hill-leak-amid-ethics-complaint-about-alleged-affairs. Accessed 4 Nov. 2019.
Diston, Mark. "*Fight Club*'s Chuck Palahniuk Is Back on Form." Review of *Make Something Up: Stories You Can't Unread*, by Chuck Palahniuk. *The Register*, 30 May 2015, www.theregister.co.uk/2015/05/30/book_review_make_something_up_water_knife_girl_at_war/. Accessed 25 Sept. 2019.
Dobozy, Tamas. "In the Country of Contradiction the Hypocrite is King: Defining Dirty Realism in Charles Bukowski's *Factotum*." *Modern Fiction Studies*, vol. 47, no. 1, 2001, pp. 43–68.
———. *Towards a Definition of Dirty Realism.* Dissertation, U. of British Columbia, 2000, open.library.ubc.ca/cIRcle/collections/ubctheses/831/items/1.0089734. Accessed 13 June 2019.
Dodge, Jason J. "Spaces of Resistance: Heterotopia and Transgression in Chuck Palahniuk's *Fight Club*." *LIT: Literary Interpretation Theory*, vol. 26, no. 4, 2015, pp. 318–33.
"Doomed." Review of *Doomed*, by Chuck Palahniuk. *Kirkus Reviews*, vol. 81, no. 2, June 2013, p. 25.
———. Review of *Doomed*, by Chuck Palahniuk. *Publishers Weekly*, vol. 260, no. 26, July 2013, p. 61.

———. Review of *Doomed*, by Chuck Palahniuk. *The New Yorker*, vol. 89, no. 42, Dec. 2013, p. 127.
"Dorothy Parker." *Americanliterature.com*, n.d., americanliterature.com/author/dorothy-parker. Accessed 5 Dec. 2019.
Dougherty, Michael Brendan. "Elizabeth Warren's Native American Problem Isn't Going Away." *National Review*, 30 Sept. 2019, www.nationalreview.com/2019/09/elizabeth-warren-native-american-controversy-not-going-away/. Accessed 4 Nov. 2019.
Douthat, Ross. "Is Pornography Adultery?" *The Atlantic*, 1 Oct. 2008, www.theatlantic.com/magazine/archive/2008/10/is-pornography-adultery/306989/. Accessed 30 July 2019.
Dowling, William C. *Jameson, Althusser, Marx: An Introduction to The Political Unconscious*. Cornell UP, 1984.
Dugdale, John. "*Porn Studies* Is the New Discipline for Academics." *Guardian*, 2 May 2013, www.theguardian.com/books/booksblog/2013/may/02/porn-studies-new-discipline-academics. Accessed 30 July 2019.
Dunne, Robert. "Beyond Grotesqueness in *Winesburg, Ohio*." *Midwest Quarterly: A Journal of Contemporary Thought*, vol. 31, no. 2, 1990, pp. 180–91.
———. "The Book of the Grotesque: Textual Theory and the Editing of *Winesburg, Ohio*." *Studies in Short Fiction*, vol. 35, no. 3, 1998, pp. 287–96.
———. *A New Book of Grotesques: Contemporary Approaches to Sherwood Anderson's Early Fiction*. Kent State UP, 2005.
Durden, Tyler. "Freshman Democrat Rep. Katie Hill Resigns Amid Sex-Scandal Ethics Probe." *ZeroHedge*, 28 Oct. 2019, www.zerohedge.com/political/freshman-democrat-rep-katie-hill-resigns-amid-sex-scandal-ethics-probe. Accessed 4 Nov. 2019.
Dworkin, Andrea. *Intercourse*. Free Press, 1987.
Dyce, Andrew. "*Fight Club 3* Makes Tyler Durden's Son the Star." *Screen Rant*, 2 February 2019, screenrant.com/fight-club-3-comic-preview/. Accessed 16 Mar. 2019.
The Editors. "The Best Adult Coloring Books, According to Hyperenthusiastic Reviewers." *The Strategist*, 10 Sept. 2019, nymag.com/strategist/article/best-adult-coloring-books.html. Accessed 6 Oct. 2019.
Edwards, Justin D., and Rune Graulund. *Grotesque*. Routledge, 2013. New Critical Idiom.
Ehrlich, David. "Why 'Fight Club' Is the Movie That 'Joker' Failed to Become—Opinion." *IndieWire*, 7 Oct. 2019, www.indiewire.com/2019/10/fight-club-is-best-joker-movie-1202179222/. Accessed 17 Oct. 2019.
Elliott, Gregory, editor. *Althusser: A Critical Reader*. Blackwell, 1994.
Ellis, Nicquel Terry, and Charisse Jones. "Banning Ethnic Hairstyles 'Upholds This Notion of White Supremacy.' States Pass Lows to Stop Natural Hair Discrimination." *USA Today*, 14 Oct. 2019, www.usatoday.com/story/news/nation/2019/10/14/black-hair-laws-passed-stop-natural-hair-discrimination-across-us/3850402002/. Accessed 31 Oct. 2019.
Ellmann, Lucy. "Love the Ones You're With." Review of *Snuff*, by Chuck Palahniuk. *New York Times*, 8 June 2008, www.nytimes.com/2008/06/08/books/review/Ellmann-t.html. Accessed 10 July 2019.
Emerson, Caryl, editor. *Critical Essays on Mikhail Bakhtin*. G. K. Hall and Company, 1999. Critical Essays on World Literature.
Emerson, Ralph Waldo. *Nature*. 1836. *Ralph Waldo Emerson: Selected Prose and Poetry*, 2nd ed., edited by Reginald L. Cook, Holt, Rinehart, and Winston, 1969, pp. 3–38.
Engels, Friedrich. Letter to Franz Mehring. 14 July 1893. Translated by Dona Torr. *Marx-Engels Correspondence 1893, Marx Engels Archive*, www.marxists.org/archive/marx/works/1893/letters/93_07_14.htm. Originally published in *Marx and Engels Correspondence*, International Publishers, 1942, pp. 510–13. Accessed 21 July 2019.
Erdrich, Louise. "Knives." *Granta: More Dirt: The New American Fiction 19*, Penguin, 1986, pp. 135–49.
Esslin, Martin. *Bertolt Brecht*. Columbia UP, 1969.
Ewen, Frederic. *Bertolt Brecht: His Life, His Art, and His Times*. Citadel P, 1969.
Faile, Jim. "Wyatt Out as Coker President." *SCNow*, 10 Sept. 2019, www.scnow.com/messenger/news/article_87a74c5c-d3f0-11e9-acd4-d762ca21fda9.html. Accessed 27 Sept. 2019.

Faludi, Susan. *Backlash: The Undeclared War Against American Women*. Three Rivers, 1991.
———. "The Money Shot." *The New Yorker*, vol. 71, no. 34, Oct. 1995, pp. 64–70.
———. *Stiffed: The Betrayal of the American Man*. Perennial, 1999.
Feis, Aaron. "Elizabeth Warren Deletes Infamous, Year-Old Native American DNA Tweet." *New York Post*, 16 Oct. 2019, nypost.com/2019/10/16/elizabeth-warren-deletes-infamous-year-old-native-american-dna-tweet/. Accessed 4 Nov. 2019.
Feller, Madison. "Katie Hill Came to Congress to Serve Southern California. Now She's Also Investigating Trump." *Elle*, 20 June 2019, www.elle.com/culture/career-politics/a27892346/katie-hill-house-oversight-committee-trump/. Accessed 4 Nov. 2019.
Fight Club. Directed by David Fincher, performances by Edward Norton, Brad Pitt, and Helena Bonham Carter, Twentieth-Century Fox, 1999.
"*Fight Club 3* #1." *Dark Horse Digital Comics*, Dark Horse, 2019, www.darkhorse.com / Comics/3003-721/Fight-Club-3-1. Accessed 16 Mar. 2019.
Fitzgerald, F. Scott. *The Great Gatsby*. 1925. Scribner's, 2003.
Fitzpatrick, Kelly. "Why Adult Coloring Books Are Good for You." *CNN*, 1 Aug. 2017, www.cnn.com/2016/01/06/health/adult-coloring-books-popularity-mental-health/index.html. Accessed 4 Oct. 2019.
Fleig, Shelby. "Pastor Accused of Being 'Practicing Homosexual' Takes Leave of Absence." *USA Today*, 14 Nov. 2019, www.usatoday.com/story/news/nation/2019/11/14/queer-iowa-pastor-takes-leave-after-charged-being-homosexual/4189426002/. Accessed 14 Nov. 2019.
Floyd, Alison. "Chuck Palahniuk Unveils Excerpt of *Fight Club 2*; Narrator of Palahniuk's Bestselling Novel Is 10 Years Older, and Struggling with Marriage and a Prescription-Drug Addiction in Comic-Book Sequel." Review of *Fight Club 2*, by Chuck Palahniuk. *Guardian*, 23 Feb. 2015. *Gale Academic Onefile*, link.gale.com/apps/doc/A402828241/AONE?u=cokercoll&sid=AONE&xid=0dcd5c3a. Accessed 18 Oct. 2019.
———. "Chuck Palahniuk's 'Close to Broke' as Agent's Accountant Faces Fraud Charges." *Guardian*, 30 May 2018, www.theguardian.com/books/2018/may/30/chuck-palahniuk-agent-accountant-faces-charges-fight-club. Accessed 25 Sept. 2019.
Ford, Richard. *Rock Springs*, Vintage, 1987.
Foucault, Michel. *Abnormal: Lectures at the Collège de France 1974–1975*. 1999. Edited by Valerio Marchetti and Antonella Salomoni, translated by Graham Burchell, Picador, 2004.
———. *The History of Sexuality, Volume I: An Introduction*. 1978. Translated by Robert Hurley, Vintage, 1990.
———. "Panopticism." 1975. *Discipline & Punish: The Birth of the Prison*, translated by Alan Sheridan, Vintage, 1995, pp. 195–228.
———. "Preface to Transgression." 1963. *Language, Counter-Memory, Practice: Selected Essays and Interviews*, edited by Donald F. Bouchard, translated by Bouchard and Sherry Simon, Cornell UP, 1977, 29–52.
Franke-Ruta, Garance. "Is Elizabeth Warren Native American or What?" *The Atlantic*, 20 May 2012, www.theatlantic.com/politics/archive/2012/05/is-elizabeth-warren-native-american-or-what/257415/. Accessed 4 Nov. 2019.
From Straight A's to XXX. Directed by Vanessa Parise, Lifetime, 2017.
Frye, Northorp. *Anatomy of Criticism: Four Essays*. 1957. Princeton UP, 1990.
Fuegi, John. *Bertolt Brecht: Chaos, According to Plan*. Cambridge UP, 1987. Directors in Perspective.
Gallagher, Brian. "Daryl Hannah and Tom Sizemore Join *Snuff*." *MovieWeb*, 8 Feb. 2011, movieweb.com/daryl-hannah-and-tom-sizemore-join-snuff/. Accessed 24 Sept. 2011.
Garrett, Greg. *Holy Superheroes!: Exploring the Sacred in Comics, Graphic Novels, and Film*. Westminster John Know, 2008.
Garrison, Justin. "'God's Middle Children' Metaphysical Rebellion in Chuck Palahniuk's *Fight Club*." *Humanitas*, vol. 25, no. 1–2, 2012, pp. 79–106.
Gearty, Robert. "North Carolina Assisted Living Facility Workers Accused of Running Dementia Resident Fight Club." *Fox News*, 14 Oct. 2019, www.foxnews.com/us/north-carolina-assisted-living-facility-dementia-fight-club. Accessed 17 Oct. 2019.

Geyh, Paula, Fred G. Leebron, and Levy Andrew, editors. Introduction. *Postmodern American Fiction: A Norton Anthology*, Norton, 1998, pp. ix-xxx.
Gibbs, Lindsay. "Megan Rapinoe isn't Asking for Permission or Forgiveness: She's Asking for People to Listen." *ThinkProgress*, 27 June 2019, thinkprogress.org/megan-rapinoe-whitehouse-908badaf6069/. Accessed 17 July 2019.
Giroux, Henry A. "Private Satisfactions and Public Disorders: *Fight Club*, Patriarchy, and the Politics of Masculine Violence." *JAC: A Journal of Rhetoric, Culture, and Politics*, vol. 21, no. 1, 2001, pp. 1–31.
Glaister, Dan. "I Dare You." *Guardian*, 12 Mar. 2004, www.theguardian.com/books/2004/mar/13/fiction.chuckpalahniuk. Accessed 10 Dec. 2019.
Golding, Bruce. "Ex-porn Star Jenni Lee Found Living Homeless in Las Vegas Tunnel." *New York Post*, 22 Aug. 2019, nypost.com/2019/08/22/ex-porn-star-jenni-lee-found-living-in-las-vegas-homeless-tunnel/. Accessed 29 Dec. 2019.
Goldsmith, Francisca. *The Reader's Advisory Guide to Graphic Novels*. 2nd ed., ALA, 2017.
Goodley, Dan. *Dis/ability Studies: Theorising Disablism and Ablesim*. Routledge, 2014.
Goodwin, James. *Modern American Grotesque: Literature and Philosophy*. Ohio State UP, 2009.
Goodyear, Dana. "Katie Hill is a New Kind of California Democrat. Can She Help Flip the House?" *The New Yorker*, 21 June 2018, www.newyorker.com/news/news-desk/katie-hill-is-a-new-kind-of-california-democrat-can-she-help-flip-the-house/amp. Accessed 4 Nov. 2019.
Graff, Keir. "Snuff." Review of *Snuff*, by Chuck Palahniuk. *Booklist*, vol. 104, no. 13, 1 Mar. 2008, p 30.
Granta: Dirty Realism: New Writing from America 8. Penguin, 1983.
Granta: More Dirt: The New American Fiction 19. Penguin, 1986.
Green, Emma. "Most People Think Watching Porn Is Morally Wrong." *The Atlantic*, 5 Mar. 2014, www.theatlantic.com/politics/archive/2014/03/most-people-think-watching-porn-is-morally-wrong/284240/. Accessed 30 July 2019.
"Guts." *YouTube*, uploaded by Jillian Freund, 14 Oct. 2013, www.youtube.com/watch?v=cYHLpEEz_8g. Accessed 25 Sept. 2019.
Haas, Susan. "Bella Thorne Posts Topless Pics to Thwart Hacker: 'I Took My Power Back.'" *USA Today*, 16 June 2019, www.usatoday.com/story/life/2019/06/16/bella-thorne-posts-topless-pics-says-hacker-might-kid/1474258001/. Accessed 20 June 2019.
Haas, Willy. *Bert Brecht*. Translated by Max Knight and Joseph Fabry, Ungar, 1970.
Hagestadt, Emma. "Doomed by Chuck Palahniuk." Review of *Doomed*, by Chuck Palahniuk. *Independent* (UK), 13 Sept. 2014. *EBSCOhost*, search.ebscohost.com/login.aspx?direct= true&db=n5h&AN=4HGINDINMLMMGLSTRY000023105697&site=eds-live&scope =site. Accessed 8 Aug. 2019.
Haller, Sonja. "Caught Your Teen Sexting? Don't 'Freak Out,' Experts Say. Study Found It Can Be Healthy." *USA Today*, 28 June 2019 (updated 20 June 2019), www.usatoday.com/story/life/allthemoms/2019/06/28/consensual-teen-sexting-could-healthy-university-of-texas-research-says/1585657001/Accessed 15 Dec. 2019.
———. "Katie Couric's New Podcast: Teens' Easy Access to Hardcore Porn Could Hurt Them … Literally." *USA Today*, 10 Oct. 2019, www.usatoday.com/story/life/parenting/2019/10/10/katie-couric-launches-new-podcast-talks-kids-access-porn/3923651002/. Accessed 15 Dec. 2019.
Harding, Natasha, and Dan Pountney. Review of *Doomed*, by Chuck Palahniuk. *The Sun*, 22 Nov. 2013, p.8. *EBSCOhost*, search.ebscohost.com/login.aspx?direct=true&db= n5h&AN=7EH79420570&site=eds-live&scope=site. Accessed 8 August 2019.
Harmon, William. "Grotesque." *A Handbook to Literature*, 12th ed., Longman, 2012, p. 223–24.
Harpham, Geoffrey Galt. *On the Grotesque: Strategies of Contradiction in Art and Literature*. Princeton UP, 1982.
Harris, Scott. "*The New Yorker*'s Visit Just a Blip to Valley." *Los Angeles Times*, 5 Nov. 1995, www.latimes.com/archives/la-xpm-1995-11-05-me-65169-story.html. Accessed 30 July 2019.

Harvkey, Mike. "Too Big to Fail: With a New Book, a New Publisher, and a New Agent, Chuck Palahniuk is Feeling Unusually Good for a Man Who's Just Survived One of the Toughest Stretches of His Career." *Publishers Weekly*, vol. 266, no. 46, 2019, pp. 48–49.
Hawthorne, Nathaniel. "Rappaccini's Daughter." 1844. www.columbia.edu/itc/english/f1124y-001/resources/Rappaccinis_Daughter.pdf. Accessed 28 Sept. 2019.
Hayes, Christal. "House Resolution Will Condemn Trump's 'Disgusting' Attacks on AOC, Tlaib, Omar and Pressley." *USA Today*, 15 July 2019, www.usatoday.com/story/news/politics/2019/07/15/pelosi-resolution-condemn-trumps-twitter-attacks-aoc-squad/1734913001/. Accessed 4 Nov. 2019.
———. "2020 Democrats are Wooing Voters at the Iowa State Fair. Here's What They're Saying." *USA Today*, 8 Aug. 2019, ww.usatoday.com/story/news/politics/elections/2019/08/08/iowa-state-fair-soapbox-2019-democratic-candidates-take-center-stage/1955161001/. Accessed 10 Aug. 2019.
Haynes, Deborah J. *Bakhtin Reframed*. I. B. Tauris, 2013. Contemporary Thinkers Reframed.
Hedegaard, Erik. "Chuck Palahniuk: A Heart Breaking Life of Staggering Weirdness." *Rolling Stone*, 30 June 2005, www.rollingstone.com/culture/culture-news/chuck-palahniuk-a-heart-breaking-life-of-staggering-weirdness-198182/. Accessed 30 Sept. 2019.
Heinecken, Dawn. "Sexed Appeals: Network Marketing Advertising and Adult Home Novelty Parties." *Studies in Popular Culture*, vol. 31, no. 2, 2009, pp. 23–43.
Hernández, Kristian, and Pratheek Rebala. "Puppies, Phones and Porn: How Model Legislation Affects Consumers' Lives." *USA Today*, 20 Nov. 2019, www.usatoday.com/in-depth/news/investigations/2019/11/20/puppies-phones-porn-meat-milk-how-model-legislation-and-copycat-bills-affect-consumers/2525454001/. Accessed 21 Nov. 2019.
Hesse, Cassandra, and Cory L. Pedersen. "Porn Sex Versus Real Sex: How Sexually Explicit Material Shapes Our Understanding of Sexual Anatomy, Physiology, and Behavior." *Sexuality and Culture*, vol. 21, no. 3, 2017, pp. 754–75.
Hirschkop, Ken, and David Shepherd. *Bakhtin and Cultural Theory*. Manchester UP, 2001.
Hobby, Blake, volume editor. *The Grotesque*. Infobase, 2009. Bloom's Literary Themes, edited by Harold Bloom.
Hollands, Neil. "Damned." Review of *Damned*, by Chuck Palahniuk. *Library Journal*, vol. 136, no. 13, Oct. 2011, p. 86.
———. "Snuff." Review of *Snuff*, by Chuck Palahniuk. *Library Journal*, vol. 133, no. 6, 1 Apr. 2008, p. 78.
Holquist, Michael. *Dialogism: Bakhtin and His World*. 2nd ed., Routledge, 2002.
———. Introduction. *Rabelais and His World*, 1965, by Mikhail Bakhtin, translated by Helene Iswolsky, Indiana UP, 1984, pp. xii–xxiii.
Holub, Christian. "Chuck Palahniuk Announces *Fight Club 3* Comic Series." *Entertainment Weekly*, 2 October 2018, ew.com/books/2018/10/02/chuck-palahniuk-fight-club-3-comic-series/. Accessed 16 Mar. 2019.
———. "Chuck Palahniuk Announces New Coloring-Book Novella, 'Legacy.'" *Entertainment Weekly*, 19 June 2017, ew.com/books/2017/06/19/chuck-palahniuk-announces-new-coloring-book-novella-legacy/. Accessed 6 Oct. 2019.
The Holy Bible, New Revised Standard Version, Holman, 1989.
hooks, bell. *Where We Stand: Class Matters*. Routledge, 2000.
Hoppenstand, Gary, editor. *Critical Insights: The Graphic Novel*. Salem Press, 2014.
Howe, Irving. "The Book of the Grotesque." *Partisan Review*, vol. 18, 1951, pp. 32–40.
Hoy, David Couzens, editor. *Foucault: A Critical Reader*. Basil Blackwell, 1986.
Hughes, Trevor, Stephanie Innes, and Jayne O'Donnell. "Is Marijuana Linked to Psychosis, Schizophrenia? It's Contentious, but Doctors, Feds Say Yes." *USA Today*, 15 Dec. 2019, www.usatoday.com/story/news/nation/2019/12/15/weed-psychosis-high-thc-cause-suicide-schizophrenia/4168315002/. Accessed 16 Dec. 2019.
Hume, Kathryn. *Aggressive Fiction: Reading the Contemporary American Novel*. Cornell UP, 2012.
Hunter, Starling, and Saba Singh. "A Network Text Analysis of *Fight Club*." *Theory and Practice in Language Studies*, vol. 5, no. 4, 2015, pp. 737–49.

Hutcheon, Linda. *Irony's Edge: The Theory and Politics of Irony.* Routledge, 1994.
———. *Narcissistic Narrative: The Metafictional Paradox.* Wilfrid Laurier UP, 2013.
———. *A Poetics of Postmodernism.* Routledge, 1988.
———. *The Politics of Postmodernism.* Routledge, 1989. *A Theory of Adaption.* Routledge, 2006.
———. *Theory of Parody: The Teachings of Twentieth-Century Art Forms.* 1985. U of Illinois P, 2000.
"I Am Charlotte Simmons Book Tour on *BookTV*." *C-SPAN*, 30 Nov. 2004, www.c-span.org/video/?185338-1/i-charlotte-simmons-book-tour. Accessed 17 July 2019.
"I Am Charlotte Simmons: Discussion on *BookTV*." *C-SPAN*, 18 Jan. 2005, www.c-span.org/video/?185340-1/i-charlotte-simmons-discussion. Accessed 17 July 2019.
"In-Depth: Tom Wolfe on *BookTV*." *C-SPAN*, 5 Dec. 2004, www.c-span.org/video/?184366-1/depth-tom-wolfe. Accessed 17 July 2019.
Iocco, Melissa. "Addicted to Affliction: Masculinity and Perversity in *Crash* and *Fight Club*." *Gothic Studies*, vol. 9, no. 1, 2007, pp. 46–56.
Isger, Sonja. "Ex-President of Medical College Spent $82,000 in School Funds for Personal Shopping Sprees." *USA Today*, 3 Jan. 2020, www.usatoday.com/story/news/nation/2020/01/03/ex-president-florida-medical-college-misused-82-000-school-fund/2803338001/. Accessed. 4 Jan. 2020.
Jabine, Angie. "Chuck Palahniuk's 'Beautiful You' Is 'Fifty Shades of the Twilight Cave Bear Wears Prada': Book Review." Review of *Beautiful You*, by Chuck Palahniuk. *The Oregonian*, 15 Oct. 2014 (updated 10 Jan. 2019), www.oregonlive.com/books/2014/10/chuck_palahniuks_beautiful_you_1.html. Accessed 3 Dec. 2019.
Jackson, David. "Trump Attacks Greta Thunberg for Being Time's 'Person of the Year,'" *USA Today*, 12 Dec. 2019. www.usatoday.com/story/news/2019/12/12/trump-mocks-greta-thunberg-being-times-person-year/4407278002/. Accessed 14 Dec. 2019.
Jakaitis, Jake, and James F. Wurtz, editors. *Crossing Boundaries in Graphic Narrative: Essays on Forms, Series, and Genres.* McFarland, 2012.
Jameson, Fredric. *Allegory and Ideology.* Verso, 2019.
"Jane Austen's Fight Club." *YouTube*, uploaded by LittleFarrahKhan, 2 Sept. 2010, www.youtube.com/watch?v=MskAK9VwDXc. Accessed 17 Oct. 2019.
"Jane Austen's Fight Club, by Emily Janice Card and Keith Paugh, 2010." *The Core Curriculum, Columbia College*, www.college.columbia.edu/core/content/jane-austens-fight-club-emily-janice-card-and-keith-paugh-2010. Accessed 17 Oct. 2019.
Jansen, Bart. "House Democrats Approve Rules for Debate on Articles of Impeachment." *USA Today*, 17 Dec. 2019, www.usatoday.com/story/news/politics/2019/12/17/house-panel-set-rules-impeachment-floor-debate-trump/2662702001/. Accessed 17 Dec. 2019.
Jaschik, Scott. "Coker University President Out." *Inside Higher Education*, 9 Sept. 2019, www.insidehighered.com/quicktakes/2019/09/09/coker-university-president-out. Accessed 29 Sept. 2019.
Jeffreys, Sheila. *Anticlimax: A Feminist Perspective on the Sexual Revolution.* Women's Press, 1990.
Jemielity, Sam. "Chuck Palahniuk: The Playboy Conversation." *Playboy*, 16 Oct. 2006, web.archive.org/web/20061016235628/http://www.playboy.com/arts-entertainment/dotcomversation/palahniuk/. Accessed 17 Oct. 2019.
Jenks, Chris. *Transgression.* Routledge, 2003.
Jennings, Scott. "Odd Couple: Marianne Williamson, Bernie Sanders Were Among the Democratic Debate Standouts." *USA Today*, 30 July 2019 (updated 31 July 2019), www.usatoday.com/story/opinion/2019/07/30/democratic-debate-williamson-sanders-warren-won-first-night-column/1867916001/. Accessed 5 Aug. 2019.
Jensen, Erin. "Whitney Cummings Shares NSFW Pic on Twitter After 'Foolish Dorks' Attempt to Extort Her." *USA Today*, 12 Aug. 2019, www.usatoday.com/story/entertainment/celebrities/2019/08/12/whitney-cummings-posts-topless-pic-twitter-amid-extortion-attempts/1987665001/. Accessed 6 Jan. 2020.
John T. *Make Life Your Bitch: Motivational Coloring Book: Turn Your Stress into Success.* CreateSpace, 2016.

Johnson, Denis. *Jesus' Son*. Picador, 1992.
Jones, Allie. "The Duke Porn Star Is Returning to Campus, Despite Threats Against Her." *The Atlantic*, 19 Mar. 2014, www.theatlantic.com/entertainment/archive/2014/03/duke-porn-star-taking-time-duke/359350/. Accessed 31 July 2019.
Jordan, Matt. "Marxism, Not Manhood: Accommodation and Impasse in Seamus Heaney's *Beowulf* and Chuck Palahniuk's *Fight Club*." *Men & Masculinities*, vol. 4, no. 4, 2002, pp. 368–79.
Joseph, Andrew. "US Fans in France Shout '(Expletive) Trump' During Fox News World Cup Report." *USA Today*, 7 July 2019, www.usatoday.com/story/sports/ftw/2019/07/07/usa-fans-expletive-trump-chant-fox-news-world-cup-report/39662065/. Accessed 17 July 2019.
Judge, Benjamin. "'A massive miscalculation of intent'—Beautiful You by Chuck Palahniuk." Review of *Beautiful You*, by Chuck Palahniuk. *Bookmunch*, 13 November 2014, bookmunch.wordpress.com/2014/11/13/a-massive-miscalculation-of-intent-beautiful-you-by-chuck-palahniuk/. Accessed 2 Oct. 2019.
Jung, Carl G. "On the Psychology of the Trickster-Figure." *Four Archetypes: Mother, Rebirth, Spirit, Trickster*, Ark, 1986, pp. 135–52. Originally published in *The Collected Works of C. G. Jung*, translated by R. F. C. Hull, Volume 9, Part 1, Princeton UP, 1969.
Kane, Tyler R. "Thanks for Sharing, Chuck Palahniuk." *Paste*, 2 June 2015, www.pastemagazine.com/articles/2015/06/chuck-palahniuk-thanks-for-sharing.html. Accessed 10 July 2019.
Kaplan, Lisa. "The Biggest Social Media Operation You've Never Heard of Is Run Out of Cyprus by Russians." *Lawfare*, Lawfare Institute, 18 Dec. 2019, www.lawfareblog.com/biggest-social-media-operation-youve-never-heard-run-out-cyprus-russians. Accessed 24 Dec. 2019.
Kaplan, Michael. "Why Chuck Palahniuk Went from Fight Club to Coloring Books." Review of *Bait*, by Chuck Palahniuk. *The New York Post*, 4 Nov. 2016, nypost.com/2016/11/04/why-chuck-palahniuk-went-from-fight-club-to-coloring-books/. Accessed 6 Oct. 2019.
Kaplan, Thomas. "Elizabeth Warren Apologizes at Native American Forum: 'I Have Listened and I Have Learned.'" *New York Times*, 19 Aug. 2019, www.nytimes.com/2019/08/19/us/politics/elizabeth-warren-native-american.html. Accessed 4 Nov. 2019.
Kavadlo, Jesse. "The Fiction of Self-Destruction: Chuck Palahniuk, Closet Moralist." *Stirrings Still: The International Journal of Existential Literature*, vol. 2, no. 2, 2005, pp. 3–26.
Kay, Sarah. *Žižek: A Critical Introduction*. Polity, 2003. Key Contemporary Thinkers.
Kayser, Wolfgang. *The Grotesque in Art and Literature*. 1957. Translated by Ulrich Weisstein, Columbia UP, 1981.
Keesey, Douglas. *Understanding Chuck Palahniuk*. U of South Carolina P, 2016.
Kellogg, Carolyn. "Chuck Palahniuk: Prophet or Profane?" Review of *Snuff*, by Chuck Palahniuk. *Los Angeles Times*, 9 June 2008, latimesblogs.latimes.com/jacketcopy/2008/06/chuck-palahniuk.html. Accessed 10 July 2019.
Kelly, Makena. "Rep. Katie Hill to Fight Revenge Porn Upon Leaving Congress." *The Verge*, 28 Oct. 2019, www.theverge.com/platform/amp/2019/10/28/20936130/katie-hill-revenge-porn-congress-resignation-advocate. Accessed 4 Nov. 2019.
Kerridge, Jake. "Piping Hot Ear, Freshly Sliced." Review of *Adjustment Day*, by Chuck Palahniuk. *Daily Telegraph*, July 2018, pp. 28–29. *EBSCOhost*, search.ebscohost.com/login.aspx?direct=true&db=n5h&AN= 8Q2139974786&site=eds-live&scope=site. Accessed 31 Oct. 2019.
Keshishoglou, Jonathan. "Morbidly Colorful Tales Fill Chuck Palahniuk's Adult Coloring Book." Review of *Bait*, by Chuck Palahniuk. *Mashable*, 14 June 2016, mashable.com/2016/06/14/palahniuk-coloring-book/#dTOzf.mIWGqU. Accessed 6 Oct. 2019.
Kestenbaum, Sam. "The Curious Mystical Text Behind Marianne Williamson's Presidential Bid." *New York Times*, 5 July 2019, www.nytimes.com/2019/07/05/nyregion/marianne-williamson.html. Accessed 5 Aug. 2019.
Kinder, Elizabeth, and Patricia Pender. "'A Copy of a Copy of a Copy': Framing the Double in *Fight Club*." *Literature/Film Quarterly*, vol. 42, no. 3, 2014, pp. 541–56.

King, Ledyard. "Hello, New Zealand: Williamson Says First Act as President Would Be a Phone Call Across the World." *USA Today*, 24 June 2019, www.usatoday.com/story/news/politics/elections/2019/06/27/democratic-debate-2019-marianne-williamson-would-call-new-zealand/1591872001/. Accessed 5 Aug. 2019.

Kirkland, Justin. "Megan Rapine, American Treasure, Slighted Trump Again at the USWNT Victory Parade." *Esquire*, 10 July 2019, www.esquire.com/entertainment/a28352682/megan-rapinoe-donald-trump-victory-parade-speech/. Accessed 17 July 2019.

Kleinman, Alexis. "Porn Sites Get More Visitors Each Month Than Netflix, Amazon and Twitter Combined." *HuffPost*, 4 May 2013 (updated 6 Dec. 2017), www.huffpost.com / entry/internet-porn-stats_n_3187682. Accessed 30 July 2019.

Knight, Rosie. "Chuck Palahniuk Talks *Adjustment Day*, His First New Book in 4 Years." Review of *Adjustment Day*, by Chuck Palahniuk. *Nerdist*, 2 May 2018, nerdist.com/article/chuck-palahniuk-adjustment-day-interview-2/. Accessed 31 Oct. 2019.

Kristeva, Julia. "Word, Dialogue, and Novel." 1966. Translated by Alice Jardine, Thomas Gora, and Léon S. Roudiez, *The Kristeva Reader*, edited by Toril Moi, Columbia UP, 1986, pp. 34–61.

Kuhn, Cynthia, and Lance Rubin, editors. *Reading Chuck Palahniuk: American Monsters and Literary Mayhem*. Routledge, 2009.

Kukkonen, Karin. *Studying Comics and Graphic Novels*. Wiley Blackwell, 2013.

Lacan, Jacques. *Écrits: The First Complete Edition in English*. Translated by Bruce Fink. Norton, 2007.

Larman, Alexander. "*Adjustment Day* by Chuck Palahniuk Review—All Punched Out." Review of *Adjustment Day*, by Chuck Palahniuk. *The Observer*, 1 July 2018, www.theguardian.com/books/2018/jul/01/adjustment-day-chuck-palahniuk-review-feeble-satire. Accessed 10 July 2019.

Lawless, Andrew. "Those Burnt Tongue Moments—Chuck Palahniuk in Interview." *Three Monkeys Online*, May 2005, www.threemonkeysonline.com/those-burnt-tongue-moments-chuck-palahniuk-in-interview/2/. Accessed 2 Oct. 2019.

The Layman with a Notebook. *What is the Oxford Group?* Oxford UP, 1933.

Leavitt, Caroline. "'Beautiful You,' by Chuck Palahniuk." Review of *Beautiful You*, by Chuck Palahniuk. *SFGate*, 7 Jan. 2015, www.sfgate.com/books/article/Beautiful-You-by-Chuck-Palahniuk-6000447.php. Accessed 4 Sept. 2019.

Lelievre, Benoit. "Book Review: Chuck Palahniuk—Fight Club 2 (2016)." Review of *Fight Club 2*, by Chuck Palahniuk. *Dead End Follies*, 29 Aug. 2016, www.deadendfollies.com/blog/book-review-chuck-palahniuk-fight-club-2-2016. Accessed 15 Oct. 2019.

———. "Book Review: Chuck Palahniuk—Make Something Up: Stories You Can't Unread (2015)." Review of *Make Something Up*, by Chuck Palahniuk. *Dead End Follies*, 21 June 2018, www.deadendfollies.com/blog/book-review-chuck-palahniuk-make-something-up?rq=Palahniuk. Accessed 27 Sept. 2019.

Lewis, William S. *Louis Althusser and the Traditions of French Marxism*. Lexington Books, 2005.

Lindgren, Simon. "A Copy of a Copy of a Copy: Exploring Masculinity Under Transformation in *Fight Club*." *Scope: An Online Journal of Film Studies*, vol. 19, 2011, www.nottingham.ac.uk/scope/documents/2011/february-2011/lindgren.pdf.

Lodge, David. *After Bakhtin: Essays on Fiction and Criticism*. Routledge, 1990.

Lo Dico, Joy. "Did Fight Club Start Snowflake Avalanche?" *Evening Standard*, 24 Jan. 2017, pp. 16–17.

Longmore, Paul "Screening Stereotypes: Images of Disabled People in Television and Motion Pictures." *Images of the Disabled, Disabling Images*. Edited by Alan Gartner and Tom Joe, Praeger, 1987, pp. 65–78.

Lopez, Kathryn Jean. "On Love, Marianne Williamson Has a Point." *National Review*, 5 Aug. 2019, www.nationalreview.com/2019/08/marianne-williamson-right-we-need-love-healing/. Accessed 5 Aug. 2019.

"Loser (Part 1)." *YouTube*, uploaded by Sarah Sprontos, 27 May 2008, www.youtube.com/watch?v=ZWrdV6P7oqw. Accessed 25 Sept. 2019.

Lukács, György [Georg]. *History and Class Consciousness*. 1920. Translator Rodney Livingstone, Merlin, 1967. *Georg Lukacs Archive, Marxist Internet Archive*, www.marxists.org/archive/lukacs/works/history/lukacs3.htm. Accessed 8 July 2019.

Luscombe, Belinda. "Porn and the Threat to Virility." *Time*, 31 Mar. 2016, time.com/4277510/porn-and-the-threat-to-virility/. 30 July 2019.

Lyotard, Jean-François. Introduction. *The Postmodern Condition: A Report on Knowledge*, 1979, translation by Geoff Bennington and Brian Massumi, U of Minnesota P, 1984, pp. xxiii–xxv. Theory and History of Literature, Volume 10.

Maasik, Sonia, and Jack Solomon, editors. *Signs of Life in the USA: Readings on Popular Culture for Writers*, 6th ed., Bedford/St. Martin's, 2009.

MacDonald, Heidi. "Comics Lure Literary Authors to Create Original Works." *Publishers Weekly*, 15 Aug. 2016, pp. 5–6.

Machell, Ben. "Dispatches from the Great Beyond." Review of *Doomed*, by Chuck Palahniuk. *The Times*, 16 Nov. 2013, p. 16. EBSCOhost, search.ebscohost.com/login.aspx?direct=true&db=n5h&AN=7EH79171206&site=eds-live&scope=site. Accessed 8 Aug. 2019.

Macherey, Pierre. *A Theory of Literary Production*. 1966. Translated by Geoffrey Wall, Routledge and Kegan Paul, 1978.

MacKinnon, Catharine A. *Toward a Feminist Theory of the State*. Harvard UP, 1989.

Madrigal, Alexis C. "Why It's Time for the Journal of Porn Studies." *The Atlantic*, 21 Mar. 2014, www.theatlantic.com/technology/archive/2014/03/why-its-time-for-the-journal-of-em-porn-studies-em/284576/. Accessed 30 July 2019.

"Make Something Up: Stories You Can't Unread." Review of *Make Something Up: Stories You Can't Unread*, by Chuck Palahniuk. *Kirkus Reviews*, 2 Mar. 2015, www.kirkusreviews.com/book-reviews/chuck-palahniuk/make-something-up/. Accessed 25 Sept. 209.

———. "Review of *Make Something Up: Stories You Can't Unread*, by Chuck Palahniuk. *Publishers Weekly*, vol. 262, no. 23, June 2015, p. 14.

Mandell, Andrea, and Bill Keveney. "Famous Friends Back Bella Thorne Over Whoopi Goldberg's 'Awful' Views on Photo Scandal." *USA Today*, 18 June 2019, www.usatoday.com/story/life/people/2019/06/18/bella-thorne-slams-whoopi-goldberg-victim-blaming-nude-scandal/1494304001/. Accessed 20 June 2019.

Marcuse, Herbert. *One-Dimensional Man: Studies in the Ideology of Advanced Industrial Society*. Beacon, 1964.

Marks, Michael, and Kassia Wosick. "Exploring College Men's and Women's Attitudes about Women's Sexuality and Pleasure Via Their Perceptions of Female Novelty Party Attendees." *Sex Roles*, vol. 77, no. 7–8, 2017, pp. 550–61.

Martin, Annie. "'Fight Club 2' Will Be a Comic Book Series, Chuck Palahniuk Says." *UPI Entertainment*, July 2014. EBSCOhost, search.ebscohost.com/login.aspx?direct= true&db= n5h&AN=B92Y4207924900&site=eds-live&scope=site. Accessed 21 Oct. 2019.

Martin, Nick. "Who Gets to Say If Warren's Apology to Cherokee Nation Is Enough." *The New Republic*, 20 Aug. 2019, newrepublic.com/article/154887/gets-say-warrens-apology-cherokee-nation-enough. Accessed 4 Nov. 2019.

Martin, Tim. "*Doomed*, by Chuck Palahniuk, Review." *The Telegraph*, 11 Nov. 2013, www.telegraph.co.uk/culture/books/bookreviews/10433985/Doomed-by-Chuck-Palahniuk-review.html. Accessed 10 July 2019.

Martinez, Nikki. "7 Reasons Adult Coloring Books are Great for Your Mental, Emotional and Intellectual Health." *HuffPost*, 24 Nov. 2015, www.huffpost.com/entry/7-reasons-adult-coloring-books-are-great-for-your-mental-emotional-and-intellectual-health_b_8626136. Accessed 6 Oct. 2019.

Marx, Karl. "Chapter 1: The Commodity." *Capital: A Critique of Political Economy*. 1867. *Value: Studies by Karl Marx*, New Park, 1976, pp. 7–40. *Karl Marx: Capital Volume One, Marxist Internet Archive*, www.marxists.org/archive/marx/works/1867-c1/commodity.htm. Accessed 8 July 2019.

Maslin, Janet. "The Road to Hell, Paved with Telemarketers." Review of *Damned*, by Chuck Palahniuk. *New York Times*, 19 Oct. 2011, www.nytimes.com/2011/10/20/books/damned-by-chuck-palahniuk. Accessed 10 July 2019.

Mason, Bobbie Ann. "Marita." *Love Life*, Harper Perennial, 1989, pp. 54–67.
Mathews, Peter. "Diagnosing Chuck Palahniuk's *Fight Club*." *Stirrings Still: The International Journal of Existential Literature*, vol. 2, no. 2, 2005, pp. 89–113.
McCampbell, Mary W. "'Paradigms Are Dissolving Left and Right': Baudrillard's Anti-Apocalypse and Chuck Palahniuk's *Survivor*." *Sacred and Immoral: On the Writings of Chuck Palahniuk*, edited by Jeffrey A. Sartain, Cambridge Scholars, 2009, pp. 146–58.
McCloud, Scott. *Reinventing Comics*. Perennial, 2000.
―――. *Understanding Comics: The Invisible Art*. Perennial, 1993.
McCracken, David. "Cassie Wright, Stormy Daniels, and #MeToo: Teaching Chuck Palahniuk's *Snuff* as a Response to Heteropatriarchy," 17 June 2019, *Chuck Palahniuk: The Treasures of Trash and Transgression*, edited by Eyal Handelsman and Chris Burlingame. Forthcoming.
―――. *Chuck Palahniuk, Parodist: Postmodern Irony in Six Transgressive Novels*. McFarland, 2016.
―――. "Chuck Palahniuk's *Beautiful You*, Alfred Kinsey's *Sexual Behavior in the Human Female*, and the Commodification of Female Sexual Desire." *Studies in Popular Culture*, vol. 39, no. 1, 2016, pp. 101–22.
―――. "Chuck Palahniuk's *Fight Club* as Working-Class Novel." *Postscript: Publication of the Philological Association of the Carolinas*, vol. 27, no. 12, 2012, pachome.wordpress.com /current-issue/27-12-david-mccracken/www.pachome.org. Accessed 17 July 2019.
―――. "Disability Studies Simulacra in Chuck Palahniuk's *Fight Club(s)*." 25 Sept. 2019, *The Midwest Quarterly: A Journal of Contemporary Thought*. Forthcoming.
―――. "The Dunning-Kruger Effect in Dirty Realism: Dorothy Allison's 'Jason Who Will Be Famous,' Larry Brown's 'Waiting for the Ladies,' and Chuck Palahniuk's 'Romance,'" 6 Jan. 2019, *Journal of the Short Story in English*. Forthcoming.
―――. "The Importance of the Support Group Chapters in Chuck Palahniuk's *Fight Club*." 7 Aug. 2018, *The Explicator*. Under review.
―――. "'Just hear that potty mouth!': An Argument for Sarah Ruden's Translation of *Lysistrata*" *Neohelicon*, vol. 45, no. 2, 2018, pp. 603–19.
―――. "Sherwood Anderson's Grotesques in Thomas Boyd's *Points of Honor*," 14 Mar. 2019, *ANQ: A Quarterly Journal of Short Articles, Notes, and Reviews*. Under review.
―――. "Teaching Postmodern Parody through Stephen King, Chuck Palahniuk, and *Fight Club*." *Teaching American Literature*, vol. 9, no. 2, 2017, pp. 39–61.
McDermott, Maeve. "Alyssa Milano Defends Attending Fundraiser for Presidential Hopeful Marianne Williamson." *USA Today*, 17 July 2019, www.usatoday.com/story/entertainment/celebrities/2019/07/17/alyssa-milano-marianne-williamson-fundraiser-bashed-over-vaccine-controversy/1753556001/. Accessed 5 Aug. 2019.
―――. "Brad Pitt Talks Sobriety, Alcoholics Anonymous: 'I removed my drinking privileges.'" *USA Today*, 4 Sept. 2019 (updated 5 Sept. 2019), www.usatoday.com/story/entertainment/celebrities/2019/09/04/brad-pitt-praises-alcoholics-anonymous-experience-talks-sobriety-struggles/2207360001/. Accessed 3 Dec. 2019.
―――. "Marianne Williamson's 'Seinfeld' Reference Was 'Bizarre,' Says Julia Louise-Dreyfus." *USA Today*, 1 Aug. 2019, www.usatoday.com/story/entertainment/celebrities/2019/08/01/marianne-williamson-julia-louis-dreyfus-side-eyes-seinfeld-quote/1886639001/. Accessed 5 Aug. 2019.
McElroy, Bernard. *Fiction of the Modern Grotesque*. St. Martin's, 1989.
McMillan, Graeme. "'Fight Club 3' Team on Bringing Tyler Durden to Comics." *The Hollywood Reporter*, 29 January 2019, www.hollywoodreporter.com/heat-vision/fight-club-3-chuck-palahniuk-explains-new-comic-1180375. Accessed 16 Mar. 2019.
"Meet Ellen Stohl." *Playboy*, vol. 34, no. 7, July 1987, pp. 68–74.
Meindl, Dieter. *American Fiction and the Metaphysics of the Grotesque*. U of Missouri P, 1996.
Mellick Carlton III, *The Haunted Vagina*. Eraserhead, 2011.
―――. *I Knocked Up Satan's Daughter*. Eraserhead, 2011.
Melville, Herman. *Moby-Dick*. 1851. Dark Horse, 2017.
―――. "The Whiteness of the Whale." *Moby-Dick*. 1851. 3rd ed., edited by Hershel Parker, Norton, 2018, pp. 151–57.

Meyers, Tony. *Slavoj Žižek*. Routledge, 2003. Routledge Critical Thinkers.
Michaelson, Jay. "Marianne Williamson, Longtime Whacko, Is Now a Dangerous Whacko." *The Daily Beast*, 22 June 2019 (updated 23 June 2019), www.thedailybeast.com/marianne-williamson-longtime-wacko-is-now-a-dangerous-wacko. Accessed 5 Aug. 2019.
"Mike Allen 7/13/19." *Saturday Midday, 700 WLW On-Demand*, iHeartMedia, 13 July 2019, /www.iheart.com/podcast/71-700-wlw-on-demand-29401446/episode/mike-allen-71319-46881755/. Accessed on 15 July 2019.
Milano, Alyssa, and Waleisah Wilson. "Why the Time is Now for #SexStrike." *CNN Opinion*, 13 May 2019, www.cnn.com/2019/05/13/opinions/alyssa-milano-sex-strike-now/index.html. Accessed 13 June 2019.
Miller, Laura. "Diary." Review of *Diary*, by Chuck Palahniuk. *Salon*, 21 Aug. 2003, www.salon.com/2003/08/20/palahniuk_3/. Accessed 10 July 2019.
Miller, Matthew, editor. *Class, Please Open your Comics: Essays on Teaching with Graphic Narratives*. McFarland, 2015.
Miller, Susan. "El Paso, Dayton Make 251 Mass Shootings in the US in 216 Days, More Shootings Than Days in the Year." *USA Today*, 3 Aug. 2019 (updated 4 Aug. 2019), www.usatoday.com/story/news/nation/2019/08/03/el-paso-walmart-shooting-250th-mass-shooting-this-year/1913486001/. Accessed 5 Aug. 2019.
Millican, Josh. "First Look: Tyler Durden Lives in *Fight Club 3* Graphic Novel Sequel by Chuck Palahniuk." *Dread Central*, Dread Central Media, 11 January 2019, www.dreadcentral.com/news/287654/first-look-tyler-durden-lives-in-fight-club-3-graphic-novel-sequel-by-chuck-palahniuk/. Accessed 16 Mar. 2019.
Mitchell, David T., and Sharon L. Snyder. *Narrative Prosthesis: Disability and Dependencies of Discourse*. U of Michigan P, 2000.
Mohan, Megha, and Yousef Eldin. "The Real (and Fake) Sex Lives of Bella Thorne." *BBC News*, 17 Oct. 2019, www.bbc.com/news/stories-50072653. Accessed 29 Dec. 2019.
Moniuszko, Sara M. "Alyssa Milano Explains Sex Strike: 'Extreme Response' Was Needed to Get National Attention." *USA Today*, 14 May 2019, www.usatoday.com/story/life/people/2019/05/14/alyssa-milano-explains-controversial-sex-strike-op-ed/3664792002/. Accessed 13 June 2019.
Montag, Warren. *Louis Althusser*. Palgrave, 2003. Transitions.
Mookerjee, Robin. *Transgressive Fiction: The New Satiric Tradition*. Palgrave, 2013.
Morin, Rebecca. "Marianne Williamson: *Vogue* Magazine is Not the 'Gatekeeper' of Who Gets to Run for President." *USA Today*, 2 July 2019 (updated 3 July 2019). www.usatoday.com/story/news/politics/elections/2019/07/02/marianne-williamson-vogue-snub-2020-democratic-hopefuls/1635830001/. Accessed 5 Aug. 2019.
Morris, Conor. "College: Those Involved in' Fight Club' Were Punished." *Athens News*, 1 Apr. 2019, p. 11.
Morris, Pam, editor. *The Bakhtin Reader: Selected Writings of Bakhtin, Medvedev and Voloshinov*. Arnold, 1994.
"NAP CLUB." *YouTube*, uploaded by Carlos Alazraqui, 20 Mar. 2018, www.youtube.com/watch?v=DTJx3AFVWic. Accessed 17 Oct. 2019.
Nelson, Sophia A. "Alexandria Ocasio-Cortez is Right, Speaker Nancy Pelosi Has a Women of Color Problem." *USA Today*, 14 July 2019, www.usatoday.com/story/opinion/2019/07/14/nancy-pelosi-learn-from-ocasio-cortez-women-of-color-column/1715320001/. Accessed 4 Nov. 2019.
Nevin, Will. "Wednesday Warrior #55: Chuck Palahniuk's 'Bait': Depraved, Disgusting, and Delightful." *AL*, 7 Mar. 2019, www.al.com/living/2016/10/wednesday_warriors_55_chuck_pa.html. Accessed 6 Oct. 2019.
"New Photo Reveals Congresswoman Katie Hill Showing Off Nazi-era Tattoo While Smoking a Bong." *MilneNews*, 24 Oct. 2019, milnenews.com/2019/10/24/new-photo-reveals-congresswoman-katie-hill-showing-off-nazi-era-tattoo-while-smoking-a-bong/. Accessed 4 Nov. 2019.
Newman, Sandra. "*Make Something Up* Review—Chuck Palahniuk at the Height of His Powers." Review of *Make Something Up*, by Chuck Palahniuk. *Guardian*, 10 June 2015, www.

theguardian.com/books/2015/jun/10/make-something-up-chuck-palahniuk-review-short-story-collection. Accessed 10 July 2019.

Ng, Andrew Hock Soon. "Muscular Existentialism in Chuck Palahniuk's *Fight Club*." *Stirrings Still: The International Journal of Existential Literature*, vol. 2, no. 2, 2005, pp. 125–49.

Nguyen, Tina. "Did Elizabeth Warren Just Neutralize Trump's Best Attack?" *Vanity Fair*, 16 Aug. 2019, www.vanityfair.com/news/2019/08/elizabeth-warren-native-american-proposal. Accessed 4 Nov. 2019.

"Nightmare, with Halsey." *YouTube*, uploaded by Halsey, 16 May 2019, www.youtube.com/watch?v=Q_dqfcvTZik. Accessed 3 Nov. 2019.

Nocera, Kate. "Rep. Katie Hill Will Resign after Details of Her Sex Life Were Published." *BuzzFeed*, 27 Oct. 2019, www.buzzfeednews.com/article/katenocera/katie-hill-resign-sex-life-published. Accessed 4 Nov. 2019.

O. Henry (William Sydney Porter). "The Gift of the Magi." 1905. *American English*, The Bureau of Educational and Cultural Affairs, n.d., americanenglish.state.gov/files/ae/resource_files/1-the_gift_of_the_magi_0.pdf. Accessed 18 Dec. 2019.

Olsen, D. M. "Book Review: Chuck Palahniuk's 'Adjustment Day.'" Review of *Adjustment Day*, by Chuck Palahniuk. *The Coachella Review*, 18 July 2019, thecoachellareview.com/wordpress/2018/07/18/review-of-adjustment-day-by-chuck-palahniuk/. Accessed 31 Oct. 2019.

Ovenden, Olivia. "Twenty Years After Its Release, What Did 'Fight Club' Achieve Where 'Joker' Failed?" *Esquire*, 12 Oct. 2019, www.esquire.com/uk/culture/film/a29386027/joker-fight-club/. Accessed 7 Nov. 2019.

Page, Susan. "Divided We Fall? Americans See Our Angry Political Debate as a 'Big Problem.'" *USA Today*, 5 Dec. 2019, www.usatoday.com/story/news/politics/elections/hiddencommonground/2019/12/05/hidden-common-ground-americans-divided-politics-seek-civility/4282301002/. Accessed 5 Dec. 2019.

Paglia, Camille. "It's a Jungle Out There." *Patterns for College Writing*. Edited by Laurie G. Kirszner and Stephen R. Mandell, 8th ed., Bedford St. Martin's, 2001, pp. 538–41. Originally published in *New York Newsday*, 7 March 1991, pp. 838–41.

Palahniuk, Chuck. *Adjustment Day*. Norton, 2018.

———. Afterword. *Fight Club*, 1996, Norton, 2005, pp. 209–18.

———. "Ah-Ha: Beginning to End with Chuck Palahniuk and Michael Bailey." *It's Alive! Bring Nightmares to Life*. Edited by Joe Mynhardt and Eugene Johnson, Crystal Lake, 2018, pp. 43–52.

———. "Author Chuck Palahniuk Tells Us Why It's Time to Re-Open Fight Club." Interview by Bryan Bishop. *The Verge*, 27 May 2015, www.theverge.com/2015/5/27/8660881/fight-club-sequel-chuck-palahniuk-interview. Accessed 21 Oct. 2019.

———. "Bait." *Bait*, pp. 105–18.

———. *Bait: Off-Color Stories for You to Color*. Illustrated by Duncan Fegredo, LeeBermejo, Joelle Jones, and Alise Gluskova, Dark Horse, 2016.

———. "Beaks and Geeks: #131: Chuck Palahniuk." Interview by Lindsay. *Soundcloud*, 1 Aug. 2016, soundcloud.com/beaks-and-geeks/131-chuck-palahniuk. Accessed 17 Sept. 2019.

———. *Beautiful You*. Doubleday, 2014.

———. "The Big Secret Why Behind Everything So Far." *The Cult*, Chuck Palahniuk Fan Website, 29 May 2018, chuckpalahniuk. net/news/the-big-secret-why-behind-everything-so-far. Accessed 25 Sept. 2019.

———. "Cannibal." *Make Something Up*, pp. 80–88.

———. "Cassandra." *Haunted*, pp. 349–54.

———. "Catching Up with ... Chuck Palahniuk." Interview by Josh Jackson. *Paste*, 26 Sept. 2008, www.pastemagazine.com/articles/2008/09/catching-up-with-chuck-palahniuk.html. Accessed 14 Nov. 2019.

———. *Choke*. Doubleday, 2001.

———. "Chuck Palahniuk: 'A Creature of Infinite Light & Love.'" Interview by Rick Kleffel. *Agony Column*, 20 May 2005, www.trashotron.com/agony/audio/chuck_palahniuk_2005.mp3. Accessed 25 Sept. 2019.

Works Cited

———. "Chuck Palahniuk Goes to Hell." Interview by Adam Weinstein. *Mother Jones*, Nov.-Dec. 2011, motherjones.com/media/2011/10/chuck-palahniuk-interview-damned/. Accessed 8 Aug. 2019.

———. "Chuck Palahniuk Hung Out with 'Separatists of Every Stripe' for New Novel." Interview by Peter Rugh. *Vice*, 1 May 2018, www.vice.com/en_us/article/paxn4z/chuck-palahniuk-hung-out-with-separatists-of-every-stripe-for-new-novel. Accessed 5 Nov. 2019.

———. "Chuck Palahniuk: 'I'm fascinated by low fiction that disgusts the reader or makes them sexually aroused.'" Interview by Ed Cumming, *Guardian*, 1 Nov. 2014, www.theguardian.com/books/2014/nov/01/chuck-palahniuk-this-much-i-know. Accessed 15 July 2019.

———. "Chuck Palahniuk Inside a Dark Mind." Interview by Ed Andrews. *Huck*, 11 Apr. 2014, www.huckmag.com/art-and-culture/print/chuck-palahniuk/. Accessed 14 Nov. 2019.

———. "Chuck Palahniuk Is Really Just a Misunderstood Romance Novelist." Interview by Jennifer M. Wood. *Esquire*, 26 May 2015, www.esquire.com/entertainment/books/interviews/a35222/chuck-palahniuk-interview/. Accessed 25 Sept. 2019.

———. "Chuck Palahniuk: *Legacy* Interview." Interview by Dana Folkard. *Impulse Gamer*, 7 Nov. 2017. www.impulsegamer.com/chuck-palahniuk-legacy-interview/. Accessed 15 Aug. 2019.

———. "Chuck Palahniuk on Fight Club 2, Dick Jokes, and the Secret to Happiness." Interview by J. Rentilly. *Men's Health*, 26 June 2015, www.menshealth.com/trending-news/a19544613/chuck-palahniuk-interview/. Accessed 21 Oct. 2019.

———. "Chuck Palahniuk on Fight Club and Its Sequel, Fight Club 2." Interview by Matthew Schniper. *Miami New Times*, 25 May 2015, www.miaminewtimes.com/arts/chuck-palahniuk-on-fight-club-and-its-sequel-fight-club-2-7639025. Accessed 28 Sept. 2019.

———. "Chuck Palahniuk on the 'Personalized,' 'Unique,' and '80s Rock-Inspired Bait: Off-Color Stories for You to Color." Interview by Russ Burlingame. *Comic Book*, 6 Sept. 2017, comicbook.com/popculturenow/2016/10/26/chuck-palahniuk-on-the-personalized-unique-and-80s-rock-inspired/. Accessed 6 Oct. 2019.

———. "Chuck Palahniuk Talks About 'Fight Club 2' and Literally Inserting Himself into the Story." Interview by Leo Johnson. *UPROXX*, 8 July 2015, uproxx.com/movies/chuck-palahniuk-fight-club-2-interview/. Accessed 18 Sept. 2019.

———. "Chuck Palahniuk Talks *Bait*, His Short Story/Coloring Book Hybrid Rated NC-17." Interview by Frannie Jackson. *Paste*, 25 Oct. 2016, www.pastemagazine.com/articles/2016/10/chuck-palahniuk-bait-coloring-book.html. Accessed 6 Oct. 2019.

———. "Chuck Palahniuk Talks 'Legacy.'" Interview by Mark Dago. *Big Shiny Robot*, 7 Nov. 2017. bigshinyrobot.com/books/chuck-palahniuk-talks-legacy/. Accessed 19 Aug. 2019.

———. "Chuck Palahniuk Wants You to Take the Bait with His New Coloring Book." Interview by Jed W. Keith. *Freak Sugar*, 25 Oct. 2016, www.freaksugar.com/chuck-palahniuk-interview-bait-coloring-book/. Accessed 6 Oct. 2019.

———. "Chuck Palahniuk: 'You Can't Just Be a Spectator.'" Interview by Johnny Adams. *The Talks*, 5 November 2014, the-talks.com/interview/chuck-palahniuk/. Accessed 5 Sept. 2019.

———. "Chuck Palahniuk's Greatest Treasures Are His Past Mistakes." Interview by Krystie Lee Yandoli and David Bertozzi. *BuzzFeed*, 26 May 2015, www.buzzfeed.com/krystieyandoli/chuck-palahniuks-greatest-treasures-are-his-past-mistakes. Accessed 24 Sept. 2019.

———. "Cold Calling." *Make Something Up*, pp. 129–35.

———. "A Collaboration." *Bait*, p. 5.

———. *Consider This: Moments in My Writing Life After Which Everything Was Different*. Grand Central, 2020.

———. "Conspiracy." *Bait*, pp. 23–41.

———. "A Conversation with Chuck Palahniuk, the Author of 'Fight Club' and the Man Behind Tyler Durden." Interview by John McDermott. *MEL*, 27 Nov. 2017, medium.com/mel-magazine/a-conversation-with-chuck-palahniuk-the-author-of-fight-club-and-the-man-behind-tyler-durden-9098e9d031fa. Accessed 25 Sept. 2019.

———. "A Conversation with Chuck Palahniuk." Interview by Tom Spanbauer. *The Believer*, no. 107, 1 May 2014, believermag.com/a-conversation-with-chuck-palahniuk/. Accessed 30 Sept. 2019.

———. "Dad All Over." *Bait*, pp. 7–22.

———. *Damned*. Doubleday, 2011.
———. "Damned If You Do: Chuck Palahniuk on His New Novel." Interview by Royal Young. *Interview*, 19 Oct. 2011, www.interviewmagazine.com/culture/chuck-palahniuk-damned. Accessed 19 Aug. 2019.
———. "Does It Make Him a Psychopath? The Millions Interviews Chuck Palahniuk." Interview by Lucia Senesi. *The Millions*, 28 Jan. 2019, themillions.com/2019/01/does-it-make-him-a-psychopath-the-millions-interviews-chuck-palahniuk.html. Accessed 5 Nov. 2019.
———. *Doomed*. Doubleday, 2013.
———. "Duel Meaning; The Writer Chuck Palahniuk on the Inspiration for Fight Club." *The Times*, 21 Nov. 2009, p. 10. *EBSCOhost*, search.ebscohost.com/login.aspx?direct=true&db=edsgao&AN=edsgcl.212587471&site=eds-live&scope=site. Accessed 9 Jan. 2020.
———. "8 Great Questions: Chuck Palahniuk." Interview by Abbe Wright. *Read It Forward*, n.d., www.readitforward.com/8-great-questions/chuck-palahniuk/. Accessed 6 Oct. 2019.
———. "Eleanor." *Make Something Up*, pp. 10–17.
———. "Exclusive Interview with Chuck Palahniuk." Interview by Alex Yarde. *The Good Men Project*, 28 May 2018, goodmenproject.com/arts/exclusive-interview-with-author-chuck-palahniuk-xela/. Accessed 5 Nov. 2019.
———. "Expedition." *Make Something Up*, pp. 211–31.
———. "Fact and Fiction: An Introduction." *Stranger Than Fiction: True Stories*. Anchor, 2004, pp. xv–xxii.
———. "The Facts of Life." *Make Something Up*, pp. 122–28.
———. "Fainting, Sequential Art & Strippers: Chuck Palahniuk and Chelsea Cain in Conversation." Interview by Sean Edgar. *Paste*, 8 Nov. 2017, pastemagazine.com/articles/2017/11/fainting-sequential-art-strippers-chuck-palahniuk.html. Accessed 11 Dec. 2019.
———. "Fetch." *Make Something Up*, pp. 195–210.
———. *Fight Club*. 1996. Norton, 2005.
———. "'Fight Club 2' Breaks the First Rule with Our In-Depth Chuck Palahniuk Interview." Interview by Alex Zalben. *MTV News*, 27 Apr. 2015, www.mtv.com/news/2143632/chuck-palahniuk-fight-club-2-interview/. Accessed 21 Oct. 2019.
———. *Fight Club 2: The Tranquility Gambit*. Illustrated by Cameron Stewart and David Mack, Dark Horse, 2016.
———. *Fight Club 3*. Dark Horse, 2020.
———. *Fight Club 3* #1. Illustrated by Cameron Stewart, Dark Horse, 2019.
———. "'Fight Club' Author Reflects on Violence and Masculinity, 20 Years Later." Interview by Maddie Crum. *HuffPost*, 6 Dec. 2016, www.huffpost.com/entry/fight-club-2-chuck-palahniuk_n_5845c35ae4b028b32338a632. Accessed 21 Oct. 2019.
———. "Fight Club for Kids." *YouTube*, 23 June 2015, www.youtube.com/watch?v=RB8sAKb9tPU. Accessed 7 Mar. 2019.
———. "'Fight Club's' Twisted Mastermind: Chuck Palahniuk on God, Men Vs. Women, and 'Fight Club 2.'" Interview by Emil Lendof. *The Daily Beast*, 27 May 2015 (updated 12 July 2017), www.thedailybeast.com/fight-clubs-twisted-mastermind-chuck-palahniuk-on-god-men-vs-women-and-fight-club-2. Accessed 25 Sept. 2019.
———. "FOG! Chats with Author Chuck Palahniuk about His New Coloring Book, 'Bait' and 'Fight Club 2.'" Interview by Stefan Blitz. *Forces of Geek*, 26 Oct. 2016, www.forcesofgeek.com/2016/10/fog-chats-with-author-chuck-palahniuk-about-his-new-coloring-book-bait-and-fight-club-2.html. Accessed 6 Oct. 2019.
———. "Foreword: The Fringe Is the Future." *You Do Not Talk About Fight Club: I Am Jack's Completely Unauthorized Essay Collection*, edited by Read Mercer Schuchardt, Ben-Bell, 2008, pp. 7–11.
———. "Ghostwriter." *Bait*, pp. 89–104.
———. "Gonzo Erotica: Chuck Palahniuk's Brutal Beauty." Interview by Kyle Dowling. *Hustler*, Feb. 2014, pp. 44–49.
———. "Guts: A Story by Saint Gut-Free." *Haunted*, pp. 12–21.
———. "The Guts Effect." *The Cult*, Chuck Palahniuk Fan Website, 5 Jan. 2008, chuckpalahniuk.net/features/essays/guts-effect. Accessed 10 Dec. 2019.

———. *Haunted: A Novel of Stories*. Doubleday, 2005.
———. "Heaven Forbid: An Interview with Chuck Palahniuk." Interview by Mandy Grathwohl. *Matador Review*, Summer 2018, www.matadorreview.com/chuck-palahniuk. Accessed 17 Sept. 2019.
———. "How a Jew Saved Christmas." *Make Something Up*, pp. 310–18.
———. "How Busy Can One Writer Be? A Conversation with Chuck Palahniuk." Interview by Z. Smith. *SLUG*, 25 Oct. 2016, www.slugmag.com/interviews-features/chuck-palahniuk-bait/. Accessed 6 Oct. 2019.
———. "How Chuck Palahniuk Became the Darling of the Alt-Right and Antifa." Interview by Maya Kroth. *GEN*, 28 Dec. 2018, gen.medium.com/how-chuck-palahniuk-became-the-darling-of-the-alt-right-and-antifa-6c2fe8a2d616. Accessed 21 Oct. 2019.
———. "How Monkey Got Married, Bought a House, and Found Happiness in Orlando." *Make Something Up*, pp. 18–27.
———. "In Her Own Words." *Stranger Than Fiction: True Stories*. Anchor, 2004, pp. 119–31.
———. "Inclinations." *Make Something Up*, pp. 255–309.
———. "Interview with Chuck Palahniuk about the Release of Fight Club 2 and His Talk of James Franco in a Comic Book." Interview by Kayla Larson. *The 1st Class Lifestyle*, 26 May 2015, the1stclasslifestyle.com/interview-chuck-palahniuk-release-fight-club-2-talk-james-franco-comic-book/. Accessed 21 Oct. 2019.
———. "An Interview with Chuck Palahniuk." Interview by Mark Dago. *Big Shiny Robot*, 1 May 2018, bigshinyrobot.com/books/wizeguy-interview-chuck-palahniuk/. Accessed 5 Nov. 2019.
———. "An Interview with Chuck Palahniuk." Interview by Mark Dago. *Big Shiny Robot*, 24 Jan. 2019, bigshinyrobot.com/comics/interview-chuck-palahniuk/. Accessed 27 Sept. 2019.
———. "Interview: 'Intelligent ca ca,' Chuck Palahniuk Talks about His Current Storm of Creativity" Interview by Davey Nieves. *The Beat*, 6 June 2016, www.comicsbeat.com/interview-creative-tornado-chuck-palahniuk-talks-about-his-upcoming-projects/. Accessed 20 Oct. 2019.
———. "Interview: Chuck Palahniuk Welcomes You to the Wonderful World of Coloring and Castration." Interview by Davey Nieves. *The Beat*, 25 Oct. 2016, www.comicsbeat.com/interview-chuck-palahniuk-welcomes-you-to-the-wonderful-world-of-color-and-castration/. Accessed 6 Oct. 2019.
———. "Interview: Chuck Palahniuk Wishes You a Happy Adjustment Day." Interview by Davey Nieves. *The Beat*, 30 Apr. 2018, www.comicsbeat.com/interview-chuck-palahniuk-wishes-you-a-happy-adjustment-day/. Accessed 5 Nov. 2019.
———. "Interview: Chuck Palahniuk—Fight Club 2." Interview by Nicole Powers. *SuicideGirls*, 19 June 2016, www.suicidegirls.com/members/nicole_powers/blog/2930555/interview-chuck-palahniuk-fight-club-2/. Accessed 21 Oct. 2019.
———. "Interview: Chuck Palahniuk." Interview by Lisa Morton. *Nightmare*, vol. 29, 2015, www.nightmare-magazine.com/nonfiction/interview-chuck-palahniuk/. Accessed 17 Sept. 2019.
———. "Interview: Chuck Palahniuk." Interview by Ross Jeffery. *STORGY*, 5 Nov. 2016, storgy.com/2016/11/05/interview-chuck-palahniuk/. Accessed 6 Oct. 2019.
———. "Interview: Chuck Palahniuk." Interview by The Geek's Guide to the Galaxy. *Lightspeed*, no. 21, Feb. 2012, www.lightspeedmagazine.com/nonfiction/feature-interview-chuck-palahniuk/. Accessed 24 Sept. 2019.
———. "Interview: Chuck Palahniuk's New Novella Inspires Musical Performances." Interview by John Soltes. *Hollywood SOAPBOX*, 6 Sept. 2017, www.hollywoodsoapbox.com/interview-chuck-palahniuks-new-novella-inspires-musical-performances/. Accessed 6 Oct. 2019.
———. *The Invention of Sound*. Grand Central, 2020.
———. *Invisible Monsters*. Norton, 1999.
———. *Invisible Monsters Remix*. Norton, 2012.
———. "It's Paula-nick." Interview. *Guardian*, 24 Mar. 2004, www.theguardian.com/books/2004/mar/24/fiction.chuckpalahniuk. Accessed 2 Oct. 2019.
———. "Knock-Knock." *Make Something Up*, pp. 1–9.

_____. *Legacy: An Off-Color Novella for You to Color*. Illustrated by Duncan Fegredo, Steve Morris, and Mike Norton, Dark Horse, 2017.
_____. "*Lemuria* Interviews Chuck Palahniuk." Interview by ADMIN. *Lemuria*, 18 Oct. 2011, lemuriablog.com/lemuria-interviews-chuck-palahniuk/. Accessed 18 Nov. 2019.
_____. "Let's See What Happens." *Bait*, pp. 43–72.
_____. "Liturgy." *Make Something Up*, pp. 176–81.
_____. "Loser." *Make Something Up*, pp. 40–49.
_____. *Lullaby*. Doubleday, 2002.
_____. *Make Something Up: Stories You Can't Unread*. Doubleday, 2015.
_____. "A Man Worth Listening to: Chuck Palahniuk." Interview by Alex Nino Gheciu. *Sharp*, 21 May 2015, sharpmagazine.com/2015/05/21/a-man-worth-listening-to-chuck-palahniuk/. Accessed 30 Sept. 2019.
_____. "Mister Elegant." *Make Something Up*, pp. 232–45.
_____. "Mud Slinger." *Bait*, pp. 119–34.
_____. "My Books Are Always about People Struggling to Gain or Maintain Power." Interview by Lara Touitou. *Feedbooks*, 16 Aug. 2012, www.feedbooks.com/interview/95/my-books-are-always-about-people-struggling-to-gain-or-maintain-power. Accessed 30 Sept. 2019.
_____. "The Nightmare Box: A Story by Mrs. Clark." *Haunted*, pp. 210–22.
_____. "Nonsense." *Bait*, pp. 73–88.
_____. "On 'Fight Club's' 20th Anniversary, Author Chuck Palahniuk Talks about the Cult Classic Book." Interview by K. W. Colyard. *Bustle*, 16 Aug. 2016, www.bustle.com/articles/178756-on-fight-clubs-20th-anniversary-author-chuck-palahniuk-talks-about-the-cult-classic-book. Accessed 21 Oct. 2019.
_____. "One or Done Interview: Chuck Palahniuk on His New Coloring Book and What People Did with the First One." Interview by Davey Nieves. *The Beat*, 9 Nov. 2017, www.comicsbeat.com/one-or-done-interview-chuck-palahniuk-on-his-new-coloring-book-and-what-people-did-with-the-first-one/. Accessed 19 Sept. 2019.
_____. "Page & Perspective: Chatting with Chuck Palahniuk about 'Stories You Can't Unread' and More." Interview by Nicole Dubowitz. *DCist*, 22 May 2015, dcist.com/story/15/05/22/page-perspective-chuck-palahniuk-on/. Accessed 21 Oct. 2019.
_____. "Palahniuk on His Adult Coloring Book & Why Reese Witherspoon Owes Him." Interview by Kristy Puchko. *CBR*, 25 Oct. 2016, www.cbr.com/palahniuk-on-his-adult-coloring-book-why-reese-witherspoon-owes-him/. Accessed 6 Oct. 2019.
_____. "Palahniuk Talks 'Fight Club 2'and His Conflicted Relationship with Tyler Durden." Interview by Kristy Puchko. *CBR*, 29 Apr. 2016, www.cbr.com/palahniuk-talks-fight-club-2-his-conflicted-relationship-with-tyler-durden/. Accessed 21 Oct. 2019.
_____. "Phoenix." *Make Something Up*, pp. 102–21.
_____. "Post-Production: A Story by Mrs. Clark." *Haunted*, pp. 140–46.
_____. "The Power of Persisting: An Introduction." *Burnt Tongues: An Anthology of Transgressive Stories*, edited by Palahniuk, Richard Thomas, and Dennis Widmyer, Medallion, 2014, pp. 1–6.
_____. *Pygmy*. Doubleday, 2009.
_____. "A Q&A with Chuck Palahniuk about Fight Club 2 and What Tyler Durden Would Think of the 2016 Presidential Election." Interview by T. E. Lyons. *LEO Weekly*, 6 July 2016, www.leoweekly.com/2016/07/chuck-palahniuk/. Accessed 30 Sept. 2019.
_____. "Q&A: Chuck Palahniuk on 'Beautiful You.'" Interview by John Nicol. *Fangoria*, 15 Dec. 2014, fangoriaarchive.com/qa-chuck-palahniuks-on-beautiful-you/. Accessed 13 Jan. 2016.
_____. "Red Sultan's Big Boy." *Make Something Up*, pp. 50–69.
_____. "Romance." *Make Something Up*, pp. 70–79.
_____. "Salvation." *Bait*, pp. 135–47.
_____. "Shelf Awareness Interviews Chuck Palahniuk: Literary Goals and Skinny Jeans." Interview by Jaclyn Fulwood. *NW Book Lovers*, 12 June 2018, nwbooklovers.org/2018/06/12/shelf-awareness-interviews-chuck-palahniuk-literary-goals-and-skinny-jeans/. Accessed 5 Nov. 2019.

———. "Smoke." *Make Something Up*, pp. 146–48.
———. *Snuff*. Doubleday, 2008.
———. *Survivor*. Norton, 1999.
———. *Tell-All*. Doubleday, 2010.
———. "Telling Funny Stories with Chuck Palahniuk." Interview by Ben Tilton. *SLUG*, 23 Oct. 2014, www.slugmag.com/book-reviews/telling-funny-stories-with-chuck-palahniuk/. Accessed 17 Sept. 2019.
———. "The Toad Prince." *Make Something Up*, pp. 136–45.
———. "Torcher." *Make Something Up*, pp. 149–75.
———. "Tunnel of Love." *Make Something Up*, pp. 246–54.
———. "Why Aardvark Never Landed on the Moon." *Make Something Up*, pp. 182–94.
———. "Why Coyote Never Had Money for Parking." *Make Something Up*, pp. 89–101.
———. "Zombies." *Make Something Up*, pp. 28–39.
"Palahniuk, Chuck: Adjustment Day." Review of *Adjustment Day*, by Chuck Palahniuk. *Kirkus Reviews*, 15 Mar. 2018. *Literature Resource Center*, link.gale.com/apps/doc/A530650889/LitRC?u=cokercoll&sid=LitRC&xid=713b95f8. Accessed 31 Oct. 2019.
Pantozzi, Jill. "Proposed Title for Chuck Palahniuk's Next Book: 'There Isn't Enough Entertainment for Men Club.'" *The Mary Sue*, 8 Aug. 2014, www.themarysue.com/chuck-palahniuk-men-entertainment/. Accessed 7 Nov. 2019.
Parker, Ian. *Slavoj Žižek: A Critical Introduction*. Pluto, 2004. Modern European Thinkers.
Pauly, Madison. "Revenge Porn Drove Katie Hill from Office. How Can She Fight Back?" *Mother Jones*, 28 Oct. 2019, www.motherjones.com/politics/2019/10/katie-hill-revenge-porn-legal/. Accessed 4 Nov. 2019.
Pechey, Graham. *Mikhail Bakhtin: The Word in the World*. Routledge, 2007.
Peck, Claude. "Chuck Palahniuk's Latest an Empowering Inferno." Review of *Damned*, by Chuck Palahniuk. *Star Tribune* [Minneapolis], 10 Nov. 2011, www.startribune.com/chuck-palahniuk-s-latest-an-empowering-inferno/133204103/. Accessed 8 Aug. 2019.
Peterson, Deb. "The Hero's Journey: Meeting with the Mentor." *ThoughtCo.*, 28 July 2019, www.thoughtco.com/heros-journey-meeting-with-the-mentor-31349. Accessed 11 Oct. 2019.
Petruski, Peter. "Beautiful You." Review of *Beautiful You*, by Chuck Palahniuk. *Library Journal*, vol. 139, no. 12, Oct. 2014, p. 78.
Picchi, Aimee. "Is This a Sign the Coloring Book Fad Has Peaked?" *CBS News*, 19 Oct. 2016, www.cbsnews.com/news/is-this-a-sign-that-the-adult-coloring-book-fad-has-peaked/. Accessed 4 Oct. 2019.
Pierce, Charles P. "The President Has Slurs for Native Peoples. Elizabeth Warren Has a Plan." *Esquire*, 16 Aug. 2019, www.esquire.com/news-politics/politics/a28722365/donald-trump-pocahontas-elizabeth-warren-native-americans/. Accessed 4 Nov. 2019.
Pirnia, Garin. "Why *Fight Club* Matters More Than Ever." *Esquire*, 9 Oct. 2014, www.esquire.com/entertainment/movies/a30361/fight-club-15-years-later/. Accessed 10 Oct. 2019.
Pitt, David. "Doomed." Review of *Doomed*, by Chuck Palahniuk. *Booklist*, vol. 109, no. 21, July 2013, p. 49.
Plato. "The Allegory of the Cave." *The Republic*, ca. 375 BC, translated by Benjamin Jowett, Vintage, 1991, pp. 253–61.
———. *The Dialogues of Plato, Volume 3 (The Republic, Timaeus, Critias)*. 1892. Translated by Benjamin Jowett, *Online Library of Liberty*, Liberty Fund, 2004–19, oll.libertyfund.org/titles/plato-dialogues-vol-3-republic-timaeus-critias. Accessed 19 Aug. 2019.
Poe, Edgar Allan. "The Purloined Letter." *The Selected Writings of Edgar Allan Poe*. Edited by G. R. Thompson, Norton, 2004, pp. 367–82.
"Pop." *Law & Order: Special Victim's Unit*, directed by Norberto Barba, season 12, episode 11, National Broadcasting Company, 11 Jan. 2011.
"Porn Star's Requiem." *Law & Order: Special Victim's Unit*, directed by Jean de Segonzac, season 16, episode 5, National Broadcasting Company, 22 Oct. 2014.
The Power of Myth. 1988. Produced by Joan Konner and Alvin H. Perlmutter, performances by Joseph Campbell and Bill Moyers, Athena, 2012.
Powers, Kristen. "Don't Mock Marianne Williamson, Democrats Need Her

Spiritual Politics in Dark Trump Era." *USA Today,* 31 July 2019, www.usatoday.com/story/opinion/2019/07/31/trump-era-calls-for-marianne-williamson-spiritual-politics-column/1878296001/. Accessed 5 Aug. 2019.

Prado, Thiago Martins. "Chuck Palahniuk's US Culture and Economic Policy Discussion in *Damned.*" *Remate de Males,* vol. 36, no. 2, 2016, pp. 503–21.

Puchko, Kristy. "Chuck Palahniuk's Salacious 'Snuff' to Become Racy TV Series." *CBR,* 29 Apr. 2016, www.cbr.com/chuck-palahniuks-salacious-snuff-to-become-racy-tv-series/. Accessed 18 Nov. 2019.

Purdue, Madeline. "How to Deal with a Long-Distance Relationship? Try This Tech." *USA Today,* 16 July 2019, www.usatoday.com/story/tech/talkingtech/2019/07/16/long-distance-relationships-bond-touch-bracelets-hugging-shirts/1561418001/. Accessed 6 Sept. 2019.

Rabelais, François. *Gargantua and Pantagruel.* 1541. Translated by Burton Raffel. *The Norton Anthology of World Literature,* edited by Sarah Lawall and Maynard Mack, 2nd ed., vol. C, 2002, 2595–2631.

Rand, Ayn. *The Fountainhead.* 1943. Bobbs-Merrill, 1962.

Rebein, Robert. *Hicks, Tribes, and Dirty Realists: American Fiction after Postmodernism.* UP of Kentucky, 2001.

Renfrew, Alastair. *Mikhail Bakhtin.* Routledge, 2015. Routledge Critical Thinkers.

Renner, Rebecca. "Everyone Misunderstand the Point of *Fight Club.*" *Literary Hub,* 26 July 2019, lithub.com/everyone-misunderstands-the-point-of-fight-club/. Accessed 4 Nov. 2019.

Resch, Robert Paul. *Althusser and the Renewal of Marxist Social Theory.* U of California P, 1992.

Reuber, Alexandra. "Identity Crisis and Personality Disorders in Edgar Allan Poe's 'William Wilson' (1839), David Fincher's *Fight Club* (1999), and James Mangold's *Identity* (2003)." *Poe: Re-Imaginings in Popular Culture,* edited by Dennis R. Perry and Carl H. Sederholm, Palgrave, 2012, pp. 93–103.

Rice, Doyle. "Great Pacific Garbage Patch is Underway, Finally." *USA Today,* 3 Oct. 2019, www.usatoday.com/story/news/nation/2019/10/03/great-pacific-garbage-patch-cleanup-underway/3854722002/. Accessed 3 Oct. 2019.

———. "World's Largest Collection of Ocean Garbage Is Twice the Size of Texas." *USA Today,* 22 Mar. 2018 (updated 28 Dec. 2018), www.usatoday.com/story/tech/science/2018/03/22/great-pacific-garbage-patch-grows/446405002/. Accessed 4 Dec. 2019.

Ring, Trudy. "Bisexual Candidate Katie Hill Challenges a Homophobe for Congress." *The Advocate,* 5 Nov. 2018, www.advocate.com/election/2018/11/05/bisexual-candidate-katie-hill-challenges-homophobe-congress. Accessed 4 Nov. 2019.

Ritzen, Stacey. "A Dem. Congresswoman, Already in Hot Water Over a Fling with a Staffer, is Now in Even Hotter Water Over an Alleged Nazi Tattoo." *UPROXX,* 25 Oct. 2019, proxx.com/viral/rep-katie-hill-nazi-tattoo/. Accessed 4 Nov. 2019.

Robert. "'Snuff' by Chuck Palahniuk." Review of *Snuff,* by Chuck Palahniuk. *Fantasy Book Critic,* 20 May 2008, fantasybookcritic.blogspot.com/2008/05/snuff-by-chuck-palahniuk.html Accessed 13 Dec. 2019.

Robertson, Adi. "Joker Imitates King of Comedy and Fight Club, but It's a Completely Different Kind of Film." *The Verge,* 14 Oct. 2019, www.theverge.com/2019/10/14/20905454/joker-movie-phillips-king-of-comedy-fight-club-scorsese-fincher-comparison-society. Accessed 17 Oct. 2019.

Rodriguez, Adrianna. "Family Outraged After a Universal Character Made 'OK' Symbol on 6-Year-Old's Shoulder." *USA Today,* 1 Oct. 2019 (updated 3 Oct. 2019), www.usatoday.com/story/news/nation/2019/10/01/universal-orlando-resort-fires-despicable-me-actor-after-ok-symbol/3791483002/. Accessed 5 Nov. 2019.

———. "Florida Man Tries to Recruit IS for Terrorist Attack on Deans After Getting Kicked Out." *USA Today,* 27 Nov. 2019, www.usatoday.com/story/news/nation/2019/11/27/florida-man-plans-isis-attack-miami-dade-and-broward-college/4316936002/. Accessed 27 Nov. 2019.

Rollin, Roger B. Introduction. *Hero/Anti-Hero,* edited by Roger B. Rollin, McGraw-Hill, 1973, pp. xiii–xxi.

Rosenbloom, Stephanie, "Travel Coloring Books for Grown-Ups." *New York Times*, 21 Nov. 2016, www.nytimes.com/2016/11/21/travel/travel-coloring-books-for-grown-ups.html?searchResultPosition=3. Accessed 4 Oct. 2019.

Rotter, Joshua. "Drag Artists Star in Live 'First Wives,' 'Fight Club' Mashup." *San Francisco Examiner*, 4 Apr. 2019, www.sfexaminer.com/entertainment/drag-artists-star-in-live-first-wives-fight-club-mashup/. Accessed 17 Oct. 2019.

"Rushdie, Burroughs, Palahniuk: Whose 'TBR' Review Was the Worst?" *New York Vulture*, 9 June 2008, www.vulture.com/2008/06/burroughs_palahniuk_rushdie_wh.html. Accessed 10 July 2019.

Safronova, Valeriya. "What's So 'Indecent' about Female Pleasure?" *New York Times*, 24 Jan. 2019, p. D4.

Said, Edward W. *Orientalism*. Vintage, 1978.

Salo, Jackie. "Leaked Nude Photo of Rep. Katie Hill Shows Her with Bong, Prompts Legal Threat." *New York Post*, 24 Oct. 2019, nypost.com/2019/10/24/leaked-nude-photo-of-rep-katie-hill-show-bong-apparent-iron-cross-tattoo/. Accessed 4 Nov. 2019.

Salter, Jim. "Charges Dropped for Alleged 'Fight Club' at Day Care Center." *US News Online*, 6 Feb. 2019. *EBSCOhost*, warehouser.coker.edu/login?url=http://search.ebscohost.com/login.aspx?direct=true&db=n5h&AN=APe6c51faae77d4c73b96fc977c9d8aece&site=-ehost-live. Accessed 10 Oct. 2019.

Sam. "Not Your Average Colouring-In Book: Chuck Palahniuk's 'Bait.'" Review of *Bait*, by Chuck Palahniuk. *Smith Journal*, 27 Aug. 2018, www.smithjournal.com.au/blogs/arts/3440-not-your-average-colouring-in-book-chuck-palahniuk-s-bait. Accessed 6 Oct. 2019.

Santucci, Jeanine. "House Committee Opens Investigation into Allegations Rep. Katie Hill Had Relationship with Staffer." *USA Today*, 23 Oct. 2019, www.usatoday.com/story/news/politics/2019/10/23/ethics-committee-investigates-rep-katie-hill-relationship-allegation/2451566001/. Accessed 4 Nov. 2019.

Sartain, Jeffrey, editor. *Sacred and Immoral: On the Writings of Chuck Palahniuk*. Cambridge Scholars, 2009.

Schaub, Michael. "Chuck Palahniuk Wrote 'Fight Club.' His Next Work of Fiction Will Be a Coloring Book." *Los Angeles Times*, 20 June 2017, www.latimes.com/books/jacketcopy/la-et-jc-chuck-palahniuk-legacy-20170620-htmlstory.html. Accessed 6 Oct. 2019.

———. "'Fight Club' Author Chuck Palahniuk Says He's 'Close to Broke' after Agent's Accountant Charged with Embezzlement." *Los Angeles Times*, 31 May 2018, www.latimes.com/books/la-et-jc-palahniuk-accountant-20180531-story.html. Accessed 1 Oct. 2019.

Schuchardt, Read Mercer. "'A Copy of a Copy of a Copy': *The Matrix, American Beauty*, and *Fight Club* as Retellings of Pink Floyd's *The Wall*." *You Do Not Talk About Fight Club: I Am Jack's Completely Unauthorized Essay Collection*, edited by Schuchardt, BenBella, 2008, pp. 157–74.

———, editor. *You Do Not Talk About Fight Club: I Am Jack's Completely Unauthorized Essay Collection*. BenBella, 2008.

Schultz, Robert T. "White Guys Who Prefer Not To: From Passive Resistance ('Bartleby') To Terrorist Acts (*Fight Club*)." *Journal of Popular Culture*, vol. 44, no. 3, 2011, pp. 583–605.

Schwedel, Heather. "Coloring Books for Adults: We Asked Therapists for Their Opinions." *Guardian*, 17 Aug. 2015, www.theguardian.com/lifeandstyle/2015/aug/17/coloring-books-adults-therapists-opinions. Accessed 6 Oct. 2019.

Scott-Hainchek, Sadye. "Chuck Palahniuk 'Close to Broke' After Alleged Embezzlement." *The Fussy Librarian*, 30 May 2018, www.thefussylibrarian.com/newswire/for-readers/2018/05/30/chuck-palahniuk-close-to-broke-after-alleged-embezzlement. Accessed 30 Sept. 2019.

Segal, Robert A. *Joseph Campbell: An Introduction*. Garland, 1987.

Sharpe, Matthew. "Slavoj Žižek." *IEP*, Internet Encyclopedia of Philosophy, www.iep.utm.edu/zizek/. Accessed 23 July 2019.

———. *Slavoj Žižek: A Little Piece of the Real*. Ashgate, 2004.

Sheehan, Jason. "'Beautiful You' Makes Sex and Death Boring." Review of *Beautiful You*, by

Chuck Palahniuk. *NPR*, 25 Oct. 2014, www.npr.org/2014/10/25/356989245/beautiful-you-makes-sex-and-death-boring. Accessed 10 July 2019.

———. "On 'Adjustment Day,' A Quick, Horrifying Descent into Madness." Review of *Adjustment Day*, by Chuck Palahniuk. *NPR*, 1 May 2018, www.npr.org/2018/05/01/605000881/on-adjustment-day-a-quick-horrifying-descent-into-madness. Accessed 31 Oct. 2019.

Shivener, Rich. "Comics Publishers Lure Bestselling Book Authors." *Publishers Weekly*, 11 Aug. 2014, pp. 6, 8.

"Shocking Video Shows Tons of Plastic Bottles and Debris Washing Ashore on South African Beach." *USA Today*, 13 Dec. 2019. www.usatoday.com/videos/news/world/2019/12/13/shocking-video-shows-tons-plastic-bottles-and-debris-washing-ashore-south-african-beach/2636951001/. Accessed 14 Dec. 2019.

Showalter, Elaine. "Peeping Tom's Juvenile Jaunt." *The Chronicle of Higher Education*, vol. 54, no. 12, 2014, p. B14.

Siacon, Aleanna, and Micah Walker. "Man Seeks $87,000 in Damages After His Parents Destroy Massive Porn Collection." *USA Today*, 15 April 2019 (updated 16 April 2019), www.usatoday.com/story/news/nation/2019/04/15/man-suing-parents-destroying-porn-collection/3479482002/. Accessed 10 Sept. 2019.

Silverblatt, Michael. "Shock Appeal—Who Are These Writers, and Why Do They Want to Hurt Us?: The New Fiction of Transgression." *Los Angeles Times*, 1 August 1993, p. Living 7.

Small Town Andrew. "#MeToo Nude Congresswoman Katie Hill Scandal Worsens: Staffer Felt Abused in 'Toxic' Relationship, Consent Questions Emerge." *MagAMedia*, 24 Oct. 2019, magamedia.org/2019/10/24/metoo-nude-congresswoman-katie-hill-scandal-worsens-staffer-felt-abused-in-toxic-relationship-consent-questions-emerge/. Accessed 4 Nov. 2019.

"Snuff." Review of *Snuff*, by Chuck Palahniuk. *Kirkus Reviews*, vol. 76, no. 5, 1 Mar. 2008, p. 213. *EBSCO*, search.ebscohost.com/login.aspx?direct=true&db=lfh&AN=31329150&site=eds-live&scope=site. Accessed 29 Aug. 2011.

Sobral, Ana. "'Hitting Bottom': Deviance in Chuck Palahniuk's *Fight Club*." *Opting Out: Deviance and Generational Identities in American Post-War Cult Fiction*, Rodopi, 2012, pp. 215–45.

Sommers, Jeff. "Today's Most Under-Appreciated Writer: Chuck Palahniuk." *Barnes & Noble Reads*, Barnes & Noble Booksellers, 7 Sept. 2015. www.barnesandnoble.com/blog/the-most-under-appreciated-writer-today-chuck-palahniuk/. Accessed 10 July 2019.

Sommers, Joseph Michael, editor. *Critical Insights: The American Comic Book*. Salem Press, 2014.

Soukhanov, Anne H. "Word Watch." *The Atlantic*, December 1996, p.128.

Spitz, Markus Oliver. "Plot, Psychosis and Protest in Chuck Palahniuk's Fight Club." *PhiN: Philologie Im Netz*, vol. 75, 2016, pp. 32–48.

Spivak, Gayatri Chakravorty. "Can the Subaltern Speak?" *Reflections on the History of Idea*. Edited by Rosalind C. Morris, Columbia UP, 2010, pp. 21–78. Originally published in *Marxism and the Interpretation of Culture*, edited by Cary Nelson and Lawrence Grossberg, U of Illinois P, 1988, pp. 271–314.

Stallybrass, Peter, and Allon White. *The Politics and Poetics of Transgression*. Cornell UP, 1986.

Stanland, Angie. "RE: A Message from the Chairman of the Board." Received by David McCracken, 6 Sept. 2019.

Staskiewicz, Keith. "I Am Jane's Pinching Corset: We Talk to the Creator of 'Jane Austen's Fight Club.'" *Entertainment Weekly*, 30 July 2010, ew.com/article/2010/07/30/jane-austens-fight-club/. Accessed 17 Oct. 2019.

Stein, Daniel, and Jan-Noël Thon, editors. *From Comic Strips to Graphic Novels: Contributions to the Theory and History of Graphic Narrative*. De Gruyter, 2013.

Steinbeck, John. *The Grapes of Wrath*. 1939. Penguin, 2002.

Stephens, Alice. "A Comic Book Drawn in Words, This is One Raunchy Novel." Review of *Beautiful You*, by Chuck Palahniuk. *Washington Independent Review of Books*, 24 Nov. 2014, www.washingtonindependentreviewofbooks.com/index.php/bookreview/beautiful-you. Accessed 4 Sept. 2019.

Stevens, Ashlie D. "'Marianne Williamson for Secretary of Crystals': The Bonkers Break-Out Character of NBC's Debates." *Salon*, 28 June 2019, www.salon.com/2019/06/28/marianne-williamson-for-secretary-of-crystals-the-bonkers-break-out-character-of-nbcs-debates/. Accessed 5 Aug. 2019.

Subramanian, Courtney, John Fritze, and David Jackson. "Trump Calls Democrats 'Deranged,' 'Spiteful' in Angry Letter to Pelosi Over Impeachment." *USA Today*, 17 Dec. 2019, www.usatoday.com/story/news/politics/2019/12/17/impeachment-trump-calls-democrats-deranged-letter-pelosi/2666116001/. Accessed 17 Dec. 2019.

Sullivan, Eric. "F*$% Chuck: The Seven Worst Sentences from the New Novel, *Damned*." *GQ*, 14 Oct. 2011, www.gq.com/story/chuck-palahniuk-novel-damned-worst-sentences-review. Accessed 5 Aug. 2019.

Syl. "Review: Chuck Palahniuk's Legacy Is a Novella That Incorporates Coloring and Fun." Review of *Legacy*, by Chuck Palahnkuk. *Wicked Horror*, 14 Nov. 2017, www.wickedhorror.com/horror-news/review-chuck-palahniuks-legacy-novella-incorporates-coloring-fun/. Accessed 6 Oct. 2019.

Tabachnick, Stephen E., editor. *Teaching the Graphic Novel*. MLA, 2009.

"Tasha Reign." *MEL*, 2019, melmagazine.com/en-us/story/author/tasha-reign. Accessed 18 Sept. 2019.

Tell, Caroline. "Coloring Books for Adults Seeking Playtime." *New York Times*, 20 Apr. 2016, www.nytimes.com/2016/04/21/fashion/adult-coloring-books-relaxation.html?searchResultPosition=7. Accessed 4 Oct. 2019.

Tennyson, Alfred, Lord. "Ulysses." *Poetry Foundation*, Poetry Foundation, www.poetryfoundation.org/poems/45392/ulysses. Accessed 5 Aug. 2019.

Thomson, Philip. *The Grotesque*. Methuen, 1972. The Critical Idiom.

Thoreau, Henry David. *Walden, or Life in the Woods*. *The Norton Anthology of American Literature*, edited by Robert Levine et al, 9th ed., vol. B, Norton, 2017, pp. 970–1144.

Thorne, Bella. *The Life of a Wannabe Mogul: Mental Disarray, Vol. 1*. Rare Bird Books, 2019.

Thrasher, Steven W. "What Tumblr's Porn Ban Really Means." *The Atlantic*, 7 Dec. 2018, www.theatlantic.com/technology/archive/2018/12/tumblr-adult-content-porn/577471/. Accessed 5 Aug. 2019.

"Tom Spanbauer on Dangerous Writing." *YouTube*, uploaded by Danny Broderick, 30 June 2009, www.youtube.com/watch?v=_wZ9vonRsYs. Accessed 30 Sept. 2019.

Trepany, Charles. "'I'm Actually Pansexual': Bella Thorne Gets Real About Her Sexuality and Struggles." *USA Today*, 22 July 2019. www.usatoday.com/story/entertainment/celebrities/2019/07/22/bella-thorne-comes-out-pansexual-talks-her-struggles/1794151001/. Accessed 24 July 2019.

Truitt, Brian. "Palahniuk Takes a 2nd Swing at 'Fight Club.'" Review of *Fight Club 2*, by Chuck Palahniuk. *USA Today*, 22 July 2014, p. 6D.

———. "Satirical 'Beautiful You' Skewers Modern Erotica." Review of *Beautiful You*, by Chuck Palahniuk. *USA Today*, 26 Nov. 2014, p. 7B.

Tucker, Reed. "Chuck Palahniuk Talks 'Fight Club 2' Comic Book Series." *New York Post*, 26 May 2015, nypost.com/2015/05/26/chuck-palahniuk-talks-fight-club-2-comic-book-series/. Accessed 21 Dec. 2019.

Twelve Steps and Twelve Traditions. 1952. Alcoholics Anonymous World Services, 1991.

"20 Years of Listening to America." *BillMoyers.com*, uploaded by Moyers & Company, 4 Oct. 1991, billmoyers.com/content/20-years-of-listening-to-america/. Accessed 15 Oct. 2019.

"Twilight Bone." *YouTube*, uploaded by CassieWrightLives, 20 May 2008, www.youtube.com/watch?v=ymok-lh9XM4. Accessed 5 Aug. 2019.

Ulrich, Nate. "Browns Notebook: With Freddie Kitchens Urging Players Not to Back Down, Final Joint Practice with Colts Turns into 'Fight Club.'" *Akron Beacon Journal*, 15 Aug. 2019. *EBSCOhost*, warehouser.coker.edu/login?url=http://search.ebscohost.com/login.aspx?direct=true&db=n5h&AN=2W61745237251&site=ehost-live. Accessed 10 Oct. 2019.

"US Soccer Star Megan Rapinoe Drops F-Bomb on Live TV." *The Quirky World of Jeanne Moos*, *CNN*, 11 July 2019, www.cnn.com/videos/us/2019/07/11/jeanne-moos-megan-rapinoe-pkg.cnn. Accessed 17 July 2019.

Vacker, Barry. "The 20th Anniversary of *Fight Club* and *The Matrix*: Two Futures All Around Us in 2019." *Medium*, 17 Mar. 2019, medium.com/@barryvacker/the-20th-anniversary-of-fight-club-and-the-matrix-two-futures-all-around-us-in-2019-511fad554864. Accessed 10 Oct. 2019.

Vadnal, Julie. "The Millennial Sex Recession Is Bullshit." *Cosmopolitan*, vol. 267, no. 1, 2019, pp. 100–07.

VanDenburgh, Barbara. "5 Books Not to Miss: 'Fight Club' Author Chuck Palahniuk's 'Consider This,' 'Hindsight.'" *USA Today*, 4 Jan. 2020, usatoday.com/story/entertainment/books/2020/01/04/new-books-chuck-palahniuk-consider-this-fight-club-hindsight/2804846001/. Accessed 4 Jan. 2020.

Van Syckle, Katie. "Sex Sells, Walmart Buys." *New York Times*, 5 July 2019, pp. B1–B3.

Vogler, Christopher. *The Writer's Journey: Mythic Structure for Writers*. 3rd ed., Michael Wiese Productions, 2007.

Wade, Peter. "Rep. Katie Hill Resigns Over Allegations of Inappropriate Relationships." *Rolling Stone*, 27 Oct. 2019, www.rollingstone.com/politics/politics-news/katie-hill-resigns-904363/amp/. Accessed 4 Nov. 2019.

Wald, Christina. "Second Selves, Second Stories: Unreliable Narration and the Circularity of Reading in Ford Maddox Ford's *The Good Soldier* and Chuck Palahniuk's/David Fincher's *Fight Club*." *Symbolism: An International Annual of Critical Aesthetics*, vol. 9, 2010, pp. 217–41.

Weida, Stacy. "Review of Becoming the New Man in Post-Post Modernist Fiction: Portrayals of Masculinities in David Foster Wallace's *Infinite Jest* and Chuck Palahniuk's *Fight Club*." *Men and Masculinities*, vol. 12, no. 4, Apr. 2010, pp. 513–15.

Whitmore, Alice. "Dirty Realism's Other Face." *Sydney Review of Books*, 16 March 2016, sydneyreviewofbooks.com/dirty-realism-feature/. Accessed 28 Sept. 2019.

Williams, G. Christopher. "Nihilism and Buddhism in a Blender: The Religion of Chuck Palahniuk." *Reading Chuck Palahniuk: American Monsters and Literary Mayhem*, edited by Cynthia Kuhn and Lance Rubin, Routledge, 2009, pp. 170–82.

Williams, Owen. "Daryl Hannah Is Up to Snuff." *Empireonline*, 9 Feb. 2011. www.empireonline.com/movies/news/daryl-hannah-snuff/. Accessed 24 Sept. 2011.

Williamson, Marianne. *A Return to Love: Reflections on the Principles of A Course in Miracles*. HarperCollins, 1992.

"The Wizard of Ass—Dorothy Is Not a Virgin Anymore" *YouTube*, uploaded by Cassie WrightLives, 7 May 2008, www.youtube.com/watch?v=gzY3r76Ax48. Accessed 5 Aug 2019.

Wolf, Naomi. *Fire with Fire: The New Female Power and How It Will Change the 21st Century*. Random House, 1993.

Wolf, Richard. "F-word Wins in Supreme Court Free Speech Case on Trademark Protection for 'Immoral, Scandalous' Material." *USA Today*, 24 June 2019, www.usatoday.com /story/news/politics/2019/06/24/fuct-supreme-court-trademark-misspelled-f-word/1367858001/. Accessed 24 June 2019.

Wolfe, Tom. "Hooking Up." *Hooking Up*, pp. 3–13.

———. *Hooking Up*. Picador, 2000.

———. *I Am Charlotte Simmons*. Farrar, Straus, and Giroux, 2004.

———. "In the Land of Rococo Marxists." *Hooking Up*, pp. 114–30.

———. "My Three Stooges." *Hooking Up*, pp. 145–71.

———. "Stalking the Billion-Footed Beast: A Literary Manifesto for the New Social Novel." *Tom Wolfe*, edited by Harold Bloom, Chelsea, 2001, pp. 151–67. Originally published in *Harper's*, Nov. 1989, pp. 45–56.

Wolter, Tyler. "*Adjustment Day* by Chuck Palahniuk." Review of *Adjustment Day*, by Chuck Palahniuk. *Open Letters Review*, 18 May 2018, openlettersreview.com/posts/adjustment-day-by-chuck-palahniuk. Accessed 31 Oct. 2019.

Woodhead, Cameron. "In Short Fiction." Review of *Beautiful You*, by Chuck Palahniuk. *Sydney Morning Herald*, 13 Dec. 2014, p. 32.

———. "In Short Fiction." Review of *Doomed*, by Chuck Palahniuk. *Sydney Morning Herald*, 16 Nov. 2013, p. 36.

Works Cited

———. "In Short Fiction." Review of *Make Something Up: Stories You Can't Unread*, by Chuck Palahniuk. *Sydney Morning Herald*, 8 Aug. 2015, p. 28.

"WRITE CLUB: A FIGHT CLUB PARODY." *YouTube*, uploaded by Noah Outlaw, 3 Nov. 2016, www.youtube.com/watch?v=oIxWPgfltK8. Accessed 17 Oct. 2019.

"Writing about Comics and Graphic Novels." *Duke University Writing Studio*, twp.duke.edu/sites/twp.duke.edu/files/file-attachments/comic.original.pdf. Accessed 1 Nov. 2019.

Wu, Nicholas. "Marianne Williamson Suggest the 'Power of the Mind' to Divert Path of Hurricane Dorian." *USA Today*, 4 Sept. 2019, www.usatoday.com/story/news/politics/elections/2019/09/04/marianne-williamson-suggests-power-mind-could-divert-dorian/2209944001/. Accessed 8 Sept. 2019.

Yancey-Bragg, N'dea, and Jordan Culver. "'Dark psychic force': Marianne Williamson's Memorable Moments from the Democratic Debate." *USA Today*, 30 July 2019 (updated 31 July 2019), www.usatoday.com/story/news/politics/elections/2019/07/30/democratic-debate-2019-marianne-williamson-memorable-moment/1874484001/. Accessed 5 Aug. 2019.

Yeats, William Butler. "The Second Coming." 1920. *PoetryFoundation.org*, Poetry Foundation, n.d., www.poetryfoundation.org/poems/43290/the-second-coming. Accessed 7 Dec. 2019.

Žižek, Slavoj. *Absolute Recoil: Towards a New Foundation of Dialectical Materialism*. Verso, 2014.

———. "The Ambiguity of the Masochist Social Link." *Perversion and the Social Relation*, edited by Molly Anne Rothenberg, Dennis A. Foster, and Slavoj Žižek, Duke UP, 2003, pp. 112–25. SIC IV.

———. "An Ethical Plea for Lies and Masochism." *Lacan and Contemporary Film*, edited by Todd McGowan and Sheila Kunkle, Other, 2004, pp. 173–86.

———. "Redemptive Violence." Afterword. *Revolution at the Gates: A Selection of Writings from February to October* 1917, by Vladimir Il'ich Lenin, edited by Žižek, Verso, 2002, pp. 250–63.

———. *The Sublime Object of Ideology*. 1989. Verso, 2008.

———. "The Violence of the Fantasy." *The Communication Review*, vol. 6, no. 4, 2003, pp. 275–87.

———. *Violence: Six Sideways Reflections*. Picador, 2008.

Zlomislić, Marko. *Žižek: Paper Revolutionary: A Franciscan Response*. Pickwick, 2018. Postmodern Ethics.

"Zombies." *YouTube*, uploaded by Bolla Rice. 9 Oct. 2013, www.youtube.com/watch?v=isJTR0MSH6Y&t=807s. Accessed 25 Sept. 2019.

Index

absent father 141, 188; *see also* Campbell, Joseph; second/secondary father
Absolute Recoil 34
Adjustment Day 1, 8, 11, 12, 15, 42, 86, 120, 200–34, 243*ch7n*1, 245*n*1
Afterword, *Fight Club* 50, 175–76, 181, 194, 245*n*5
Alcoholics Anonymous 208, 241*ch*1*n*1, 244*n*2; *see also* Big Book
Allison, Dorothy 121, 143, 242*n*2
Althusser, Louis 1, 2, 11, 12, 14, 33–35, 41, 44, 61, 70, 81, 82, 89, 96, 104, 115, 119, 120, 147, 154, 192, 212, 225, 231, 238*n*13, 238–39*n*14; *see also For Marx*; "Ideology and the Ideological State Apparatus (Notes Towards an Investigation)"; *Philosophy of the Encounter*
Anatomy of Criticism 20–21, 236*n*3; *see also* Fry, Northrop
Anderson, Sherwood 27–28, 32, 37, 237*n*8; *see also Winesburg, Ohio*
Aristophanes 93, 95, 116; *see also Lysistrata*

"Bait" 153, 159
Bait: Off-Color Stories for You to Color 1, 11, 41, 125, 146–63, 167, 178, 243*ch7n*1, 123*n*2; *see also* "Bait"; "A Collaboration"; "Dad All Over"; "Ghostwriter"; "Let's See What Happens"; "Mudslinger"; "Nonsense"; "Salvation"
Bakhtin, Mikhail 1, 2, 11, 12, 14, 20, 22–23, 26, 28–32, 46, 50–52, 70, 72, 77, 82, 89, 99, 109, 114, 120, 134, 143, 157, 171, 183, 211, 231–32, 236*n*2, 238*n*10, 238*n*12, 241*n*6, 242*n*5; *see also* carnival, dialogism, heteroglossia; *Problems of Dostoevsky's Poetics*; *Rabelais and His World*
Barth, John 209–210, 238*n*10, 246*n*4
Barthelme, Donald 130
Barthes, Roland 32, 89, 235*n*3
Baudrillard, Jean 240*n*5, 244*n*2
Beautiful You 1, 11, 15, 17, 19, 93–116, 121, 125, 129, 159, 169, 208, 209, 211, 241*ch*5*n*3, 242*n*4, 242*n*5
Big Book 208–09

bizarro fiction 73
Blume, Judy 68, 76, 125, 241*ch*4*n*2, 241*ch*4*n*3
Bomer, Paula 17–18, 32, 97
Brecht, Bertolt 229–30, 246*ch*10*n*1
Brown, Larry 143, 242*n*2
Buford, Bill 127–28
Bukowski, Charles 54–55, 121, 126–27, 143, 242*n*2

Campbell, Fiona Kumari 24–25, 236*n*4
Campbell, Joseph 73–74, 88, 90, 95, 139, 141, 149, 165, 175–77, 179–86, 188, 191–92, 197–98, 242*ch*6*n*4, 244*n*2, 244*n*3; *see also* hero's journey (monomyth)
"Cannibal" 132–33
Capital 33
carnival/carnivalesque 1, 11–14, 20, 26, 28–32, 42, 47, 51–53, 59–60, 62, 70, 82, 86–87, 89, 96, 105, 107, 109, 114, 120, 136–37, 143, 147, 153, 157–58, 166, 171, 173, 183, 186, 189, 198, 200, 211, 214–15, 218, 227, 231–33, 236*n*1, 238*n*10, 242*n*5
Carver, Raymond 121, 127, 128, 143
Cassandra (mythology) 40
"Cassandra" (story) 39–40
Chong, Annabel 49, 52, 56–57, 62, 240*n*3; *see also* Quek, Grace
"Cold Calling" 133–34
"A Collaboration" (Preface to *Bait*) 154
coloring 146–54, 157, 160, 161, 163, 167, 172, 208, 234, 243*n*1
comedy 13, 17, 20–23, 26, 30, 32, 34, 39, 52, 73, 79, 80, 105, 131, 133, 161, 166, 195, 205, 224, 231
comic grotesque 1, 2, 10–11, 13, 14–15, 28, 32–33, 38, 46, 50, 62, 69–70, 72, 80, 81–82, 87, 95–96, 99–100, 104, 110, 115–16, 120, 123–24, 128, 131, 136, 138, 143, 147, 153, 160–61, 164, 171, 178, 180, 185, 192, 194–96, 202, 204, 207–08, 210–13, 220, 228, 229, 231–34, 241*ch*5*n*3, 242*ch*6*n*5, 246*n*3
Corpora, Lisa Ann 54, 55, 201
Cummings, Whitney 4, 160, 201, 202

Index

"Dad All Over" 151, 153–55
Damned 1, 11, 15, 66–92, 99, 100, 115, 121, 122, 125, 129, 156, 186, 211, 212, 241ch4n2
dangerous writing 15, 122–23, 127
Dante Alighieri 58, 68–72, 74, 78, 86, 89–90, 241ch4n2, 241ch4n3; see also *The Divine Comedy*
Deleuze, Gilles 239n16
dialogism 77, 141, 238n10
Dirty Realism 2, 117, 120–21, 126–29, 143, 172, 180, 242n2
disability studies 24–25, 45, 244n2
The Divine Comedy 70–72
Dobozy, Tamas 242n2
Donadio & Olson 122
Doomed 1, 11, 15, 66–92, 99, 100, 115, 121, 125, 129, 156, 186, 211, 213
Dunne, Robert 27, 237n8
Dworkin, Andrea 47, 62, 101–02, 219, 240n4

Écrits 239n15
Edwards, Justin D. 25, 26, 67, 238n12
"Eleanor" 125, 130
Ellmann, Lucy 17–18, 32, 46, 236n1
Emerson, Ralph Waldo 67
Erdrich, Louise 121, 143
"An Ethical Plea for Lies and Masochism" 240n17
"Expedition" 125, 138, 139–41, 149, 182–83, 188, 191, 197

"The Facts of Life" 134–35
Faludi, Susan 49–50
"Fetch" 138
Fifty Shades of Grey 98, 107
Fight Club (film) 36, 168, 244n2, 245–46n3
Fight Club (novel) 1, 9, 15, 36, 37, 38, 39, 41, 50, 61, 62, 63, 85, 87, 88, 97, 98, 99, 100, 115, 120, 124, 130, 137, 139, 140, 141, 149, 151, 153, 157, 163, 164, 167, 168–99, 204, 205, 206–07, 209, 216, 217, 226, 227, 233, 235n1, 235n2, 236n1, 239n17, 239–40n17, 242n1, 242n3, 243n2, 244n2, 245n4, 245–46n3
Fight Club 2 1, 11, 15, 100, 139, 148, 152, 153, 163, 165, 168–99, 202, 205, 211, 212, 214, 214, 226, 243n2, 243n3, 234ch8n1, 245n4
Fight Club 3 125, 324
"Fight Club for Kids" 168, 198
Fire with Fire 103
Fitzgerald, F. Scott 16, 175, 205, 206; see also *The Great Gatsby*
For Marx 238n13
Ford, Richard 121, 143
"Foreword: The Fringe Is the Future" 8–9, 10, 12, 13, 41, 232
Foucault, Michel 19, 26, 204, 226. 237n5
The Fountainhead 205, 208, 227

Frye, Northorp 20–21, 236n3; see also *Anatomy of Criticism*

Gargantua and Pantagruel 22, 29, 32, 212, 231, 238n10
"Ghostwriter" 153, 158–59
Goodley, Dan 24, 236n4
The Grapes of Wrath 205, 222, 227
graphic novel (genre) 172–74, 179, 192, 202, 243ch7n1, 243ch8n1
Graulund, Rune 25, 26, 67, 238n12
The Great Gatsby 138, 175, 205, 227
grotesque 13, 14, 20, 23–29, 31, 38, 50, 53, 62, 73, 75, 78, 80, 106, 109, 114, 125, 138, 139, 141, 152, 156, 159, 160, 161, 165, 189, 191, 193, 195, 211, 231, 236n2, 237n5, 237n7, 237n8, 237–38n9, 238n12, 238n13, 241ch5n3, 242–43ch6n5, 245–46n3
Guattari, Félix 239n16
"Guts" 14–15, 18, 32, 125, 128, 132, 169

Haunted: A Novel of Stories 14, 39, 73, 125, 129, 193; see also "Cassandra"; "Guts"; "The Nightmare Box"; "Post-Production"
Hawthorne, Nathaniel 182; see also "Rappaccini's Daughter"; *The Scarlet Letter*
Hero/Antihero 21
hero's journey (monomyth) 88, 180–81; see also Campbell, Joseph
heteroglossia 29, 46, 52, 109, 130, 213, 238n10
Hill, Katie 200–03, 210–11, 219, 223
History and Class Consciousness 237n6
hooks, bell 110–11, 225
"How a Jew Saved Christmas" 142–43
"How Monkey Got Married, Bought a House, and Found Happiness in Orlando" 142
Hutcheon, Linda 246n4

I Am Charlotte Simmons 6, 9, 12, 22, 52, 235n2
identity politics 203, 205, 210, 220, 226
ideological discordance 11, 37–38, 39, 40, 46, 51, 60, 69, 75, 87, 114, 115, 117, 120, 126, 129, 131, 133, 136, 137, 138, 142, 153, 165, 167, 213, 218, 227, 231, 233
ideology 2, 8, 9, 10, 11, 13, 14, 18, 24, 25, 27, 33–38, 39, 40–41, 45, 52, 55, 57, 61, 62, 63, 67, 68, 69, 71, 77, 78, 82, 85, 86, 87, 88, 90, 92, 94, 95, 96, 101, 103, 104, 110, 113, 114, 115, 116, 119, 128, 131, 132, 133, 134, 137, 138, 144, 154, 156, 157, 158, 159, 160, 162, 163, 168, 171, 177, 179, 180, 183, 184, 185, 186, 187, 191, 192, 196, 197, 199, 202, 204, 208, 209, 212, 215, 216, 221, 223, 224, 225, 226, 227, 229, 230, 234, 237n5, 237n6, 238n13, 238–39n14, 239n16, 240ch4n1, 241n3, 246n1
"Ideology and the Ideological State Apparatus (Notes Towards an Investigation)" 33–34, 238–39n14

Incel 209, 245*n*3, 246*n*3
"Inclinations" 135, 136, 137–38
Invisible Monsters 41, 134, 234, 236*n*1
Invisible Monsters Remix 209

Jameson, Fredric 238*n*13
Jeffreys, Sheila 102–03
Johnson, Denis 121, 128, 143
Jung, Carl G. 183, 188, 244*n*3, 245*n*4

Keesey, Douglas 26–27, 47, 51, 236*n*1, 242*n*1
"Knock-Knock" 132, 133, 135, 142, 153
Knox, Belle (Miriam Weeks) 57, 63
Kristeva, Julia 26, 238*n*10

Lacan, Jacques 36, 113, 239*n*15; *see also Ècrits*
Law & Order: Special Victims Unit 63, 169
Legacy: An Off-Color Novella for You to Color 1, 11, 146–67, 178, 243*ch*7*n*1, 243*n*2
"Let's See What Happens" 153, 156–57
"Liturgy" 124, 130–31, 153
"Loser" 128, 130, 133–34, 136, 143
Lukács, György 25, 237*n*6; *see also History and Class Consciousness*
Lullaby 73, 122, 234
Lyotard, Jean-François 27–28; *see also The Postmodern Condition*
Lysistrata 22, 52, 93, 95, 100, 106, 114, 116, 241*ch*5*n*2; *see also* Aristophanes

Macherey, Pierre 238*n*13
MacKinnon, Catharine A. 62, 102; *see also Toward a Feminist Theory of the State*
Make Something Up: Stories You Can't Unread 1, 11, 16, 117–45, 152, 153, 160, 173, 243*ch*7*n*2; *see also* "Cannibal"; "Cold Calling"; "Eleanor"; "Expedition"; "The Facts of Life"; "Fetch"; "How a Jew Saved Christmas"; "How Monkey Got Married, Bought a House, and Found Happiness in Orlando"; "Knock-Knock"; "Liturgy"; "Loser"; "Mister Elegant"; "Phoenix"; "Red Sultan's Big Boy"; "Romance"; "Smoke"; "The Toad Prince"; "Torcher"; "Tunnel of Love"; "Why Aardvark Never Landed on the Moon"; "Why Coyote Never Had Money for Parking"; "Zombies"
Marcuse, Herbert 230–31, 232, 235*n*1; *see also One-Dimensional Man* 230, 235*n*1
Marx, Karl 33, 34, 238*n*13; *see also Capital*
Mason, Bobbie Ann 121, 143
#MeToo 66, 93, 103, 113, 116, 134, 160, 201, 202, 240*n*4, 241*ch*5*n*1, 242*n*2
Melville, Herman 18, 172
Messalina 56–57, 62, 106
Milano, Alyssa 66, 93, 103, 106
Minimalism 122, 127, 128, 182
"Mister Elegant" 133, 134

Moyers, Bill 139, 175–77, 180–81, 184
"Mud Slinger" 151, 159–60

The Nightmare Box (object) 39, 40–41, 42, 163, 234
"The Nightmare Box" (story) 39, 125
"Nonsense" 151, 157–58

One-Dimensional Man 230, 235*n*1

Paglia, Camille 102, 219
Palahniuk, Chuck (biography) 121–23, 138
Parody 4, 19–20, 29, 41, 43, 71, 74, 83, 88, 107, 112, 124, 134, 139, 140, 148, 156, 171, 179, 186, 194, 198, 208, 209–10, 226, 227, 234, 235*n*4, 241*ch*4*n*2, 246*n*4
Philosophy of the Encounter 238*n*13
"Phoenix" 134, 135–36
Plato 84, 162
Poe, Edgar Allan 125, 161, 182, 185, 244*n*2
Porn Studies 47
"Post-Production" 39
The Postmodern Condition 27–28
Postmodernism 27–28, 90, 246*n*4
"The Power of Persisting" 10, 235*n*4
Problems of Dostoevsky's Poetics 31–32
Pygmy 15, 42

Quek, Grace 57, 240*n*3; *see also* Chong, Annabel

Rabelais, François 1, 17, 22–25, 28–32, 41, 50, 52–53, 70, 77, 79, 82, 96, 106, 115, 180, 212, 231, 238*n*10; *see also* Gargantua and Pantagruel
Rabelais and His World 29–30, 89, 109, 114, 241*n*6
Rand, Ayn 205–206, 208, 245*n*1; *see also The Fountainhead*
Rapinoe, Megan 4–6, 9–10, 13, 18, 21–22, 36, 52
"Rappaccini's Daughter" 138–39
Rebein, Robert 127–28
"Red Sultan's Big Boy" 135, 136, 153, 155
"Redemptive Violence" 239*n*17
A Return to Love 90
Rollin, Roger B. 21; *see also* Hero/Antihero
"Romance" 1, 133–34

Said, Edward W. 237*n*4
"Salvation" 151, 153, 160–63
The Scarlet Letter 21–22
Schuchardt, Read Mercer 8, 236*n*1, 244*n*2
second/secondary father 141, 181, 198, 214–15, 217, 244*n*3
"Smoke" 130–31, 153
Snuff 1, 11, 12, 15, 17–18, 43–65, 70, 74, 93, 94, 96, 98, 99, 100, 106, 109, 112, 115, 121, 125,

129, 152, 157, 158, 169, 208, 211, 212, 213, 234, 240n2, 240n4, 240n5, 241ch4n1, 242n2
Spanbauer, Tom 122–23, 127
Spivak, Gayatri Chakravorty 237n4
Steinbeck, John 205–06; *see also The Grapes of Wrath*
The Sublime Object of Ideology 34–36, 37–38, 128
Survivor 91, 96, 209, 244n2

Tell-All 15, 41, 71, 157, 209, 243n4
Tennyson, Alfred Lord 54–55
Thoreau, Henry David 110
Thorne, Bella 3–6, 9–10, 13, 18, 21–22, 36–37, 41, 43–45, 52, 55, 160, 201, 234
"The Toad Prince" 138–39, 143, 153
"Torcher" 135, 136–37, 157, 242–43n5
Toward a Feminist Theory of the State 102
transgression 12, 14, 17, 19–20, 23, 25–26, 29, 39, 80, 212, 236n2, 238n10, 240n4, 241ch5n1, 242n2, 244n2
trickster archetype 140, 177–79, 182–84, 186, 188–89, 195–98, 207, 217–19, 244n3, 245n4
Trump, Pres. Donald 163, 167, 202–05, 227, 234
"Tunnel of Love" 135
Twelve Steps 123, 241n1, 242ch6n4, 244n2

Violence 240n17
"The Violence of the Fantasy" 198, 239n17

Warren, Elizabeth 203
"Why Aardvark Never Landed on the Moon" 142
"Why Coyote Never Had Money for Parking" 142, 143
Williamson, Marianne 66–68, 70, 71, 86, 89–90, 111–12; *see also A Return to Love*
Winesburg, Ohio 27, 237n8
wise old man/mentor archetype 110, 176–78, 181, 183, 185, 188–89, 197, 207, 214, 216–18, 220, 226, 244–45n3
Wolf, Naomi 103; *see also Fire with Fire*
Wolfe, Tom 6–10, 11, 22, 120, 123, 235n2; *see also I Am Charlotte Simmons*

Žižek, Slavoj 1, 2, 11, 12, 14, 33–38, 40–41, 44, 58, 61, 81, 87, 91, 96, 113, 114, 115, 119, 128–29, 154, 156–57, 159, 160, 184–85, 198, 225–26, 231, 239n15, 239n16, 239–40n17; *see also Absolute Recoil*; "An Ethical Plea for Lies and Masochism"; "Redemptive Violence"; *The Sublime Object of Ideology*; *Violence*; "The Violence of the Fantasy"
"Zombies" 133, 134, 160

www.ingramcontent.com/pod-product-compliance
Lightning Source LLC
Chambersburg PA
CBHW021349300426
44114CB00012B/1141